CYLINDER
OF
VISION

CYLINDER OF VISION

The Fiction
and Journalistic Writing
of Stephen Crane

MILNE HOLTON

LOUISIANA STATE UNIVERSITY PRESS / BATON ROUGE

For Sylvia

ISBN 0-8071-0045-5
Library of Congress Catalog Card Number 79-181358
Copyright © 1972 by Louisiana State University Press
All rights reserved
Manufactured in the United States of America
Printed by The Parthenon Press, Nashville, Tennessee
Designed by Albert Crochet

Each man sat in his own little cylinder of vision, so to speak. It was not so small as a sentry-box nor so large as a circus tent, but the walls were opaque, and what was passing beyond the dimensions of his cylinder no man knew.

Stephen Crane, "London Impressions," 1897

Je veux seulement y voir clair.

Albert Camus, *Le mythe de Sisyphe*, 1942

Preface

In recent years the work of Stephen Crane has again become the subject of renewed interest. The first full-length study of the fiction appeared in 1966—Eric Solomon's *Stephen Crane: From Parody to Realism*—followed by Donald B. Gibson's *The Fiction of Stephen Crane*. In a sense, both of these studies represent radical departures from the main body of Crane criticism. It is my intention here to develop my own critical position by building upon that body of criticism rather than by departing from it. I have considered all of Crane's fictional writing and extant journalism, and have thereby attempted to approach an understanding of the development of Crane's imagination. I have also considered the complex of interrelationships among these individual works and have attempted to suggest something of the nature of the impact of Crane's work upon modern literature.

To this end I have made use of some significant achievements in the development of Stephen Crane scholarship which were unavailable to both Gibson and Solomon. In the first place, I have had the good fortune to be able to build my study upon the comprehensive biography recently presented by R. W. Stallman in *Stephen Crane: A Biography*. Stallman's biography accumulates much of the factual information already known about Crane, adds much that is new, and provides a convenient single source for reference.

Secondly, I have had the advantage of the recent and important work of Crane's editors. It has therefore not been necessary for me to rely exclusively upon Wilson Follett's often erroneous and now archaic 1925–27 Knopf edition of *The Work of Stephen Crane.*

The recent editions of Crane's works correct Follett's errors and make available much new material, and it has therefore been possible for me to examine critically, in addition to the standard works, some new stories and a considerable body of important journalistic writing. The relationships between Crane's journalistic writing and his fiction have never before been systematically explored, yet such exploration is necessary in order to come to a real understanding of the full import and implication of Crane's prose. Through the examination and comparison of the newly established canons of fiction and of journalism I have attempted to demonstrate more completely than has been done before both the preoccupations and the process of Stephen Crane's literary imagination. However, because of their special nature, Crane's poems have not been considered here. The poetry has been carefully edited and studied by Joseph Katz in *The Poems of Stephen Crane* and by Daniel G. Hoffman in *The Poetry of Stephen Crane.* In my opinion, the poetry, because of its idiosyncratic nature, lies beyond the scope of this study.

The University of Virginia Edition of the Works of Stephen Crane, edited under the direction of Fredson Bowers, is presently in preparation, four volumes having appeared at this writing. This edition should certainly be definitive, and I have used it wherever possible. Where it is not, I have used several recent collections, all of which are superior to Follett's Work. Notable among them are *The New York City Sketches of Stephen Crane* and *The War Dispatches of Stephen Crane,* both volumes edited by R. W.

Stallman and E. R. Hagemann, *Stephen Crane: Sullivan County Tales and Sketches,* edited by R. W. Stallman, and *Stephen Crane in the West and Mexico,* edited by Joseph Katz. These have been used as texts in cases in which the Virginia edition is not available.

When a work does not appear in any of these collections, I have turned to *Stephen Crane: Uncollected Writings,* edited by Olov Fryckstedt, an excellent Swedish collection which is unfortunately not always available in the United States. And for work not otherwise collected I have used Thomas A. Gullason's less formally edited collections, *The Complete Short Stories and Sketches of Stephen Crane* and *The Complete Novels of Stephen Crane.* Gullason's collections correct many of the errors and idiosyncrasies of Follett's *Work* and take into account recent scholarly discoveries concerning the texts of *Maggie* and of *The Red Badge of Courage.* For a review and evaluation of several of these texts, see Maurice Bassan, "Our Stephen Crane," *Mad River Review,* I (Spring–Summer, 1965), 85–90.

As for secondary material, any student of Crane must, because of the practical problems consequent to the preparation of a manuscript for publication, interrupt at some arbitrary point his consideration of the virtually unceasing flow of Crane scholarship and criticism. I established January 1, 1970, as the date beyond which I would consider no more material. Of course, there must always be exceptions to such a rule, and the two most recent volumes of the Virginia edition and Joseph Katz's collection have already been mentioned as such.

Acknowledgments

I wish to thank R. W. B. Lewis of Yale University, under whose wise direction this study was originally conceived and executed. I am grateful to the staff of the Library of Congress for providing me with research facilities and otherwise assisting me during the course of this study. Mary Milne Holton has taken an active interest in my work, and A. Dayle Wallace, of Wayne State University, and his wife, Marguerite, have been a steady source of encouragement.

I have been the fortunate beneficiary of the expert advice of William Peden of the University of Missouri. The Graduate Research Board of the University of Maryland has generously supported my work, and my colleagues and students in the Department of English at Maryland have provided me with invaluable advice and assistance.

I would also thank Albert S. Winer for his advice and encouragement. Robert Greene has been of invaluable assistance in the final preparation of the manuscript. Carol Joan Sharlip has over several years provided loyal and imaginative assistance, both in research and in the preparation of the manuscript.

Contents

Preface   vii

Acknowledgments   xi

I.   The Exile from Reality   3

II.   "The Marvellous Boy"   17

III.   A Sparrow's Fall and
a Sparrow's Eye: *Maggie*   35

IV.   Experiments In Misery   55

V.   "The Curtain of the Style"   75

VI.   "To the Destructive Element":
The Red Badge of Courage   86

VII.   New Directions   119

VIII.   "The Color of the Sky"   147

IX.   "War is Kind"   169

X.   Past and Present: Whilomville and London   195

XI.   Showdowns: Crane's West Remembered   225

XII.   "The Glazed Vacancy": Crane's Last Wars   244

XIII.   Conclusions   273

       Notes   287

       References Cited   331

       Index of Crane's Writings   343

       General Index   350

CYLINDER
OF
VISION

I

The Exile from Reality

The world is silly, changeable, any of it's [sic]
decisions can be reversed.
> Stephen Crane in a letter to
> Nellie Crouse, January, 1896.

In the last seven decades Stephen Crane has become one of
America's most explicated and most elusive writers. In 1900,
the year of his death, Crane was regarded as a homegrown
Chatterton, a "marvellous boy" whose career had been cut
off at its budding.[1] Before long he began to fade into obscu-
rity. But with the advent of World War I, readers again
began to notice Stephen Crane; and now it was Crane the
realist, the remarkable technician, the poetic innovator, who
was the object of attention.[2] In the twenties Crane was admired as a rebel against Victorian conformity and hypocrisy.
"It was a fashion in America among the younger writers,"
said Alexander Woollcott, "to spend ten minutes each day
in severely admiring Stephen Crane." [3]

Crane came to academic respectability in the late twenties
and early thirties, first as an example of a "school of American
writing." There were by then two biographies (one the note-
worthy but undocumented life by Thomas Beer)[4] and Wilson Follett's edition (Knopf, 1925–27), the first general col-

3

lection of Crane's work. Yet, although many aspiring writers read Crane, these works provoked no great general response in the reading public during the decade which ensued. Some of the more societally aware critics of the later thirties were displeased by what they considered to be his insensitivity to social causation.[5] But then came the forties and another war, and with Stephen Crane thoroughly established and classified in books such as Alfred Kazin's *On Native Grounds*,[6] readers remembered and reread America's war classic, *The Red Badge of Courage*.[7]

By the late forties, when the important World War II novels were being published, reviewers and critics began to draw inevitable comparisons, and Stephen Crane was up for another major critical rediscovery.[8] John Berryman's psychoanalytically oriented biography and R. W. Stallman's symbol-conscious readings of the fiction soon turned Stephen Crane into a major academic light industry.[9] Since 1952 there have been well over two hundred publications dealing wholly or in part with his life and work. Some critics, disciples of Stallman, have searched Crane's fiction for symbols, Christian and otherwise.[10] Other critics have focused their attention upon Crane's irony,[11] or his imagery.[12] There have been exhaustive source studies,[13] and many new facts concerning his life have lately come to light. New critical orientations have been developed; his work has been examined by anthropological critics;[14] more recently some have tried to show his stories to be prototypes of existential fiction.[15] And two full-length studies of Crane's fiction have attempted to establish it, respectively, as parody and as enactment of psychic conflict.[16] Indeed, critics of almost every prejudice and method have turned to Crane for their subject.

Not all of the important scholarship on Crane has been critical, however. Lillian Gilkes's remarkable biography of

Cora Crane is a valuable collateral source;[17] Joseph Katz's edition of the poems certainly establishes their texts,[18] and R. W. Stallman's biography is sufficiently comprehensive, if occasionally erroneous.[19] Perhaps most important of all—and unfortunately late in arriving—are the editors and collectors, Stallman, Hagemann, Gullason, Fryckstedt, and, most recently and significantly, Fredson Bowers. Only in the late sixties have serious efforts been undertaken to establish a text for the heavily criticized prose of Stephen Crane.

Yet for all this effort, the centers of Crane's stories somehow remain obscure. One can never quite settle on meanings appropriate to the allegedly symbol-bearing images. One can never be entirely sure whether, at a given moment, Crane is being ironic. One can never quite characterize the style or explain the almost unbelievable unevenness in the quality of his later work. And many excellent and difficult stories, somehow inconvenient to the usual generalizations, remain unconsidered or only fleetingly examined. Too often an understanding of one story, when finally arrived at, contradicts a seemingly sound assertion about another. The critics retreat to biography and intellectual history, while Crane's fiction remains elusive, its meanings still unclear.

From this confusion, however, there have emerged two consistently recurrent lines of critical opinion about Stephen Crane. One is the notion that he is the virtual embodiment of literary naturalism. From the time that the word came into currency among American critics, it has been employed to describe Crane. V. L. Parrington called Crane a naturalist in 1930.[20] C. C. Walcutt redefined the term and studied Crane as a "Naturalist and Impressionist" in 1956.[21] In 1965 Donald Pizer, in an article which explores the conflict between Crane's irony and the conventions of literary naturalism, concludes by speaking of Crane's "uniquely personal style and vision within naturalistic conventions." [22]

Naturalism has always been a confusing term in American literary criticism. No one is quite sure whether it is to be taken to mean a kind of fatalistic pessimism (the assumption of Parrington, Harry Hartwick, and Oscar Cargill)[23] or an optimistic reformer's faith in a progress born of scientific knowledge (George W. Meyer's position)[24] or something in between, a vision at once pessimistic and optimistic (C. C. Walcutt's argument).[25] But whatever is meant, all of the critics using the term seem to be in agreement upon one point: they recognize in the naturalist a writer committed to an objective, scientific, positivistic attitude toward his subject—to an attempt to represent the thing before him in a manner which is objectively and absolutely true.[26]

Some of these same critics also use the word *impressionist* to describe Stephen Crane. In fact, it is with Crane as the most obvious example—in American literature, at least— that literary historians have begun to include impressionism as a characteristic of literary naturalism. In any event, Crane has been consistently described as an impressionist—though with varying intentions—by many critics, some during his own lifetime, and an increasing number writing in the 1960's. Edward Garnett, Crane's contemporary, called him "the chief impressionist of our day." [27] Joseph Conrad had said the same thing in a letter to Garnett in 1897: "He is *the only* impressionist and *only* an impressionist." [28] It was as an impressionist that Crane began to make his appearance in American literary histories, and in the introduction to Thomas Beer's biography of Crane in 1923 Conrad reminded Crane's readers of Garnett's dictum.[29]

Thus it is no surprise that both John Berryman, in his 1950 biography, and R. W. Stallman, in *Stephen Crane: An Omnibus* of 1952 (the two books which announced the most recent and most sustained Crane revival), gave considerable attention to Crane's "impressionism," [30] and the interest has continued. Orm Øverland's full restatement and intelligent development of the position of those critics who emphasize the significance of Crane's impressionism appeared in 1965.[31]

As Øverland points out, implicit to impressionism is an attitude toward reality which is radically different from that implicit to naturalism. For the impressionist regards the sensorily received impressions of reality to *be*, and not to *represent*, reality itself. Reality—the reality with which the artist is to be concerned—is essentially subjective, and not objective. There is no objective and final truth which it is the artist's duty to assert. Rather it is for the artist simply to render the impression of the thing as it is apprehended by the senses. In doing so, he has come as close as is humanly possible to representing the thing itself.

Indeed, if Stephen Crane was both an impressionist and a naturalist, there is implicit in his sensibility an inherent contradiction which must either diminish the value of his work or must generate from it a statement implicit in which is a kind of double vision, an ironical paradox. It is interesting that Crane repeatedly engaged that contradiction or confronted that paradox. The confrontation is so complete, the unblinking examination of the opposition so repeated, that one might even see that confrontation in Crane's work as a pervasive theme, a doubled awareness which informs contradiction and achieves irony, not invalidation.

One can see Crane's concern in his recurring subject. For his stories and novels, many of his poems, and much of his more imaginative journalistic writing repeatedly represent and turn upon some event of visual apprehension. Sometimes a character for the first time sees something—perhaps the situation in which he finds himself. Sometimes the protagonist's safety depends upon how he is seen, or whether he is seen, by others. In one celebrated story two characters confront one another; one sees clearly, and the other does not. But almost everywhere, in one way or another, Crane is concerned with the capability of the eye.

Stephen Crane's style reflects this concern. His frequent use of color images, his careful and consistent commitments to points of view, his use of synaesthetic figures in his descriptions of excited activity, all suggest an imagination engaged in recording the event of perception and in asserting reality as it appears to the objective eye. There is another side to Crane's style—the deliberate heightening of descriptive language, the frequent use of ironic figures of comparison, the deliberate denial of meaning at a moment of high emotion—which receives less comment. Yet these devices work to deflate impressionistic techniques, or naturalistic formulations, to emphasize the inaccuracy of the character's apprehension of an objective reality. It is the juxtaposition of these techniques which articulate Crane's ironic awareness.

Crane's concern with the ironies of apprehension often determined his choice of characters and his attitude toward them. His fiction is filled with cognitive innocents—characters who, in the course of the story, come to see something for the first time—untried soldiers, reporters in their first war, children. Very frequently Crane's are initiation stories; stories in which the way a character apprehends a thing for the first time is crucially important. The capacity of a character to see clearly is admired by Stephen Crane, delusion or inadequacy of vision is often ridiculed or treated with contempt or, if more gently, with patronizing good humor. For Crane is not concerned only with subjective reality; he holds his characters to some extent responsible for their vision. And he is concerned with the causes of visual incapacity. Although an inadequacy of the eye is sometimes presented as being determined (as in *Maggie*) by one's environment, clear seeing can also be learned or forgotten, can be acquired or lost.

The capacity for vision can, of course, have dramatic significance in Crane's stories. Clear seeing can put one in danger or protect one from difficulty. Climaxes often turn around moments of apprehension or of confrontation. Often —especially in the early sketches—comic effects are achieved through exposures of characters' delusions. Everywhere— from the early Sullivan County sketches to *The Red Badge of Courage,* to the western stories, to "The Monster," and even to the profound apprehensions of the men in "The Open Boat" and of Lieutenant Timothy Lean in "The Upturned Face"—Stephen Crane's stories are dramas of vision.

Out of Crane's concentration upon and evaluation of the sensory apprehension of his characters arises an obvious metaphor, a metaphor almost as old as the language itself. In describing his characters' capacities for vision, Crane is also often describing their capacities for understanding. Seeing can mean comprehension as well as apprehension. Maggie's capacity to see refers inevitably to her capacity to understand the reality of which she is a part. *The Red Badge of Courage,* as has often been said, is really a *Bildungsroman,* a novel of education, one of Crane's stories of cognitive innocence. It is "the apprehension of life through the play of perceptions" which is so often at the center of Crane's fiction.[32]

Such a metaphor was, of course, not original with Stephen Crane. One has only to remember Hawkeye, or the "transparent eyeball" of which Ralph Waldo Emerson spoke, or the doubled vision of whales which commanded Ishmael's attention in *Moby Dick* to recognize that the literature which was Stephen Crane's as a national heritage seems unusually committed to vision. And it is also obvious to the reader of American fiction that along with the concern for vision as a metaphor for understanding, a whole panoply of devices emphasizing visual experience—the whiteness of whales and of polar landscapes, scarlet letters—are familiar landmarks to the imagination.

Perhaps more important than these landmarks was Crane's own experience in the serving of his literary apprenticeship. For Stephen Crane began as a reporter, a hired observer of events, whose job it was to apprehend and objectify experience. For the reporter the eye is terribly important; for the novice in the late eighties and early nineties a "professional" attitude existed, involving a certain cynicism toward generalization and a commitment to actuality, to "things as they are." [33]

When Crane moved away from New York and settled in England in 1897, he found himself in the company of other visually oriented writers, who were interested in impressionism and its implications for literature. In the very summer that Crane arrived in England, Joseph Conrad was writing the preface to *The Nigger of the "Narcissus."* In the autumn the two were to meet and begin their close friendship with a long ramble through London and an excited literary discussion. In the preface mentioned above, Conrad had just written: "All art, therefore, appeals primarily to the senses, and the artistic aim when expressing itself in written words must also make its appeal in the senses, if its high desire is to reach the secret spring of responsive emotions. . . . My task which I am trying to achieve is, by the power of the written word to make you hear, to make you feel—it is, before all, to make you *see*." [34] Stephen Crane undoubtedly agreed. He had been for several years instinctively applying the very principles in his writing which Conrad and the other formulators of literary impressionism were setting down. But Crane had, in a sense, gone beyond impressionism even before it was formulated. For he had committed to his concern with seeing, not only his literary method, but also the very theme central to his fiction. His commitment to vision was procedural, but it was also substantive.

This substantive commitment is perhaps the key to another important awareness—the awareness of the nature of Crane's place in the development of what has been variously identified as "modern" literature. In *Poets of Reality*, a remarkable book which has established a recent and significant definition for modernity in twentieth-century literature, J. Hillis Miller has identified a dramatic change in the literature of our century, a change equivalent in degree to the appearance of romanticism a hundred and fifty years before. Professor Miller has traced the sources of that change to an emergent nihilistic vision embodied in the works of Joseph Conrad. This nihilism, according to Miller, was a natural development of romantic subjectivism in which Nietzsche's notion of the death of God was only one inevitable step. Following his discussion of that notion as set forth in Nietzsche's *The Joyful Wisdom*, Professor Miller describes the nihilism thus:

> Man has killed God by separating his subjectivity from everything but itself. The ego has put everything in doubt, and has defined all outside itself as the object of its thinking power. Cogito ergo sum: the absolute certainty about the self reached by Descartes' hyperbolic doubt leads to the assumption that things exist, for me at least, only because I think them. When everything exists only as reflected in the ego, then man has drunk up the sea. If man is defined as subject, everything else turns into object. This includes God, who now becomes merely the highest object of man's knowledge. God, once the creative sun, the power establishing the horizon where heaven and earth come together, becomes an object of thought like any other. When man drinks up the sea he also drinks up God, the creator of the sea. In this way man is the murderer of God. Man once was a created being among other created beings, existing in

an objective world sustained by its creator, and oriented by that creator as to high and low, right and wrong. Now, to borrow the passage from Bradley which Eliot quotes in the notes to "The Waste Land," "regarded as an existence which appears in a soul, the whole world for each is peculiar and private to that soul."

When God and the creation become objects of consciousness, man becomes a nihilist. Nihilism is the nothingness of consciousness when consciousness becomes the foundation of everything. Man the murderer of God and drinker of the sea of creation wanders through the infinite nothingness of his own ego. Nothing now has any worth except the arbitrary value he sets on things as he assimilates them into his consciousness. Nietzsche's transvaluation of values is the expunging of God as the absolute value and source of the valuation of everything else. In the emptiness left after the death of God, man becomes the sovereign valuer, the measure of all things.[35]

The "special place" which Professor Miller assigns to Joseph Conrad "lies in the fact that in him the nihilism covertly dominant in modern culture is brought to the surface and shown for what it is." Conrad, Miller goes on to say,

can best be understood as the culmination of a development within the novel, a development particularly well-marked in England, though of course it also exists on the continent and in America. After the attempt to recover an absent God in nineteenth-century poetry, a subsequent stage in man's spiritual history is expressed more fully in fiction than in poetry. The novel shows man attempting to establish a human world based on interpersonal relations. In the novel man comes more and more to be defined in terms of the strength of his will, and the secret nihilism resulting from his new place as the source of all value is slowly revealed.

Thus Professor Miller devotes sixty pages of his *Poets of Reality* to a study of the prose fiction of Joseph Conrad. However, when a student of Stephen Crane reads Miller's discussion of the sea stories, of "Heart of Darkness," and of *The Secret Agent*, he is struck by the remarkable similarity of the techniques and concerns of the American writer to those which are being identified in Conrad's work. And when Professor Miller generalizes as to the purpose of Joseph Conrad's fiction, that generalization would seem to him to apply to the fiction of Stephen Crane as well.

> If civilization and each man in it move farther from reality the more completely the humanizing of the world succeeds, is there any chance to escape from the falsity of the human? How can man be liberated from his dream? The aim of all Conrad's fiction is to destroy in the reader his bondage to illusion, and to give him a glimpse of the truth, however dark and disquieting that truth may be. His work might be called an effort of demystification. It attempts to rescue man from his alienation. His problem in reaching this goal is double: to lift the veil of illusion, and to make the truth appear.[36]

Professor Miller also points out that, for Conrad, "The human world is a lie. All human ideals, even the ideal of fidelity, are lies. They are lies in the sense that they are human fabrications. They derive from man himself and are supported by nothing outside him." Yet the commitment of Conrad's characters to these ideals, and the ironic if sometimes partial awareness of Conrad's narrators as to their invalidity, is not unlike a similar commitment and awareness to be found in Stephen Crane's characters and narrators. It obtains for Henry Fleming and for the narrator of *The Red Badge of Courage*, for the Swede and for Mr. Blanc of "The Blue Hotel," for Scratchy Wilson and for the narrator of "The Bride Comes to Yellow Sky," to take the most obvious examples. The exile from reality as an inevitable condition of humanity, which Professor Miller sees as a recurrent theme in Conrad's fiction, can also be found as a theme in "The

Monster" and "The Open Boat." Conrad's repetitive effort
to bring his reader to engage reality with a hallucinatory intensity, an intensity which sharpens apprehension as it diminishes interpretation and which is often achieved by detached images or by metaphor, is also identified by Miller
and can also be found in *Maggie* or in *George's Mother.*
Conrad's awareness of the fragile absurdity of civilization
as it is set against an omnipresent and dark natural chaos
is apparent not only in "Heart of Darkness" but in Crane's
Sullivan County sketches and in "The Blue Hotel" and in
several of his western stories. The threatening quality of the
apprehension of uninterpretable experience which Miller
recognizes for Conrad's characters is also very real for Crane's
characters in "The Monster" and in "The Upturned Face."

For a single striking analogy, consider what Professor Miller
has to say about the ending of *The Secret Agent* in light of
what happens at the end of Crane's *Maggie.* In discussing
Winnie Verloc's suicide by drowning in the Channel, Miller
notes how Winnie's death is a conclusion of a process of
gradual depersonalization, how Conrad "shows her progres-
sively approaching a state of anonymity and melting into the
blackness of death," how "everything seems to have come
out of this fluidity and to be in danger of returning to it
on any dark, rainy night." [37] It is also a dark, rainy night
upon which Maggie kills herself by drowning, after a surreally
rendered walk across the city. In Conrad's novel Comrade
Ossipon also goes on a rather fully rendered walk in the city;
it occurs just after he has abandoned Winnie to her final
train ride. In his discussion of that walk Professor Miller
speaks of the motif of walking in Conrad's novel and shows
how it "signifies man's inability to escape from himself." In
Maggie there are two chapters following Maggie's suicide,
one concerned with her seducer's escape into the oblivion
of alcohol, the other with her mother's escape into self-

delusion. If Professor Miller's evidence of Conrad's nihilistic vision is valid, and I believe that it is, it would seem that there is evidence of a similar vision in Crane's fiction.

It is well known that after Crane settled in England in 1897, he and Joseph Conrad were drawn to one another by what Conrad himself recognized as an almost magnetic attraction.[38] That attraction, a result of Crane's reading *The Nigger of the "Narcissus"* and of Conrad's reading *The Red Badge of Courage*, ripened into an intense literary friendship, perhaps not unlike Melville and Hawthorne's; Crane and Conrad were to remain friends and to support one another's literary endeavors until Crane's untimely death in 1900. The facts surrounding that friendship are well known; they have been set forth by Eric Solomon in some detail, and they need not be repeated here.[39] Unfortunately, the significance of that friendship to the work of the two writers has not been so carefully or so closely studied.[40] From a look at dates alone, however, it is obvious that any similarities between Crane's early work and the work of Conrad are the result of natural affinities rather than of influence. *The Nigger of the "Narcissus,"* which first drew Crane's attention to the older writer, did not begin to appear until August of 1897, and by then Crane had already completed *Maggie, The Red Badge of Courage, George's Mother, The Little Regiment* stories, most of the New York sketches, "The Open Boat," and *The Third Violet*. The impact of Crane's work upon the imagination of Joseph Conrad is much less clear, and much more interesting. But whatever else may be said, it is clear that when Crane and Conrad met, the greater part of the younger writer's career lay behind him, or, to put it differently, that Crane's nihilistic vision had already come to him.

Thus Stephen Crane might well be said to occupy a place in the history of the beginnings of modern fiction which anticipates—even prefigures—that of Joseph Conrad. Crane's sense of man's inability to see, his simultaneous effort—by use of an impressionism both procedural and substantive—to make his readers apprehend reality clearly, his ironic awareness of the impossibility of man's sustaining that apprehension, his arrival at an ultimately nihilistic vision— all are antecedent to similar awarenesses in Conrad, awarenesses which Professor Miller has set forth as crucial to the development of modern literature. Perhaps Stephen Crane's contribution to the development of modern fiction is also of crucial significance. In part it will be my purpose here to suggest Crane's importance by defining his significance.

It is my primary intention, however, to establish the presence of his doubled and opposed commitment—a commitment to vision which generated his irony and laid the foundation for Crane's nihilism. That commitment is doubled because it is both thematic and methodological; it is opposed in that it implies both a subjective and an objective view of reality. For if Crane's concerns are the impressionistic concerns, his understanding assumes both an impressionist's and a naturalist's orientation. By examining the whole body of Crane's fiction I hope to define more clearly the nature of this complex commitment. I shall examine the source of the paradoxical irony which emanates from his opposed orientation. I shall attempt to characterize and to illustrate the devices peculiar to his impressionistic technique. I shall explore the thematic implications of Crane's visual metaphor, and establish his evaluations and standards for clear seeing. I hope thereby to move closer to the center of Stephen Crane's imagination. I shall seek readings for his stories, sketches, and novels which will expose more of their elusive meanings and which will specify more clearly the proper place for their author in modern literature.

peer at the deck of a passing ship. A man stands with his hand on a lever and changes the scene at will.[9]

New York City Sketches, 270

For an instant the reader almost feels that he is not on an American boardwalk at all but in Plato's cave. It is a sense which is to recur when he reads Crane's "London Impressions" of 1897.

Another such moment appears in an ironic representation of how one Asbury Park resident sees. In "On the Boardwalk" of August 14 Crane described the beneficent presence of James A. Bradley, the founder of the resort, as he walks upon the boardwalk and—like the Lord of Creation—surveys his handiwork: "It warms his heart to see the thousands of people tramping over his boards, helter-skeltering in his sand and diving into that ocean of the Lord's which is adjacent to the beach of James A. Bradley." [10]

The most notorious of Stephen Crane's contributions to the *Tribune* of 1892 is the one which seriously damaged the Crane brothers' relationships with the newspaper. In the August 21 issue of the Sunday *Tribune* and under the headline of "On the New Jersey Coast" there appeared an account, written by Stephen Crane, of the parade of the Junior Order of United American Mechanics before a crowd of middle-class Asbury Park resorters. Whether the account, which elicited an irate letter to the editor from an offended union member and required an apology from the *Tribune,* actually got both Cranes fired (it almost certainly did) or really brought about the election of Grover Cleveland (it almost certainly did not) are still matters of some dispute, but there can be no doubt, when we read the sketch, that Crane's own concern was hardly political.[11] For his representation is designed to show two groups of people confronting one another without any comprehension of what the other is all about. It is not the union but the radical innocence of the American middle class ("Asbury Park creates nothing") which is the subject of Crane's sardonic sketch. His concern is manifest in the concluding paragraph.

> The bona fide Asbury Parker is a man to whom a dollar, when held close to his eye, often shuts out any impression he may have had that other people possess rights. He is apt to consider that men and women, especially city men and women, were created to be mulcted by him. Hence the tan-colored, sun-beaten honesty in the faces of the members of the Junior Order of United American Mechanics is expected to have a very staggering effect upon them. The visitors were men who possessed principles.*
>
> *New York City Sketches,* 272–73

The summer of 1892 was also the summer of Stephen Crane's first meeting and infatuation with Lily Brandon Munroe. The infatuation was not easily put aside by Crane; although he was unsuccessful in persuading Mrs. Munroe to elope with him, he remembered and even pursued her until late in 1898.[12] The infatuation manifested itself in his writing in that first summer, for Mrs. Munroe figured in his sketch of a confrontation between resort ladies and a local fisherman-fireman in "The Captain." And she continued to haunt his writing a year later, when Crane produced a graceful little fantasy-romance (Stallman calls it a "wish-fulfillment of what might have happened to himself and Mrs. Lily Monroe")[13] rather obviously set in an amusement park at Asbury Park and around the merry-go-round, which Crane had already represented in a piece for the *Tribune* of July 17, 1892, entitled "Joys of Seaside Life."[14]

That story, "The Pace of Youth," was not written until

---

* A similar confrontation—between two uncomprehending groups of people whose failure to understand one another is the result of their social conditioning—was to be described by Crane in one of the Mexican stories, "The Five White Mice" of 1898. But of course the most notable example of this theme would occur in "The Bride Comes to Yellow Sky."

the spring of 1893, and it must be regarded as one of Crane's most graceful early works.[15] It is established in the illusory world of summer romance and is an account of the courtship and elopement of a merry-go-round attendant and the boss's daughter (named, not "Lily," but "Lizzie"). But its freshness and charm is enhanced because the courtship that precedes the elopement is conducted, not with speech, but with the eyes.

> Often the dark-eyed girl peered between the shining wires, and, upon being detected by the young man, she usually turned her head away quickly to prove to him that she was not interested. At other times, however, her eyes seemed filled with a tender fear lest he should fall from that exceedingly dangerous platform. As for the young man, it was plain that these glances filled him with valor, and he stood carelessly upon his perch, as if he deemed it of no consequence that he might fall from it. In all the complexities of his daily life and duties he found opportunity to gaze ardently at the vision behind the netting.
>
> This silent courtship was conducted over the heads of the crowd who thronged about the bright machine. The swift, eloquent glances of the young man went noiselessly and unseen with their message. There had finally become established between the two in this manner a subtle understanding and companionship. They communicated accurately all that they felt. The boy told his love, his reverence, his hope in the changes of the future. The girl told him that she loved him, that she did not love him, that she did not know if she loved him. Sometimes a little sign saying "Cashier" in gold letters, and hanging upon the silvered netting, got directly in range and interfered with the tender message.
>
> *Virginia*, V, 4–5

The story is considerably more mature than the 1892 pieces. It is stylistically succinct; its images are fresh and their symbolic implications are unobtrusive (as in the case of the "Cashier" sign above, for the father's greed is to be an obstacle to the relationship); it is told from a delicately controlled ironic distance. "The Pace of Youth" concludes with a delightful (and symbolic) chase, a futile pursuit of youth by age. And it ends on a note of negation (the father, after losing the chase, "made a gesture. It meant that at any rate he was not responsible"). The story has a quality reminiscent of a first rate silent movie.*

Crane's curious attitude toward his own material is also apparent in another New Jersey piece, published in the New York *Sunday Press* of November 11, 1894, and presumably written earlier that autumn. "Ghosts on the New Jersey Coast" consists of a compilation of local ghost stories, which at first are treated ironically, indeed are even parodied by the author. But if Crane begins by scoffing at the stories he tells, he ends (in recounting the tale of a phantom black dog similar to the dog of the Sullivan County tale) by almost frightening himself. "Ghosts on the New Jersey Coast" is a remarkable exercise in tonal control in which the narrator is represented as being unbelieving but nonetheless frightened.[16]

Stephen Crane was not to write directly out of his experiences at Asbury Park again except in a single journalistic piece which appeared first in the New York *Journal* of August 16, 1896, long after the author of *The Red Badge* had made his reputation. The sketch—a much more mature and contrapuntal performance in which Crane remembers once again the perambulations of James A. Bradley, opens with two paragraphs in which the now mature journalist sets forth his earlier rather ambitious journalistic intentions. In these paragraphs there is ascertainable a certain sense of

---

* *Virginia*, V, 12. Also note the motifs in this story recurring in "The Blue Hotel," for both the symbolically suggestive cash register and the denial of responsibility in the final sentence reappear in the later story.

disappointment at the results.* And indeed Crane's early Asbury Park sketches were of no particular distinction and showed no particular promise. Even the early attempts at fiction, although at least one of them is gracefully executed, demonstrated no unusual imaginative capacity. It is difficult to realize that the same Stephen Crane in 1892 had already completed preliminary drafts of *Maggie*. But his writings of that summer are significant for the directions in which they point. In them the concerns and preoccupations of the young writer began to become apparent.

Stephen Crane as a writer of fiction, however, had had his real beginning earlier in that same year of 1892, a beginning which can be traced to the appearance of the first of the Sullivan County sketches in the New York *Tribune*. Crane had shown two of these pieces to Willis Johnson as early as the summer of 1891, but it was not until February 21, 1892, that the first of them was printed in Johnson's paper.[17] Eleven more appeared throughout the spring and early summer. "A Tent in Agony," appearing in December, was Crane's first professional magazine publication. Another was published in the Syracuse *University Herald* on Decem-

---

* It is a sad thing to go to town with a correspondent's determination to discover at once wherein this particular town differs from all other towns. We seek our descriptive material in the differences, perhaps, and dismay comes upon the agile mind of the newspaper man when the eternal overwhelming resemblances smite his eyes. We often find our glory in heralding the phenomena and we have a sense of oppression, perhaps, when the similarities tower too high in the sky.

The variations being subtle, and the resemblances being mountainous, we revenge ourselves by declaring the subject unworthy of a fine hand. We brand it with some opportune name, which places it beyond the fence of literary art, and depart to earn our salaries describing two-headed pigs. Asbury Park somewhat irritates the anxious writer, because it persists in being distinctly American, reflecting all our best habits and manners, when it might resemble a town in Siberia, or Jerusalem, during a siege.

"Stephen Crane at Asbury Park," *New York City Sketches*, 283

ber 23, and several others remained unpublished for the time being.[18]

These sketches were set in the forested mountains near Hartwood, New York, where Crane had spent winter school vacations and holidays, and where he had visited as recently as September of 1891.[19] The writing which these visits occasioned is clearly the most significant of Crane's preliminary work; in fact, the Sullivan County sketches occupy a place in the Crane canon which is roughly the equivalent of the *In Our Time* sketches of Ernest Hemingway. Like Hemingway's, Crane's sketches are camping sketches, frequently stories of hunting or fishing. Also like the young man in Hemingway's stories, Crane's characters reappear in later sketches. But most important, in the Sullivan County sketches, just as in *In Our Time*, we can observe a young writer emerging from an apprentice journalism to attempt an experimental fiction in which—with an artistic method that was to become characteristic—he engaged directly and for the first time the themes and questions he would repeatedly confront as a mature artist.

The first several sketches were hardly fictional undertakings. Rather, they were ironic journalistic essays which undertook—in a sometimes deliberately overblown prose—to underline the discrepancy between art and life as it was to be seen in Sullivan County. "The Last of the Mohicans" (the first of the sketches to appear) asserted in a final paragraph the reality of Uncas, who was not Cooper's noble Indian at all, but rather a drunken beggar of Sullivan County. "Hunting Wild Hogs" and "The Last Panther," the next two sketches, were also reportorial. They were realistic descriptions of hunting, descriptions always held in an ironic opposition to the "tales of the panther's gleaming eyes and sharp claws" to be told afterwards by the old hunters—

stories of which the described event was surely to become the subject.

Crane achieved an articulated awareness of the discrepancy between fact and fancy in "Sullivan County Bears," the next sketch which followed. "It is difficult to reconcile the bear of fiction with the bear of reality," he wrote.[20] In "Sullivan County Bears" Crane took the first step toward representing the difference between these two bears—toward confronting, if not reconciling this discrepancy—by telling us what Sullivan County bears and bear hunting are really like. It is in the next journalistic sketch that Crane confronted the nature and causes of the Sullivan County hunting tales' misrepresentations.

"The Way in Sullivan County" is in a sense the fulcrum of the sketches. For in it Crane turned away from journalistic descriptions of reality to devote his attention to the folklore of the county. In this sketch Crane began to consider the theme which was to be of major significance throughout his career as a writer of fiction. Here he took a first direct look at human distortion of reality, or how men see and how they refuse or fail to see. Here Crane looked at the causes of misapprehension and misrepresentation of reality; later he would consider consequences. But in either case, the examination involved the problem of the narrator and how he apprehends reality; Crane's own style often suggests a narrating *persona* who is always a bit distanced from his story and sometimes rather clearly ironic in relating it. But throughout Crane's works it is the apprehending eye and its capabilities—his own as well as his character's—which was constantly of concern to him.

"The Way in Sullivan County" begins very simply as "A Study in the Evolution of the Hunting Yarn" (or so it is subtitled). Crane mentions at the outset the "enjoyment" felt by the hunters "when the unoffending city man appears," but he moves closer to the complex causes of misapprehension when he tells us, "In a shooting country, no man should tell just exactly what he did. He should tell what he would have liked to do or what he expected to do, just as if he accomplished it" (*Sullivan County Tales*, 60).

Crane then concludes in narrative (indeed, Crane's shift from journalism to fiction can be said to have taken place within this sketch) when he tells his reader two tales, "one of great execution done by the liar, the other in which the bear figures as one who saw great things." But in the second, Crane leaves his reader, not with the sense of the "great thing" of a battle between panther and bear, but rather with a sense of the beastliness of the hunters who have observed it. The sentence concluding the story has the flat and undercutting factuality of many of Crane's later endings. "Then they shot the victor." Two months later, on July 17, there would appear a third hunters' story, "Bear and Panther," a somewhat naturalistic account of the revenge of a mother panther upon a bear who killed her kittens. In this sketch the hunters again take their place in a red-in-tooth-and-claw natural cycle by shooting the victorious panther. And on July 24 there appeared in the *Tribune* a sketch called "Two Men and A Bear," in which a realistic account of how dogs fight bears is followed by a hunter's tale of how a bear frightened two men.[21]

Before the *Tribune* published either, however, Crane began to turn the Sullivan County material to purposes which were clearly fictional. Now he would tell hunters' tales himself—in a way which would simultaneously and ironically expose the reality of the situation and the false apprehension of it by those characters who were participants. In July, 1892, five such stories appeared in the *Tribune*. In December two more appeared, one in *Cosmopolitan* and one in the Syracuse *University Herald,* and at least three other stories remained unpublished until after the year of Crane's death.[22]

All of the ten stories have at their centers one or more of the same characters, four hunters from the city who generally remain nameless and are identified only by epithets.[23] All of the stories turn on events of confrontation or of misapprehension, in which a reality is seen for the first time or in which something is mistaken for something else. Indeed, of the ten, four follow almost identical plot patterns. In each of these the protagonist, whose perception is distorted by fear, acts inappropriately or simply discovers that the object of his fear is less dangerous than it originally seemed to be. Fear is dissipated in a comic anticlimax.[24]

Thus in "Four Men in a Cave" (the first of these stories to appear in the *Tribune*) Crane's four men, determined to explore a cave, discover inside an ominous figure who threatens one of them ("the little man"), force him to play poker, then dismisses him. The story concludes with the four men being told that the figure they have confronted was not a "vampire," a "ghost," a "Druid before the sacrifice," or "the shade of an Aztec witch doctor," as they had first believed, but only Tom Gardner, a local eccentric.[25] In "A Tent in Agony" the "little man," left alone to protect the camp while the others seek supplies, is chased by an intruding bear. The bear becomes entangled in a tent and is seen by the three other returning campers. Crane tells us, "It seemed to them like a white-robed phantom pursued by hornets. Its moans rifled the hemlock twigs" (*Sullivan County Tales*, 108).[26] But again the story concludes comically as the illusory fear is dispelled.

In "The Cry of a Huckleberry Pudding" three campers in the forest are frightened by terrifying cries in the night. They believe they are hearing a monster who has seized their companion, but they discover that the cries are from the "little man" himself, who is crying out because of the pain of an upset stomach. And in "A Ghoul's Accountant" the "little man" is frightened by an apparent madman, a "ghoul," who turns out to be only a Sullivan County native who needs assistance in arithmetic.

The pattern of action established by Crane in these stories was to be an important one in his later work; *The Red Badge of Courage* is, among other things, an account of the dissipation of distortions of apprehension induced by fear. Besides these four stories, several other Sullivan County sketches followed patterns of action which, though not precisely identical, were closely similar. In a story not published until 1949, "An Explosion of Seven Babies," the "little man" climbs a stone wall in the forest to confront an enraged giant of a woman whose anger causes her to mistake him for another and to attack him. Only later does he discover that the intended victim was the seller of the flypaper which the woman's children have eaten. In "The Octopush" the plight of the four men, stranded on stumps in a swamp by a drunken fisherman's guide, is relieved when the guide, in his alcoholic hallucination, flees to the "little man's" stump and exclaims, "Stump turned inter an octopush. I was asettin' on his mouth." "The Black Dog"—perhaps a deliberate parody of Ambrose Bierce's "The Boarded Window"[27]— is a half-ironic account of the appearance of a traditional spectral black dog at death and the fear of Crane's four hunters who are terrified and yet deny the possibility of such strange happenings.

"The Mesmeric Mountain" (published posthumously in *Last Words* of 1902) is a second story bordering on fantasy, but here the fantasy is more clearly delusionary—the product of the "little man's" solipsistic delusion that a mountain has "been follerin' me." Crane was to use the relationship of a man to a mountain in several of the *Black Riders* poems which appeared in 1895.[28] "The Holler Tree" is another prototypal story; it describes a man (the "little man") who, though he is frightened, is driven to a foolish and dangerous undertaking to make good a boast.[29] Crane would tell a similar story in "A Mystery of Heroism," a considerably more mature and more profound tale. "The Holler Tree" simply concludes in another comic anticlimax. Another significant prototype—that of the simple account of an initiation, a rite of passage—comes in one of the most perfect of the sketches, "Killing His Bear." But even here the description of the initiate's fear is of major importance.

Thus Crane's Sullivan County stories are evidence of the discovery of patterns of action and of themes which were to be of increasing importance to him later. Throughout, Crane's concern with the way men see is apparent. But the way men tell is also important in Crane's Sullivan County. "Four Men in a Cave," the story which Willis Johnson so admired,[30] begins with a motive for action expressed by the "little man": " 'We can tell a great tale when we get back to the city if we investigate this thing' " (*Sullivan County Tales*, 71). When we read Crane's conclusion to the story, an ironic echo of these words, we remember that in Sullivan County but also in the city the telling of the tale is sometimes more important to men than the event. From here it is but a short step to the profounder implications of the final sentence of "The Open Boat."

As the tale is important to Crane's characters, the telling of it was important to Crane himself. And as the tale and its antecedent reality are ironically juxtaposed, so it is with the reality which he reported and the language with which he reported it. For the language in the Sullivan County stories —the "somber-jocular, sable, fantastic prose," as John Berryman characterizes it,[31] is entirely inappropriate to Crane's subject. An obvious example is from "The Cry of a Huckleberry Pudding":

"Oh, thunderation," wailed the little man. Suddenly he rolled about on the ground and gave vent to a howl that rolled and pealed over the width of forest. Its tones told of death and fear and unpaid debts. It clamored like a song of forgotten war, and died away to the scream of a maiden. The pleadings of fire-surrounded children mingled with the calls of wave-threatened sailors. Two barbaric tribes clashed together on a sun-burnt plain; a score of bare-kneed clansmen crossed claymores amid grey rocks; a woman saw a lover fall; a dog was stabbed in an alley; a steel knight bit dust with bloody mouth; a savage saw a burning home.

Sullivan County Tales, 120

And all to describe a stomachache. This is obviously deliberate overwriting, and it is not sufficient to characterize it simply as a parody of romantic fiction.[32] For implicit in this kind of overwriting—graceless though it may be—is an awareness of man's tendency to inflate experience to grandiose dimensions.

This implication is everywhere in Crane's Sullivan County writing. It is in a description of a pratfall in the dark in "Four Men in a Cave" ("The fat man, having lost the support of one pillar-like foot, lurched forward. His body smote the next man, who hurtled into the next man. Then they all fell upon the cursing little man.") or in a phrase like "eyes that saw the unknown" to describe a drunken guide's frightened face or "the glare of a tigress" to describe the face of an angry country woman.[33] And everywhere Crane was ironic. Crane the reporter was deliberately overstating, and his overstatement suggests something of his character's apprehension.

But deliberate overwriting is not the only means by which Crane served this suggestion. For throughout the sketches Crane undertook experiments with adjectives and descriptive metaphors which will bear considerable fruit in later works. Synaesthetic adjectives abound. Sounds are frequently colored ("crimson oaths" or "lurid oaths which blazed against the sky") and often emotions are concretized ("white terror").[34] Crane would gradually develop control of these images—in *Maggie* and elsewhere (notably in *The Red Badge*)—as elements in a developed and responsive style. Here again the Sullivan County stories serve as prototypes.

Crane later put his Sullivan County experience to use in two other stories, neither of which utilized the four characters who figured in the others.[35] One of these, "Across the Covered Pit," was probably also written in 1892 (for, as Stallman suggests, it is a companion piece to "Four Men in a Cave")[36] and is also an account of fear. It describes a preacher-spelunker and his Negro guide as they cross a hitherto untested pit cover. The other, "The Snake," is the result of an experience in the summer of 1894, and is in a more mature style.[37] But here again is a story of confrontation, fear, and primitive response; "The Snake" is the account of what happens when man and dog meet a snake, of the almost physical fear, and of the battle which follows. Man and snake are natural enemies; each strikes at the other, and the snake is killed. In this short sketch, a *tour de force* with Crane writing in a language which seems restrained and compressed after the earlier sketches, there is a representation of a confrontation with an ultimate reality—a rational, absurd, yet terribly dangerous reality. Here is a confrontation conditioned by emotions which go deep, deeper than individual psychology. "And now the man went sheer raving mad from the emotions of his forefathers and from his own. He came to close quarters. He gripped the stick with his two hands and made it speed like a flail. The snake, tumbling in the anguish of final despair, fought, bit, flung itself upon this stick which was taking its life" (*Sullivan County Tales*, 137).

After such a confrontation the response is ritual, and the ritual is one of telling. At the story's end, the man decides to "carry Mr. Snake home to show the girls." Even though "The Snake" is generally ignored by Crane's critics and editors, it is as perfect a piece of short writing as appears in the Crane canon. And even in this sketch, it is apprehension, the snake's and the man's, which is at the center. "The Snake" prefigures the later Crane of "The Upturned Face."

In only a few years Crane—committed to his own understanding of the "realism" advocated by William Dean Howells and Hamlin Garland—would be somewhat apologetic for the Sullivan County sketches.[38] And thereafter they have been of interest only to the serious student of Crane. Few of the sketches are richly imagined, and, like much of the writing which Crane did in the early years, they are largely derivative; they are not executed with the flawlessness which marks much of his best later work. Crane later spoke of them as being written in what he called his "Rudyard-Kipling style," and one cannot be entirely sure that the very attitude which Crane himself struck in these stories is not a bit artificial and contrived as well.[39] But the early writing manifests certain attitudes and concerns which were to characterize Crane's writing throughout his short career. If for no other reason, the Sullivan County sketches are important as prototypes for the later stories.

III

A Sparrow's Fall and a Sparrow's Eye: *Maggie*

> *Sin and suffering and shame there must always be in the world, I suppose, but I believe that in this new world of ours it is still mainly from one to another one, and oftener still from one to one's self....*
>
> *Dig anywhere, and do but dig deep enough, and you strike riches.*
>
> William Dean Howells
> *Criticism and Fiction* (1891)

At certain moments Stephen Crane was his own finest critic. In a letter to Lily Brandon Munroe in 1894, he reported,

> My career has been more of a battle than a journey. You know, when I left you, I renounced the clever school in literature. It seemed to me that there must be something more in life than to sit and cudgel one's brains for clever and witty expedients. So I developed all alone a little creed of art which I thought was a good one. Later I discovered that my creed was identical with the one of Howells and Garland and in this way I became involved in the beautiful war between those who say that art is man's substitute for nature and we are most successful in art when we approach the nearest to nature and truth, and those who say— well, I don't know what they say. They don't, they can't say much but they fight villianously [sic] and keep Garland and I [sic] out of the big magazines. Howells, of course, is too powerful for them.[1]

35

Thus by August of 1892, at the end of his first summer on his own as a reporter-writer, with a handful of published newspaper sketches and stories to his credit (and probably already in trouble with his paper),[2] and with perhaps a draft of an as-yet-unnamed novel,[3] Crane felt that it was time for a fresh start.

Actually the seeds of this renunciation had been sown somewhat earlier—probably as early as August of 1891, when Crane, then in Asbury Park, covered Hamlin Garland's lecture on William Dean Howells. Garland, impressed by Crane's newspaper story, arranged to meet the young reporter the next day—at first to pitch baseball. Out of the summer meetings that year and the next (Garland found the youth "a capital catcher of curved balls") there developed a friendship. Garland was later to introduce Crane to Howells, then a considerable literary kingmaker. And Howells' *Criticism and Fiction* appeared in 1891. It is no accident that both the "realist" and the "veritist" are mentioned in Crane's letter.[4]

But Garland and Howells were not the only influences. Even earlier that same summer Crane had also heard Jacob Riis lecture. Presumably he had read Flaubert at Syracuse, and by 1892 he had most probably also read Zola—*Nana* (1880) or *L'Assomoir* (1887) or *La Débâcle* (1892)—or even Tolstoy.[5] Also, of course, all of this took place in and around New York City on the eve of the depression of 1893.

It was in the fall and winter of 1893 that Crane undertook the final rewriting of the novel which was to be called *Maggie: A Girl of the Streets*. This novel was the first product of his renunciation. E. H. Cady says, "What differentiates it from *The Sullivan County Sketches* both in style and in 'perspective'" is *Maggie's* "turn toward realism."*[6] And

---

* Crane did some city writing before *Maggie,* and not all of it was "clever." Although "The Broken Down Van" of the summer of 1892 is

throughout 1893 and into 1894 Crane was to be involved in writing sketches, short stories, newspaper pieces, and at least two novels which in some ways partly conformed to standards asserted in such manifestoes of realism as Howells' *Criticism and Fiction*. In the stories and sketches which Crane wrote in 1893 there were still occasional examples of "cleverness" ("Why Did the Young Clerk Swear" of that year, for instance, is devoted to parodic comment— possibly to a parody of Zola).[7] Generally, however, in most of the writing after *Maggie* and through *George's Mother* Crane was involved in trying to come "nearest to nature." The nature which Crane was most often interested in getting near to, the reality which he now most vigorously pursued, was one of the critical realities of modern America—specifically, the reality of man in the city. For in 1893 and in 1894 Stephen Crane was writing, not of comically deluded hunters lost in the woods of Sullivan County nor of the innocence of resort life in New Jersey, but of slum dwellers and Bowery derelicts, of impoverished children and of tenement dandies, all trapped in their environment by their poverty and their delusions.

Over the years, Stephen Crane's *Maggie: A Girl of the Streets* has been almost universally regarded as the first work of unalloyed "naturalism" in American fiction. But the precise nature of *Maggie*'s naturalism and the exact qualities in the book which make it "naturalistic," are subjects of some dispute. Earlier critics, like V. L. Parrington, simply assumed *Maggie* to be naturalistic.[8] To C. C. Walcutt *Maggie*'s "pure" naturalism, admittedly "naturalism in a restricted and special sense," was to be found in Crane's attitude to-

---

clearly pre-"renunciation" writing, "The Landlady's Daughter" (a sketch unpublished in Crane's lifetime which has recently come to light) might ultimately prove to antedate the final *Maggie*. See Stallman, 57, 59, 82, 178; *New York City Sketches*, 3–14; *Stories and Sketches*, 70–74; and Solomon, *Stephen Crane*, 34n.

ward received values, in his impressionism, and in the intensity with which Crane rendered the grotesque reality of *Maggie*'s apprehended world.[9] To Lars Åhnebrink, *Maggie*'s naturalism was evidenced by the extent to which it was imitative of the work of continental naturalists—specifically of Zola's *L'Assomoir* and *Nana*.[10] More recently, David Fitelson has called *Maggie* "Darwinistic," and has emphasized the "primordial struggle for existence" in which he sees *Maggie*'s characters to be involved, and William T. Lenehan believes *Maggie* is flawed by Crane's "failure to master the techniques of the tradition of literary naturalism." [11]

No wonder so many critics, some of them concerned with other issues, seem loath to look beyond the tradition which tells them that Stephen Crane's *Maggie* is some sort of naturalistic prototype.[12] Perhaps Crane himself had after all really established the tradition at the very beginning in his inscription for Hamlin Garland's issue of the 1893 edition of *Maggie*. There he wrote:

> It is inevitable that you will be greatly shocked by this book but continue please with all possible courage to the end. For it tries to show that environment is a tremendous thing in the world and frequently shapes lives regardless. If one proves that theory one makes room in Heaven for all sorts of souls (notably an occasional street girl) who are not confidently expected to be there by many excellent people.
> It is probable that the reader of this small thing may consider the Author to be a bad man, but, obviously, this is a matter of small consequence to
>
> The Author[13]

It is determinism—for many a *sine qua non* of literary naturalism—that Crane seems to be emphasizing here.

But in spite of Crane's possibly unintended emphasis there have been some critics, particularly in recent years, who have found more in *Maggie* than "the truism that young girls in the slums are more apt to go bad than young girls elsewhere." [14] Many have dissented from the purely naturalistic approach, and in their readings of *Maggie* have minimized the significance of its naturalistic elements. R. W. Stallman, perhaps, introduced this interpretation of *Maggie* with his own "Reassessment," in which—though he dutifully acknowledged that "*Maggie* is par excellence the exemplar of literary naturalism"—he also asserted that "the paradox is that it is also a work of art," and devoted most of his attention to such problems as "Illusion versus Reality," and "Double Mood." [15] James B. Colvert later characterized *Maggie* as "an ironic study of vanity and conceit," [16] and Edwin H. Cady explicitly minimized Crane's naturalism in *Maggie* and emphasized instead "the moral vitality of its irony," which, he believed, was of central significance.[17] And there have been others—Joseph X. Brennan, Janet Overmyer, Max Westbrook, and, notably, Donald Pizer.[18]

Pizer has made an attempt to resolve the issue. He calls *Maggie* "a novel primarily about the falsity and destructiveness of certain moral codes," and goes on to say: "Crane, then is a naturalistic writer in the sense that he believes that environment molds lives. But he is much more than this, for his primary concern is not a dispassionate, pessimistic tracing of inevitable forces but a satiric assault on weaknesses in social morality. He seems to be saying that though we may not control our destinies, we can at least destroy those systems of value which uncritically assume we can." [19]

Stephen Crane, in a letter to John Northern Hilliard in January of 1896, wrote, "I go ahead, for I understand that a man is born into the world with his own pair of eyes, and he is not at all responsible for his vision—he is merely responsible for his quality of personal honesty. To keep close to this personal honesty is my supreme ambition." [20] In this letter Crane announced the metaphor appropriate to his concerns.

And in *Maggie,* and for the first time explicitly in Crane's writing, we discover that Crane is employing the event of seeing to represent the achievement of understanding. And the failure of understanding, "the falsity of moral codes" of which Pizer speaks, is throughout represented by the failure of vision.

The metaphor is intrinsic to Crane's method as well as to his theme. For Crane's impressionism, his "apprehension of life through the play of perceptions," as Sergio Perosa calls it,[21] is certainly the most apparent of the characteristics of Crane's prose in *Maggie.* Probably the most frequently quoted passage offered as evidence of Crane's impressionism is one from chapter two of the novel.

> Eventually they entered into a dark region where, from a careening building, a dozen gruesome doorways gave up loads of babies to the street and the gutter. A wind of early autumn raised yellow dust from cobbles and swirled it against an hundred windows. Long streamers of garments fluttered from fire-escapes. In all unhandy places there were buckets, brooms, rags and bottles. In the street infants played or fought with other infants or sat stupidly in the way of vehicles. Formidable women, with uncombed hair and disordered dress, gossiped while leaning on railings, or screamed in frantic quarrels. Withered persons, in curious postures of submission to something, sat smoking pipes in obscure corners. A thousand odors of cooking food came forth to the street. The building quivered and creaked from the weight of humanity stamping about in its bowels.[22]
>
> *Virginia,* I, 11

This is certainly an impressionistic rendering, a rendering of a reality by the representation of selected sensory impressions. Some of the images approach symbolic significance, it is true ("gruesome doorways gave up loads of babies to the street and the gutter," "Withered persons, in curious postures of submission," for example). But what is peculiarly characteristic of this paragraph is the fact that in it the seeing is being done, not by Crane or by the reader, but by a character—in this case by Jimmie. Jimmie, his street fight ended, is being brought home by his father, and this paragraph, which opens the second chapter, describes the route which Jimmie is to take from the street to the apartment. Jimmie and his father will leave the street and enter a courtyard through an entryway ("a dark region"). He will cross the courtyard and enter the building and feel it tremble beneath his feet. In his passage across the courtyard, he will see drying laundry as "streamers" (he has just been involved in the chivalric activity of fighting for the honor of Rum Alley, of giving and receiving challenges, and Crane's language and metaphor in the first chapter have suggested already that the boy has romanticized his struggle). To such a child, younger children seem stupid. To a boy expecting punishment from a ferocious mother, all women seem "formidable." The boy's fear also, perhaps, will cause him to see the building as "careening," or the doorways as "gruesome."

This is indeed impressionism of a rather special kind. Crane is not describing a courtyard in a slum; he is describing a frightened boy's apprehension of that courtyard. By presenting the way a frightened boy sees the tenement in which he lives, Crane shows us how the boy's sensibility is being shaped by his environment. The courtyard is not realistically pictured, but is grotesque, distorted by the boy's fear.[23]

It is convenient at this point to seek a label for Crane's method. One is tempted to call it *expressionism*, but if one understands the expressionist as attempting to render *his own* emotional or subjective response to an object or event, the term is not precisely appropriate here. Nor is the term *impressionism,* if we mean by that term the attempt of the artist to vitalize the descriptive process by dramatizing the event of his own or of his reader's apprehension of the described reality. For in this description Crane himself is at a great distance; his own emotions in no way alter the apprehended image.[24] Nor is his main concern here the vitalization of the described scene. Rather, he is concerned with vitalizing his character's apprehension of the scene. For want of a better term, I shall call Crane's method *dramatic impressionism.*

As a number of critics, Pizer most recently, have pointed out, there are two recurring patterns of imagery in *Maggie* —chivalric imagery and animalistic imagery. Both are present in this paragraph; one is Jimmie's, the other Crane's. The boy associates drying laundry with streamers; Crane likens the halls of a tenement to "bowels." It is the disparity between these two associations and between the understanding and evaluation of a reality which they imply that produces the irony, the "double mood" which so many critics have noted in *Maggie.* Crane's dramatic impressionism produces this irony as a result of the fact of the disparity between the associations which the author attaches to represented images and those which the character attaches. Crane's irony is really the result of a disparity between two different ways of seeing.*

Since William Dean Howells in *Criticism and Fiction* set for the realistic novel a patternless structure by describing "a big book" as "necessarily a group of episodes more or less loosely connected," critics have tended to regard Crane as having had no conscious program of organization in *Mag-*

---

* This ironic disparity is everywhere reinforced by Crane's language, by the disparity between the heightened, plurasyllabic, abstract, almost elegant diction of the author and the monosyllabic mutterings of his characters. See Gibson, *The Fiction of Stephen Crane,* 31.

gie.[25] But though it may be true that there is no consciously developed progression of development in the book, yet there is rude symmetry in the novel. In the first place, Crane generally alternates his concern between Maggie and Jimmie and invests his point of view, first in one, then in the other (Jimmie seems to me to be of considerably more importance than has been previously acknowledged). Secondly, Crane devotes roughly the first half of his book (the first nine chapters) to a portrayal of Maggie and Jimmie and the world in which they live. Jimmie attempts to assert himself and to achieve a sort of individuality in the slum. Maggie tries to escape it at the end of the ninth chapter. The results of these attempts are the concern of the second half of the book. To put it differently, if we are to assert that central to Crane's concern is the representation of Maggie's and Jimmie's illusions, then it is the causes of those illusions which are set forth in the first half of the book, their consequences in the second.

It is interesting to note that in the first half of *Maggie* nearly every scene presents an event and a character observing it; each scene is a description of the recording of experience upon a consciousness. And more often than not the experience is one of violence or disorder.[26] Throughout these chapters there are statements such as "from a window . . . there leaned a curious woman" or "the engineer of a passive tugboat hung lazily over a railing and watched" or "curious faces appeared in doorways" (*Virginia*, I, 7, 18). Someone is always watching the street fights or the domestic violence which so characterize the world of *Maggie*. And the identity of the observer is often of some significance— "The babe sat on the floor watching the scene," for instance (*Virginia*, I, 12). Even more important (for "The babe, Tommie, died," Crane later tells us. *Virginia*, I, 20) is Jimmie, who lives, and who is being conditioned by what he sees. In the third chapter, as Jimmie confronts the results of his family violence, Crane builds to his first climax of description in a silent, highly colored, sharply defined scene that has that quality of intensified reality which is familiar in the painting of Edvard Munch or Henri Rousseau, or perhaps also in the dream experience of all of us.

> Jimmie stood until the noises ceased and the other inhabitants of the tenement had all yawned and shut their doors. Then he crawled up stairs with the caution of an invader of a panther den. Sounds of labored breathing came through the broken door-panels. He pushed the door open and entered, quaking.
>
> A glow from the fire threw red hues over the bare floor, the cracked and soiled plastering, and the overturned and broken furniture.
>
> In the middle of the floor lay his mother asleep. In one corner of the room his father's limp body hung cross the seat of a chair.
>
> The urchin stole forward. He began to shiver in dread of awakening his parents. His mother's great chest was heaving painfully. Jimmie paused and looked down at her. Her face was inflamed and swollen from drinking. Her yellow brows shaded eye-lids that had grown blue. Her tangled hair tossed in waves over her forehead. Her mouth was set in the same lines of vindictive hatred that it had, perhaps, borne during the fight. Her bare, red arms were thrown out above her head in an attitude of exhaustion, something, mayhap, like that of a sated villain.
>
> The urchin bended over his mother. He was fearful lest she should open her eyes, and the dread within him was so strong, that he could not forbear to stare, but hung as if fascinated over the woman's grim face.
>
> Suddenly her eyes opened. The urchin found himself looking straight into an expression, which, it would seem, had the power to change his blood to salt. He howled piercingly and fell backward.

Virginia, I, 18–19

Here again is Crane's dramatic impressionism. Is there any wonder that, in the next chapter when the results of Jimmie's childhood conditioning are set forth, Jimmie's dreams of women are "blood-red," or that it is the capacity for violent destruction for which Jimmie has a particular admiration? Crane devoted a whole chapter to Jimmie's vision, opening it with "The inexperienced fibres of the boy's eyes were hardened at an early age" (*Virginia*, I, 20), and developing it in a set of quickly rendered scenes in which Jimmie is seen observing and reacting to his environment. Jimmie is described at the mission church, observing the man of quality, driving his truck in traffic. Crane reports that "his sneer grew so that it turned its glare upon all things" (*Virginia*, I, 21). Then there is represented the one object commanding Jimmie's respect—the fire engine. And, at the very end of the chapter, Crane redeems Jimmie from the reader's complete contempt. "Nevertheless, he had, on a certain star-lit evening, said wonderingly and quite reverently: 'D' moon looks like hell, don't it?' " (*Virginia*, I, 23).

It is not until Crane has accounted for the way of vision, or the fate, of her two brothers that he turns his full attention upon his title character. Maggie has appeared earlier, it is true. In the second chapter she observes the damage suffered by her surviving brother, and in the third, after her brother has confronted his sleeping mother, Maggie also has a significant visual experience. "The small frame of the ragged girl was quivering. Her features were haggard from weeping, and her eyes gleamed from fear. She grasped the urchin's arm in her little trembling hands and they huddled in a corner. The eyes of both were drawn, by some force, to stare at the woman's face, for they thought she need only to awake and all the fiends would come from below" (*Virginia*, I, 19). But although Maggie has gradually begun to emerge from the darkness of her tenement, she does not take the center of the stage until, at the beginning of the fifth chapter, Crane reports that "The girl, Maggie, blossomed in a mud puddle" (*Virginia*, I, 24).

Unlike her brother, the fibres of whose eyes are hardened, and who accepts a violent animalistic world with aggression as the only meaningful activity, Maggie's fear leads her to seek escape. If Jimmie, in his fight for the honor of Rum Alley was "saved" by Pete, it is the same Pete to whom Maggie will turn in her search for a way out.[27] But, for Crane, properly to represent Maggie's way of dealing with reality is to describe her vision. And in the fifth chapter, when Crane has undertaken to present the effects of Maggie's childhood upon her understanding, he describes how she sees Pete:

> Maggie observed Pete.
>
> He sat on a table in the Johnson home and dangled his checked legs with an enticing nonchalance. His hair was curled down over his forehead in an oiled bang. His pugged nose seemed to revolt from contact with a bristling moustache of short, wire-like hairs. His blue double-breasted coat, edged with black braid, was buttoned close to a red puff tie, and his patent-leather shoes looked like weapons.
>
> His mannerisms stamped him as a man who had a correct sense of his personal superiority. There was valor and contempt for circumstances in the glance of his eye. He waved his hands like a man of the world, who dismisses religion and philosophy, and says "Rats!" He had certainly seen everything and with each curl of his lip, he declared that it amounted to nothing. Maggie thought he must be a very "elegant" bartender.
>
> He was telling tales to Jimmie.
>
> Maggie watched him furtively, with half-closed eyes, lit with a vague interest.
>
> *Virginia*, I, 26

And Maggie continues to watch:

With Jimmie in his company, Pete departed in a sort of a blaze of glory from the Johnson home. Maggie, leaning from the window, watched him as he walked down the street.

Here was a formidable man who disdained the strength of a world full of fists. Here was one who had contempt for brass-clothed power; one whose knuckles could defiantly ring against the granite of law. He was a knight.

Virginia, I, 27–28

If Jimmie finally comes to understand his world as a jungle, and if his way of asserting himself in it is by aggression, Maggie understands her world in chivalric terms, and her mode of response is flight, for in a chivalric fantasy the lady customarily flees, or is carried away. Maggie allows herself to be carried away by her knight at the end of the ninth chapter. When her brother hears of Maggie's flight, he attempts to deal with the situation in the only way he knows, in the only way his eyes have taught him. He will fight. Of course, both responses, both ways of seeing, prove inadequate. These inadequacies and their consequences are Crane's subjects in the latter half of his book.

Thus it is no surprise that the quality which nearly all of the scenes of the final ten chapters of *Maggie* have in common is a quality of distortion. Reality is never seen clearly in the second half of *Maggie*. Characters are often drunk, or confused by rumor. Scene after scene takes place in bar, beer hall, or theater. The air is continually smoky, and images are blurred by glare, or sudden movement, or rain, or darkness.*

* Note, for instance, the smoky atmosphere to which Crane invariably refers in his beer hall scenes—"clouds of tobacco smoke" (30), "boys . . . tried to find the girl's eyes in the smoke wreaths" (52), "the usual smoke cloud was present" (57), "the smoke eddied and swirled like a shadowy river" (57). In Pete's bar mirrors multiply reality (45). On the streets, or inside, there is glare—"the glare of gas jets" (31), "a yellow glare upon the pavement" (45), "electric lights, whirring softly, shed a blurred radiance"

The inadequacy of Jimmie's eyes is made immediately apparent, but the results are less dire and less dramatic for him than are the consequences of his sister's delusion for her. Yet immediately after Maggie's fall from virtue Crane turns his attention to Jimmie and devotes two chapters of his book to the demonstration of Jimmie's inadequacy. Jimmie's confusion is portrayed with understatement ("Jimmie had an idea it wasn't common courtesy for a friend to come to one's home and ruin one's sister." *Virginia*, I, 42). But again the crucial image, the trope which sums up Jimmie's condition, concerns seeing. For at the moment in which Crane really establishes Jimmie's ethical confusion—the brother's inability to accept the implications for himself of his sister's difficulty or to understand a morality more complicated than that implicit to aggressive action—it is Jimmie's obscured vision which Crane represents. "Jimmie walked to the window and began to look through the blurred glass. It occurred to him to vaguely wonder, for an instant, if some of the women of his acquaintance had brothers. Suddenly, however, he began to swear" (*Virginia*, I, 43). Jimmie's environment and his conditioning have provided him with only two possible responses: he may fight, or he may negate with cynical indifference ("'what d' hell?'"). And, of course, neither response is adequate to the challenge with which he is now confronted. Thus, when he provokes a fight with Pete in the saloon in which Pete works, Jimmie finds that ultimately it is the police, an overpowering opponent, with whom he must contend. So now there is only one response: "'Ah, what d' hell?' he demanded of himself" (*Virginia*, I, 50).

This is the end of Jimmie's capacity for self-assertion, and

(68). Often rapid movement distorts vision—"swiftness that blurred the view of the cocoanut palms" (57). And, of course, as we shall see later, there is light-and-darkness distortion on the rainy night of Maggie's suicide (68–70).

damn good f'ler.' "), and, when his female companions leave him, he remains behind, unconscious in the house of illusion. "The smoke from the lamps settled heavily down in the little compartment, obscuring the way out. The smell of oil, stifling in its intensity, pervaded the air. The wine from an overturned glass dripped softly down upon the blotches on the man's neck" (*Virginia*, I, 74).

Maggie is in a sense a bipolar novel; at one polarity is illusion, at the other, blind chaos. At the center of the novel's chaos is Mary, Maggie's mother. Thus if Pete, the purveyor of illusion, is in the eighteenth chapter left trapped in his own fantasy, so in the final chapter Crane leaves Mary as she is avoiding the real reasons for her daughter's death by a retreat to self-delusion and pietistic cliché. Mary is drunk and violently aggressive in most of her earlier appearances, but she is at least relatively sober in this final chapter. But even in her sobriety, when she is informed of her daughter's death by Jimmie (who now is only "a soiled, unshaven man" who submits sullenly to his mother's demands) Mary chooses to weep self-righteous tears rather than to understand. Crane's irony rises to a new stridency as he tells us that Mary's "good, motherly face was wet with tears," and it is Mary's hypocrisy, her failure—like all the others—to confront and to come to terms with reality, which fills the whole novel as Crane concludes it: "The tears seemed to scald her face. Finally her voice came and arose in a scream of pain. 'Oh, yes, I'll fergive her! I'll fergive her!'" (*Virginia*, I, 77). Thus Crane leaves his reader with a sense of the supreme and horrible irrelevance of slum life. One perhaps feels some relief that Maggie is now far away from her mother's violent self-deceit. And yet, with Mary's final cry, we feel that the world of Maggie's tenement is a world still lost in illusion and self-deception.

In a letter to an admirer written late in 1896, five months after Appleton republished *Maggie*, Crane said:

> Thank you very much for your letter on Maggie. . . .
> I do not think that much can be done with the Bowery
> as long as the [word blurred] are in their present state
> of conceit. A person who thinks himself superior to the
> rest of us because he has no job and no pride and no
> clean clothes is as badly conceited as Lillian Russell.
> In a story of mine called "An Experiment in Misery"
> I tried to make plain that the root of Bowery life is a
> sort of cowardice. Perhaps I mean a lack of ambition
> or to willingly be knocked flat and accept the licking.
> The missions for children are another thing and if you
> will have Mr. Rockefeller give me a hundred street
> cars and some money I will load all the babes off to
> some pink world where cows can lick their noses and
> they will never see their families any more. . . . I had
> no other purpose in writing "Maggie" than to show
> people to people as they seem to me. If that be evil,
> make the most of it.[31]

Conceit is always a tricky word, and *cowardice* here is a curious one. If Crane is talking about the slum dweller's inability or refusal to understand his environment—a failure of apprehension which is engendered in that environment—I should be inclined to suggest that "An Experiment in Misery" is not the only work which Crane composed on the subject. For—if we extend the metaphor which Crane has employed so consistently in the book—*Maggie* is also about an incapacity of vision, about the fear or ignorance or confusion which brings about that incapacity, about the escapes available in avoiding clear seeing and the consequences of those escapes. *Maggie* is about the fall of a Bowery sparrow, but it is also about the failure of her eye. And of the two, in the book at least, it is the latter—the illusion of Maggie and of all the others—which is the more important.

IV
Experiments In Misery

*I decided that the nearer a writer gets to life
the greater he becomes as an artist.*
Stephen Crane in a letter to
an editor of *Leslie's Weekly*, 1895

George's Mother is in a sense the companion piece to
Maggie. Also a story of a slum family, *George's Mother* describes a relationship between a mother and son who live in
Maggie's tenement. Maggie herself, in fact, makes a brief
yet crucial appearance in the novel. And curiously enough,
this novel, like *Maggie*, also received its title late; it was
known as late as 1895 as *A Woman Without Weapons*.[1]

Although *George's Mother* was not published until 1896,
Crane began it early—perhaps as early as 1891 or 1892—and
was at work on it soon after *Maggie* went to press in 1893.[2]
But as he became disillusioned with *Maggie* he put the second slum novel aside and wrote *The Red Badge*. He returned to *George's Mother* in 1894 and completed it in
November of that year.[3] Thus, as Harry Thurston Peck was
the first to point out, *George's Mother* is an early work; "its
first draft must belong to the time when [Crane] wrote and
published *Maggie*." [4]

What has perhaps seemed more important, however, is

the fact that Crane's conception of *George's Mother* must have occurred around the time of Crane's own mother's final illness and death.[5] For *George's Mother* has long been the subject of biographers' conjectures. Richard Chase has said that "George and his mother are not too remote projections of Crane and his own mother, a strong Methodist and lecturer on religious subjects."[6] And both Beer and Berryman have made similar suggestions, though Stallman sees the novel's George Kelcey as a presentation of Crane's own drunken brother Townley.[7]

I do not wish to press the biographical parallel too far, for in spite of Crane's own testimony any such parallel must at best remain conjectural.[8] But I should note that the recently discovered and conclusive evidence of *George's Mother*'s early inception does lend some support to those who argue that Crane's second "New York book" is not that at all, but rather a psychological study—the representation of a mother and a son, their visions and illusions and abilities and inabilities to understand one another.

If there is a remarkable biographical identity between Crane and his novel, there is at the same time a remarkable distance of candor. Eric Solomon, in his discussion of *George's Mother*, has shown how the book proceeds out of a parody of what Solomon calls "The Alger stereotype" and a burlesque of the temperance novel into a meaningful and profound and acute study of a complex and destructive love-hate relationship between mother and son.[9] Indeed, it would seem that it is Crane's use of parody and burlesque that enables him to place himself at a great distance from his subjects, to refuse to moralize about them, and at the same time to render their blindnesses and their delusions with a sharp irony. Moreover, this irony not only attacks characters; it parodies a literature which would deal with such characters so unrealistically. Crane is unconcerned with the immediate social causes of his characters' failures of vision. Nowhere does he consider—even to the extent he does in *Maggie*—slum conditions, economic duress, or the exploitation of the poor. *George's Mother* could have happened in Asbury Park as easily as it could in Maggie's tenement. For it is the failure of apprehension and understanding—of characters and of those who write about them—which is Crane's subject.[10]

Despite Crane's curious relationship to his book, *George's Mother* is in many ways much less complex than *Maggie*. More economical in plot and character, *George's Mother* confines itself to two characters and does not attempt to treat, as does *Maggie* in less than a hundred pages, of the childhood, maturity, and downfall of both brother and sister.[11] And in the second book Crane also avoids the use of shifting points of view. George Kelcey is the sole perceiver of events, and by having him so, Crane was able to achieve a unity of effect which escaped him in *Maggie* and which approaches that of *The Red Badge of Courage*.

But if *George's Mother* is less complex than *Maggie*, Crane's method in the two books is similar in many ways. Like *Maggie*, *George's Mother* is full of drinking scenes (there are seven chapters of eighteen in which drinking or its aftermath is the central action). The bars are still smoky, and the drinker's vision distorted. The streets still glitter with reflected light. And *George's Mother* is filled with the metaphor as well as the imagery of illusion. As is the case with *Maggie*, *George's Mother* is committed to dramatic impressionism, and in it the recurring chivalric-military metaphor is consistently used to display the delusions of Crane's two principal characters. As in *Maggie*, it is the characters who do the perceiving.

Thus, when Crane describes George Kelcey's mother doing

her housework, it is by means of metaphor that we discover
how she regards herself.

> In her arms she bore pots and pans, and sometimes a
> broom and dust-pan. She wielded them like weapons.
> Their weight seemed to have bended her back and
> crooked her arms until she walked with difficulty. Often
> she plunged her hands into water at a sink. She splashed
> about, the dwindled muscles working to and fro under
> the loose skin of her arms. She came from the sink,
> steaming and bedraggled as if she had crossed a flooded
> river.
> There was the flurry of a battle in this room. Through
> the clouded dust or steam one could see the thin fig-
> ure dealing mighty blows. Always her way seemed beset.
> Her broom was continually posed, lance-wise, at dust
> demons. There came clashings and clangings as she
> strove with her tireless foes.
> It was a picture of indomitable courage.
>
> *Virginia*, I, 119–20

Though *The Red Badge of Courage* may have provided this
metaphor, it is its incongruity and what that incongruity
suggests which is important. Mrs. Kelcey's association of her
housecleaning with battle is as delusionary as George's apprehension of the mirrored bars which he frequents ("Drink
and its surroundings were the eyes of a superb green dragon
to him. He followed a fascinating glitter. . . ." *Virginia*, I,
159) or as his view of himself at Old Bleeker's party as "an
enthusiast, as if he were at a festival of a religion" (*Virginia*,
I, 146).

Again illusion and its consequence are Crane's concern.
And the consequence of George's bedazzled eye and his
mother's moralistic misunderstanding of herself and her son
is isolation. It is no accident that in scene after scene of
George's Mother George constantly moves away from company—away from his home, away from his companions, and

into isolation. As in *Maggie* and in late works such as "The Blue Hotel," isolation—and the uncorrected vision of the isolated man—often means vulnerability to danger. In *Maggie* and in the later works the danger is explicit and physical; in *George's Mother*, in which Crane does not take his protagonist beyond isolation, one senses only an anticipation of danger, one sees only George's fear.

George Kelcey first appears in the novel as an innocent, a "brown young man" fresh from the country, wandering in a glistening, rainy city. As the imagery in the opening chapter suggests, George is full of illusions and naiveté and is unable to know his place in the strange and mutable world of which he is now a part. As a protection, he seeks acceptance—by Old Bleeker and "the boys"—but it is never quite achieved. His fumbling overtures to Maggie are rejected. Even in the streetcorner society, of which he is for a time a part, his relationships are tentative and marred by hostility. And in the final scene George is deprived of his mother, his only real companion in a continuous if imperfect relationship. George is left terrifyingly alone and vulnerable by her death.

Throughout this process of isolation the reader is constantly reminded of George's naiveté, of his imperfect understanding, of his incomplete vision. George's illusions are, of course, fed by his mother's fatuousness and Old Bleeker's hyperboles, and soon the youth comes to regard himself in a most unreal fashion. Crane's language in the description of George's self-delusion is richly imagistic and rendered in "scenes he took mainly from pictures."

> The world was obliged to turn gold in time. His life was to be fine and heroic, else he would not have been born. He believed that the common-place lot was the sentence, the doom of certain people who did not know how to feel. . . . He thought that the usual should fall to others whose nerves were of lead. Occasionally he

wondered how fate was going to begin in making an enormous figure of him; but he had no doubt of the result. A chariot of pink clouds was coming for him. His faith was his reason for existence. Meanwhile he could dream of the indefinite woman and the fragrance of roses that came from her hair.

Virginia, I, 137–38

It is no wonder that Pete's appearance shatters such a fragile and unreal vision of Maggie. But George is undeterred and moves on to another illusion—that of nobility of comradeship among drinking companions. This illusion, shattered in the most strikingly rendered scene in the novel, is recorded through the alcohol-distorted vision of George and rendered in increasingly grotesque stages as he slowly drinks himself into unconsciousness. "He felt them hurl him to a corner of the room and pile chairs and tables upon him until he was buried beneath a stupendous mountain. Far above, as up a mine's shaft, there were voices, lights, and vague figures" (*Virginia*, I, 149). When George awakens the next morning the very process of apprehension is painful to him. And Crane's images are almost painful for his reader.

At first the gray lights of dawn came timidly into the room, remaining near the windows, afraid to approach certain sinister corners. Finally, mellow streams of sunshine poured in, undraping the shadows to disclose the putrefaction, making pitiless revelation. Kelcey awoke with a groan of undirected misery. He tossed his stiffened arms about his head for a moment and then leaning heavily upon his elbow stared blinking at his environment. The grim truthfulness of the day showed disaster and death. After the tumults of the previous night the interior of this room resembled a decaying battle-field. The air hung heavy and stifling with the odors of tobacco, men's breaths, and beer half filling forgotten glasses. There was a rack of broken tumblers, pipes, bottles, spilled tobacco, cigar stumps. The chairs and tables were pitched this way and that way, as after some terrible struggle. In the midst of it all lay old Bleecker stretched upon a couch in deepest sleep, as abandoned in attitude, as motionless, as ghastly as if it were a corpse that had been flung there.

A knowledge of the thing came gradually into Kelcey's eyes. He looked about him with an expression of utter woe, regret, and loathing. He was compelled to lie down again. A pain from above his eyebrows was like that from an iron-clamp.

Virginia, I, 150

George's confrontation with the reality of his condition in all its agonizing clarity is similar to certain scenes in *Maggie*. Here is a moment in which Crane's dramatic impressionism is particularly manifest, and in which Crane's peculiarly distanced attitude toward his protagonist and toward his story is manifest as well. George cannot bear to confront for long "the grim truthfulness of the day" and the devastated nature of his world, and Crane is ironic as George turns away from the confrontation to an inward acknowledgment of his pain. But Crane's irony is softened by the vividness of his imagery, a vividness which is almost an acknowledgment of a sympathy for George's remorseful state.

The moment of clarity is perhaps too much for George. He retreats from the spoiled dream of comradeship to the world of illusion offered by his mother. George's mother, failing to see her own world as it is, and escaping from it to the false promises offered by her church, has an illusionary conception of her son as well. But her imaginings are of no benefit to her son. The prayer meeting to which she takes him only makes George guilty and uncomfortable. Soon he grasps again at his own romantic fantasy and escapes to return to the dreamworld of the saloon. "The saloons contained the mystery of a street for him. When he knew its saloons he comprehended the street. Drink and its surroundings were the eyes of a superb green dragon to him. He followed a fascinating glitter, and the glitter required no explanation" (*Virginia*, I, 159). Even when George, returning to the saloon, begins his *fin de siècle* rake's progress, his mother's illusions remain unimpaired. When the women of the tenement come to commiserate with her over George's wildness, "She told them of his wit, his cleverness, his kind heart."

Trapped in his own illusions, George soon descends to the company of street gangs (these gangs are paradoxically quite arrogant; "their feeling for contemporaneous life was one of contempt"), and his relationship with his mother degenerates from failure of understanding to open quarrelling. George is gradually isolated. Dismissed from his job, he appeals to Bleecker and his saloon friends for money and is refused. Soon George finds himself in the violent world of the slum street. The street gang sets one of its members on its new cohort, and its members ridicule George when he breaks off the fight to attend his failing mother.

The final scene, Crane's representation of the moment of the mother's death—the moment in which George is definitively isolated, in which he is deprived of final protection and escape—is particularly vivid. George watches impotently as his mother sinks into her own last illusion, a pastoral fantasy. She believes she is back on the farm which she and her son left for the city. Crane reports, laconically, "She was at a kitchen-door with a dish-cloth in her hand. Within there had just been a clatter of crockery. Down through the trees of the orchard she could see a man in a field ploughing. 'Bill—o-o-oh, Bill—have yeh seen Georgie? Is he out there with you? Georgie! Georgie! Come right here this minnet! Right—this—minnet!'" (*Virginia*, I, 177). But Crane has one more visual horror for his reader. Just after George's mother dies in the throes of her fantasy, George, now experiencing the isolation and vulnerability which results from the final separation, also slips for a moment into a fantasy—not of escape but of sheer terror, a terror achieved by a final grotesquerie, a monstrous juxtaposition of the imagery of reality and fancy. "Kelcey began to stare at the wall-paper. The pattern was clusters of brown roses. He felt them like hideous crabs crawling upon his brain" (*Virginia*, I, 178).

Although in 1893 Crane was writing in his inscriptions of *Maggie* of environment being "a tremendous thing in this world," in 1896, the year of publication of *George's Mother*, he was saying that "the root of Bowery life is a sort of cowardice." And *George's Mother*, with its intense psychological realism, its sharply focused point of view, and its grotesque and vivid dramatic impressionism, is much more concerned with the nature of that cowardice than with the environment. One cannot deny that Crane was concerned with social issues, but *George's Mother* is much more psychologically than socially committed. It is fear, not environment, which drives George to his final and terrible isolation.

Between the private publication of *Maggie* in March of 1893 and Crane's departure in January of 1895 for a trip to the American West and Mexico, he spent most of his time in and around New York. He was to return to New York in June of 1895 and would remain there until November of the following year when he departed again—this time for Jacksonville. Afterwards, he was to be in New York again only briefly, and upon only three occasions.* So it was out of

* Crane spent a week there in March of 1897, after the *Commodore* experience and before his departure for Greece. He stopped over again a year later, but only for a few days and en route to Cuba and the Spanish American War. And late in the same year, after his sojourn in Havana, Crane spent about a month in the city and a week in New Jersey with his brother Edmund. See Stallman, 260–66, 350–51, 435–42.

the early experiences in the city—in 1893 and 1894—that Crane produced—besides *George's Mother*—a number of short stories and sketches as well as a quantity of journalistic writing.

Except for *Maggie*, Crane published little of this city writing in 1893.[12] But Maggie's tenement was the source for several other stories which were written in that year and perhaps early in the next—stories about the adventures of Maggie's and Jimmie's little brother, who dies in the novel, but who was here briefly resurrected. Crane called them his "baby sketches" and in them employed as protagonist a character whose vision is even more naive than Maggie's or George's. Tommie of the "baby sketches" is Crane's first child protagonist; he anticipated by several years the children of Whilomville.

The first of the sketches is entitled "An Ominous Baby"; it was published in the *Arena* in May of 1894, almost a year after its composition.[13] In it Tommie confronts a world of social inequality for the first time—in the person of a child from a wealthy quarter of the city. Tommie responds by stealing a toy fire engine (he and his brother Jimmie apparently have similar tastes). "A Great Mistake" describes a similar apprehension and response; in it Tommie is "left face to face with the horrid joys of the world" when he sees the fruit on an Italian's fruit stand. "For a time he was a simple worshiper at this golden shrine," but Crane's story turns upon the moment when Tommie touches, then takes. At the end, when Tommie is caught, the reader discovers that the boy had chosen to steal a lemon.[14]

Although the sketches reveal the class tensions in the city which were to erupt in the labor troubles of 1893–94, they also describe—with considerable vitality of impressionistic image—the beginnings of a Bowery education. Crane was clearly a writer with a strong sense of social injustice—

stronger perhaps than is manifest in *Maggie*. Yet he maintained considerable ironic distance from his subject. Even in these stories the significant event is an event of seeing.*

There was one other tenement story, possibly written as early as 1893, and certainly drawn from the material set down originally in *Maggie*. "A Desertion" is a piece of elaborately lighted Biercian melodrama concerning a slum girl who returns home to talk jauntily to her unresponsive father, her one protector from the danger of her world, only to discover that her silent father is dead, slumped over a table. Crane concludes this slight and artificial experiment with a rather forced irony, as the tenement dwellers mistake the girl's cries of discovery for a family fracas. "But over all this came the shrill shrewish tones of a woman. 'Ah, th' damned ol' fool, he's drivin' 'er inteh th' street—that's what he's doin'. He's drivin' 'er inteh th' street' " [15] (*New York City Sketches*, 192). As a piece like "A Desertion" so forcibly reminds us, the young writer in 1893 was still very much a beginner.

The fierce and tragic winter of social unrest in 1893–94 offered little to diminish Crane's awareness of social injustice. Early in the new year Crane wrote two slum sketches which

---

* The last of the "baby sketches," "A Dark Brown Dog" (which is the longest and the most complete), is possibly a later work or the subject of a later revision. Perhaps it attained its final state at a time when Crane, under serious economic pressure and much more the "professional" writer, was more prepared to accommodate his reader's taste for sentimentality and sensationalism. At the same time it represents a more psychologically sophisticated and subtly ironic treatment of Crane's subject: the formation of the slum sensibility. In the sketch Tommie consistently brutalizes a stray dog, before and after he drags the creature home. And when, in the course of the violent life in the Johnson tenement, the dog is hurled to his death by Tommie's drunken father, the boy is grief-stricken. ("When they came for him later, they found him seated by the body of his dark-brown friend.") Crane's final irony here lies in the fact that the brutality which Tommie has learned from his father does not preclude human feeling. See *New York City Sketches*, 132–37; Stallman, 101–102; and Gibson, *The Fiction of Stephen Crane*, 55–56.

manifest more sharply an awareness of the effects of environment upon the human being, which demonstrate more clearly a social conscience in Crane, than any of his earlier works.
Both are the result of direct experience. In a blizzard toward
the end of February, Crane joined a Bowery breadline and
wrote "The Men in the Storm," and a night in a flophouse
was to serve the young writer as "An Experiment in Misery." [16]

In "The Men in the Storm" Crane describes, with boldly
impressionistic imagery, a crowd of derelicts who suffer in
a blinding snowstorm and await shelter in a charity lodging-
house. Because of the pressure of those in the rear of the
crowd who cannot see well enough to understand the difficulty that they are creating, the doors to the charity house
cannot be opened. Now Crane's images seem to transcend
even the special brand of dramatic impressionism which was
his at times in *Maggie* and *George's Mother,* and to approach
something new, an investment in the image of symbolic meaning which almost anticipates his later writing. Crane had
begun the description of the scene with this kind of suggestion ("A street lamp on the curb struggled to illuminate,
but it was reduced to impotent blindness by the swift gusts
of sleet crusting its panes." *New York City Sketches,* 93).
At the end of the scene, when Crane pauses for a moment to
represent a random observer of the event, he sums up in a
single ironic image a whole social attitude.

> In the brilliantly-lighted space appeared the figure of
> a man. He was rather stout and very well clothed. His
> whiskers were fashioned charmingly after those of the
> Prince of Wales. He stood in an attitude of magnificent
> reflection. He slowly stroked his moustache with a cer-
> tain grandeur of manner, and looked down at the
> snow-encrusted mob. From below, there was denoted
> a supreme complacence in him. It seemed that the

sight operated inversely, and enabled him to more clearly regard his own environment, delightful relatively.*

New York City Sketches, 95

Like "The Men in the Storm," "An Experiment in Misery"
is an example of the *fin de siècle* journalistic habit of seeing
for one's self how the other half lived. For in the piece,
Crane was certainly following the lead of Jacob Riis, Josiah
Flynt Willard, and others.[17] But although "An Experiment
in Misery" demonstrates Crane's commitment to the accurate
representation of social realities, it manifests other artistic
concerns as well. Crucially important in the story is the fact
that Crane's protagonist in "An Experiment in Misery" is
not a derelict at all; rather, he is a young man who "was
going forth to eat as the wanderer may eat, and sleep as the
homeless sleep." Indeed, Crane's young man figures even
more largely in the story as it first appeared in the New
York *Press* of April 22, 1894.[18] In the *Press* version he appears in a frame story, an account of conversation between
himself and an older man in which (at the beginning)
the young man takes up the challenge to conduct his experiment and (at the end) reports on its results. And those
results expose the center of Crane's concern. " 'Well,' said
the friend, 'did you discover his point of view?' 'I don't
know that I did,' replied the young man; 'but at any rate
I think mine own has undergone a considerable alteration' "
(*New York City Sketches,* 43).

Thus if "An Experiment in Misery" is a representation of
reality, it is at least equally a representation of an apprehension of reality. Or, as Maurice Bassan has it, the story is an
initiation both of the reader and "the latter-day Goodman
Brown who is its hero . . . into the reality of evil." Bassan

---

* It is interesting to observe here an early experiment in the ironic
manipulation of two points of view. These early experiments point the way
to later works like "The Bride Comes to Yellow Sky." See Stallman, 95–96.

has pointed out the geographic circularity of the story, has identified the moment of the initiation to evil—when the boy, lying in a Bowery flophouse, hears the wails of one of his companions. He has noted the moment the next morning when the youth confronts the thing itself, the naked men, distorted by the society whose victims they are. He has observed the contradictory central metaphors—one of a society grinding down its victims, the other of the vertical distance which separates an unconcerned society from the vagrants of the slums.

It remains for me only to observe the part which the imagery of sensory apprehension plays in the total effect of "An Experiment in Misery." Crane's young man apprehends the evil of the Bowery life with all of his senses. He sees in the darkness the yellow flesh of the sleepy men, he hears their cries, he tastes their soup and their beer, he touches the cold brother of his cot, and smells the "unholy odors." But as is usual in Crane, it is the seeing which is most important. The youth's eyes must be prepared for his initiation. When the youth has been ushered into the sleeping chamber by "the man with the benevolent spectacles" and is alone on his cot, Crane reports that "it was some time before the youth's eyes were good in the intense gloom." It is only after "the young man's eyes became used to darkness" that the real initiation —the central apprehension of which Bassan speaks—can occur. And it occurs in a moment of apprehension which is visual as well as auditory. The scene is rendered as grotesque with all the power which Crane's dramatic impressionism can generate. "Within reach of the youth's hand was one who lay with yellow breast and shoulders bare to the cold drafts. One arm hung over the side of the cot and the fingers lay full length upon the wet cement floor of the room. Beneath the inky brows could be seen the eyes of the man exposed by the partly opened lids. To the youth it seemed that he and this corpse-like being were exchanging a prolonged stare and that the other threatened with his eyes" (*New York City Sketches*, 38). Here is a moment which, as it is a part of the multi-sensory apprehension which culminates in the youth's hearing of the wail of "one fellow off in a gloomy corner" (a wail which the youth interprets as "the wail of a whole section, a class, a people"), is near the very center of "An Experiment in Misery." It is a moment which anticipates several of the climactic confrontations which are to recur in Crane's later fiction.*

"An Experiment in Luxury," the companion piece, was published the following week in the *Press*. Artistically inferior to its predecessor, it is rather rigidly didactic, and though it employs the same frame, and perhaps even the same protagonist, the understanding which the youth achieves of "the eternal mystery of social condition," is more explicitly described than dramatized.[19] Yet "An Experiment in Luxury" comes as close as Crane ever does to the explicit articulation of his own awareness of social inequity and of the terrible fact that he can find no one who is consciously and individually responsible. The disturbing image of the "famous millionaire," the amiable father of the family, playing with his kitten, in complete innocence of his economic role, is perhaps the most memorable in Crane's sketch.

For the youth, the experiment in luxury is a second step into the mystery of social reality. And that second initiation is at the center of the sequel. As Crane insists at the end of the story,

> Indicated in this light chatter about the dinner table there was an existence that was not at all what the youth had been taught to see. Theologians had for a long time told the poor man that riches did not bring happiness, and they had solemnly repeated this phrase

* And again there is the doubled point of view. See Stallman, 102.

until it had come to mean that misery was commensurate with dollars, that each wealthy man was inwardly a miserable wretch. And when a wall of depair or rage had come from the night of the slums they had stuffed this epigram down the throat of he [sic] who cried out and told him that he was a lucky fellow. They did all this because they feared.*

New York City Sketches, 50-51

In 1894 Crane was to make use of city subjects while moving in a number of new directions. Much of the writing was feature journalism, done for the most part on assignment from the New York *Press*. There were two stories—"Stories Told by an Artist" and "The Silver Pageant"—which came out of little bohemia which Crane inhabited in the old Art Students' League building on East 23rd Street,[20] stories which would anticipate *The Third Violet* of a year later. And there was even straight reportage, an interview with William Dean Howells, for example.[21]

In the feature writing Crane found a real medium for experiment. There were the most conventional holiday tributes,[22] original exercises in point of view and in tonal control and, at times, fully developed short fictions. One of the most remarkable is a description of a Pennsylvania coal mine, which Crane did with C. K. Linson as his illustrator. It is rather flamboyant writing, seething with ironic anger at the conditions which Crane confronted. Indeed, like "An Experiment in Misery," "In the Depths of a Coal Mine" dramatizes its author's rage at what he saw in his visit. But if Crane was concerned here with social conditions (and indeed his antibusiness assertions were too much for McClure, who excluded some from the printed version), he was also con-

---

* Crane made another attempt in journeying within the walls of the urban establishment in a rather banal satire upon the exclusiveness of a Manhattan men's club, which he called "A Night at the Millionaire's Club" and which appeared in *Truth* of April 21, 1894.

cerned with the process of his own apprehension. Throughout the piece there are references to the disordering of perception which life in the mine brings about. On his descent into the mine in an elevator,

> The dead black walls slid swiftly by. They were a swirling dark chaos on which the mind tried vainly to locate some coherent thing, some intelligible spot. One could only hold fast to the iron bars and listen to the roar of this implacable descent. When the faculty of balance is lost, the mind becomes a confusion. The will fought a great battle to comprehend something during this fall, but one might as well have been tumbling among the stars. The only thing was to await revelation.
>
> *New York City Sketches*, 292

Later Crane reports, "In our first mine we speedily lost all ideas of time, direction, distance," and it is this disorientation—the offense to the senses and its results, manifest in the mine donkeys—with which Crane concludes as the mine's ultimate horror. Toward the end, Crane tells of a mule whose sensory apprehensions of life on the surface after long deprivation lead him to a kind of rebellion.

> Usually when brought to the surface, the mules tremble at the earth radiant in the sunshine. Later, they go almost mad with fantastic joy. The full splendor of the heavens, the grass, the trees, the breezes, breaks upon them suddenly. They caper and career with extravagant mulish glee. A miner told me of a mule that had spent some delirious months upon the surface after years of labor in the mines. Finally the time came when he was to be taken back. But the memory of a black existence was upon him; he knew that gaping mouth that threatened to swallow him. No cudgellings could induce him. The men held conventions and discussed plans to budge that mule. The celebrated quality of obstinacy in him won him liberty to gambol clumsily about on the surface.

Like the Bowery, the root of mine life seems a sort of cowardice, a refusal by men, though not by this illustrious mule,
to acknowledge the objective reality to be apprehended by
the senses and to act boldly in confirmation of it.

Although they were perhaps less dramatically rendered,
other feature pieces contained other experiments. In several
pieces Crane made use of a narrating character, a "stranger"
who accompanies the reporter and who participates in the
comment.[23] This character's presence is less significant in
the more formally narrated account of a fire ("When Every
One is Panic Stricken"), he becomes only a rather intimate
first-person narrator in "Matinee Girls"; he is altogether
absent in "When a Man Falls a Crowd Gathers," a sketch
presented as a short story.[24] On the other hand, "Heard
on the Street Election Night" is without literary device and
is simply a collection of direct quotations, and "In the
Broadway Cars" uses the chronology of a day to describe a
variety of events occurring in a trolley.[25]

Some of the pieces are in fact short stories, and in them
Crane experimented in plot types and in methods of development which were to be used again in later stories.[26] In
"The Duel That Was Not Fought" Crane turns his story
upon an event of confrontation and near-battle between two
East Side denizens with opposed attitudes toward honor.[27]
In another, "A Lovely Jag in a Crowded Car," Crane manip-
ulates for ironic and comic effect three ways of seeing—that
of a drunk boarding a streetcar, that of the shocked lady
passengers who "stared out of the little windows which cut
the street scenes in half and allowed but the upper parts
of people to be seen," and that of the man over in the corner
who, with the conductor, watches "this wavering figure"
after he disembarks and "until observation was no longer
possible." [28] "Billy Atkins Went to Omaha" is comic picaresque, and "A Christmas Dinner Won in Battle" is a

sentimental Christmas story with a setting which anticipates some of the less successful writing to come out of the western trip.[29] And in "Mr. Bink's Day Off" Crane juxtaposes a representation of city life ("The sense of a city is battle") with the placidity of the New Jersey countryside.[30]

In January of 1895 Crane left New York to travel in the West and in Mexico for the Bacheller syndicate and did not return until May. In these five months there would occur a perceptible maturation in Crane's prose fiction. Before his departure, and since the termination of the "clever period" (with the single significant exception of *The Red Badge of Courage*) Crane's writing—both as journalist and as fiction- ist—was devoted to experiences set in a geographical area which he himself knew. Writing on city subjects developed his skills as a writer and taught him to control his irony, to render impressionistically and at times to turn his impres- sionistic skills to dramatic advantage in scenes of remark- able, if not at times grotesque, vitality. And it was also in the years after the "clever" period that Crane was able to make more functional use of his awareness of color, to learn to control an impulse toward a heavy-handed and sometimes self-consciously "clever" irony and to turn a deadening arch- ness toward his subjects into a distanced and balanced sympathy—an attitude which was to be a prerequisite to the success of his later works.

But if the early years of Crane's career were marked by a rapid development of control and maturity, in the writings of those years there can be noted a recurrent figure and a recurrent pattern of action. Repeatedly apparent are the figures of naifs—children, tenement girls, unsophisticated hunters, bumpkins. And repeatedly these naifs are seen in moments of confrontation, in moments in which they see that which they have not seen before.

This development, this learned control, this recurrence,

was to be of real significance in the shape and quality of Crane's literary identity. *Maggie, George's Mother,* and several of the early city sketches and stories, as well as *The Red Badge* and the work which was yet to come, show Crane to be consistently interested in how his characters saw—in how reality was recorded upon their sensibilities. This concern on Crane's part is manifest in the emphasis with which he repeatedly rendered scenes of confrontation. It is apparent in his concern for delusion in his characters, in his interest in its causes and consequences. It is apparent in his repeated presentation of naive characters, whom we observe as they confront an experience for the first time. Indeed, for all of Crane's undoubtedly sincere and intense concern for the "eternal mystery of the social condition" and his anger— often apparent in his writings—at the economic and social inequalities so terribly obvious in his New York of the mid-nineties,[31] it seems that even more central to the city writing was his interest in the way in which that social condition was apprehended.

V

"The Curtain of the Style"

I began to write special articles and short stories for the Sunday papers and one of the literary syndicates, reading a great deal in the meantime and gradually acquiring a style.
Crane in a letter to an
editor of *Leslie's Weekly*, 1895

Although I have considered Stephen Crane's subjects and themes in his early stories, I have, so far, ignored that aspect of his art which is of crucial importance in the understanding of his work—his superlative style.[1] His most direct influence upon American writing is a stylistic one,[2] and more significantly, as R. W. Stallman has so sharply asserted, that which is permanent in Crane's work is his use of language.[3] As James Colvert has said, it is in style that meaning exists in Crane's fiction.[4] So before I consider *The Red Badge of Courage*, the novel which is, in a sense, the achievement and the transcendence of Crane's early style, I shall undertake to identify the determining characteristics of that early style itself.

Whenever Crane's style is described, one word always recurs—the word *impressionism*.[5] I have used the word repeatedly myself thus far, although without elaborate or careful qualification. For it seems clear that the great ironic distance which Crane always keeps from his subject prevents the word from being more than roughly suggestive. Perhaps the term *dramatic impressionism* is more useful, as I have already suggested. But regardless of the label, it is true that, like the work of the French impressionist painters—Monet, Pisarro, Renoir—who in Crane's time were just beginning to attract American attention, Crane's prose was marked by an intense concern with the rendering of the immediate and the individual visual experience. Such a method was particularly appropriate for Crane, whose typical action centered upon an event of seeing. And for other critics Crane's dramatic impressionism seems also appropriate to his subject; at least one critic has described it as a form of extreme psychological realism.[6] But Crane's style, as it emerged in the early years of his career, is too individual merely to be identified by label. His literary technique, the functioning of that technique, and its effect upon his theme deserve a closer look.

The question of whether Crane's dramatic impressionism, with its elaborate color effects, is the result of the experience of living with artists in New York in 1893 and 1894 is still unsettled.[7] But it is clear that, whatever the influence, one of Crane's principal literary tools was the palette. His concern for color throughout his career is apparent in his titles— "A Dark Brown Dog," "An Illusion in Red and White," "The Bride Comes to Yellow Sky," "The Blue Hotel," and, of course, *The Red Badge of Courage*. From the very beginning the bright primary colors set against a contrasting background are everywhere apparent. On the third page of *Maggie* there appears, "A worm of yellow convicts came from the shadow of a grey ominous building and crawled slowly along the river's bank." "The Cry of a Huckleberry Pudding," one of the Sullivan County sketches, opens with "A great blaze wavered redly against the blackness of the night in the pines," and in "An Ominous Baby" there appears:

"The child from the poor district made way along the brown street filled with dull gray shadows. High up, near the roofs, glancing sun-rays changed cornices to blazing gold and silvered the fronts of the windows" (*New York City Sketches,* 60).

Stephen Crane's way of using color was highly unusual. He never used a variety of colors in elaborate descriptions; rarely did he use color as a device of characterization.[8] Color, when used descriptively by Crane, occurs in quick, bold strokes. Usually the colors are primary, and they are carefully chosen in twos or threes for contrast and balance of composition. Whether or not Crane's painterly concern with colors is attributable to the influence of artists, the similarity to the paintings of the American impressionists has always been a striking one. Take for example this passage from "An Experiment in Misery," which certainly suggests one of James McNeill Whistler's city paintings.[9] "It was late at night, and a fine rain was swirling softly down, covering the pavements with a bluish luster" (*New York City Sketches,* 34). Or this one:

> The mists of the cold and damp night made an intensely blue haze, through which the gaslights in the windows of stores and saloons shone with a golden radiance. The street cars rumbled softly, as if going upon carpet stretched in the aisle made by the pillars of the elevated road. Two interminable processions of people went along the wet pavements, spattered with black mud that made each shoe leave a scar-like impression. The high buildings lurked a-back, shrouded in shadows. Down a side street there were mystic curtains of purple and black, on which lamps dully glittered like embroidered flowers.
>
> *New York City Sketches,* 34–35

In Crane's early writing, colors were used primarily for descriptive or pictorial effects. But sometimes—notably in

The Red Badge of Courage—colors were used synaesthetically; sometimes the sensations attendant upon a character's apprehension of something were described in color images.* Thus, as such a technique would suggest, Crane early saw possibilities for colors which transcended mere description. For though none of the work before *The Red Badge of Courage* suggests anything approaching a symbolic schematization of colors, it is clear that before 1895 he was prepared to use colors to suggest not only what his characters saw, but how they saw it.

"Crane with nervous meticulousness excises and excises," said Ford Madox Ford.[10] It is certainly true that what is left out of Crane's prose characterizes it as much as any other quality. From the very first he wrote with a deliberate simplicity. Sentences are usually simple or compound; adjectives, prepositional phrases have been pared away; and there are few participles or gerunds. Crane set this syntactical norm early—in "On the New Jersey Coast": "Asbury Park creates nothing. It does not make; it merely amuses. There is a factory where nightshirts are manufactured, but it is some miles from town. This is a resort of wealth and leisure, of women and considerable wine. The throng along the line of march was composed of summer gowns, lace parasols, tennis trousers, straw hats, and indifferent smiles. The procession was composed of men, bronzed, slope-shouldered,

* I have noted some eighteen synaesthetic descriptions in the work before *The Red Badge*, of which some of the more striking are "yellow discontent" and "flame-colored anger" (*Virginia*, I, 24, 48) and "sunlight is noise" of "A Ghoul's Accountant" (*Sullivan County Tales*, 91). Usually the synaesthetic effects in the early work are achieved with color adjectives, notably red and yellow, but occasionally other transfers are attempted. In most cases, however, synaesthesia occurs to describe the vision of a character under emotional stress. W. Gordon Milne and Robert L. Hough (see footnotes 2 and 7 of this chapter) have commented on Crane's synaesthetic effects. Milne points out that Crane's synaesthesia is anticipatory of F. Scott Fitzgerald. It would seem that Crane's synaesthetic effects could well be a proper subject for closer study by one of his many students.

uncouth and begrimed with dust" (*New York City Sketches*, 272). Here is an angular, sharply defined sentence, short and clear and relatively undecorated—prophetic of Hemingway and of other writers of the twenties, but hardly in a style one would associate with the American eighteen nineties.[11] Rather, Crane's is a style which asserts its image sharply and brings the reader to a vivid, dramatic, and immediate apprehension of the described reality as it is perceived by narrator or character. Moreover, here is a syntax marked by a periodicity which later became a characteristic of Crane's prose. The repetition of structure in the penultimate sentence quoted above emphasizes the contrast between the images which the two sentences contain. Toward the end of Crane's career this same periodicity would recur, but by then it would be less angular and more maturely handled. Take, for example, this passage in "The Clan of No-Name," a war story of 1899: "But something controlled him; something moved him inexorably in one direction; he perfectly understood, but he was only sad, sad with a serene dignity, with the countenance of a mournful young prince" (*Virginia*, VI, 131).

Crane's style is also marked, from the very beginning, by special selections of words, which give individuality to his diction. Gorham Munson characterized these selections as "resensualization";[12] it is certainly true that Crane's words, although not unusual and frequently monosyllabic (Crane's vocabulary was not extensive and his spelling atrocious),* appear in new relationships. Notable are the unusual adjectives and adverbs—the "yellow discontent," the "responsible horses" of Maggie's brother's wagon, the "insipid" water which George Kelcey drinks after his debauch, the "impas-

---

* An examination of the letters demonstrates repeatedly that Crane could never be sure whether *i* or *e* should come first. See *Letters*, 94, 231. And he never learned the difference between *it's* and *its*.

sioned carbuncles" to which frightened eyes are compared in "Four Men in a Cave." Crane's verbs—concrete and image bearing—also vivify his prose and command his reader's attention. In "The Pace of Youth," Crane described a young lover's gaze upon his beloved in these words: "With his eyes he supplicated her to telegraph an explanation" (*New York City Sketches*, 277). In *Maggie*, "A baby falling down in front of the door, [sic] wrenched a scream like that of a wounded animal from its mother" (*Virginia*, I, 64), and, in "An Ominous Baby" (of the child regarding his theft), "His little form curved with pride" (*New York City Sketches*, 62).

This diction, by its very uniqueness, does have the effect of vitalizing Crane's language, of bringing the reader to fresh association with word and image. Crane's diction established new standards for denotative use of language which were to be observed by Hemingway, Fitzgerald, and other writers of the twenties and thirties.[13] But Crane's new word combinations, bearing as they do connotative and metaphoric implications, also suggest another characteristic of the prose which should not be ignored.

One is immediately struck in reading Crane, even in his early prose, by the rich and unusual figurative language which is employed. Crane's figures—for the most part similes and occasionally implicit metaphors—achieve comparisons which demonstrate an incredible finesse of imagination. Often, especially in the early writing, many of these far-fetched similes are little more than virtuosity, a virtuosity nonetheless conducted within the docorum of Crane's "plain style." [14] Frequently Crane's early similes, although they are striking in their originality, were derived from his own limited experience—from domestic or athletic life, from simple anatomical associations.

I remember that the flashing white waves looked like teeth when they swallowed me.

Icicles dangled from the trees' beards, and fine dusts of snow lay upon their brows.

Some of the gusts of snow that come down on the close collection of heads cut like knives and needles.[15]

There are, however, occasions in which the experience of association dramatized by the simile is not Crane's but his character's, and these most often occur when Crane arranges similes in groups to achieve particular effects. Joseph X. Brennan has called our attention to such an occasion in *George's Mother*. Brennan says of that work, "As the plot moves from a conflict of romantic illusions to one of savage realities, as the mother and her fond dreams decline and a bitterly disillusioned George takes the ascendancy, the language shifts perceptively from that derived in general from medieval romance to that descriptive of the jungle." [16] This shift is achieved mainly through a manipulation of similes and metaphors. We are told of George's mother's dustpan and broom: "She wielded them like weapons"; Crane says that the broom "was continually posed, lance-wise, at dust demons," that "her voice was often raised in a long cry, a strange war-chant, a shout of battle and defiance." Eric Solomon, perhaps more sensibly than Brennan, has seen in this "overblown language" evidence of Crane's parodic method;[17] at least the change in figure seems to bear him out. For, later on, when George confronts a gang, one member is described as being "like a savage who had killed a great chief." And a pillage of the city captures the gang's imagination "as the image of Rome might have lain small in the hearts of the barbarians"; one member is seen "gibbering like a wounded ape." [18]

Crane began early to use such organic figures. Indeed, as early as "The Octopush" of the Sullivan County sketches Crane was grouping metaphors to suggest the fear of the men stranded on the pond. "A ghost-like mist came and hung upon the waters. The pond became a graveyard. The gray tree-trunks and dark logs turned to monuments and crypts. Fireflies were wisp-lights dancing over graves, and then, taking regular shapes, appeared like brass nails in crude caskets" (*Sullivan County Tales*, 89). In *Maggie* Crane has also utilized figurative language to achieve his dramatically impressionistic renderings. Indeed, such descriptions as that of Pete as seen through Maggie's eyes ("his patent-leather shoes looked like weapons") are achieved as often by clusters of inflated figures as by heightened diction.

Of course, one effect of such manipulation of figures is a sense of doubled perception—an awareness that the narrator's apprehension of a thing or of a situation by the reader is different from its apprehension by the perceiving character. And such doubled perception, such irony, is the quality which most sharply characterizes Crane's fiction. Critics from Edward Garnett to the present have recognized the importance of irony to Crane's work, and a proper consideration of this phenomenon of Crane's style could be adequately treated only in a separate study.[19] Indeed, here I cannot even catalog the stylistic varieties of Crane's irony. For irony in Crane extends from the situational ironies of the Sullivan County sketches and "The Blue Hotel" (where the Swede's fear and the delusions resulting from it actually bring about the feared event—an irony at once situational and dramatic) to the irony implicit in the image of Scratchy Wilson's New York-made maroon shirt or in the haloed figure on the beach in "The Open Boat," from the irony of Crane's endings, which so often deny the very story they conclude,* to the irony achieved sometimes with a single word (Jimmie's "responsible" horses in *Maggie*). Crane's irony is ubiquitous. But it is also necessary here to suggest something of the directions which Crane's uses of irony were to take. For upon its successful control and use depends the success or failure of Crane's work.

In his best writing Crane was to strike an ironic balance which was truly to express the doubleness of his own vision; here would be manifest evidence of John Berryman's assertion that "this author is simultaneously *at war with* the people he creates and *on their side.*" [20] Crane would later express this ambivalence more fully in "The Open Boat," "The Clan of No-Name," "The Bride Comes to Yellow Sky," and "Death and the Child." He just failed to achieve it completely in *The Red Badge*. But in the early works he was still an apprentice ironist. In *Maggie* the hand was still a bit heavy: "When he paused to contemplate the attitude of the police toward himself and his fellows, he believed that they were the only men in the city who had no rights" (*Virginia*, I, 22). "Maggie observed Pete. . . . His mannerisms stamped him as a man who had a correct sense of his personal superiority. There was valor and contempt for circumstances in the glance of his eye" (*Virginia*, I, 25). In *George's Mother* Crane was more subtle. By then he had

* In the final sentence of "The Five White Mice," for example, Crane concludes a story of hairbreadth escape from death with the sentence, "Nothing had happened" (*Stories and Sketches*, 419). In "Flanagan and His Short Filibustering Adventure" Crane concludes with "The expedition of the *Foundling* will never be historic" (*Stories and Sketches*, 377). At the end of "War Memories," Crane says, "And you can depend upon it that I have told you nothing at all, nothing at all, nothing at all" (*Work*, IX, 258). "An Episode of War," "the story of how the lieutenant lost his arm," ends with the lieutenant's statement, " 'I don't suppose it matters so much as all that' " (*Stories and Sketches*, 656). These sentences—which seem so much like Hemingway's ending of "A Clean, Well-lighted Place" (" 'It is probably insomnia. Many must have it.' ")—throw considerable light on the half-ironic endings of *The Red Badge of Courage* and "The Open Boat."

learned to group and to arrange figures to achieve ironic effects. In fact, the very opening of the novel—so important in immediately establishing the emotional situation of Crane's protagonist and that protagonist's failure to use that situation for what it is—is delicately wrought. Here is the dramatic impressionist at work, but with a description which is concise and succinct:

> In the swirling rain that came at dusk the broad avenue glistened with that deep bluish tint which is so widely condemned when it is put into pictures. There were long rows of shops, whose fronts shone with full, golden light. Here and there, from druggists' windows or, from the red street-lamps that indicated the positions of fire-alarm boxes, a flare of uncertain, wavering crimson was thrown upon the wet pavements.
>
> The lights made shadows, in which the buildings loomed with a new and tremendous massiveness, like castles and fortresses. There were endless processions of people, mighty hosts, with umbrellas waving, bannerlike, over them. Horse-cars, aglitter with new paint, rumbled in steady array between the pillars that supported the elevated railroad. The whole street resounded with the tinkle of bells, the roar of iron-shod wheels on the cobbles, the ceaseless trample of the hundreds of feet. Above all, too, could be heard the loud screams of the tiny newsboys, who scurried in all directions. Upon the corners, standing in from the dripping eaves, were many loungers, descended from the world that used to prostrate itself before pageantry.
>
> *Virginia*, I, 115

And in "An Experiment in Misery," as I noted earlier, Crane introduces a young man whose innocence of vision provides an irony very muted indeed.

But what is even more curious in Crane's early writing is the ironic attitude he takes toward the material of the story itself. And in pieces like "Ghosts on the New Jersey

Coast" that attitude is elusive indeed. As we have seen in "Ghosts," at the beginning he seems to be parodying the very story he tells, yet at the end he seems fearfully engaged. And one even senses another Crane, still further removed, sardonically observing the narrating Crane's becoming frightened by his own words. In *Maggie* and in *George's Mother* the reader is always a bit unsure whether he should take Crane's protagonist—or, indeed, any of the characters—seriously. It is almost as if Crane might be somewhat ill at ease in the recording of his own fantasies. Yet such a recording is inevitable in the writing of fiction.

Sometimes Crane lost control of the complex apprehensions and attitudes manifest in his gigantic irony so often apparent in the early writing. He had yet to achieve the consistent *"ton juste"* for which Gorham Munson praised him.[21] But even in those works the characteristic quality of Crane's irony is apparent. It was achieved out of the disparity between what the narrator or his characters think they perceive and what the reader or the narrator knows they confront. Crane's irony is directed—as James Colvert has it—against "heroes [who] rarely have . . . a clear insight into their own limitations for seeing the world clearly and truly."[22]

H. G. Wells said of Crane, "He began stark." Yet Crane's early "starkness"—his boniness of syntax—had about it a strikingly bright and dramatic quality. And it had an organic quality as well, for Stephen Crane's early style, almost from the first, was clearly wedded to statement. It is the fusion of style with content, the functional quality of the language, which has made him important to his successors. But it is also significant to his successors that Crane was forging, in his early years, a style capable of representing events of perception, full of color and empty of rhetoric, always in the service of the eye. He was, in the early years, developing a language of vision appropriate to his action and his theme.

VI

"To the Destructive Element": *The Red Badge of Courage*

> *A youth in apparel that glittered*
> *Went to walk in a grim forest.*
> *There he met an assassin*
> *Attired all in garb of old days;*
> *He, scowling through the thickets,*
> *And dagger poised quivering,*
> *Rushed upon the youth.*
>
> Crane, *The Black Riders*, 1895

> *War is neither magnificent nor squalid; it is*
> *simply life.*
>
> Crane, "War Memories," 1899

The *Red Badge of Courage* was probably the most difficult of his books for Stephen Crane to write. Its creation was even a more arduous process than the writing of *Maggie* or *George's Mother*. Nearly three years elapsed between its original conception and its publication, and during those years the war novel was in a state of almost constant change. There were three drafts and at least as many revisions by its author. But the game was certainly worth the candle; the September, 1895, publication of *The Red Badge*, first by Appleton and then by Heinemann's in London two months later, brought Crane almost immediate fame.[1]

The agonizing composition of *The Red Badge* suggests that Crane's conception of the novel was a dynamic one and that expansion progressed not merely from pot-boiler to serious novel (which he came to feel must be done "my own way");[2] the conception expanded and became more complex as his awareness of the nature of the relationship be-

86

tween individual apprehension and objective reality matured.

Maggie had shown how "environment is a tremendous thing in the world and frequently shapes lives [and apprehensions] regardless." [3] *George's Mother* was leading Crane into an awareness of the shaping influence of primal family relationships upon a person's vision. Yet when Crane confronted the fact of man in battle, and when Crane addressed himself to the question of "how they *felt* in those scraps," [4] he was coming to an awareness that man's apprehensional process is shaped, not only by his environment, not only by his family relationships, but by his imagination as well—an imagination drenched in myth, filled with distorted images generated by the memory, wrenched by fear, capable of concretizing emotion into image and inserting it into that which is seen. To assert these awarenesses Stephen Crane had to develop creative and stylistic capabilities of a sophistication beyond those he had previously known.*

Discussions of *The Red Badge of Courage* by Donald Gibson and Eric Solomon, two of the book's more recent critics, reveal a disagreement crucial to Crane criticism that is still unresolved. Gibson sees *The Red Badge* as a mythic enactment of a psychic drama, and is concerned primarily with the question of whether Henry Fleming "undergoes meaningful change." [5] Solomon, on the other hand, sees *The Red Badge* as realism, albeit realism of a very special kind. For Solomon, Crane's realism is achieved by means of a sort of parodic irony, by a form of denial of all of the heroic and romantic attitudes which established the conventions for the war novel. [6] I would argue that *The Red Badge*

---

* It is also probably the case that, as James B. Colvert asserts (*Virginia*, VI, xi-xxiii), by the time of the completion of *The Red Badge* in 1894, Crane was beginning to move beyond an apprentice's commitment to the realism and veritism of Howells and Garland and in the direction of a more personal statement.

describes both a psychic and an external action. For me it seems certainly the case that the vitalizing center of *The Red Badge of Courage* is established in an oppositional tension, but this center occupies a specific ground. In *The Red Badge of Courage* it would seem that the omnipresent irony is the direct result of the tension in the novel between Crane's commitment to things as they are and things as they are seen and felt to be, between reality as it statically is and as it dynamically is apprehended, or, to put it differently, between a novel conceived as realism and a novel conceived in terms of Crane's evolving dramatic impressionism.

This tension in Crane's writing *The Red Badge* provoked some new undertakings which are not so apparent in his earlier writing. One of them is the effort for an intensity of focus. This effort can be seen, not only in Crane's imagery (although single images often generate new intensities in the war novel), but also in such matters as the intensity achieved by the use of what seems to be a single point of view throughout. Everything *appears* to be seen through the eyes of Henry Fleming, so much so that at times Crane commits himself to a kind of "substitutionary speech" as a means of representing more closely the perceptions of Henry Fleming.[7] The form of the novel supports this intensity of focus; one critic has called *The Red Badge* a sort of *tondo*.[8] Yet, for all of the novel's focused intensity, its ironic doubleness is still apparent; one senses that there is someone else watching. As one critic puts it, "The point of view is dual: we are both spectators on a scene where the main character is one of the actors, and we experience the same scene, to a large extent, through this main character. We do not only see him in action; we have access to his innermost thoughts and feelings."[9] To state it differently, we do not see the war only through Henry's eyes; we see the war through our own as well. The experience of war is presented not only by means of an intensified dramatic impressionism but by means of a pure realism; it is presented not only as it objectively is but as it is subjectively apprehended.

Thus *The Red Badge of Courage*, like so much of Crane's early work, is conceived with a critical awareness of apprehensional possibility. And yet Crane here is not only an ironic impressionist, concerned with doubly representing facts and events. For in *The Red Badge* he has chosen for the main action an apprehensional initiation, and he has conducted that event in a style which, in spite of its new achievements, remains an intensely apprehensional style. Before I examine that theme, I shall consider the new capabilities of that style.

The Red Badge shows Crane's vital early style approaching its full maturity. All of the clearly recognizable stylistic idiosyncrasies—the colorings, the similes, the sharply sensualized images, the ironies, the elaborate figurations—are immediately apparent and are here clearly functional to Crane's purpose. And—although in the later work Crane's style becomes somewhat less obtrusive and more restrained—in *The Red Badge* the reader is confronted by an imagery and language which exploits associational possibilities and generates an intensified and revitalized concreteness.

The most immediately apparent evidence of this vigorous concreteness is Crane's repeated use of sharply effective sound imagery. *The Red Badge* is a very noisy book, and Crane's onomatopoeiae underline this fact.[10] The result is an intensification of apprehensions, the reader's apprehension of the sounds of war and Henry Fleming's apprehension of these same sounds. For even as the onomatopoeiae vitalize experience for the reader, they dramatize the significance which the experience of hearing suggests to Crane's protagonist. When Henry visits the forest, "swishing saplings" mark his presence. After the boy has seen the rotting corpse in the forest "chapel," Crane again uses alliteration to imitate forest sounds. "The trees about the portal of the chapel moved soughingly [*sic*] in a soft wind. A sad silence was upon the little guarding edifice" (*Novels*, 236).[11] There are two paired *s* alliterations here. One intensifies the experience for the reader; the other suggests Henry Fleming's evaluation of it.

If *The Red Badge of Courage* is a shockingly noisy novel, it is even more vital to the sight. From the opening cinematic image of the book to its final sun, showing itself "through hosts of leaden rain clouds," Crane has selected and arranged his images to achieve an acute visual intensity. And, as we shall see, the images of battle shock Henry's eyes as well.

The impact of Crane's imagery upon the vision of his protagonist and his reader is not only for dramatic or for emphatic effect, however. In *The Red Badge* he was also beginning to exploit the significative potential of imagery.[12] This exploitation can be regarded as a departure on Crane's part from the "objective" realism which was so characteristic of the earlier work. For in his movement toward symbolism he was showing himself to be more willing to deal in the ambiguities of subjective apprehension.

It does not seem to me that in *The Red Badge* Crane showed himself to be a full-fledged symbolist. I cannot accept the novel as a Christian allegory, for example; I am more inclined to believe that *The Red Badge* is about what it seems to be about. Yet, although I have no intention of reopening the rather fruitless disputes as to the brand of wafer to be found pasted in the sky of chapter nine, it does seem that Crane is from time to time presenting images as embodiments of conceptions. Even as symbolist, however, Stephen Crane is still the impressionist first; as such, he is concerned less with what an image signifies to his reader than with what an apprehended fact suggests to the perceiving character.[13] The fact which is so little understood about the novel is that in it Henry Fleming's and not Stephen Crane's imagination directly generates symbolic meanings.

A notable example of Henry's symbol-making is the small animal which Henry Fleming sees just before entering his forest "chapel." "Pausing at one time to look about him he saw, out at some black water, a small animal pounce in and emerge directly with a gleaming fish" (Novels, 235). This image is supported throughout the novel by similes and metaphors which compare soldiers to fish, the war to a beast. The soldiers call their untried companions " 'Fresh fish' " (Novels, 206). At the end of the novel, the lieutenant is a larger, less vulnerable fish—a "whale" (Novels, 298), but on at least two earlier occasions, war has been represented as a "red animal." [14] This arrangement of images and figures suggests that Crane is using Henry's recent memory and his present perception of the animal and the fish to represent one understanding available to the boy of the relationship of war to the soldier.[15] Edward Stone has also pointed out the recurrence of the image of the sun in the novel, and William Howarth's demonstration of Crane's having repeatedly revised the chapter endings gives evidence of Crane's intentions.[16] The sun's symbolic function is not unlike that of Crane's small animal and the fish; the sun represents the center of the universe to Henry. Its significance depends upon how Henry sees it and how he responds to it. And there are other similarly functioning symbols in the novel; the flag and the boy's wound are two.[17]

This is, of course, a rather light-handed symbolism—really no more than the exploitation of recurring images, and hardly the ponderous symbol-forging which Stallman and Daniel Weiss suggest. But The Red Badge of Courage also manifests an experiment with another symbolical pattern, a new way of using colors. Frank Noxon, Crane's friend and fraternity brother at Syracuse, writing to Max Herzberg in 1926, said of *The Red Badge*, "Incidentally, the use of the word 'Red' in this title was part of a program. After the book appeared he and I had somewhere a talk about color in literature. He told me that a passage in Goethe analyzed the effect which several colors have upon the human mind. Upon Crane this had made a profound impression and he had utilized the idea to produce his effects." [18] The "passage in Goethe," as Robert L. Hough has pointed out, is almost certainly from *Farbenlehre*, published in 1810 and translated into English by Charles Locke Eastlake in 1840 as *Goethe's Theory of Colours*.[19] Noxon was referring to section six of this translation, "Effect of Colour with Reference to Moral Associations." In this section Goethe suggested that the effects of colors "are immediately associated with the emotions of the mind." [20] Crane had also read Emerson— as early as 1893 [21]—and presumably was aware with Emerson that "Nature always wears the colors of the spirit." [22] But in *The Red Badge* it was Goethe's more often than Emerson's color values which Crane followed.

Of course Crane's methods here are neither consistent nor simple, and the assertion that Crane is using colors in *The Red Badge* to signify emotional states must necessarily be complicated by the fact that Crane is also using color imagery to transmit experience directly to the reader. The opening paragraph of the novel contains a particularly rich example of this more usual imagery. "A river, amber-tinted in the shadow of its banks, purled at the army's feet; and at night, when the stream had become of a sorrowful blackness, one could see across it the red, eyelike gleam of hostile camp-fires set in the low brows of distant hills" (*Novels*, 201). It is no wonder that Orm Øverland, in his definitive essay on Crane's impressionism, says that Crane's use of color "on many points bears close resemblance to the technique of the impressionist painters." [23] And it is also no wonder that such passages as Crane's opening attract intense analyses. R. W. Stallman, for example, has commented,

> A striking analogy is established between Crane's use of colors and the method employed by the impressionists and the neo-impressionists or divisionists, and it is as if he had known about their theory of contrasts and had composed his own prose paintings by the same principle. Their principle, as one writer defines it, is this: "Each plane of shade creates around itself a sort of aura of light, and each luminous plane creates around itself a zone of shade. In a similar way a coloured area communicates its 'complementary' to the neighboring colour, or heightens it if it is 'complementary.' " [24]

Rather than Crane being a "divisionist" however, it seems more likely that, as Robert L. Hough points out, Crane is again simply following Goethe, who advocated such contrasting juxtapositions. [25]

It is, however. reasonable to expect that in describing the coloration of Henry Fleming's vision Crane is often symbolically representing the young soldier's emotional state. Yellow, "the colour nearest the light" [26] for Goethe, is the color of the light in the barracks hut to which Henry withdraws to consider his situation in the opening pages of the novel. And yellow is also the color associated with the boy's feeling toward his mother's bustling practicality ("this yellow light thrown upon the color of his ambitions," *Novels*, 203). As Goethe tells us that yellow is "extremely liable to contamination" and is sometimes "not undeserving the epithet foul," so Crane suggests Henry's response to the rotting corpse which the boy encounters on the march to the battle by dressing it "in an awkward suit of yellowish brown" (*Novels*, 217). And the mouth of the corpse in the forest "chapel" is seen as "appalling yellow" (*Novels*, 235). [27]

Red, which for Goethe "includes all the other colours" predominates when an excited Henry experiences the emotional intensity of combat. Goethe tells us that "the red glass exhibits a bright landscape in so dreadful a hue as to inspire sentiments of awe," and Henry sees the "red eyes" of the rebel campfires as "a row of dragons advancing" (*Novels*, 210). We are told that the soldiers will look at the "red animal—war" (*Novels*, 218). Blue, for Goethe, is a passive color. Blue "in its highest purity is, as it were, a stimulating negation." For Emerson, "the blue sky in which the private earth is buried, the sky with its eternal calm, and full of everlasting orbs, is the type of Reason." [28] Henry Fleming, seeing blue, feels his own insignificance—he sees war as a "blue demonstration," [29] himself only a part of an impersonal military machine, and he sees tiny soldiers gesticulating "against the blue and sombre sky" (*Novels*, 253).

Crane in *The Red Badge* was attempting to write, perhaps according to Emerson's precepts, but certainly upon Goethe's suggestion that "colour may be employed for certain moral and aesthetic ends" and that "such an application, coinciding entirely with nature, might be called symbolical." [30] * And the symbolic values assigned these colors are, for the most part, generated by the imagination, not of the author, but of the apprehending character. And, of course, there were the efforts on the part of Crane for a sharpened intensity, for a tighter unity in the war novel. But for the most part his style in *The Red Badge* remains clearly recognizable. Here is the same syntactically spare angularity (even if a bit softened), the same vitality of diction, the same striking and original figures, the same irony, and all of these characteristics are working together—even more smoothly now—to describe a process of apprehension. In *The Red*

---

* Crane occasionally remembered Goethe's color values in later work, notably, in "The Blue Hotel."

Badge Crane began to seek for new possibilities in his apprehensional style.

If Crane's impressionistic and visually oriented style in *The Red Badge* seems to be moving to a new subjectivism, a new distrust of assertions about objective reality, his theme in the novel still assumes an objectively apprehendable universe. For, although it is to be doubly evaluated and doubly seen, initiation—the initiation of a private—is the event which occupies the novel's center.[31] Like Robin, of Hawthorne's "My Kinsman, Major Molyneux," Henry Fleming is a bumpkin, a boy from the country, who stands innocent and alone at the threshold of a confrontation which is of crucial importance to him. Both Robin and Henry in their progress to initiation stop at chapels (Henry's is a "natural" chapel), and both, ironically, experience fear, not reassurance, on their visits.[32] Both are led to their final confrontation by kindly but unnamed strangers. And, incidentally, both are provided with stockings by their respective mothers. Both are stories of coming-of-age.

But here the resemblance stops. For if Hawthorne's reader, at the end of his story, is convinced that he has observed Robin's coming-of-age as an event of confrontation which symbolically frees the boy from his own psychic and cultural past,[33] Crane's reader is more ambiguously aware of Henry's experience. He observes the youth's first battle, his lonely confrontation with the realities of war, and his return to the securities of communal illusion, yet simultaneously he sees battle as a boy sees it who is to believe, at battle's end, that "He had been to touch the great death, and found that, after all, it was but the great death. He was a man" (*Novels*, 298). If Henry's view is that his initiation to battle is conclusive, however, the reader is not so sure. One result of Crane's dual orientation is that he leaves his reader with an understanding of the events which is ironic, and in which acceptance is considerably qualified.[34]

Thus the theme of *The Red Badge of Courage* is informed by an ironic tension—a tension between what a character learns and what he thinks he has learned—and it is informed by another opposition as well. Everywhere in *The Red Badge* is to be found Crane's awareness of the doubled nature of human experience, a double nature intensified by conditions of battle. A man is an individual and at the same time he is a member of a community, and if he receives experience privately, his acts in response to those apprehensions have public consequence and generate public response. This doubled nature of the human condition can shape the very process of apprehension as well. It is this shaping process with which *The Red Badge of Courage* is centrally concerned.

Stephen Crane opens his novel with a preparation of his novice for rites of passage which involve a change in the patterns of apprehension appropriate to both kinds of experience. Before Crane's protagonist can be initiated into the experience of war, he must purge himself of deluding preconceptions acquired in the community of his childhood. Crane's first attention is upon his protagonist as he returns to the "light yellow shade" of his hut and withdraws from his companions, who are abuzz with rumors of impending action. We first see Henry in the process of shaking off a number of his illusions concerning the reality of war. One set of illusions most dramatically vitiated are his assumptions about the nature of the enemy; these are wiped away by his contact with one individual, a rebel picket. Another concerns the soldier's life, which, Henry has discovered, involves much more waiting than fighting.[35]

But the illusion with which we are most concerned is Henry's misunderstanding of the true nature of war itself and of his own place in it. This confusion is self-contradictory. At first Henry's notion of war is highly romanticized; he sees battle as the individual action of brave men, a "Greeklike struggle." Henry's mother has "thrown yellow light . . . upon the colour of his ambitions," however, and the ridicule to which Henry has been subjected by "a certain light-haired girl" who was present at his heroic departure from his schoolmates has further shaken the boy's fantasy. But Henry also sees himself and war in another way. He sees himself to be only "a part of a vast blue demonstration," only a unit in a huge, impersonal war machine. This awareness, in its simplistic fatalism, comforts the boy, but it contradicts his expectation of a hero's role in the war.

As Henry Fleming approaches his baptism of fire, he vacillates between his two understandings, between his romantic pride which separates him from his fellows, and his sense of lost identity and of insignificance. At first, as his regiment moves to the place of battle, Henry's self-awareness is heightened to an exaggeration of his own importance, to an almost solipsistic pride. "In his great anxiety his heart was continually clamoring at what he considered the intolerable slowness of the generals. They seemed content to perch tranquilly on the river bank, and leave him bowed down by the weight of a great problem. He wanted it settled forthwith. He could not long bear such a load, he said. Sometimes his anger at the commanders reached an acute stage, and he grumbled about the camp like a veteran" (*Novels*, 210). This arrogance brings alienation ("The youth kept from intercourse with his companions as much as circumstances would allow him"), and Henry feels himself to be different in nature from his fellows ("He felt that every nerve in his body would be an ear to hear the voices [of 'a thousand-tongued fear'] while other men would remain stolid and deaf"). Indeed, "he was a mental outcast," and with this alienation comes fear, fear as he stares at the redness in the center of the fire.

But soon Henry discards his sense of specialness. As the regiment before the battle is casting aside unnecessary equipment, Henry tries to escape from the burdensome feeling of loneliness and fear, and returns "to his theory of a blue demonstration." He surrenders his sense of separateness ("He felt carried along by a mob") to become a part of the war machine, an atom in a deterministic universe. But this way of looking at his situation is also uncomfortable for him. "He instantly saw that it would be impossible for him to escape from the regiment. It enclosed him. And there were iron laws of tradition and law on four sides. He was in a moving box" (*Novels*, 216).

Thus neither of these untested generalizations seems adequate to the situation. Yet when Henry is first engaged in battle, he finds that his capacity to surrender identity, his ability to lose concern for himself and become "not a man but a member," makes him able to act under fire with reasonable success. It is only when the awareness of individuality returns—and when fear for his own safety distorts his perception—that he leaves the relative safety of the group. Upon the second charge of the enemy, Henry, frightened, and sure that the charge presages a rout, throws down his weapon and flees the battle.[36]

When Henry becomes aware of what he has done, his understandings of war and of himself are invalidated. He is certainly neither a hero nor a will-less atom. At least, he believes, he can trust his own understanding of what has taken place. Then, almost immediately, the boy is confronted with the inadequacy of his understanding as well. Amidst a "gleaming of yellow and patent leather," a general exults in victory and Henry overhears. Now the front is seen to be in a "yellow fog," and Henry "cringed as if discovered in a crime." Now he is isolated and racked with guilt. But what is even more painful, he is aware of his own vulnerability. He knows that he is alone and that he can no longer trust his own capacities to understand.

In his agony, Henry seeks a solution that is characteristic of the romantic imagination which Crane has already subjected to sharp irony. Henry seeks solace in Nature. The boy moves even farther away from his fellows and deeper into the forest. "The landscape gave him assurance," Crane ironically tells us. If Henry cannot be an epic hero or a disciplined member, he can at least attempt to see himself as a romantic isolate seeking his solution in a transcendental communion.* Nature even gives him signs, or so it seems to Henry. He throws a pine cone at a squirrel and sees the squirrel's retreat as an indication of the futility of standing to fight.[37]

But the indifferent Nature which Crane has already introduced to Henry as having "gone tranquilly on with her golden process in the midst of so much devilment" is hardly Thoreauesque and benevolent. "Once he found himself almost into a swamp. He was obliged to walk upon bog tufts and watch his feet to keep from the oily mire. Pausing at one time to look about him he saw, out at some black water, a small animal pounce in and emerge directly with a gleam-

---

* Earlier in the novel Henry has had another romantic impulse, that time to a bucolic escape. Alone and waiting for the march to begin,

> He wished, without reserve, that he was at home again making the endless rounds from the house to the barn, from the barn to the fields, from the fields to the barn, from the barn to the house. He remembered he had often cursed the brindle cow and her mates, and had sometimes flung milking stools. But, from his present point of view, there was a halo of happiness about each of their heads, and he would have sacrificed all the brass buttons on the continent to have been enabled to return to them. He told himself that he was not formed for a soldier. And he mused seriously upon the radical differences between himself and those men who were dodging implike around the fires.

Novels, 212–13

Gibson (in The Fiction of Stephen Crane, 74–75) suggests the similarity between this impulse to go home again and the seeking of the protection of Mother Nature.

ing fish" (*Novels*, 235). Confronting Henry is a post-Darwin-ian Nature, a Nature red in tooth and claw. And any "sign" which Henry can properly discover in this Nature is not, as the boy would believe, in the discretion of a jovial squirrel. The emblem for Henry to observe is the gleaming fish.[38]

Nature does, however, provide for Henry a glimpse at reality. But the reality is not, as Crane's ironically religious imagery would indicate, a religious insight.[39] In a horribly grotesque and distorted rendering Crane dramatizes Henry's terror as he enters Nature's chapel, a chapel which offers something less than eternal life.

> At length he reached a place where the high, arching boughs made a chapel. He softly pushed the green doors aside and entered. Pine needles were a gentle brown carpet. There was a religious half light.
>
> Near the threshold he stopped, horror-stricken at the sight of a thing.
>
> He was being looked at by a dead man who was seated with his back against a column-like tree. The corpse was dressed in a uniform that had once been blue, but was now faded to a melancholy shade of green. The eyes, staring at the youth, had changed to the dull hue *to be seen on the side of a dead fish*. The mouth was open. Its red had changed to an ap-palling yellow. Over the gray skin of the face ran little ants. One was trundling some sort of bundle along the upper lip.*
>
> *Novels*, 235

* Emphasis mine. Here is the kind of grotesque rendering that we have seen in *Maggie* and in *George's Mother*, but now Crane's ability in reproduc-ing already charged images ("the dull hue to be seen on the side of a dead fish") manifests a new sophistication of technique. Note also that it is a threat to the eye which really terrified Henry here and provides the climax to this little grotesquerie. "At last he burst the bonds which had fastened him to the spot and fled, unheeding the underbrush. He was pursued by a sight of the black ants swarming greedily upon the gray face and venturing horribly near to the eyes" (*Novels*, 235).

Henry has seen death before; on the march to the battle-field he had passed a corpse and had felt that "it was as if fate had betrayed the soldier." But here is another, more chilling betrayal. For now Henry sees man's real place and relationship with Nature, a relationship engaged only through death. Now, alone in the forest, separated from his fellows, he confronts that moment of engagement, the process of natural death itself. And he sees simultaneously how alien and unimportant he is to the natural process—at least as long as he is alive.[40]

The terror of this experience in the chapel, hardly a feeling of renewal or of regeneration, turns Henry back in the direction of the "crimson roar" and the community of soldiers at the front.* Henry's confrontation in the forest has at least given him some awareness of the inadequacy of his understanding and the absurdity of his situation. Henry now knows with an almost existential wryness that he is, in Camus' phrase, no tree among the trees. "Reflecting, he saw a sort of a humor in the point of view of himself and his fellows during the late encounter. They had taken themselves and the enemy very seriously and had imagined that they were deciding the war" (*Novels*, 236). But when Henry leaves the forest and comes upon a column of wounded, he is at the threshold of a visual confrontation which will deprive him of his last illusion of protection. For in that column of wounded he encounters Jim Conklin, and Henry

---

It is undoubtedly this kind of grotesque which Warner Berthoff has most vividly in mind when he says of Crane, "It may be said that everything convincing in Crane's work turns on visionary images which have, as they succeed one another, the hallucinatory serenity and intactness of dream images" (*The Ferment of Realism*, 232).

* Kermit Vanderbilt and Daniel Weiss have suggested ("From Rifleman to Flagbearer: Henry Fleming's Separate Peace in *The Red Badge of Courage*," 371-80) that Henry in *The Red Badge* is manifesting the soldier's commitment to battle as a means of overcoming the fear of death, is displaying a primitive instinct to overcome death by means of murder. To me what is shown here can as well be regarded as an instinct to herd.

must watch helplessly as Conklin succumbs to his mortal wound.

R. W. Stallman, on rather flimsy evidence it would seem, has argued that Crane intends Jim Conklin (with appropriate initials) as a Christ figure.[41] More recently it has been proposed that Conklin—far from being a Christ figure—is a horrible example of that primitive military virtue of stoicism which Henry must transcend.[42] But both, it would seem, have missed the direction of Crane's irony here. Isaac Rosenfeld, perhaps closer to the truth, says, "Henry, deep in the guilt of his desertion, cannot help but regard Jim Conklin as a Christ figure." [43] Rosenfeld is at least aware of the disparity between Conklin's significance to Henry and to Crane. But what is important about Jim Conklin is not his sense of duty but his humanity and the illusory protection which that humanity offers. Henry on several occasions earlier in the novel has turned for aid and comfort to Conklin and in his desperate search for his old companions turns again to him now. But Crane's point in presenting so vividly Conklin's death is the very fact that Conklin, like any other soldier, is ultimately unable even to protect himself. If Henry in the chapel confronted the nature of death, here he confronts the actuality of human dying.[44]

Conklin first appeared in the novel as Henry saw him, a "tall soldier" informing others of the rumor that the regiment would move. Before the first chapter was over he reassured Henry when Henry had doubts of his own courage. On the march, Henry looked to Jim Conklin almost as an older brother, and just before Henry's first combat, it was Jim to whom he turned for reassurance.* So it is only natural

---

* At that moment Henry sees Conklin touch the color which is for Henry the color of war. "The tall soldier, having prepared his rifle, produced a red handkerchief of some kind. He was engaged in knitting it about his throat with exquisite attention to its position, when the cry was repeated up and down the line in a muffled roar of sound" (*Novels*, 224).

that the discovery of Jim in the line of wounded should attract the boy to him. But Jim is dying, and for Jim, dying is a private matter. As Conklin moves away from Henry and lurches toward his fate, seeking a place to die, his is hardly the role of a redeemer.[45]

"The youth, aghast and filled with wonder at the tall soldier, began quaveringly to question him. 'Where yeh goin', Jim? What you thinking about? Where you going? Tell me, won't you, Jim?' The tall soldier faced about as upon relentless pursuers. In his eyes there was a great appeal. 'Leave me be, can't yeh? Leave me be fer a minnit' " (Novels, 242). Henry can only stand by, helpless and apart, and watch in horror the grotesque rite of his friend's death. And—with phrases like "the tremor of his legs caused him to bounce a little way from the earth" or "the teeth showed in a laugh" or "the side looked as if it had been chewed by wolves"— the rendering is grotesque indeed. Here again, as in the earlier works, the grotesque rendering records the distortion of the protagonist's emotions. For now Henry is at a moment of intense isolation and intense awareness.[46] His only relief is in gesture. It is here that Henry curses the sun, the implacable and distant center of his universe.[47]

Henry's paradoxical generalizations about the reality of war have thus been tested in the heat of private experience and in individual confrontations. He has seen the process of death amid Nature's indifference to it. He has come as close as one can to the experience of dying—he has watched a friend die. But, although he has lost the illusions and the protections provided by the group, he still risks the distortions of subjective vision. Yet, gratuitously, there remains one man who thrusts himself upon Henry as a companion—the tattered man.

It is this man's perception which leads the reader into the tenth chapter. Crane opens that chapter with, "The tattered soldier stood musing." Here is the common soldier who cannot comprehend the rite of death which he and Henry have just witnessed. " 'Besides, if I died, I wouldn't die th' way that feller did. That was th' funniest thing. I'd jest flop down, I would, I never seen a feller die th' way that feller did.' " (*Novels*, 244–45).

Later in Crane's career, when apprehension of mystery seemed to him less possible, he celebrated the common soldier as a hero. But here in *The Red Badge* the common soldier is only a foil, albeit a very important foil. For even here, it is not about death but about life that Henry Fleming must finally learn. And it is the reality of the common soldier, and of all of the other ordinary men like him, and the reality of their limited awareness and the limits which they impose upon his own, with which Crane's protagonist must ultimately come to terms. At their meeting here Henry's guilt alienates him from the tattered soldier's innocence. When the tattered soldier asks solicitously of Henry's wound, his presence becomes intolerable, and Henry abandons him to his fate. With this breach Henry's isolation and guilt are complete—so much so that in the eleventh chapter he hopes for the defeat of his own army as vindication of his own acts, and in the twelfth chapter he is wounded, not at the hands of the enemy but at the hands of federal troops.* His is a red badge not of bravery in battle but of awareness and of alienation.

The first twelve chapters of *The Red Badge of Courage* have followed a penetrating movement, a movement downward and inward to reality. Henry has confronted with his

---

* Gibson (*The Fiction of Stephen Crane*, 78) sees no irony in the circumstances of Henry's wound. And it is true that the wound is received from soldiers fleeing the fight, a flight which Henry opposes. Perhaps also, it could be said that Henry's wound is a badge of courage because he is opposing flight and attempting to return to his regiment when he receives it. But for me, the significant fact is the identity of him who gives the wound. As is usual with Crane, there are several possibilities.

eyes the reality of his place in the natural universe and the reality of death itself. But his confrontation has not been without cost. He has paid for his apprehension with his innocence, and he has experienced consequent alienation and guilt. As we shall see in the last half of Crane's novel, Henry will move upward and outward; he will regain his place in the community of his regiment, but by that very return he will lose something of his newly and privately earned awareness of reality.

At the moment of Henry's wound in the twelfth chapter of *The Red Badge of Courage*, the movement of Crane's novel turns upward. The wounding also provides the image for Crane's title, and because of its climactic position in the novel, the moment is elaborately presented. All of Crane's colors come into play—the "faded yellow" of Henry's fear, the red of intense and excited emotion, the blue which signals Henry's feeling of insignificance. And in this moment, amidst the celebration of color, Henry remembers moments of the past. One is a moment of eating, an anticipation of the renewal which will come to him. The other is clearly preparatory to an event of purification, to a washing away of guilt, to a return to a kind of innocence. "Too, he remembered how he and his companions used to go from the schoolhouse to the bank of a shaded pool. He saw his clothes in disorderly array upon the grass of the bank. He felt the swash of the fragrant water upon his body. The leaves of the overhanging maple rustled with melody in the wind of youthful summer" (*Novels*, 254). For the very wound which marks Henry's alienation paradoxically serves the boy also as an atonement for his sin of flight and as a ticket of readmission to the community of soldiers. But if it is a ticket of admission, it is also the means to the surrender of the awareness which is the result of that isolation.

At the beginning of the second half of the novel, Henry finds himself less isolated than he was earlier. Shortly before, the boy was befriended by a man identified only as "the owner of the cheery voice." This shadowy figure—Henry never sees his face—ebullient, jovial, and compassionate, leads Henry back to his regiment, guides him in a return to his kind. It is a return home, the beginning of a completion of a cycle which, as Eric Solomon says, "in war fiction has stood for homecoming from Kipling's 'The Man Who Was' to Jones' *From Here to Eternity*, [and] marks the completion of Henry Fleming's isolation and the start of the conquest of glory for himself and the regiment." [48]

Upon Henry's return he is greeted first by Wilson, formerly a "loud soldier" but now changed, perhaps by a first confrontation with war which was not too emotionally different from Henry's.[49] It is this Wilson who will be, for the remainder of the novel, Henry's counterpart and his companion, and it is, therefore, certainly proper that Henry's first contact with his regiment should be with him. Wilson leads his friend back to his place in the military community; at the end of the chapter, as Henry sleeps, we are told, he "was like his comrades."

As Henry's isolation is thus diminished, he loses some of his self-concern, and the intensity of his guilt decreases. After his meeting with Wilson, Henry finds himself standing before his corporal, who accepts the boy's explanation of his absence. Henry's fear of ridicule is lessened, his shame is alleviated, and—or so Crane ironically would have it seem—the very reality of his flight seems to have diminished. Now the reality of Henry's own past action is being replaced in his understanding with reality as it is constructed in the imaginations of his comrades. Now communal apprehension supersedes individual perception as a test of reality. "He had performed his mistakes in the dark, so he was still a man" (*Novels*, 264), as Crane ironically puts it.

Thus, by his return to community and to corporate understanding, Henry's whole sensibility is altered. It is as the corporal inadvertently suggests, almost a rebirth which Henry is experiencing. " 'Why, I thought you was dead four hours ago! Great Jerusalem, they keep turnin' up every ten minutes or so!' "* (*Novels*, 256). Upon Henry's reawakening from his sleep at the beginning of the next chapter, "it seemed to him that he had been asleep for a thousand years." Crane is ironically suggesting that Henry, in several senses, feels like a new man.

But this rebirth, this return to innocence, is necessarily incomplete. In the very first encounter with Wilson, Henry, in lying to his friend, had preserved for himself the guilty knowledge of his flight (" 'Over on th' right, I got shot. In th' head. I never see sech fightin'.' " *Novels*, 256). And the private awareness which this misrepresentation protects will remain more or less important throughout the rest of the novel. For even though Henry's acceptance by his fellows may somewhat alleviate his guilt, the boy remains in part sharply and privately aware of his flight from the first day's battle. This awareness serves as a check to Henry's blustering arrogance. The result is a new qualification of a new capacity for relationship. Now Henry shows a new sympathy and re-

---

* It is interesting to note how closely this incident parallels a less ironic but otherwise similar "rebirth" at a similar point in another two-part novel. After Huckleberry Finn flees the Grangerford feud and rejoins Jim on the raft, Jim greets him with " 'Laws bless you, chile, I 'uz right down sho' you's dead agin.' " Mark Twain, *The Adventures of Huckleberry Finn*, Autograph Edition, 22 vols. (Hartford, Conn., 1899), XIII, 159. Although Beer, 113, reports that Crane had read *Huckleberry Finn* (and criticized its ending) at the Art Students' League in 1893–94, the reading was not too late to have affected *The Red Badge*. See also David L. Evans, "Henry's Hell: The Night Journey in *The Red Badge of Courage*," *Proceedings of the Utah Academy of Sciences, Arts, & Letters*, XLIV (1967), 159–66.

spect, yet some restraint, in his treatment of his friend Wilson.

Henry's new capacity leads him, inevitably, to a closer identification with his regiment. As Eric Solomon points out, those who before battle were his "companions" are now his "comrades." Soon Henry's instinct for self-glorification—an instinct which had isolated him earlier—is transformed. His pride in his regiment overshadows his private sense of guilt; his delusion of self-importance joins him to his fellows rather than isolates him from them.*

Likewise, Henry's private fury, his rage at the realities of his universe—manifest in his curse at the sun—is now transformed into a share in a corporate fury, a hatred for the enemy.[50] "He had a wild hate for the relentless foe. Yesterday, when he had imagined the universe to be against him, he had hated it, little gods and big gods; to-day he hated the army of the foe with the same great hatred" (*Novels*, 270). If Henry's rage is illogically directed, it is at least efficient. In the first engagement of the day after his

---

* Henry's pride, the sense of specialness which isolated him from his fellows, is thus mitigated upon his return. In a passage which Crane canceled in the "long manuscript" version the new attitude was made too explicitly clear.

He decided that he was not as he had supposed, a unique man. There were many in his type. And he had believed that he was suffering new agonies and feeling new wrongs. On the contrary, they were old, all of them, they were born perhaps with the first life.

These thoughts took the element of grandeur from his experiences. Since many had had them there could be nothing fine about them. They were now ridiculous.

However, he [considered *canceled*] yet considered himself to be below the standard of traditional man-hood. He felt abashed [in the *canceled*] when confronting [the *canceled*] memories of some men he had seen. [There *canceled*]

These thoughts did not appear in his attitude. He now considered the fact of his having fled, as being buried. He was returned to his comrades and unimpeached. So despite the little shadow of his sin upon his mind, he felt his self-respect growing strong within him. His pride had almost recovered it's [*sic*] balance and was about—*unfinished*.

The Red Badge of Courage, ed. Stallman, 218–19

return, he fights with a fury which is almost excessive and thus finds himself in a new role—that of hero. But Henry's is not to be the individualized, romantic heroism which he had anticipated before the battle. Rather he becomes a hero of quite another sort, for as flagbearer-hero, Henry embodies the regiment itself.

When Henry and Wilson are on a mission to refill canteens, they overhear an officer report to a general the incompetence of the regiment. " 'But there's th' 304th. They fight like a lot 'a mule drivers. I can spare them best of any' " (*Novels*, 275). It is Henry's rage at the lack of concern and the contempt which these officers, the omnipotent gods of the war (the reader recalls Henry and the red wafer of the sun), show for his regiment that drives him to his heroism. Memory of the phrase "mule-drivers" continually rankles Henry. And soon the boy urges his comrades to battle. Then, as he acquires the flag,* he becomes the very symbol of his

* Within him, as he hurled himself forward, was born a love, a despairing fondness for this flag which was near him. It was a creation of beauty and invulnerability. It was a goddess, radiant, that bended its form with an imperious gesture to him. It was a woman, red and white, hating and loving, that called him with the voice of his hopes. Because no harm could come to it he endowed it with power. He kept near, as if it could be a saver of lives, and an imploring cry went from his mind.

Novels, 280

It is interesting to note that Henry conceives of the flag as a woman. There are few women in *The Red Badge*. For Henry there is first the mother, whose concern for her son's safety is ineffectual, and then there is "a certain light-haired girl," who mocks him. Henry also seeks solace and protection from a nature which he "conceived . . . to be a woman with a deep aversion to tragedy" (*Novels*, 234). In each case, Henry is disappointed by women.

It is this kind of awareness which had made of the flag, and of the fact of Henry's flagbearing, the last symbolic ambiguity of the book and the most recent subject for critical controversy. See Vanderbilt and Weiss, "From Rifleman to Flagbearer," who argue that the flag is a symbol of illusory protection, and Norman Lavers, "Order in *The Red Badge*," who sees the flag and Crane's association of it with birds, as a symbol of achieved manhood. I shall later assert only that the flag suggests the identity and actual protection which the soldier finds in the group, yet it gives him also

regiment's corporate emotions, of its morale. Henry's "heroism," however, is ironically a subjective thing, the product of
an apprehension. It is achieved only after the regiment's igno-
minious retreat and in spite of rebukes to the regiment, when
Henry hears himself praised by his commander and thus can
assume the hero's mantle. Now again he accepts the very
identity to which he is assigned, this time by the godlike
officers.

The direction which the last half of the novel is taking is
by now clear. Henry's return to his regiment is a complexly
ironic event, doubly to be apprehended by Crane's readers.
On the one hand—and viewed from one perspective—it is
an act of courage, a return to the human condition of participation. On the other hand, it is a retreat from apprehension, a turning away from the awareness achieved in the
privacy of flight. Yet there is still another paradox. The
reader sees the return both through Henry's eyes and
through his own; it is received simultaneously as objective
event and as subjective experience.

For Henry the return is simultaneously a return to innocence and an initiation, a private, yet a shared experience.
His reintegration is achieved, not only by his putting "the
sin at a distance," but by his identification with what is happening to the regiment itself. Indeed, from Crane's increased
use of the pronoun *they* as opposed to *he*, and from the
assertion of a corporate point of view in the final chapters,* one might even regard the regiment and Henry as al-

---

an heroic identity—as embodiment of the regiment's idealized image of
itself—which makes him at once more vulnerable and less capable of protect-
ing himself. Fortunately—and gratuitously—Henry survives. See also John J.
McDermott, "Symbolism and Psychological Realism in *The Red Badge of
Courage.*"

  * For example: "Presently, the regiment seemed to draw itself up and
heave a deep breath. None of the men's faces were mirrors of large thoughts.
The soldiers were bended and stooped like sprinters before a signal. Many
pairs of glinting eyes peered from the grimy faces toward the curtains of

most equal protagonists in the last half of *The Red Badge*. And, just as Henry's military career is following a pattern of flight, alienation, and return, so his regiment follows a similar pattern. The regiment's failure in its first charge, met with ridicule from the veterans and anger from the general, is to be redeemed by a second, victorious assault. It is after this final battle action that the regiment "joined its fellows." In this process of reunion the regiment merges into the brigade, and the brigade into division; thus the regiment completes its return, and its part in the novel concludes.

Henry's return, his integration into the spirit and the way of comprehension of his regiment, is achieved in the final battle action itself. This synthesis—so complete that Henry loses all sense of himself—begins as he watches the action in which he is about to participate, "He did not know that he breathed; that the flag hung silently over him, so absorbed was he" (*Novels*, 291). With the confused, distorted, and fragmentary description of the final action, and with Henry's heroic participation in the capture of the rebel flag in the twenty-third chapter, the final, upward movement of the novel is completed. But, as he had paid the price of guilt and isolation for the confrontation with reality which he experienced in the first half of the book, so his return to the human community is costly as well.

When Henry was alone in his flight, he experienced two confrontations. One, the sudden and grotesque reality of the corpse in the forest chapel, and the other, the macabre death dance of Jim Conklin. These were moments of terrible insight for Henry, awarenesses of his own lonely and absurd nonrelation to his universe. But gradually his universal apprehension fades. After he rejoins his regiment, such revelatory confrontations, such moments of cosmic insight, no

the deeper woods. They seemed to be engaged in deep calculations of time and distance" (*Novels*, 276).

longer occur. After that reunion, of course, Crane ironically talks of Henry's seeing the world with "new eyes" (this is the way Henry believes he sees it). But, as Henry's delusionary pride returns, "his panting agonies of the past he put out of his sight."* It is not only the surrender to corporate vision but the passage of time itself which obscures his memory, and Crane dramatizes this loss by pointing out before the first engagement following Henry's return that he could see "for but a short distance" and by commenting later (*Novels*, 272) on the "glazed vacancy of his eyes." Ironically, however, Henry, before the next fighting, is quite sure of the validity of his vision. After he hears his regiment denigrated, and realizes its ultimate insignificance, "new eyes were given to him" (*Novels*, 275). Henry rejoices in his new clarity of vision; yet with a taciturn but unmistakable irony, Crane indicates that this new vision is at best imperfect.

> It seemed to the youth that he saw everything. Each blade of the green grass was bold and clear. He thought that he was aware of every change in the thin, transparent vapor that floated idly in sheets. The brown or gray trunks of the trees showed each roughness of their surfaces. And the men of the regiment, with their starting eyes and sweating faces, running madly, or falling, as if thrown headlong, to queer, heaped-up corpses—all were comprehended. His mind took a mechanical but firm impression, so that afterward everything was pictured and explained to him, save why he himself was there.[51]

Novels, 277

* In an uncanceled passage from the "long manuscript" version which nevertheless did not appear in the first published book version, Crane, in four overwritten paragraphs, described Henry's "new eyes" thus:

> But he was now, in a measure, a successful man and he could no longer tolerate in himself a spirit of fellowship for poets. He abandoned them. Their songs about black landscapes were of no importance to him since his new eyes said that his landscape was not black. People who called landscapes black were idiots.

In these final engagements, however, Crane repeatedly refers to the smoky haze which obscures Henry's battle vision. Henry's eyes are "almost closed" just before the reader is told of his fondness for the flag. On the smoky, impressionistically rendered battlefield, "His eyesight was shaken and dazzled by the tension of thought and muscle. He did not see anything excepting the mist of smoke gashed by the little knives of fire" (*Novels*, 293). If the first battle was a "battle-sleep" (*Novels*, 226), now the second battle is a "frenzy"; the men are "dazed and stupid"; and Henry himself is compared to an "insane soldier" and a "madman" and runs, "his head ducked low" and "his eyes almost closed" (*Novels*, 277, 278, 280).[52] In both battles, soldiers are compared to "babes" (*Novels*, 226, 295). If Henry's earlier flight into isolation has brought him to confront the thing itself, now he has turned away and returned.

The reader who considers what has gone before reads the last chapter with a sense of disappointment. In that chapter there is a tonal flatness—an unsureness of authorial attitude which comes with the failure to resolve the complexities of the author's points of view. In the final chapter Crane undertook to represent the completion of Henry's return and the final reformation of the Union army, to dramatize the distancing by time which comes as Henry moves away

---

He achieved a mighty scorn for such a snivelling race.

He felt that he was the child of the powers. Through the peace of his heart, he saw the earth to be a garden in which grew no weeds of agony. Or, perhaps, if there did grow a few, it was in obscure corners where no one was obliged to encounter them unless a ridiculous search was made. And, at any rate, they were tiny ones.

He returned to his old belief in the ultimate, astonishing success of his life. He, as usual, did not trouble about processes. It was ordained, because he was a fine creation. He saw plainly that he was the chosen of some gods. By fearful and wonderful roads he was to be led to a crown. He was, of course, satisfied that he deserved it.

Novels, 264, 803–804

with his companions from the lonely center of the experience of war. Yet the task was too great for him; for in the final chapter Crane fails to provide a position from which the reader can evaluate the events which have been reported to him. In this chapter the convolutions of Crane's irony finally get the better of him.

Throughout *The Red Badge of Courage* and up until the final chapter, Crane has assumed a posture of narrative anonymity. He has presented experience directly to the reader; he has dramatized Henry's apprehension of it. He has never evaluated but has commented only indirectly, through the ironies implicit in the contrast between the paradoxes of represented fact and the protagonist's one-dimensional apprehension of it. But in the last chapter Crane seems to come on stage to comment upon the meaning of Henry's experience. Or are we reading only Henry's understanding, and is Crane still at his bemused and ironic distance? Or is the ambiguity deliberate? The reader cannot be sure.[53]

Thus the critical dispute rages over Crane's final chapter. The critics who are disposed to read Crane's novel as naturalistic—C. C. Walcutt or Winifred Lynskey, for example—see it as ironic, and, for quite different reasons, Daniel Weiss and Kermit Vanderbilt, Clark Griffith, and Donald Gibson seem disposed to agree.[54] At the opposite extreme are the "symbolist" critics, who read *The Red Badge* as a *Bildungsroman*, a novel of completed education, or of a learning to see. One of these critics, R. B. Sewall, says, "In this closing scene there is none of the saving irony that played about the earlier passages of Henry's rationalizing; Crane gives us no hint that his moral victory is anything but complete." [55] There are a number of positions between these extremes. R. W. Stallman, who is clearly at the vanguard of the symbolist critics of *The Red Badge,* and who sees the novel as replete with Christian symbolism, inconsistently perhaps, reads the final chapter as ironic and argues that Henry's soul has not changed, although, presumably, his character has.[56] James Trammell Cox also asserts Crane's Christian symbolism, but follows Bernard Weisberger[57] in reading these symbols as ironic. Cox, curiously enough, sees no irony—only paradox—in the concluding chapter. Eric Solomon sees the final chapter as anticlimactic and ambiguous.[58] Stanley Greenfield and more recently Thomas M. Lorch, in particularly sophisticated readings, recognize the half irony of Crane, the deliberate ambiguity which suggests multiple and possibly contradictory meanings.[59]

For Crane's final chapter is neither directly ironic nor clearly the unqualified assertion of a victory for Henry—whether of the eye, the understanding, or the morale. That Henry has experienced initiation—that after his first experience in battle "his eyes seemed open to some new ways"—can hardly be denied. Henry is now a veteran, has experienced fear and seen death, and is now at once more familiar with them and more resistant to them than before. His capability for efficient and useful action as a member of the corporate military machine is undoubtedly sharpened. But whether there remains to Henry any of the understanding which might have been the result of his lonely and terrible visions is at best unclear. And Crane's ultimate evaluation of such understanding never emerges. There are only tautologies—ironic or otherwise—for conclusion. "He had been to touch the great death, and found that, after all, it was but the great death. He was a man"* [60] (*Novels*, 298). The rest is rhetoric—three paragraphs of symbolist bombast. The twenty-fourth chapter is

---

*R. W. Stallman has discovered three and perhaps four endings which Crane considered in the final holographic manuscript alone. See his *The Red Badge of Courage*, 220; Stallman, 171; and *Novels*, 805.

an unfortunate and useless coda to an otherwise skillfully achieved novel. It bothered Crane and has confused his critics.

In a story which appeared in *McClure's* of August, 1896, Crane undertook a clarification. "The Veteran" is really a kind of gloss on *The Red Badge*.[61] Henry Fleming, the reader discovers, received a promotion (but not to major general), has survived the war to become a grandfather (the grandson is named Jim—for Jim Conklin?).[62] Now the reader is informed that "that was at Chancellorsville." [63] More important, the reader also discovers how Henry Fleming himself has been affected.*

Most important, perhaps, is the fact that Henry has "put the sin at a distance," that the distance of time has decreased the emotional distortion of his battle vision. Now he can report without shame, " 'I thought every man in the other army was aiming at me in particular' " (*Virginia*, VI, 83). He also remembers Jim Conklin. But there is no mention of the forest chapel, no reference to Conklin's horrible death. Henry Fleming has now truly become a veteran, but there is no evidence that his initiation is either perfect or complete.

Thus, when he is confronted with the gratuitous and destructive barn fire, he can behave bravely—he can act efficiently and courageously to save horses and the Swede— but he cannot save himself. Instead of accepting the absurd and horrible fact of the destruction of the colts which remain in the burning barn, Henry recklessly plunges again into the fire to save them. And he perishes in the attempt.

---

* As we shall see, Henry Fleming will also make a brief appearance in "Lynx-Hunting" (one of the Whilomville stories), but the appearance is not important as an elucidation of *The Red Badge*. See *Virginia*, VII, 137–43.

It is interesting to note that "The Veteran" also contains within it seeds for later stories. The Swede of "The Veteran" is not unlike the Swede of "The Blue Hotel." And the absurd and destructive fire and the phrase "his face ceased instantly to be a face" (*Virginia*, VI, 84) anticipate "The Monster."

We see Henry's courage, the courage which he earned at Chancellorsville, but we also see the ultimate uselessness of that courage. And again, and it seems to me deliberately this time, Crane's closing rhetoric has an ironically hollow ring. "When the roof fell in, a great funnel of smoke swarmed toward the sky, as if the old man's mighty spirit, released from its body—a little bottle—had swelled like the genie of fable. The smoke was tinted rose-hue from the flames, and perhaps the unutterable midnights of the universe will have no power to daunt the color of this soul" (*Virginia,* VI, 86). Wilson Follett (and other editors) had the good sense to publish "The Veteran" in the same volume with *The Red Badge of Courage,* for it was in that story that Crane finally achieved the conclusion to his war novel.[64]

The Red Badge of Courage is the story of the gaining of courage. But also, and more significantly, it is the account of a momentary confrontation—first of isolation and the stripping away of delusion, then of moments of clear apprehension, and finally of the return to community and the qualification of vision which must follow. The presentation of this confrontation is complex; the experience is rendered in a way in which event is directly apprehended even as experience is reported. And out of the disparity between apprehension and event is produced a kind of irony which had perhaps already become Stephen Crane's identifying characteristic.

In fact, the novel itself seems to provide a kind of identity for Crane. It is his most famous, and in many ways his most ambitious book. Yet it is not a perfect book. One way to view its unresolved problems is to consider them problems of Crane's time. *The Red Badge* begins as a modern novel; in the early chapters his concern seems to be primarily with how his protagonist is to engage the reality of an imperfectly apprehended and almost intolerable world. But the second half of the novel seems to be Victorian fiction; here Crane's concern is with establishing a place in a community for his protagonist. And when Crane arrives at the end of the novel, and comes to the inevitable question of evaluation, he seems incapable either of taking up a position as to which of these concerns is the more important or of refusing clearly to do so.

Nevertheless, *The Red Badge of Courage* is crucial in Crane's career. In writing it, he was forced to extend his talent to its full capacity; in conceiving it he found a pattern of action to fit his recurring concern. For if the movement from initiation to isolation, from isolation to confrontation with reality, and from confrontation to a return to community had its beginnings in *The Red Badge*, it would recur in many of Crane's later stories. "The Open Boat" is only the most obvious and most immediate example.

VII
New Directions

I always want to be unmistakable. That to my mind is good writing.

> Crane in a letter to
> Clarence Loomis Peaslee,
> February 12, 1895

When Stephen Crane set out in January of 1895 on a trip through the American West—a first journey in a life of travel which would take him far beyond his original destinations—he also began a period of new literary directions, a period during which many new experiences and imagined possibilities would infuse his writing. In 1894 he had established himself in New York as a remarkably and sometimes uncomfortably honest young reporter. By 1896—with both *The Black Riders* and *The Red Badge of Courage* out—Crane's literary reputation was considerably broadened and his image more complex than they were a year earlier. In the intervening year, his imagination had matured and expanded as well. By the time he set out for Florida in the fall of 1896, Stephen Crane was a writer of considerable maturity and dimension.

The maturation of 1895 was forged in the heat of Crane's own experience. In that year he was to feel the disorientation and reaffirmation of reality which comes with first travels, and he confronted in those travels environments with po-

119

tential for destructiveness which he had only fitfully seen, perhaps, in his explorations in the Bowery and only read about or imagined for *The Red Badge.* When he returned to New York, that city rapidly showed to him its own potential for destructiveness, a potential which would ultimately drive him to expatriate himself. In 1895 Crane's own experience validated and sharpened his vision of objective reality and of man's apprehension of it.

The trip west, partly under the auspices of the Bacheller syndicate, was for Crane the satisfaction of a long-standing project. He had begun to talk about a trip to the West in 1892, and in 1894—in anticipation of the trip—he had written two stories with western settings. "Billy Atkins Went to Omaha" is a compulsive peripatetic tramp's account of his misfortunes while riding the rails from Denver to Omaha, and "A Christmas Dinner Won in Battle" is an adventure tale of antiunion heroics set in "Levelville," a prairie town which was becoming urbanized and socially stratified ("Levelville had developed about five grades of society") with the advent of the railroad.[1] Crane's attention was here directed toward an American cultural phenomenon which had also drawn the attention of a number of American intellectuals—the fast-disappearing American frontier, its new communities, and their contrast to those of the dominant eastern culture. Neither story was of much consequence, but in the two Crane dramatized his own fears and interests concerning his impending trip.*

Crane set out on his American grand tour in late January of 1895, and after stops in Philadelphia, Chicago, and St. Louis,[2] he reached Lincoln, Nebraska, on February 1. Here he confronted what Katz calls a "Situation." For now—after

* See Joseph Katz's introduction to his *Stephen Crane in the West and Mexico,* ix–xxv. Katz also says, "Like Henry Fleming before Chancellorsville, Crane before his journey was essentially unfinished" (ix). I am indebted to Professor Katz for his perceptive introduction.

the drought and dust storms and heat of the summer of 1894—lack of fodder and exceptionally harsh blizzards in January had destroyed livestock and in many counties had created conditions for farmers in which simple survival was problematical. To make matters worse, the distribution of aid to the victims was hampered by blatant corruption. Crane was confronting on the snow-swept Nebraska plains a reality perhaps more ominous and overpowering than any he had hitherto seen.[3]

He apprehended the situation clearly and reported it sharply in "Nebraska's Bitter Fight for Life." [4] The piece is strikingly vivid in its description and sympathetically aware of a community which depended—in the face of a ferocious nature and an absurd relief system "upon their endurance, their capacity to help each other and their steadfast and un-yielding courage." Yet this confrontation with social injustice and the destructive indifference of the universe left Crane rather seriously shaken; the contemporary accounts of Crane in Nebraska represent him to be a writer with discomposed imagination and empty pocketbook.[5] Both conditions would recur repeatedly after Crane left Lincoln on February 14.*

On his way south he stopped in Hot Springs, Arkansas (where he reported ironically on a favorite subject, the naive apprehension of a resort crowd),[6] then he went on to New Orleans. Here he did his best to restore a rather travel-worn spirit by visits to the performances of the French Opera Company and by enjoying the festivities of Mardi Gras, and he reported on both spectacles.[7] He soon set out for Mexico City by way of Galveston and San Antonio. But he was still somewhat travel-weary after his rapid passage through so many contrasting environments. Crane reflected upon this

---

* It is, of course, obvious enough that "The Blue Hotel" was conceived out of the Nebraska experience. For a precise account of the germinal events, see "Stephen Crane: A Portfolio," 192–99.

disorientation in a rather tired little piece about Galveston.[8] And the piece about San Antonio and the Alamo had a similar, rather flattened, routine quality.[9] Crane's eyes were tired; he seemed now to be unable to approach his material with any clear or consistent point of view.*

For a time the Mexican sketches were no better, although the first, in which Crane attempted to impose a dual, fictionalized point of view—that of a "Chicago capitalist" and an "archeologist from Boston"—had some remarkably vivid colorings.[10] † After his arrival in Mexico City the reportage suffered from Crane's disorientation. It almost seemed as if Crane's eyes were bedazzled, as if he were incapable of ordering his apprehensions, of bringing them all together into a coherent whole. The sketches of Mexico City are rather flat travel writing for the most part—accounts of street traffic, of currency and the costs of things, of the local drink, of the look of the buildings.[11]

One sketch, however, "The Viga Canal," really seems to catch fire, and it does so because it expresses Crane's awareness of the inconsequence and squalor of humanity playing out its petty concerns in a Nature which, if it is much more beautiful, is just as supremely indifferent as a Nebraska snowstorm.[12] And there is another piece which, like "The Viga Canal," seems to bring something of the essence of Crane's experience to expression. In "Above All Things,"

* Curiously, however, his stay in and around San Antonio would later generate some remarkable fiction—the unfinished "Apache Crossing," "The Bride Comes to Yellow Sky," and its sequel, "Moonlight on the Snow," among others. See "Stephen Crane: A Portfolio," 184–86.

Stallman says that Crane wrote "A Mystery of Heroism" in San Antonio (Stallman, 136–37, 580). But see Colvert, *Virginia*, VI, p. xxv, who says the story was written after Crane's return. Colvert's position seems the more plausible.

† Crane was the "archeologist"; the capitalist was a Chicago engineer named Charles Gardner. Gardner was also the model for the "San Francisco Kid" in the Mexican short stories; Crane was the "New York Kid." See Levenson, *Virginia*, V, pp. xxxvi–xxxvii. But see Berryman, 112.

Crane's recurring interest in the feelings of the bottom dog
—the interest which had taken him to Maggie's Bowery,
imaginatively to the Civil War private's first battle, or more
recently to starving farmers in Nebraska—now took him to
consider the wretched of Mexico City.[13] And the essay
which resulted is something of an exercise in disengagement,
a disengagement of rage in a commitment of apprehension.

> Yet, indeed, it requires wisdom to see a brown woman
> in one garment crouched listlessly in the door of a low
> adobe hut while a naked brown baby sprawls on his
> stomach in the dust of the roadway—it requires wisdom
> to see this thing and to see it a million times and yet
> to say: "Yes, this is important to the scheme of nature.
> This is part of her economy. It would not be well if it
> had never been."
>
> It perhaps might be said—if any one dared—that the
> most worthless literature of the world has been that
> which has been written by the men of one nation con-
> cerning the men of another.
>
> It seems that a man must not devote himself for a
> time to attempts at psychological perception. He can
> be sure of two things, form and color. Let him then see
> all he can but let him not sit in literary judgment on
> this or that manner of the people. Instinctively he will
> feel that there are similarities but he will encounter
> many little gestures, tones, tranquilities, rages, for which
> his blood, adjusted to another temperature, can possess
> no interpreting power. The strangers will be indifferent
> where he expected passion; they will be passionate where
> he expected calm. These subtle variations will fill him
> with contempt.
>
> *Stephen Crane in the West and Mexico,* 74

Crane then proceeds to contrast the poor of Mexico City
with the American urban poor.

> The people of the slums of our own cities fill a man
> with awe. That vast army with its countless faces im-

movably cynical, that vast army that silently confronts
eternal defeat, it makes one afraid. One listens for the
first thunder of the rebellion, the moment when this
silence shall be broken by a roar of war. Meanwhile
one fears this class, their numbers, their wickedness,
their might—even their laughter. There is a vast national
respect for them. They have it in their power to become
terrible. And their silence suggests everything.

They are becoming more and more capable of defining their condition and this increase of knowledge
evinces itself in the deepening of those savage and
scornful lines which extend from near the nostrils to the
corners of the mouth. It is very disturbing to observe
this growing appreciation of the situation.

I am venturing to say that this appreciation does not
exist in the lower classes of Mexico. No, I am merely
going to say that I cannot perceive any evidence of it.
I take this last position in order to preserve certain hand-
some theories which I advanced in the fore part of this
article.

Crane maintains his precarious ironic distance with a rather
forced ironic argument about the opportunity to be virtu-
ous; then he concludes with this final apprehension: "But
yet their faces have almost a certain smoothness, a certain
lack of pain, a serene faith. I can feel the superiority of their
contentment."

This was pretty strong stuff for popular journalism in
1895, and, not surprisingly, Bacheller refused to use it. Nor
did he use "The Viga Canal." Yet, although neither would
appear during Crane's life, they were important to him—
important for their articulated awareness of natural indifference, important also for the commitment to apprehension as
a means to moral toleration. The writing of them seemed to
serve Crane as a kind of apprehensional reorientation.

After Crane's rather sudden return from Mexico to New
York in mid-May of 1895, he would continue to write out of

his experiences in the West, now in fictional form. Almost immediately he wrote three curious fables, apparently in another attempt to bring the experience together into some sort of coherence.[14] And over the coming years there would be a number of short stories. Most were written sometime later, however. There was only one in 1895; it was entitled "One Dash—Horses."

"One Dash—Horses," which was written in September, was the product of an actual experience in Mexico, when Crane, on a trip to the badlands, had encountered a Mexican bandit and had made a hairbreadth escape on horseback.[15] As he had done in *The Red Badge*, Crane employs here a sharply unified point of view—through the eyes and ears of the protagonist, Richardson. This point of view is used both to produce irony and to record events. Point of view makes it possible to report fear and experience simultaneously (as Richardson overhears unsurely the Mexican bandits plot his death in Spanish), to report the experience of escape, to describe the perception of a frightened man in flight on horseback. As in *The Red Badge*, here is an account of an apprehension affected by fear. For again Crane is concerned not only with telling his story but with recounting the experience of confronting alone a new, terrifying, and not entirely understandable reality. And, as in *Maggie*, the inability to comprehend that reality is dangerous; here accuracy of vision provides protection. In "One Dash—Horses," when Richardson lies in bed, waiting for the Mexican bandits who, he knows, threaten him, he looks at a blanket-covered door and is unable to see the bandits on the other side.

> The blanket over the door fascinated him. It was a vague form, black and unmoving. Through the opening it shielded was to come, probably, menace, death. Sometimes he thought he saw it move.

> As grim white sheets, the black and silver of coffins,
> all the panoply of death, affect us because of that which
> they hide, so this blanket, dangling before a hole in an
> adobe wall, was to Richardson a horrible emblem, and
> a horrible thing in itself. In his present mood Richard-
> son could not have been brought to touch it with his
> finger.
>
> *Virginia*, V, 18

Here again is a representation of fear-distorted vision, but
instead of the presentation of a grotesque image as the object
of vision, Crane simply makes reality unavailable to his protagonist. Now Crane is relying directly upon symbolic meaning rather than upon assigned connotations to an image. And
in later stories he will again return to the terror of the unseen—to the power of blankness.

That horror can perhaps sometimes be overcome by a
momentary detachment, an awareness of human inconsequence, which can come from the unblinking apprehension
of what is; perhaps this was the real lesson of "Above All
Things." In any event, in "A Man and Some Others," one
of the western stories which Crane wrote in the spring and
summer of 1896, this theme is dramatized.[16] "A Man and
Some Others" is also a story of the badlands, and in it Crane
juxtaposed and contrasted the ways of seeing of Easterners
and Westerners, of Mexicans and Americans, as he told the
story of a Bowery saloon bouncer-turned-sheepherder named
Bill, whose assertive resistance to a group of Mexicans who
would run him off the range finally leads to a gun battle
in which he is killed. But, more significantly, it is about an
innocent Easterner who, seeking a place to camp, becomes
Bill's companion and disciple and is ultimately implicated
in the dispute. This eastern "stranger," who is not present
at first, establishes the point of view from which the final
events are recounted. Indeed, as the story develops it becomes

clear that it is not Bill and his gun battle which are at the story's center, but rather the engagement of the stranger's imagination in those events. For the stranger, who is first horrified by the killing, gradually becomes involved, comes to feel "for Bill, this grimy sheepherder, some deep form of idolatry," and discovers for himself "that it was easy to kill a man" (*Virginia*, V, 66). Then, after his bloody initiation, he confronts what he has done.

> Finally he arose and, walking some paces, stooped to loosen Bill's gray hands from a throat. Swaying as if slightly drunk, he stood looking down into the still face.
> Struck suddenly with a thought, he went about with dulled eyes on the ground, until he plucked his gaudy blanket from where it lay, dirty from trampling feet. He dusted it carefully, and then returned and laid it over Bill's form. There he again stood motionless, his mouth just agape and the same stupid glance in his eyes, when all at once he made a gesture of fright and looked wildly about him.
> He had almost reached the thicket when he stopped, smitten with alarm. A body contorted, with one arm stiff in the air, lay in his path. Slowly and warily he moved around it, and in a moment the brushes, nodding and whispering, their leaf-faces turned toward the scene behind him, swung and swung again into stillness and the peace of the wilderness.

With this grotesque apprehension the stranger's vision, dulled by violence, is suddenly revitalized, and it is in this apprehension that the full implications rush upon him as the story ends.

Joseph Conrad, undoubtedly recognizing Crane's intentions in his vividly rendered account of emotion-charged apprehensions, called the story "immense" and said "I admire it without reserve." Indeed, "A Man and Some Others" is frequently praised by Crane's critics—early and late.[17] Certainly "A Man and Some Others" is a distinguished performance. And the story also prefigures some of the significant achievements of Crane's later writing—stories like "The Blue Hotel," "Death and the Child," and "The Upturned Face."

In 1896 Crane also wrote "A Texas Legend" (sometimes called "A Freight Car Incident" or "Caged With a Wild Man") and here again considered how individual sensibilities are affected by a meeting of East and West.[18] Here again is the account of the city man inadvertently involved in western violence, and here again are images of obscured vision. Like "A Man and Some Others," "A Texas Legend" also prepares the way for Crane's two later and memorable western stories—"The Blue Hotel" and "The Bride Comes to Yellow Sky." And like several of the later stories, in the violent environment of "A Texas Legend," an ability to see clearly is of more protective value than an ability to fight.

Set in a western town becoming "easternized," and with a dispassionate "railroad man" as narrator, "A Texas Legend" is the story of Luke Burnham, a gunfighter who is trapped and unable to see in another of Crane's adroitly chosen and symbolically suggestive settings, a darkened freight car. Even when he bursts out of the car and into the sunlight, Luke is unable to find his enemy. Our last impression of the gunman anticipates Scratchy Wilson of "The Bride Comes to Yellow Sky." Here is represented—through dispassionate eastern eyes—his frustrated rage as he searches for his enemy ("He went among them, bellowing in bull fashion, and not a man moved"). But unlike "The Bride" (and perhaps similar to "The Blue Hotel"), "A Texas Legend" ends in a tragic death—a death which is the result of a failure of apprehension. " 'And so they didn't kill him, after all,' said someone at the end of the narrative. 'Oh, yes; they got him that night,' said the major, 'in a saloon somewhere. They got him all right' " (*Stories and Sketches*, 275-76).

Crane wrote two more western stories in Hartwood in 1896, but he left them behind when he went into the city that summer, and he did not reclaim the manuscripts until he had settled in England in 1897; so neither appeared in print until 1898.[19] Both were generated out of Crane's memories of his friendship with Charles Gardner in Mexico City. "The Five White Mice"—which Ford Madox Ford regarded as "one of the major short stories of the world" (though he could not remember its title)—merits first attention.[20] The tale is one of those stories centering around and using as point of view a character known as the New York Kid, Crane's *persona* in his Mexico City stories. And, probably more clearly than any of the other early western stories, "The Five White Mice" reflects Crane's growing awareness of the randomness of events and his interest in patterns of causation and the absence of them.[21] Here the New York Kid is caught in a series of gratuitous yet dangerous circumstances, and as a result of his ability to deal successfully with them he comes to a new understanding of his relationship to his universe and his fellows.

The story opens in Mexico City as the Kid's ritual repetition of a gambling slogan (about "five white mice of chance") fails to bring him luck, and he loses a dice game. The loss obliges him to entertain the others at a circus, and this obligation results in his late arrival for a previously arranged meeting with two other companions. When he does arrive the other two have become quite intoxicated. One of them lurches into a passing Mexican and, drunkenly unaware of the danger, challenges him to fight.

> The New York Kid could not follow Spanish well, but he understood when the Mexican breathed softly: "Does the señor want fight?"
> Benson simply gazed in gentle surprise. The woman next to him at dinner had said something inventive.

His tailor had presented his bill. Something had occurred which was mildly out of the ordinary, and his surcharged brain refused to cope with it. He displayed only the agitation of a smoker temporarily without a light.

The New York Kid had almost instantly grasped Benson's arm and was about to jerk him away when the other Kid, who up to this time had been an automaton, suddenly projected himself forward, thrust the rubber Benson aside and said: "Yes!"*

Virginia, V, 47

Thus the New York Kid finds himself and his two drunken companions confronted by a trio of hostile, knife-bearing Mexicans. Two causal sequences have led to this event. One of them is gratuitous in origin; a throw of dice determined subsequent events.[22] But the other—the capacity for clear apprehension—is within human control. And here, in Crane's absurd but dangerous universe, a deluded drunkenness† has created a situation in which Crane's protagonist confronts a reality which he must comprehend if he is to remain unharmed. His first reaction is inefficient, for in his delusion, which comes not from fear, not from alcohol, but from false conceit (the human characteristic which has proved so dangerous to Maggie Johnson, to Henry Fleming, and later to the Swede of "The Blue Hotel"), the New York Kid has fantasies concerning the significance of his own death. "The Eastern lad suddenly decided that he was going to be killed. His mind leaped forward and studied the aftermath. The story would be a marvel of brevity when first it reached the far New York home." And the fantasy spins itself out for several paragraphs. But ultimately the New York Kid recognizes the raw facts of his situation, and

* The incident is prefigured in a sketch which Crane wrote before he ever saw Mexico—"The Duel That Was Not Fought." See Chap. 4, *supra*.

† Drunkenness is frequently a trope for delusion in Crane. Consider *Maggie*, *George's Mother*, or "The Bride Comes to Yellow Sky."

is able, by confronting one more gratuitous fact, to save himself and his friends. "He suddenly knew that it was possible to draw his own revolver, and by a swift manoeuver face down all three Mexicans. If he was quick enough he would probably be victor. If any hitch occurred in the draw he would undoubtedly be dead with his friends. It was a new game. He had never been obliged to face a situation of this kind in the Beacon Club in New York."

The New York Kid succeeds in facing down the Mexicans, and, in doing so, learns something new about the human condition. "Thus the Kid was able to understand swiftly that they were all human beings. They were unanimous in not wishing for too bloody a combat. There was a sudden expression of the equality" (*Virginia*, V, 50).

The outcome of Crane's story is not only in the hands of chance (the five white mice), but is affected by a protagonist who can see and understand his situation. The New York Kid's apprehension has saved his life. After this consideration of chance and causation, after the dice game, the near-fatal fight, the achievement of a new awareness, Crane's flat final statement is richly ironic: "Nothing had happened." *

"The Wise Men," the other 1896 Mexico City story, is little more than a sardonic report of a remembered event, "A Detail of American Life in Mexico," as the subtitle asserts. Crane here describes another game played in Mexico City, this time less grimly, for the game is a footrace between two bartenders. The characters and setting are much the same as those of "The Five White Mice." Unfortunately, however, and in spite of H. G. Wells's praise ("I cannot imagine how it could possibly have been better told"),[23] "The Wise Men" fails to catch fire. As was the case with

---

* Crane's ironic denial of the very significance of his story at its end is increasingly to be seen in the late work. The cowboy's " 'Well, I didn't do anythin', did I?' " at the end of "The Blue Hotel" (*Virginia*, V, 170), although it has another meaning, has perhaps a similarly negative effect.

much of the Mexico City journalism, Crane fails here to develop the material of the story into meaningful statement, and no coherent point of view is apparent. It would be another year before Crane's experiences in the West would cohere in a consistently generative vision.*

Crane's return to the East in May also marked a return to his city writing. But there were few sketches[24] for in those busy months, when he was caught up in the activities of Lanthorne Club, in the *Philistine* affair, and in the shepherding of both *The Black Riders* and *The Red Badge of Courage* through the presses, whatever time was left was being devoted to a novel.

This book, which Crane called "pretty rotten work," [25] was his first attempt at a novel of society. *The Third Violet* is set in the resort country around Port Jervis and Hartwood and in the Art Students' League building in the city. It tells the story of an impressionist painter, William Hawker, who falls in love with an heiress, Grace Fanhall. In it Crane undertook to sustain for over a hundred pages the sympathetic yet lightly ironic distance of "The Pace of Youth." But the result demonstrates only Crane's archness toward his characters, an attitude which simply diminishes his reader's concern.

Although *The Third Violet* is a vivid enough record of Crane's experiences with his artist friends, of his life around

* John Berryman has suggested (*Stephen Crane*, 112) that the New York and San Francisco Kid stories manifest a *doppelgänger* theme. The idea has been alluded to elsewhere. See Austin M. Fox, "Stephen Crane and Joseph Conrad." There is one story, of uncertain date, entitled "A Man by the Name of Mud," which, as Levenson suggests, might give some support to this notion. "A Man by the Name of Mud" tells a last story of the two Kids, now in New York. In this story the two have lost their gaiety, and a woman comes between them. See *Virginia*, V, pp. cxxx–cxxxi. The story was published posthumously in an unfinished state in *Last Words* (1902). See *New York City Sketches*, 197–99.

Hartwood and Port Jervis, and of his love affairs there for Berryman to call it "honest, often charming," [26] although H. G. Wells, Ford Madox Ford, and Henry James were all pleased by it, to the reader today, the novel seems poorly plotted and badly constructed.[27] But there is another unsolved problem apparent in *The Third Violet* and that is a problem of theme. For Crane seems here to be attempting to conduct an impressionistic novel—a work committed to the process of apprehension—within the conventions of American realism. Crane never seems to decide whether his book is to be a Howells-like story of New York or a record of an artist's vision. The reader is never sure what is the point of the studio scenes; or, on the other hand, if they are important, there is too little about Florinda O'Connor, the artist's model whose love for Hawker is apparently in vain, yet who is the obvious alternative to Miss Fanhall.* And if it is the way that men see which is important, Crane wasted too much time in the first half of the novel on descriptions of country resort life. Without focus, without direction, without firm control of point of view, Crane's irony frequently misfires or becomes petulance. And the theme which could have saved *The Third Violet*, the theme of Hawker's failure in seeing his beloved Miss Fanhall for what she is and of the pain which his illusion causes him, does not clearly emerge. The failure of the novel is a failure of commitment.

Yet if *The Third Violet* can sustain little critical interest today, it at least indicates something of the nature of Crane's own concerns at the time in which he was writing it. For the novel dramatizes not only Crane's life with artists but the artistic concerns which he shared with them. When in the

* Stallman (122, 426) reports James G. Huneker as praising a story, now lost, written in 1898, which concerned an artist's model who marries an artist. The name of the story was "The Cat's March."

early pages there occur phrases like "Hawker saw his two sisters shading their eyes and peering down the yellow stream" as a representation of the protagonist's nocturnal approach to a lighted farmhouse (*Novels*, 353), it becomes obvious that many of the preoccupations of characters and several of the discussions between them, both in and around the Hemlock Inn and in the New York studio, reproduce Crane's own intense concern with how people see. In these passages he is translating the conventional concerns of the impressionist painters into prose fiction. Crane's protagonist is such a painter. And when his point of view is assumed, color becomes vitally important and is recognized as essentially a subjective phenomenon, to be recorded as it is seen. "Hawker encamped in front of some fields of vivid yellow stubble on which trees make olive shadows, and which were overhung by a china-blue sky and sundry little white clouds. He fiddled away perfunctorily at it. A spectator would have believed, probably, that he was sketching the pines on the hill where shone the red porches of Hemlock Inn" (*Novels*, 355). Hollander (Hawker's "writer friend") shares this recognition. "He perched on a boulder and began to study Hawker's canvas and the vivid yellow stubble and the olive shadows" (*Novels*, 355–56). Sometimes there is direct discussion of impressionistic technique between them:

> "Say, does that shadow look pure purple to you?"
> "Certainly it does, or I wouldn't paint it so, duffer. What did she write?"
> "Well, if that shadow is purple my eyes are liars. It looks a kind of slate colour to me. Lord! if what you fellows say in your pictures is true, the whole earth must be blazing and burning and glowing and . . . ."
> Hawker went into a rage. "Oh, you don't know anything about colour, Hollie. For heaven's sake, shut up, or I'll smash you with the easel." [28]
>
> *Novels*, 392–93

After such discussions, when, later, another painting, of "the landscape of heavy blue, as if seen through powder-smoke, and all the skies burned red," is represented, the allusion and the demonstration of method seem almost deliberate.*

In 1896 Crane's name began to reappear as a city journalist. There were, in various newspapers throughout the year, a number of descriptive sketches of some rather intriguing aspects of city life. There were descriptions of a New York sailing, of the opium smoker's New York, of bicycle riding on the West Side, and of dinner in a roof-garden restaurant.[29] Crane also described a mongrel which associated himself with demolition workers; he returned to Asbury Park for another look at resort life; and he wrote of a visit to Sing Sing and to the execution chamber there.[30] These sketches are shot through with evidences of Crane's impressionistic concern—the effect of a single source of light on the faces of opium smokers, the "glittering wheels" of bicycles, the "flaming parasols" of the resort girls in the sun. But for all his aesthetic distance, Crane's ironic awareness of social injustice is never entirely suppressed (at the end of "An Evening on the Roof" Crane turns away from roof-garden restaurants to another kind of evening on another kind of roof; "An evening upon a tenement roof, with that great golden march of the stars across the sky and Johnnie gone for a pail of beer, is not so bad if you have never seen the mountains nor heard, to your heart, the slow, sad song of the pines." *New York City Sketches*, 156).

On at least one occasion in these sketches, Crane achieved the grotesque vitality of description which was earlier apparent in *Maggie* and *George's Mother*, and again the vitality

* One of the best reviews of Crane's work, "Mr. Stephen Crane's New Book," which appeared in *The Academy* of May 22, 1897 (541), early identified the keen impressionistic preoccupations of Crane's novel. Although the review is probably the most sensitive appreciation of the novel yet written, it has been generally ignored. See Stallman, 295–98.

is generated by emotion, although this time it is the narrator's. Now the protective and distancing irony is absent; Crane here confronted directly the significance of that which he had seen in a moment of intense apprehension. "In the middle of the graveyard there is a dim but still defiant board upon which there is rudely carved a cross. Some singular chance has caused this board to be split through the middle, cleaving the cross in two parts, as if it had been done by the demoniac shape weaved in the clouds, but the aged board is still upright and the cross still expresses its form as if it had merely expanded and become transparent. It is a place for the chanting of monks" (*New York City Sketches*, 301–302). In order to achieve the confrontations of his final stories, Crane had at some point to come to terms with the irresponsibilities of ironic distance and take the risk of seeing with his own eyes. Here at least is a movement in that direction.[31]

In 1896 Crane was also writing a number of city stories, though only a few of them were published in that year. "A Self-Made Man" shows Crane at his parodic best in his treatment of the Horatio Alger success story,[32] and another was a rather unsuccessful experiment in turning the tables on the western stories and representing a night "on the town" in a French restaurant as seen through the eyes of a Westerner (in its ironic ending "The Man from Duluth" prefigures "The Blue Hotel").* And there were other experiments—in one story of social comment, "A Detail," Crane described the confrontation between a hungry old woman looking for work and two young women on the street; in another, "The Auction," a parrot's talk disrupts an auction of his owner's property.[33] But where the first of these stories

---

* It is probable, however, that the ending of "The Man from Duluth" was not written by Crane but by his wife, Cora, who finished the story after her husband's death. See Gilkes, *Cora Crane*, 286; *Stories and Sketches*, 779–85; and Stallman, 207–209, 611.

succeeds, the second fails. For in "A Detail" Crane's re-strained and objective description strikes just the right balance between ironic involvement and aesthetic distance, yet in "The Auction" the pathos of the account is utterly violated by the ironic comedy of the parrot's mindless chattering. Crane's success in these stories depends as always upon tonal control, and in 1896 Crane's control of tone was not yet quite sure.*

In September, Crane concluded an agreement with Hearst's *Journal* to do a series of sketches on New York police and the underworld. It was an agreement leading to events which changed the very course of his life. It led him first to the police courts, and then to his meeting with Dora Clark. There followed his quixotic (or noble?) defense of her and, finally, his notoriety and harassment and expatriation.[34] Crane's own account of the affair—at least of the events which were later to produce such unfortunate results for him—was set forth in the first of the *Journal* sketches, "Adventures of a Novelist." † But out of his visits to police courts and to New York's night-town (the infamous "Tenderloin") came also some of his most impassioned city writing.

Even the most reportorial of the sketches for Hearst were at least semificitional.‡ In the first sketch, "The 'Tenderloin'

---

* In one other story of the year, "A Poker Game," Crane abandoned irony for dramatic suspense, but here Crane's description bears no significant theme. See *Stories and Sketches*, 325–27; Solomon, *Stephen Crane*, 290; and Gibson, *The Fiction of Stephen Crane*, xiv, 23, 59ff.

† Crane was deeply moved by the events and by the social corruption and injustice which they dramatized. There have recently come to light three intensely straightforward descriptive accounts, all in manuscript (one of them a fragment of a story), which indicate the acute involvement which Crane felt. See "A Blackguard as a Police Officer," "Notes About Prostitutes," and "A Desertion," *New York City Sketches*, 259–61.

‡ There was one rather ironic report of the denizens of Minetta Lane (then a refuge for criminals and not a thoroughfare), but it was not written for Hearst and did not concern the night world of the Tenderloin but rather

As It Really Is," Crane combined an account of a dance-hall brawl in the old Haymarket with a representation of the more sedate barroom drinking of the contemporary Tenderloin to give a sense of the history of the quarter.[35] The second is also distanced; "In the Tenderloin" is simply an impressionistic description of the talk overheard in a Tenderloin restaurant.[36] Here again Crane was the dispassionate, objective colorist: "The innumerable tables represented a vast white field, and the glaring electric lamps were not obstructed in their mission of shedding a furious orange radiance upon the cloths" (*New York City Sketches*, 167).

Presumably Crane wrote "An Eloquence of Grief" after his disillusioning experience at Dora Clark's trial on October 15, for this sketch manifests considerably more *engagement*. In this account of the arraignment of a servant girl upon the complaint of theft, brought by her employer before a magistrate's court, there is none of the restrained sympathy of "A Detail," but rather a furious satire at the hypocrisies and cruelties of American police court justice. Crane's sardonic anger at what he had seen in Dora Clark's trial is apparent in this opening description: "The windows were high and saintly, of the shape that is found in churches. From time to time a policeman at the door spoke sharply to some incoming person. 'Take your hat off!' He displayed in his voice the horror of a priest when the sanctity of a chapel is defied or forgotten" (*New York City Sketches*, 261–62). Hearst did not publish this one; it was not until 1898 in *The Open Boat and Other Stories* that "An Eloquence of Grief" saw print.

There were also three fully fictional Tenderloin stories, accounts of how the denizens of the district live, love, cheat, and help one another. "Diamonds and Diamonds" is an

---

the less sophisticated world of Negro criminals. See "Stephen Crane in Minetta Lane," *New York City Sketches*, 178-84; and Stallman, 105-107.

inside look at a confidence game, and "Yen Nock Bill and His Sweetheart" tells how a loyal girl friend comes to the aid of an opium addict in distress. But certainly the most striking of the Tenderloin stories is the one curiously entitled "In the Tenderloin: A Duel Between an Alarm Clock and a Suicidal Purpose." Here Crane tells the story of an attempt to save a girl from suicide by morphine. The climax of the story turns around an absurdly intense apprehension—the focusing of the drugged attention of the girl upon a housefly which she has accidentally injured. Crane ironically intensified his representation of the girl's rather distorted concern and at the same time adroitly exploited it (her concern for the fly's life parallels her lover's concern for her own) and saves his story from melodrama. Eric Solomon sees the story as an attack upon "the conventions of contemporary popular fiction," [37] but it seems more likely that in "A Duel" Crane was simply exploring a new possibility for his fiction of apprehension.

Even as he was writing of the West and the city, Stephen Crane was aware of another subject which was available to him. This was the subject of man at war, the subject of his popular success.* Beginning almost immediately after his return to New York, he wrote a number of Civil War stories, two of which appeared in 1895. He collected six such stories in a volume he was to call *The Little Regiment* and offered them to Appleton, and Appleton, fresh from the success of *The Red Badge*, accepted them in March of 1896 and published the collection in November.[38]

The collection is too markedly inferior to *The Red Badge* to be appropriately compared to it. Crane's return to New

* Indeed, war and the city seem to have been closely intertwined in Crane's imagination. As he once remarked to Emile Stange, when looking at a painting, "The sense of a city is war." Stallman, 221.

York was, to some extent at least, a return to realism, and *The Little Regiment* stories show little of the remarkably rendered dramatic impressionism, the grotesque apprehensions of external reality on the part of Crane's characters which so sharply established point of view in *The Red Badge* and elsewhere. As James B. Colvert puts it, the hallucinatory sense is notably subdued.[39] There is a resultant gain in a kind of narrative realism and objectivity but a loss of intensity and focus. Indeed, the sense of Crane's disorientation with his material which I have noted in some of the western writing is not entirely absent here.

Four of the stories—"A Mystery of Heroism," "A Gray Sleeve," "The Little Regiment," and "The Veteran" (which I have already discussed)—turn around an ironic tension which is critical to *The Red Badge of Courage*, the tension between the private experience of war and the communal understanding of it; of them, the first written is the most notable. That story, "A Mystery of Heroism," is set into motion by a dare. A private soldier, Collins, is goaded by his companions at the front into a foolhardy act of crossing no man's land to fetch water at a well. He is driven to this foolishness by his own boastfulness and his fear of loss of face. The situation is by now a familiar one (remember the "little man" in "The Holler Tree," Maggie's Pete, Private Fleming). Crane would continue his accounts of unwished-for confrontations—in "Yellow Sky," in "The Blue Hotel," and elsewhere—but in the later stories the showdowns would be for higher stakes.

In all of these showdown stories, however, it is the characters' feelings at the moment of confrontation which interest Crane. "He had blindly been led by quaint emotions, and laid himself under an obligation to walk squarely up to the face of death. But he was not sure that he wished to make a retraction even if he could do so without shame. As a matter

of truth he was sure of very little. He was mainly surprised"
(*Virginia*, VI, 53). And especially, Crane was interested in
the effect of fear upon apprehension. There have been times
when fear has sharpened the apprehension and has intensified
the experience of confrontation and thus rendered it meaningful. In *The Red Badge*, however, the reader could not be
sure, and "The Veteran" is not much help in this matter.
For Crane equally recognized the possibility—especially in
battle—that fear can overpower experience and leave a confrontation gratuitous, meaningless, even absurd. Such is the
case with Private Collins in "A Mystery of Heroism": "And
now as he lay with his face turned away he was suddenly
smitten with the terror. It came upon his heart like the grasp
of claws. All the power faded from his muscles. For an instant
he was no more than a dead man."

Here, however, Crane's purpose was not to examine Collins'
coming to awareness of his foolish conceit and his pointless
heroism. Instead Crane wished to present objectively the
absurd meaninglessness of the event itself. In his terrified
return from the well, Collins refused water for a dying soldier
until too late. When he is finally safe behind the lines, the
water which he has so daringly carried is spilled before it can
be drunk. Here again Crane demonstrates his growing interest in the gratuitous nature of reality and in what happens after this absurdity is confronted. Thematically, "A
Mystery of Heroism" anticipates not only "The Open Boat"
but a number of other later stories as well.

In "The Little Regiment," the title story, Crane again
tries—but this time with less success—to turn the events of a
historical battle into fiction.[40] Here Crane places sharply
in opposition the private sensibility and the public assertions
about war, the self as it apprehends reality and the self as it
presents itself to be apprehended. The plot of "The Little
Regiment" turns on two brothers' rivalry and concern for

one another and their attempts to determine one another's fate in the dangerous confusion which is the reality of the supposed "pageantry" of battle. "A Gray Sleeve" is similarly concerned with the private sensibility in a public situation; it is a rather implausible account of the infatuation of a Union officer with a Confederate girl.*

"Three Miraculous Soldiers" is based upon another irony of opposed apprehensions. It is an adventure story of escape, the escape of three Confederate soldiers hidden in a barn by a romantic young Confederate belle. In the story Crane was particularly interested in the disparity between the fantasizings of the girl, from whose point of view the story is told and who casts herself in the story as "heroine," and the reality of the situation which confronts her. Crane treated with characteristic irony the girl's "carefully constructed ideals which were the accumulation of years of dreaming":

> Heroines, she knew, conducted these matters with infinite precision and dispatch. They severed the hero's bonds, cried a dramatic sentence, and stood between him and his enemies until he had run far enough away. She saw well, however, that even should she achieve all things up to the point where she might take glorious stand between the escaping and the pursuers, those grim troopers in blue would not pause. They would run around her, make a circuit. One by one she saw the gorgeous contrivances and expedients of fiction fall before the plain, homely difficulties of this situation.
>
> *Virginia*, VI, 33

Crane's "heroine" in her naiveté is not unlike Henry Fleming before his induction with his "large pictures extravagant in color, lurid with breathless deeds" (*Novels*, 203). In the final sentence, when the girl acts so out of her "heroic"

---

* Crane described "A Gray Sleeve" as "not in any sense a good story" and its protagonists as "a pair of idiots" (*Letters*, No. 127, p. 97; No. 129, p. 99).

character as to weep over the Yankee who has been knocked unconscious in the escape, Crane's irony is keenly apparent.[41]

"An Indiana Campaign" is reminiscent of Crane's earlier writing and follows a plot pattern similar to that which Crane employed in the Sullivan County sketches. Here the heroic bravery of "the Major" and the fear of the people of an Indiana town innocent of the realities of war prove to be illusory when the "rebel," whom they hunt in the woods, turns out to be only Jacoby, the town drunk. If "An Indiana Campaign" is reminiscent, however, it is also anticipatory. In the Whilomville stories Crane is often concerned not so much with individual delusion as with communal misapprehension.

Crane himself misjudged (or misrepresented) *The Little Regiment* on two counts. He said of it that it "represents my work at its best I think and is positively my last thing dealing with battle." [42] For in these first war stories Crane was not only establishing a new subject but also was experimenting with new themes and new possibilities for his short fiction. It was becoming increasingly apparent that the subject of man at war could serve him as a trope for the absurd and dangerous confusion which he saw as the condition of human experience. He developed in these stories his interest in the individual and communal emotions—especially the emotion of fear, and he found challenging possibilities in the ironic contrast between the individual and the communal battle vision. The war stories—in spite of their common subject and the fact that they are haunted by Crane's impressionistic preoccupations—are disparate indeed.

Crane wrote one other Civil War story in 1896, but too late to be included in *The Little Regiment*. Thus, Crane's most distinguished short story about the Civil War remained unpublished until 1899.[43] This story, modestly titled "An

Episode of War," is also the most hallucinatory of these stories, the least committed to the representation of an objective reality. Here, as in *The Red Badge*, Crane is concerned with the process of gaining an apprehension, with earning the capacity to see the thing itself. And, as in *The Red Badge of Courage*, in "An Episode of War" apprehension is associated with isolation and injury. But now the isolation seems more permanent, and the injury is real.

"An Episode of War" concerns a lieutenant who receives a maiming wound and must retire from his command at the front. At the story's beginning Crane's lieutenant is fully a part of the community of soldiers (he is first seen dividing coffee among his men). In fact, the wound he suffers becomes a reality to him only when seen by his men. The lieutenant seeks an explanation for his misfortune ("He looked sadly, mystically, over the breastwork at the green face of a wood," *Virginia*, VI, 89) and finds none. But if the cause is unclear, as the story develops, the effect of the wound soon becomes apparent.

The effect is threefold. First, the lieutenant becomes vulnerable and almost inadequate to his earlier responsibilities (his clumsy attempt to return his sabre with his left hand is only one example). But, paradoxically, it is also reported that "A wound gives strange dignity to him who bears it," and the lieutenant is invested with this dignity. Finally—and most significantly—the lieutenant, now different from the others, also acquires a special vision. "It is as if the wounded man's hand is upon the curtain which hangs before the revelations of all existence—the meaning of ants, potentates, wars, cities, sunshine, snow, a feather dropped from a bird's wing; and the power of it sheds radiance upon a bloody form, and makes the other men understand sometimes that they are little" (*Virginia*, VI, 90).

Curiously enough, this new vision is achieved as the lieutenant moves away from the battle (Henry Fleming could not see clearly at the front, either); from the new perspective the lieutenant can see war clearly for the first time. Now he apprehends a sequence of images (not unlike the sequence in the seventeenth chapter of *Maggie*) which, together, constitute the totality of war. First he sees the forest, then "a general on a black horse," then "a battery, a tumultuous and shining mass." But there is the other side of war: the stragglers, the "low white tents of the hospital," an "interminable crowd of bandaged men," a dying man who is unaware of his condition.

The ultimate apprehension is not shared with the reader and is resisted by the lieutenant himself. It takes place, appropriately enough, in a schoolhouse that is being used for surgery. And the lieutenant is literally dragged to this final confrontation. " 'Let go of me,' said the lieutenant, holding back wrathfully, his glance fixed upon the door of the old schoolhouse, as sinister to him as the portals of death."

The reader does not go with the lieutenant inside the schoolhouse. Instead, the story leaps forward in time ("And this is the story of how the lieutenant lost his arm") to a final and now a negative awareness for Crane's protagonist (" 'I don't suppose it matters so much as all that' "). Here is the sort of negation—an ironic denial of significance to the event of the story itself—which ends so many of Crane's stories. Ultimate knowledge for Crane always involves an awareness of one's ultimate insignificance, but more important, the story has ended upon a diminishing intensity of an apprehension, an apprehension which for Crane cannot be shared. Or perhaps it is the fading of that apprehension, as the maimed lieutenant at the end of the story rejoins his family, that makes the apprehension at all humanly bearable.[44]

Stephen Crane's departure from New York in November of 1896 marked in a sense the end of an apprenticeship.[45] From now on he would be a man in motion, running against time from place to place and from war to war—private as well as public. Under the conditions of his final years, any writing which would survive must be from an already accomplished pen. Yet, though it is of uneven quality, the work of the final two years of that apprenticeship served well to prepare him for his later work.

If in those years Crane expanded his capabilities with disparate subject matters, he also made other important steps forward. He confronted the absurd dangerousness of the universe and man's inconsequence in it, and then he began to consider what he had seen. He suffered a certain aesthetic and personal disorientation as a result of his confrontation, but from his sense of disorientation he began to discover new possibilities for his fiction. Now he recognized that confrontation is often a dual, and sometimes a communal or cultural experience. Now he developed his impressionistic style in nondramatic as well as in dramatic contexts. Now he began to learn to control his ironies and by doing so to risk for himself new and unprotected awarenesses. Later out of these new awarenesses he would achieve for his writing new symbolic capabilities, and in the sometimes hurried and irregular writing of 1895 and 1896 there are often found seeds of his later brilliance.

VIII
"The Color of the Sky"

*It seems a pity that this should be—that art
should be a child of suffering; and yet such seems
to be the case.*
> Stephen Crane in a letter to
> *DeMorest's Family Magazine,* May, 1896

In much of his fiction written before 1897 Stephen Crane
manifested an interest in those emotions and attitudes which
blocked or distorted human perception—in the illusions of
preconception or pride or fear. For the most part, he was
asserting these interests in writing on four subjects: man in
Nature (the Sullivan County sketches or "The Snake," for
example), man in the city (*Maggie, George's Mother,* and
other sketches), man confronting the myth and reality of
the American West (Crane was beginning to exploit the
experiences of his trip), and, in the work upon which his
reputation was made, man at war. It was in his war novel,
The Red Badge of Courage, that he found a new pattern of
action within which he could articulate his concern. For in
The Red Badge there also emerged a story of initiation—of
a movement away from community, of a first confrontation
with a reality, and of a return afterward to a community in
which the initiate bears the consequences of that confrontation. This pattern of action, as we have seen, created a major
discordance in *The Red Badge of Courage,* and Crane's

147

more successful works of 1895 and 1896 did not exploit the pattern fully, although he often developed its thematic implications. It was not until "The Open Boat" that the discordance was fully resolved. Afterwards, this pattern of confrontation and return was to recur frequently in Crane's later fiction. Whether inverted, truncated, or reasserted in its original shape, the pattern was to be repeatedly recognizable as the archetypal cycle of action which he found appropriate to his concern.

The discovery of this action also enabled Crane to come to terms with his ironic awareness. From the beginning of his career—even in the Sullivan County sketches or in "On the New Jersey Coast"—he was aware of and sought to assert the difference between the way things are and the way things are seen—at times he even seemed to distrust his own apprehension of the reality which he reported. His prose style was shaped by these awarenesses, and in *Maggie* we can see the development of a kind of dramatic impressionism by which Crane articulated his awareness and his distrust. But he first objectified his distrust, and gave his awareness thematic and narrative significance, in the cyclical action of *The Red Badge of Courage*. It was only after these discoveries of a theme and a device appropriate to his concern that the great stories of the final years could be written.

In 1896, as Crane's artistic skills matured, his world also increased its dimensions. After the success of *The Red Badge* he explored new subjects and new approaches to those subjects. Thus, at the moment of his departure from New York in November, he stood at a point of artistic embarkation as well.[1] The geographical route which Crane followed in the next year was a circuitous one indeed. After his rather forced departure from New York,[2] there was a trip to Florida to report the Cuban insurrection. Failing to reach Cuba, and finding New York again intolerable, he was soon off to

England, to Greece and the war, and then again to England. There he and his new "wife," Cora, found new friends, and felt new influences.[3] Now he was separated from Garland and Howells and his painter friends by at least an ocean; in October of 1897 in England he began a friendship with Joseph Conrad. Soon Harold Frederic, Ford Madox Hueffer, Edward Garnett, and even Henry James—all of them writers seriously concerned with the technique and the critical evaluation of prose fiction, and most of them seriously concerned with the problem of man's engagement with reality—were within Crane's immediate acquaintance.[4] These experiences and these associations had a marked effect upon his work.[5] With "The Open Boat" of 1897, Crane had already begun to discover new subjects, to resolve problems, and to recognize potentials which had remained unrealized in earlier writing.[6] But it was in the years after "The Open Boat" that his art achieved its fullest realization.

Paradoxically, the fiction of Crane's last years contained much of his worst and his best work. Plagued by debts, disease, and the extravagant demands of visitors and household, Crane wrote hurriedly and sometimes without care or self-criticism.[7] As his letters convincingly demonstrate, in his eagerness for publication, Crane, although nobly responsible to his wife in the final years, was at times irresponsible to his muse. Too often the result was hack work (*Great Battles of the World*, for instance) or slight, imperfect, hurriedly written, or simply ill-considered stories and novels. But Crane was also capable on certain occasions—especially before the tragedy of his final months—of a heightened attention to his art which yielded such results as "The Open Boat," "The Blue Hotel," "The Bride Comes to Yellow Sky," and "The Upturned Face." In these stories he examined with an expanded and experienced awareness the old subjects—man in Nature, man in the American West. Also he would draw new potentials of meaning from the matter of war. And these subjects were now also to manifest more surely and with more imaginative capability Crane's newly conceived and resolved cycle of action—the cycle of confrontation and return. In these final years Crane found himself more perceptively committed to the figure of the innocent as protagonist, and now with more frequency he was to develop as his central perceiving character that most innocent of seers, the child. Crane had only briefly concerned himself with children earlier (in the "baby sketches"). In 1898 and 1899 he was to produce both the Whilomville stories and "The Monster."

Thus in the years between 1892 and 1900 Crane occasionally showed a capability for a fiction of increasingly broad and deep dimensions. Now events and capabilities of confrontation could have ethical and social or aesthetic significances as well as merely practical or ironic importance. Now, on occasion, Crane's characters would apprehend for a moment realities which were of broad and profound significance. In the last years, when he was at times writing under the worst of conditions, he was moving by fits and starts in the direction of a major statement.[8]

When Stephen Crane wrote "The Open Boat," his prose style also came of age. All of the promise of *The Red Badge* and of the other, earlier pieces was being fulfilled, and the young man had now made of his prose an instrument which could perfectly serve his art. He did this to a great extent by the simple exercise of restraint and by the development of a selective editorial taste. This refinement of taste was manifest in many ways, and I can mention here only the most striking instance. It became apparent after *The Red Badge* that the rather heavy-handed and mannered use of epithet— a habit so consistent that anonymity of character had come to be a distinguishing characteristic of his style—had sharply diminished. Occasionally in place of a name a common noun was used (as in "The Open Boat") but now at best the rather pretentious epithets were less frequent. Also Crane had learned control over what, after Øverland, one might call the synechdochal mannerism.[9] And along with these evidences of restraint, Crane also had come to write in a less distorted, less grotesque syntax, and to employ more active constructions with somewhat more energetic verbs. These changes achieved a closer control of connotations and also generated a more unified, more controlled tone.

As Crane was developing more skill in the use of his stylistic devices, he was also becoming more committed to the use of dramatic impressionism as a technique for the representation of reality as apprehended. Indeed, his late prose seems to have become more clearly purposive on those occasions in which he sought to dramatize his character's emotion in describing an event of apprehension. In the late stories Crane made a more frequent and more overt use of symbol. The grotesque descriptions of fear-distorted apprehension were coming to be more closely integrated to theme in the stories after 1896.

Throughout his career Crane continued his interest in colors. But after he left New York he began to mute his colors—to use them with more literary ability, if with less painterly bravura. In *The Red Badge* Crane, experimenting with Goethe's color theory, had explored the symbolic potential of primary colors; after *The Red Badge*, however, these experiments were largely at an end. And after 1896 Crane's colors were no longer only primary; now they were more exactly realistic and were used associatively rather than symbolically and for more specific and pragmatic purposes. Although color is so important in "The Open Boat" that it figures in the story's opening statement, there are none of the gaudy flashes of *The Red Badge* or the arbitrarily sudden and only barely relevant colors of *The Third Violet* or *Maggie*.[10] Now instead of red and yellow we have subtlety and exactness: "slate," "Canton flannel gulls," "lights of emerald and white and amber." When Crane does use particular colors symbolically, as in "The Blue Hotel," the color symbols suggest qualities of emotional atmosphere or metaphysical circumstance. Again in "The Blue Hotel," he made his intention known in the opening sentence. "The Palace Hotel at Fort Romper was painted a light blue, a shade that is on the legs of a kind of heron, causing the bird to declare its position against any background" (*Virginia*, V, 142).

As the story develops, the color values become clearly apparent. Light blue, the surface color, the color of the exterior of the hotel, makes the environment of the hotel special, sets it apart from its background. Red, the color of anger and heightened emotion, is dominant inside the hotel; the travelers "burnished themselves fiery red" with water from a washbasin. In the saloon in which the Swede is later killed, a "red light was burning," and outside, vision is obscured by the whiteness of the snow. Although the system may have changed, there was yet in Crane's method the long logic, kept carefully out of sight.[11]

As Crane's sentences in the later stories began to move with a greater syntactic clarity and directness, they came also to be increasingly marked by patterned verbal repetitions. Sometimes these repetitions were used ironically, to suggest automatic, patterned responses on the part of perceiving characters, and thus to provide tacit comment upon those presuppositions which affect characters' capacities for apprehension.* One such example occurs in "The Clan of No-

---

* Sometimes it seems that Crane's sole purpose in these syntactic recurrences was to achieve rhythmical periodicity. It is true that in the later years Crane's sentence rhythms took on a new smoothness.

Name" and describes the protagonist's quality of mind. "There was a standard and he must follow it, obey it, because it was a monarch, the Prince of Conduct" (*Virginia*, VI, 127). In "The Open Boat," the repetition is used as a device of description. Here the reiteration is reproduced by Crane to create a rhythmical sameness which charges a scene with an almost mesmeric quality of exhaustion: " 'Keep her head up! Keep her head up!' . . . 'Keep her head up, sir.' The voices were weary and low" (*Virginia*, V, 81).

Sometimes in this mature work these patterns became formalized or ritualized into repetitions which almost seem to function, rhythmically, dramatically, and thematically, as prose refrains. In "The Open Boat" Crane reported the correspondent's increasingly irrelevant thoughts in one of these refrains. " 'If I am going to be drowned—if I am going to be drowned—if I am going to be drowned, why, in the name of the seven mad gods who rule the sea, was I allowed to come thus far and contemplate sand and trees?" (*Virginia*, V. 77, 81, 84). The refrain appears three times in the story. In "The Clan of No-Name," the catalogue "on peak or plain, from dark northern ice-fields to the hot wet jungles, through all wine and want, through all lies and unfamiliar truth, dark or light" occurs twice with similar purpose.[12] If Crane's style can sometimes achieve a spare purity (certain exchanges in "The Open Boat" seem to anticipate Hemingway),[13] the later prose can also approach an ironically baroque formality.

Crane's representation of the speech of his characters was also to become more adroit. The dialect of the slum was clumsily handled in *Maggie*; later he was more successfully to imitate in English the speech rhythms of Spanish and of other languages.* But in the late work Crane was also to

---

* See "The Clan of No-Name" and "Death and the Child." Ernest Hemingway, in *For Whom the Bell Tolls* and in stories like "The Gambler, the Nun and the Radio," imitated Crane successfully in this technique.

turn increasingly to indirect discourse in which the author in his own voice describes the contents of his character's speech and thought. This substitutionary speech places Crane's reader precisely in the middle ground between what is and what is seen, and as the distance between the two diminishes, the irony inherent in their disparity sharpens.[14]

In spite of their more normal syntactic appearance, Crane's brilliantly vivid and curiously selected adjectives lose none of their force in the later works. And the verbs also become more evocative. His early style does not prepare us for his use of such a string of verbs as the following, in "The Upturned Face": "They tugged away; the corpse lifted, heaved, toppled, flopped into the grave" (*Virginia*, VI, 298).

There also remained the same energy in the individual image. In fact, some images—like the towers in "The Open Boat" or the interior of the Pullman car in "The Bride Comes to Yellow Sky"—even achieve with more compression and significance the grotesque intensity which Crane achieved in the image of the corpse in Henry Fleming's forest chapel.[15] For in addition to serving as emblems these images are now used with the clear purpose of exposing more subtle states of mind of their perceivers or, more significantly, to suggest something which Crane himself feels toward the described event. His imagistic symbols have been traced back at least as far as *Maggie*,[16] but now they are increasingly present— from the cash register of "The Blue Hotel" or the cuckoo clock in "Twelve O'Clock" to the upturned face itself.

In the fiction beginning with "The Open Boat," Crane also demonstrates a new sophistication in his use of figurative language. His later similes are seldom only bizarre comparisons which merely arrest the reader's attention. Now these figures are carefully arranged and patterned in groups to achieve effects organic to theme. Indeed, very frequently in Crane's later fiction, similes and metaphors are consciously organized to suggest a particular quality of perception in his speaker, to assert a theme, or to develop certain ironic attitudes toward material. In "The Open Boat," for instance, the analogies which a landsman would draw to the described experiences are set in similes to establish a narrative viewpoint which distances Crane from his castaways.[17] In "The Blue Hotel" hyperbolic metaphors and similes suggest the paranoid delusion of the Swede.[18] In "The Bride Comes to Yellow Sky," homely similes ("as that of a man shoeing his first horse," "like a man waiting in a barber's shop") establish a narrator whose prosaic imagination contrasts ironically with Jack Potter's anxiety and Scratchy Wilson's violent blundering.

The development of Crane's style—the regulation of his syntax, the controlling of his color, the organization of his figures of speech—can to some extent be described as a movement away from the reference of image and in the direction of the more purely verbal. One might conjecture that this change, which was a gradual one, was brought about by a change which began between 1895 and 1897, when Crane left behind his associations with visual artists and began to find himself more exclusively in the company of writers, publishers, and literary critics.[19] The direction and extent of Crane's verbal development is sharply apparent in a single paragraph written in 1897 and found in "The Monster." In the horrible moment before the burning of Henry Johnson's face, the narrator pauses to take an ironically naive look at the fire itself. Simile, color, syntax, all contribute to effect. But now, though the passage has lost none of its visual vitality, its predominant power is associational. The horror is not a horror of the senses but a horror of irony—a horror of the mind. "The room was like a garden in the region where might be burning flowers. Flames of violet, crimson, green, blue, orange, and purple were blooming everywhere. There was one blaze that was precisely the hue of a delicate coral. In another place was a mass that lay merely in phosphorescent inaction like a pile of emeralds" (*Virginia*, VII, 24). When, in a few lines, Crane calls the fire "a delicate, trembling, sapphire shape like a fairy lady [who] with a quiet smile . . . blocked his path," the ironic horror is complete.

Indeed, it was in the later years and when he was writing at his best that Stephen Crane really became the artist of *"le ton juste."* [20] And that tone is predominantly one of controlled irony. Like the style, the irony also matured. It is no longer pervasive as it was in *Maggie*, where Crane very nearly destroyed any concern which the reader might have for the girl's plight. No longer does his zealously ironic scorn for delusion dominate whole stories (or confuse his reader in its inconsistency, as it does in *The Red Badge*). Now his irony is controlled, compressed, reasonable. When it flashes out to ridicule Martha Goodwin, the village gossip in "The Monster," the reasons are clear. And in "Death and the Child," when he represents the innocence of Peza's uncompleted vision, Crane is restrained and sympathetic. Moreover, the late irony is tightly compressed—sometimes in a single image (like Scratchy Wilson's maroon shirt), sometimes (as in "The Blue Hotel") in a single word.*

It was not until the final years, however, that Crane's skill in opening his stories came to be fully developed. There was, of course, the beginning of *Maggie*—with the battle of the boys and the "worm of yellow convicts" which set the conditions of struggle and servitude in which Maggie must live. But Crane here refused to rely solely upon these images to announce his theme, so *Maggie's* opening remains only a promise. In the later stories he was to develop an ability to

---

* James Trammell Cox (in "Stephen Crane as Symbolic Naturalist") discusses the irony implicit in the "square" at the end of the story, and he points out imagery which supports this tightened irony.

assert surely—in one image, in the setting of a single scene, in a single symbolically charged and dramatically integrated statement—a theme for an entire story.

Crane's newly developed capacity is first apparent in "The Open Boat." In the opening sentence ("None of them knew the color of the sky") Crane asserts for the story a theme of initiatory seeing. And there are others. In the openings of "The Bride Comes to Yellow Sky" and "Death and the Child," themes and symbolic relationships are suggested by a closing focus of scene or by a shifting perspective—cinematic techniques which Crane first employed expressionistically in the compressed time sequence of Maggie's walk to the river. There is the opening sentence of "The Blue Hotel" which explicitly assigns separative significance to the color of the title building. And, at the very end of his career, there is the curiously flat opening of "The Upturned Face," which asserts so succinctly the thematic importance which ritual will have for that story. All of these openings are different in method, yet each asserts brilliantly the central concern of its story.

The author who developed such a style in his later years cannot be understood if he is regarded only as hurried and careless. For whenever Crane was working under reasonable conditions he was producing fiction in a style consciously achieved, succinct, closely developed, and organic to theme. Such a style is not easily won. But more significantly, Crane's style in the later fiction is functionally developed to articulate his preoccupations with his character's apprehension and to place his reader at an exact point of ironic stasis between the presentation of an actuality and the representation of its apprehension. The style was developed to communicate to Crane's readers events of apprehension, and those consequences to apprehension which follow upon a return to community. It is Crane's style which also takes us that significant step beyond realism which I discussed in the first chapter. The possibility of the ultimately subjective reality, the nihilistic vision of which J. Hillis Miller speaks, arises in the style. It is this unsureness about the nature of reality which will cause Crane's style to reverberate throughout the American fiction of the post-realist twentieth century.

In many ways "The Open Boat" marks for Stephen Crane an end as well as a beginning. It was Crane's last work in America before the departure for Crete, which just preceded his settling in England with Cora and new friends. And it is a fictional account of an event in Crane's life after which, as John Berryman says, Crane lived actively with death.* [21] But

* The incident of the foundering of the *Commodore*, which is too well known to recount here, occurred in the night of January 1–2, 1897, and the dinghy finally capsized in the surf near Daytona Beach on the morning of January 3. Crane returned to Jacksonville and Cora's Hotel de Dream on the 4th; he wrote and filed his famous report of the foundering (over 3000 words) with remarkable speed, for it appeared on page one of the New York *Press* on January 7. This account ("Stephen Crane's Own Story," *Writings*, 234–43) has been thoroughly studied by other Crane scholars and critics (see W. T. Going, "William Higgins and Crane's 'The Open Boat': A Note about Fact and Fiction," *Papers on English Language and Literature*, I (Winter, 1965), 79–82; Andrew Lytle, " 'The Open Boat': A Pagan Tale," *The Hero with the Private Parts* (Baton Rouge, 1966), 60–75; etc.), and since Crane does not describe his nights at sea ("The history of life in an open boat for thirty hours would no doubt be instructive to the young, but none is to be told here and now"), and since my concern with "The Open Boat" is more with its apprehensional and communal themes and its symbolic aspects than with its potential as realistic description of what happened, I shall not consider the journalistic piece here.

Crane wrote the short story in the course of the following month. In May of 1897 (after he had left for Greece) there appeared another piece about Cuban filibustering, and "The Open Boat" appeared in *Scribner's Magazine* in June. See B[ernice] D. S[lote] (ed.), "Stephen Crane: Two Uncollected Articles," *Prairie Schooner*, XLIII (Fall, 1969), 287–96; Levenson, *Virginia*, V, pp. lvi-lxi; and "Textual Introduction," *Virginia*, V, pp. clxvi-clxvii.

In August of 1897 there appeared yet another story which came out of Crane's experiences during the foundering of the *Commodore* and after. "Flanagan and His Short Filibustering Adventure" is a death-wish fantasy; though a comic story, it recounts imaginatively the darker side of Crane's experience in the open boat. It tells the story of a captain who goes fili-

"The Open Boat" is also the first of Crane's major short stories. And in this story he functionally established his cycle of action and related it clearly to his thematic concern with significance of apprehension.

Like *The Red Badge of Courage,* "The Open Boat" is the story of an initiation. But in "The Open Boat" Crane directly comments upon its significance. To the initiates the consequences of Henry Fleming's initiation are, in spite of Crane's efforts, never entirely clear, but for the men in the open boat the consequences of the experience are less accidentally ambiguous. As Peter Buitenhuis puts it, "Unlike Henry Fleming, . . . the correspondent, the protagonist of 'The Open Boat,' is no stripling. He is represented as an experienced, cynical, somewhat dogmatic individual. His initiation is not into manhood, as is Fleming's, but into a new attitude towards nature and his fellow-men." [22]

If "The Open Boat" is an account of an initiation, it is also the story of a return. It tells of four men separated from the human community—alone at sea in an open boat—and of their finding their way back to their community on shore. After these men have confronted the reality of the sea and its essential indifference to them, they must arrive at the beach if they are to survive. In "The Open Boat" Crane is follow-

---

bustering because he "gets the ant of desire-to-see-what-it's-like stirring in his heart." It is an almost absurdly unfortunate trip; the captain, in spite of incredibly clever maneuver and seamanship, loses his ship and drowns. In the final scene Flanagan's body floats ashore in Florida at the feet of vacationers who have come from a dance and are completely unaware of Flanagan's adventure. Therefore, "The expedition of the Foundling will never be historic." *Virginia,* V, 108. "Flanagan" is a slight work if set beside "The Open Boat" (Levenson says that it shows what could happen when Crane worked hurriedly under pressure), but perhaps after the qualified and tragic affirmation of "The Open Boat," the darkly comic negation of "Flanagan" was inevitable. See Stallman, 309; and Levenson, *Virginia,* V, pp. lxx—lxxii. See also Joseph Katz, "Stephen Crane to William Howe Crane: A New Letter," *Stephen Crane Newsletter,* II (Fall, 1967), 9, which suggests strongly that "Flanagan" was written in March of 1897.

ing the pattern of *The Red Badge*; like Henry Fleming the four isolated men first confront the thing itself, then they rejoin their fellow creatures.

But even more significantly, the story is a report of an experience of confrontation conducted within the metaphor of vision.[23] "The Open Boat" begins with an assertion of its characters' visual innocence ("None of them knew the color of the sky") and proceeds immediately to describe the quality of that innocence in each of the four characters.[24] The cook "invariably gazed eastward over the broken sea," and he is terribly afraid; the oiler, concerned with the business at hand, "sometimes raised himself suddenly to keep clear of water that swirled in over the stern"; the intellectual, ruminative correspondent "watched the waves and wondered why he was there"; the captain "was at this time buried in that profound dejection and indifference which comes, temporarily at least, to even the bravest and most enduring when, willy-nilly, the firm fails, the army loses, the ship goes down . . . this captain had on him the stern impression of a scene in the greys of dawn of seven turned faces, and later a stump of a topmast with a white ball on it, that slashed to and fro at the waves, went low and lower, and down." Here four men confront the fact of their situation in a "bathtub" in the middle of the ocean. Each reacts in a human way—the captain with *tristesse* and indifference, the cook with fear, the correspondent with abstract questioning, and only the oiler with hard work in an attempt to stay alive.[25]

"The Open Boat" is the story of how these four men come to terms with their situation, with the reality by which they are confronted. Therefore, it is their vision to which Crane frequently returns. The correspondent emerges as the character from whose point of view Crane tells most of his story. But first there is another point of view, that of a "concealed narrator," [26] a landsman, apparently, since he describes events in homely similes or similes taken from the language of the West (for him the boat is a "bath-tub," and "A seat in this boat was not unlike a seat upon a bucking bronco"). This landsman narrator is detached; after his description of the open boat, he moves away from it. Thus again, but without intruding himself into the story, Crane balances his reader neatly between two apprehensions and achieves his inevitable irony:[27] "Viewed from a balcony, the whole thing would doubtlessly have been weirdly picturesque" (*Virginia*, V, 69).

If Crane's tone is ambivalently ironic, his attention is nevertheless steadfast upon the four men and their response to their situation. And their first response, a debate over whether or not the lighthouse which they see is occupied (not unlike an argument over the sentience of God) is largely irrelevant to their immediate problem of what to do.

> The cook had said: "There's a house of refuge just north of the Mosquito Inlet Light, and as soon as they see us, they'll come off in their boat and pick us up."
> "As soon as who sees us?" said the correspondent.
> "The crew," said the cook.
> "Houses of refuge don't have crews," said the correspondent. "As I understand them, they are only places where clothes and grub are stored for the benefit of shipwrecked people. They don't carry crews."
> "Oh, yes, they do," said the cook.
> "No, they don't," said the correspondent.
> "Well, we're not there yet, anyhow," said the oiler, in the stern.

The next three sections of "The Open Boat" describe a shift in the attitude of the four men from the despair suggested by the captain's question, " 'Do you think we've got much of a show now, boys?' " [28] to an attitude of hope and finally to one of almost ridiculously high spirits. Here is an

exuberance resulting from a new sense of comradeship, but
it is an illusory pomposity, and at the end of the third section Crane's concealed narrator,[29] again distanced from the
four men, summarizes with "thereupon the four waifs rode
impudently in their little boat and, with an assurance of an
impending rescue shining in their eyes, puffed at the big
cigars and judged well and ill of all men. Everybody took a
drink of water." Like Henry Fleming, the men in the open
boat vacillate between blinding fear and illusory arrogance.

The narrating voice almost immediately punctures their
pomposity. "It was fair to say that there was not a life-saving
station within twenty miles in either direction." Comrades
or not, the men are still faced with the possibility of drowning. As they discover, at the beginning of the fourth section,
that no assistance is forthcoming from the lifesaving station—
that they must save themselves—the men see their real condition, their essential alienation from their universe, if only
for a moment. That awareness is the first step in their initiation.

This first awareness is accompanied by anger. In what Peter
Buitenhuis[30] has called a "choral lament," to be partly re-
peated twice in the story and now repeated in this chapter,
Crane's narrator conjectures of his four men:

> There was a great deal of rage in them. Perchance
> they might be formulated thus: "If I am going to be
> drowned—if I am going to be drowned—if I am going
> to be drowned, why, in the name of the seven mad gods
> who rule the sea, was I allowed to come thus far and
> contemplate sand and trees? Was I brought here merely
> to have my nose dragged away as I was about to nibble
> the sacred cheese of life? It is preposterous. If this old
> ninny-woman, Fate, cannot do better than this, she
> should be deprived of the management of men's for-
> tunes. She is an old hen who knows not her intention.
> If she has decided to drown me, why did she not do it

in the beginning and save me all this trouble. The whole affair is absurd."

Virginia, V, 77

The comprehension of the absurdity of their situation, however, is not permanent. <u>The men cannot tolerate the perception of their own insignificance in an absurd universe in which they are not regarded as important.</u> The paragraph continues, " 'But no; she cannot mean to drown me. She dare not drown me. She cannot drown me. Not after all this work.' Afterward the man might have had an impulse to shake his fist at the clouds, 'Just you drown me, now, and then hear what I call you!' "

The oiler, doing the necessary work of saving himself and the others, continues his rowing, but in the remaining pages of the fourth section the other characters are reduced to an acting out of their own delusions. Crane's narrator and the characters simultaneously observe the events taking place on shore. It is a doubled and an ironic perception, for although the characters see all of the activities on shore as somehow referent to themselves and to their situation, it is made apparent to the reader that these events are either entirely random (we never discover the intentions of the waving man, for instance)[31] or are without significance to the men in the boat. We are merely observing from a distance the comings and goings of life at a resort (the "lifeboat" turns out to be a beach omnibus). The final absurdity is the cook's remark, "apropos of nothing": " 'Billie,' he murmured, dreamfully, 'what kind of pie do you like best?' " (*Virginia*, V, 81).

It is only during the long night at sea[32] that the reader's attention is focused upon a single character, as the correspondent experiences privately a second stage in his confrontation with reality. Now point of view is narrowed, and ironic distance is shortened so that the reader sees with the correspondent's eyes only. Believing the others to be asleep, Crane's correspondent considers his situation and again is enraged. But this time he passes beyond the impotence and frustration of anger. After a repetition of the refrain ("If I am going to be drowned . . ."), the narrator becomes explicit. "When it occurs to a man that nature does not regard him as important, and that she feels she would not maim the universe by disposing of him, he at first wishes to throw bricks at the temple, and he hates deeply the fact that there are no bricks and no temples. Any visible expression of nature would surely be pelleted with his jeers" (*Virginia*, V, 84–85).

The narrating voice is still ironic. But faced with the disillusioning apprehension of his situation, the correspondent is able to recognize one more fact: "Then, if there be no tangible thing to hoot, he feels, perhaps, the desire to confront a personification and indulge in pleas, bowed to one knee, and with hands supplicant, saying, 'Yes, but I love myself.' "

Here is the second step—the recognition of one's own ultimate concern. It is only after this recognition that the correspondent remembers, imperfectly, a poem from his childhood, Lady Caroline Norton's "Bingen." [33] As he recalls the pathos of the dying soldier in the poem, the correspondent is "moved by a profound and perfectly impersonal comprehension. He was sorry for the soldier of the Legion who lay dying in Algiers."

This is the last step in the correspondent's initiation. Now he can accept his awareness that the sea is not cruel, "nor beneficent, nor treacherous, nor wise. But she was indifferent, flatly indifferent." And now he can accept his place on such a sea in such a universe. For, as is so frequently to be the case in Crane's writing, the absurdity of the human condition can be tolerated only when one senses that it is shared. Immediately following the correspondent's recognition, two events occur. The shark, which has been following the boat, departs, and the captain, who has been awake all the time, makes his wakefulness known to the correspondent. Now the correspondent can become aware of the fact that his experience, though private, is not unique. And the rest of this penultimate section is a dramatization of the newly discovered sharing of the human condition in the face of universal absurdity, as the correspondent and the oiler "spell" one another in the task of rowing the boat.

At the moment of the correspondent's recognition much of the irony, the result of discrepancies between the points of view from which the story is recorded, disappears from "The Open Boat." And in the final section Crane achieves a sure, unambiguous assertion of the kind which he was unable to establish at the end of *The Red Badge.* The last section of "The Open Boat" opens with a statement which, answering as it does the story's opening sentence, clarifies Crane's attitude toward his characters. "When the correspondent again opened his eyes, the sea and the sky were each of the gray hue of the dawning. Later, carmine and gold was painted upon the waters. The morning appeared finally, in its splendor, with a sky of pure blue, and the sunlight flamed on the tips of the waves" (*Virginia*, V, 87). The correspondent can now know the color of the sky.

Now the men, recognizing that they will receive no help in landing, turn the boat for the beach. Now the correspondent can see; he can apprehend, without fear and without conceit, the significance of the tower before him. "The boat was headed for the beach. The correspondent wondered if none ever ascended the tall wind-tower, and if then they never looked seaward. This tower was a giant, standing with its back to the plight of the ants."

The correspondent turns away from his initiatory confrontation and, with the others, makes the effort necessary for survival. But he has seen enough for his initiation to have a number of ambiguous, perhaps ironic implications. One of them is ethical, or perhaps a diminution in the significance of ethical meaning.* "It is, perhaps, plausible that a man in this situation, impressed with the unconcern of the universe, should see the innumerable flaws of his life and have them taste wickedly in his mind and wish for another chance. A distinction between right and wrong seems absurdly clear to him, then, in this new ignorance of the grave-edge, and he understands that if he were given another opportunity he would mend his conduct and his words, and be better and brighter during an introduction or at tea." Another is a sharpening—or is it a limiting—of the senses which comes as the emotions become calm and objective. Maybe the moment of pure apprehension, unaltered by emotion, was a fleeting one; in any event, it seems that Crane's irony has returned. And it remains, even in the final moment of excitement; as the boat swamps, the correspondent's apprehension seems curiously disengaged. "The January water was icy, and he reflected immediately that it was colder than he had expected to find it off the coast of Florida. This appeared to his dazed mind as a fact important enough to be noted at the time. The coldness of the water was sad; it was tragic. This fact was somehow mixed and confused with his opinion of his own situation, so that it seemed almost a proper reason for tears. The water was cold" (*Virginia*, V, 90).

Yet the correspondent's initiation (and perhaps a drop of

* William Bysshe Stein, in an essay perceptively aware of the existential world view apparent in Crane's fiction, has suggested that this statement constitutes an ironic rejection of old values ("Stephen Crane's *Homo Absurdus*," *Bucknell Review*, VIII [May, 1959], 171, also 168–88). Whether or not Crane meant to suggest this much, he is asserting one effect of the correspondent's visual initiation—an effect upon his relations with his fellows.

sea water in the eye) makes it possible for him to see human creature in a new and fundamental way. When a man on the shore comes to offer assistance, he is described: "He was naked, naked as a tree in winter, but a halo was about his head, and he shone like a saint." Here, in one of Crane's intensely apprehended moments, is man—and perhaps also the saint—in Crane's universe, a vulnerable creature ("as a tree in winter"), who is inadequate to help against the continuing absurdity of a Nature that leaves the quietly competent oiler face down in the sand, but who is present to assist the correspondent in his exit from the shallow water.[34] Though muted, the simile is a grotesque one; Crane's saint is almost as powerless as is Henry Fleming at the death of his friend Jim.

Crane's ambiguities at the end of "The Open Boat," however, do not stand in the way of his moving to a clear conclusion. For in the final sentence—and with the assertion of a final ambiguity*—Crane's theme and intention come clear. "When it came night, the white waves paced to and fro in the moonlight, and the wind brought the sound of the great sea's voice to the men on the shore, and they felt that they could then be interpreters" (*Virginia*, V, 92). They (the point of view is again collective) *felt* that they could then be interpreters. Can they? If Crane's ending is ironic, it is only a half irony. For Crane is rightly aware that it is ultimately in interpretation that private perception

---

* This ambiguity, which Stallman has ignored (258), and which William Going ("William Higgins in Crane's 'The Open Boat' ") and William Randel ("The Cook in 'The Open Boat,' " *American Literature*, XXXIV [November, 1962] 405–11) have both recognized, seems—along with many others—deliberate, especially if the ending is compared to that of "Stephen Crane's Own Story." And such deliberate ambiguity suggests that Crane, far from accepting a view of an objectively real world, as Charles Metzger has suggested ("Realistic Devices in Stephen Crane's 'The Open Boat' "), has here moved beyond realism to a more qualified, subjective, and even existential understanding of reality and thus has anticipated an orientation of many writers who were to follow him. But more of this later.

achieves social significance. And the correspondent, having confronted the absurd unconcern of Nature, having recognized that in spite of it he loved himself, having also recognized his concern for the soldier of the Legion and for his shipmates, having learned to see for himself—at least a color of the sky—now can complete his return by the communication of the fruit of his vision to his fellows. Thus Crane resolves the discordance of *The Red Badge of Courage.*[35]

Henry James, in Crane's own time, was asserting in his stories of writers and artists the significance of interpretation of experience. But, for American literature at least, his was only a reiteration. Emerson long before had claimed that "The man is only half himself, the other half is his expression," and Walt Whitman had realized that "Speech is the twin of my vision, it is unequal to measure itself,/It provokes me forever, it says sarcastically,/*Walt you contain enough, why don't you let it out then?*"[36] At the end of "The Open Boat" Stephen Crane joins their number.[37]

IX

"War is Kind"

But some who this blithe mood present,
  As on in lightsome files they fare,
Shall die experienced ere three days be spent—
  Perish, enlightened by the vollied glare;
Or shame survive. . . .

Herman Melville
"The March into Virginia," 1866

Stephen Crane's experience in an open boat at sea was one of initiation for the young writer. Those thirty hours brought him, perhaps more intensely than any previous experience, into confrontation with what he had come to consider the "reality" of the universe. He expressed the nature of that experience in "The Open Boat," and thus it provided the material for one of his most perfect stories. Moreover, the writing of that story was an event critical to Crane's later writing. But he was to know yet another initiation in another "reality," and—given his choice of subject in a considerable body of later writing—this initiation would be an equally crucial one. This second initiation was to the reality of war.

When Stephen Crane wrote *The Red Badge of Courage* in 1893 and 1894 he had never seen a battle. This fact has been ritually observed by almost every commentator on the book since its earliest reviewers. It is also well known that Crane did finally see battle in 1897, on a battlefield far away from Chancellorsville. He recorded his experiences in that foreign battle on several occasions, first in journalistic writing, then, definitively, in one short story, and later, fragmentarily, in other fiction. A close examination of the short story "Death and the Child," in light of Crane's own battlefield experience, helps explain, not only one of the writer's most enigmatic works, but also an alteration in his understanding which was another result of his confrontation with war's actuality in Greece.

Crane found his first war only after he had abandoned his search for another. It was in Jacksonville during his recuperation from his night at sea and his rendering of that experience into "The Open Boat" that he gave up his search for passage to Cuba and the fighting there. On the other side of the world another war was brewing, this one in Crete and in Greece. Greek nationalists were pressing their struggle against the Turks, as the young Greek nation sought to assist the Cretans in their struggle for independence and at the same time to make certain adjustments in their Thessalian and Epirot frontiers. It promised to be a romantic war, especially for English and American journalists. So Crane saw here a second opportunity. On March 11, 1897, he wrote to his brother William: "I have been for over a month among the swamps further south wading miserably to and fro in an attempt to avoid our derned U.S. navy. And it cant be done. I am through trying. I have changed all my plans and am going to Crete. I expect to sail from NY one week from next Saturday." [1] Thomas Beer has quoted Crane in another letter. "I am going to Greece for the *Journal* and if the Red Badge is not all right I shall sell out my claim on literature and take up orange growing." [2] Everyone was going to Greece, and Crane's principal rival, the glamour boy of American journalism, Richard Harding Davis, was among them. It was not difficult for Crane to persuade the New York *Journal* to send to Greece, not only himself, but his

new friend Cora Stewart, as "the first female war correspondent." [3]

I am concerned here with the writing—both journalistic
and fictional—which was the direct result of Crane's first
real war. For in this writing he recorded some new awarenesses about the reality of war which were to affect his later
work, such as his Spanish-American War writing and "The
Upturned Face." The Greek war was also important to
Crane because, for better or worse, his major subject throughout his career was war. From 1896, when he first set out for
Cuba from New York, his career was repeatedly marked by
recurrent efforts to find battlefields, to report wars for
newspapers, to imagine wars for himself—if at the last only
for "sure, quick money." Perhaps war came to be really a
kind of escape—and certainly his frequent immersions in
battle experience were often associated with a turning from
unpleasant circumstances, whether from the harassments of
the police or from the perhaps too-complex difficulties of
his later domestic life in England with Cora. As his life
developed, this escape seemed almost an obsession. Perhaps,
also, especially in the turbulent last years of Crane's career,
writing about war was simply a return to a subject which,
in an earlier and surer period, had yielded good results, and
profit.

Whether war was an escape or a retreat, it was also a subject nicely commensurate with his talents. On the battlefield he could focus his impressionist's eye on vivid action
and his attention upon the individual soldier's apprehension of that action. Here he could observe and record how
the soldier saw and understood, or failed to see and understand, the events around him and the essence of the battle
experience itself. Here he could consider how the soldier's
understanding or failure to understand separated him from
or brought him together with his fellows, and how the horrors

of battle created for the individual a situation of sufficient agony and stress to wash away his previous assumptions and prejudices about the nature of war's reality. But before Crane could fully articulate the soldier's "mental attitude," he had to come to terms with his own attitude toward the reality of war. This is what he did in the Greek war.

The Greek war which Crane saw was comically short in duration. But it was a long time in coming about. For many years Greece, free from Turkish domination since 1829, had taken a rather aggressive posture toward its former master. Greece had supported the Cretan efforts for independence from the Turks in 1866–69, and, although the Congress of Berlin in 1878 had ignored the situation, that island had remained smoldering in revolt. Thus, when insurrection on Crete again broke out, with the Christian Cretans rising against the Turks in 1895, it was a Greek nationalist society which lent them support, and before long the Greeks on the mainland were also clamoring for a war against the hated Turks, a war which would, they hoped, gain them Thessaly. By January of 1897 Crete was again in flames.

The Great Powers imposed peace on the island with a naval blockade for a time.[4] But on March 27 Prince Konstantinos left Athens for the Thessalian frontier, and hostilities commenced on the mainland when Greek irregulars crossed the Thessalian and Epirot frontiers into Turkish territory. The Greeks—lacking an intelligence department, adequate maps, field glasses, signaling equipment, or even competent officers—could at best be described as engaged upon a foolhardy venture, but the English and American journalists, Byronic and romantically partial to the Greeks, wished for and expected a Greek victory.

Crane had arrived in Athens by April 17, after a trip which had begun in New York and had taken him first to London, where he arranged to report to the *Westminster Gazette*, then to Paris for a day of sightseeing, then to Brussels, Frankfurt, Munich, Budapest, and finally across the Balkan peninsula to the Black Sea port of Varna, where he sailed on the *Danae* to Istanbul. From here Crane and Cora boarded a French ship, the *Guadiana*, which sailed for Athens, stopping in Crete at the Bay of Suda for a mail delivery. And it was here that Crane gazed uncomprehendingly at the fleet of the Concert of Europe and wrote his first dispatch.[5]

In Athens, Crane, still rather disoriented, concerned himself with the Greek citizens' enthusiasm for battle while other journalists were making their own battle predictions and comparisons of battle forces.* But the war was not in Athens. Rather, it was being conducted on two fronts. One front was in Epirus, the southwesternmost province of Turkish Macedonia, where the Greeks had crossed the border to launch a campaign directed at Ioannina. They got as far as Arta and crossed the Arta River, but their position was attacked on April 28 and 29, and soon they were in a panic-stricken flight back across the river. Crane had left Athens with the Greek army moving toward Ioannina, but, hearing of sharper fighting in Thessaly, he returned to Athens, filed his report,

---

* As usual, Crane was concerned less with what happened than with how it was seen. The first two pieces about Athens were entitled "The Spirit of the Greek People" (editors' title; published for the first time in *War Dispatches*, 19–21) and "Stephen Crane Says Greeks Cannot be Curbed," *War Dispatches*, 21-22. "Half a Day in Suda Bay" (also published as "Stephen Crane's Pen Picture of the Powers' Fleet Off Crete"), the first dispatch, will be discussed later.

As Stallman points out, Crane's naive account of Greek enthusiasm, and certainly his prediction, were inaccurate (see Stallman, 276). Throughout the war Crane remained committed to the Greek cause. "The Greeks I can see and understand, but the Turks seem unreal," he said to John Bass (*War Dispatches*, 43). Indeed, Crane's last report from the front, written after the armistice which proved the end of the war and entitled "Greeks Waiting at Thermopylae," still reports the Greeks' eagerness for battle and predicts a Greek victory. In the piece, Crane concluded, "I would like to write a dispatch telling of a full blown Greek victory for a change" (*War Dispatches*, 48–49).

and remained there from the 22nd through the 29th. Then he headed toward Thessaly.

The Thessalian campaign was more significant than the Epirot fighting. The Greeks advanced as far as Melouna, and at first threatened to outflank the Turks and separate them from their main force at Elasson. But at Melouna the tide turned; here the Turks drove the Greeks back and recaptured this gateway to Thessaly when the crown prince ordered a Greek retreat. Again retreat turned into rout, when the Greeks fled like a mob past Larissa to Pharsalia and Volos. The Turks, baffled at this unexplained flight, feared a trap and failed to pursue. This was the situation as Crane and Cora left Athens on April 29 and headed for the eastern front.

They traveled north by ship from Athens to Stylis, then overland to Domokos and Pharsalia, and finally arrived at the resort town of Volos on May 1. Now Crane was only twelve miles east of Velestinon, where the Greeks were making a belated but noble stand against the advancing Turkish army, repulsing on three successive days three vigorous Turkish attacks. But Crane, stricken with dysentery, could go no farther. It was not until May 5, after the crown prince naively split his forces between Pharsalia and Velestinon, and after the consequent rout of his troops and their retreat from Pharsalia to Domokos, that Stephen Crane finally saw a battle. On that day he was strong enough to travel the twelve miles to witness the second battle at Velestinon and the retreat of the Greek forces to Volos.

There were two reports of Stephen Crane on that battlefield. One, by his rival, Richard Harding Davis, even denied that Crane was at the front. But another and more reliable report was written by Crane's colleague for the *Journal*, John Bass.

Your correspondent sought shelter in a trench and cautiously watched the pale, thin face of the novelist as the latter seated himself on an ammunition box amid the shower of shells and casually lighted a cigarette. Crane did not appear surprised, but watched with a quiet expression the quick work of the artillerymen as they loaded, fired, and jumped to replace the small cannon overturned by the recoil. I was curious to know what was passing in his mind, and said: "Crane, what impresses you most in this affair?" The author of *The Red Badge of Courage* lighted another cigarette, pushed back his long hair out of his eyes with his hat and answered quietly: "Between two great armies battling each other the interesting thing is the mental attitude of the men." [6]

War Dispatches, 43

Things were going well for the Greeks when again the crown prince blundered. He ordered a retreat, and the Greek general, Smolenski, wept as he led his forces back to Volos. It was now obvious that the resort town could not be held. The Greek army evacuated by sea, with Stephen Crane and Cora managing to get aboard just as the Turks were reaching the slopes of Mt. Pelion above the town. Then Crane and Cora traveled back to Chalkis by crowded refugee ship and filed their reports by courier to Athens. Crane interviewed soldiers on his way to Athens, and once there, traveled north again by steamer to report on the evacuation of the wounded soldiers and refugees. This last experience provided him with the material for one of his most vivid reports for the *Journal*.*

* "War's Horrors and Turkey's Bold Plan" was co-authored with Julian Ralph, another Hearst correspondent. Ralph did the first part, and in it he reported the movement of troops, the political situation at the Turkish court, and the real power in Turkey and its purposes. But none of these were Crane's concerns. Here is a bit of Crane's part: "Near the hatch where I can see him is a man shot through the mouth. The bullet passed through both cheeks. He is asleep with his head pillowed on the bosom of a dead

Crane again joined the Greek army as it prepared a last-ditch stand—at Thermopylae. From the acropolis at Lamia he watched with field glasses the Turks as they took up their positions for their assault. He discussed the situation with Greek officers at Lamia while everyone waited. But, although Crane did not know it, the thirty days' war was over. The Russian Czar had intervened with a personal appeal to the Sultan, and an armistice was arranged on that very day, May 20. So at the second battle of Velestinon, Stephen Crane had his one real opportunity to see war closely enough to record the "mental attitude of the men" during battle. Yet he came away from his first war with an awareness distinctly altered, and that alteration is recorded in his writing of the Greek war.

There were, of course, a number of dispatches for the *Journal*, filed for immediate publication.[7] And there was—written in the same notebook as that in which Crane composed at least one of his war articles for the *Journal*—a remarkable poem entitled "The Blue Batallions." Daniel G. Hoffman calls it Crane's "most significant poem," [8] and it is certainly one of Crane's most germinal works, perhaps the first evidence for a shortening of aesthetic distance to a real engagement with experience which was to be a necessary ingredient of his future writing.[9]

Perhaps the best of Crane's Greek war reporting were the

---

comrade. He had been awake for days, doubtless, marching on bread and water, to be finally wounded at Domokos and taken aboard this steamer. He is too weary to mind either his wound as his awful pillow. There is a breeze on the gulf and the ship is rolling, heaving one wounded man against the other" (*War Dispatches*, 40).

As in *The Red Badge* Crane is here again the impressionist, the master of sentence rhythms and of image sequence. But now his awareness of horror is sharper and more subtle. For now one is simultaneously aware of the horror of the situation and the dream of the sleeping soldier, and the final impression is that of fact mixed with dream.

pieces he selected from his dispatches, and some of which he reworked, for appearance in the *Westminster Gazette* in May and June of 1897.[10] They numbered seven in all and appeared serially under the common generic title of "With Greek and Turk." An underlying logic of arrangement provides the pieces with a sequential unity and a unifying theme. If one reads the first piece, "An Impression of the Concert," [11] as a symbolic introduction to the causes of the war, and the three episodes following (all titled "A Fragment of Velestinon") as a representation of the thing itself, one day of battle, then the next episodes ("Some Interviews") exist as representations of this experienced event as it takes on private meaning for individual Greek soldiers, and "The Man in the White Hat" (the final piece in the set) explores some of the political consequences of those individual understandings of the event.

"An Impression of the Concert" is an account of an arrival on the scene, a record of Crane's first glimpse of war from a distance. It is achieved in Crane's now familiar impressionistic style: "This headland was rough and gaunt, a promontory that one would expect in Iceland. It was of a warm color, resembling rusted iron. It towered grandly until one found in the sky above it some faint crystalline markings which later turned into a range of exalted snow-draped mountains. The blue sea glimmered to the foot of the rusty cape and the sun shone full on the silver peaks" (*War Dispatches*, 12).

Again here is Crane recording with a painter's eye—or perhaps with that of a motion picture cameraman—changes in light and color as his ship approaches port. And throughout the sketch there is maintained this sense of varying perspective as the *Guadiana* approaches the harbor and the warships, makes its mail deliveries, and at the end, moves slowly away. In the final paragraph, "The Guadiana at last hove anchor and departed from Suda Bay, and behind her the fleet again blended gradually into a hedge. For a long time the tall tan stacks of the Camperdown and the long, gray hull of the Kaiserin Augusta remained distinct, but eventually, in the twilight, the fleet was only a great black thing, and afterward it was nothing" (*War Dispatches*, 19).

But if Crane's apprehension of Suda Bay is a "moving picture," it is for him something more, "a painting from that absurd period when the painters each tried to reproduce the universe on one canvas" (*War Dispatches*, 12). Crane here is trying to reproduce, if not the universe, at least the fullness of the political fact of the war, a fact which includes the great powers of Europe, their characteristics as nations, and their complex interrelationships. Thus "at any time when a Russian boat was near a French one, the Frenchman smiled with bright friendliness," the Austrian torpedo boat "was a bottle-green scorpion," and the English torpedo ship, the *Boxer*, "came in from the sea" and "did not join the collection of bottle-green scorpions on the Suda side of the harbor, but slid slowly over to an anchorage near the Revenge." The Italian officers "had pistol practice from the stern"; the Russians "played an uncanny melody." And at the very end comes the Turk. "He was fit for problems and he was fit for war, this fellow."

So Crane's "Impression"—his record of his first apprehension of the situation in Crete just after the insurgency there which touched off the Greek war—is an apprehension which at once records visual experience and symbolizes an awareness of the friendship of France and Russia, of the danger of the sudden involvement of the Austrian Empire, of the very maritime interests which Britain protected, of the importance of Russia to pan-Slavic movements, of the serious role of the Italians, of the diplomatic adroitness of the Turks. As Crane's final sentence records, "The hand of

Europe was hidden by the hills lying in evening peace."

"An Impression of the Concert" is an initial, distanced look at the war—in part a disguised political allegory. "A Fragment of Velestino," however, is quite different; in it Crane describes the close look, the participants' experience of a day in battle.[12] Crane begins it as he began *The Red Badge of Courage*—with the image of a landscape. Yet his landscape here is rich in the suggestion of his own disorientation. "The sky was of a fair and quiet blue. In the radiantly bright atmosphere of the morning the distances among the hills were puzzling in the extreme. The Westerner could reflect that after all his eye was accustomed to using a tree as a standard of measure, but here there were no trees" [13] (*War Dispatches*, 70). The road—it was historically important as the route of the Greek retreat from Velestinon—is soon occupied by a lone figure, a wounded Greek soldier. And again Crane's purpose is symbolical as well as impressionistic. "Behind him was the noise of battle, the roar and rumble of an enormous factory. This was the product, not so well finished as some, but sufficient to express the plan of the machine. This wounded soldier explained the distant roar. He defined it. This—this and worse—was what was going on. This explained the meaning of all that racket. Gazing at this soldier with his awful face, one felt a new respect for the din."

Having thus described his initial orientation to the fact of war, Crane proceeds to represent his experience of the event itself. In the next part are represented the sights and sounds of battle—a dead horse beside blood-red poppies, a captain with a bottle of wine, the destruction of a roadside shrine. And Crane describes his reorientation to a new background of landscape whenever he changes his position on the battlefield. Yet, because a participant's sense of direction or of progress or of the success of his cause in a battle is usually unclear, Crane provides his reader with no clear narrative development. At the end is represented the only really apprehendable result of battle, death.

> To the rear lay the body of a youth who had been killed by a ball through the chest. This youth had not been a regular soldier, evidently; he had been a volunteer. The only things military were the double cartridge belt, the haversack, and the rifle. As for the clothes, they were of black cloth with a subtle stripe or check in it, and they were cut after a common London style. Beside the body lay a black hat. It was what one would have to call a Derby, although from the short crown there was an inclination to apply the old name of dicer. There was a rather high straight collar and a little four-in-hand scarf of flowered green and a pin with a little pink stone in it.

Here is a remarkable and almost grotesquely sharp sartorial accuracy, an almost too-careful visual and verbal precision. But the intense clarity of Crane's apprehension leads the reader also to an imagined understanding of the dead youth's motives which makes his death vivid and intensely, almost personally, significant.

> The dead young Greek had nothing particularly noble in his face. There was expressed in this thing none of the higher thrills to incite, for instance, a company of romantic poets. The lad was of a common enough type. The whole episode was almost obvious. He was of people in comfortable circumstances; he bought his own equipment, of course. Then one morning news sped to the town that the Turks were beating. And then he came to the war on the smoke, so to speak, of the new fires of patriotism which had been immediately instilled in the village place, around the tables in front of the cafe. He had been perhaps a little inclined to misgiving, but withall anxious to see everything anyhow, and usually convinced of his ability to kill any number of Turks.

He had come to his height, and fought with these
swarthy, hard-muscled men in the trench, and, soon or
late, got his ball through the chest. Then they lifted
the body and laid it to the rear to get it out of the way.

War Dispatches, 70

This sense of shared experience, this empathy so carefully
balanced by distance and control and objectivity and even
the suspicion of irony directed at the naive idealism of the
young man, is all that is left of the triumphant note of battle
brotherhood with which Crane—albeit somewhat uncertainly
—had concluded *The Red Badge of Courage.* And now
initiation into war ends in death, not in the achievement
of manhood.

The last section of "A Fragment of Velestino," like that of
The Red Badge, is a record of the communal experience of
a military unit under fire. In it the Turks assault the Greek
position, the attack fails, and, as the day ends, the Greek
soldiers settle in their camp for the night. Here Crane presents the community of soldiers and the ordered music of
their song, which for the moment seems to replace the
cacophanous noises of battle. But even as the soldiers' song
is being described, there is apparent an overpowering darkness, the unseen but lurking dangers of war, the terrible
fragility of this little knot of men.

There were some mountaineer volunteers in great
woolly grey shepherds' cloaks. They were curious figures
in the evening light, perfectly romantic if it were not for
the modernity of the rifles and the shining lines of
cartridges. With the plain a sea of shadow below, and
the vague blue troops of Greece about them in the
trenches, these men sang softly the wild minor ballads
of their hills. As the evening deepened many men curled
in their blankets and slept, but these grey-cloaked moun-
taineers continued to sing. Ultimately the rays of the
moon outlined their figures in silver light, and it was not

infrequently that shells from the persistent Turco-German batteries threw a sudden red colour on their curious garb and on the banner of their village which hung above them.*

The next two sections of "With Greek and Turk" comprise a set of six interviews with veterans of the battle.[14] These interviews, conducted with mercenary and patriot, with shepherd and bourgeois youth, with the wounded and the unharmed—make use of as broad a spectrum of experience as possible in establishing the political implications of the war. All agree that the crown prince was to blame, and the last interview, with an Athenian youth, suggests something of the threat which the crown prince's military incompetence has caused to the Greek king.[15] But these interviews are also accounts of the experience of war as it is recorded on various sensibilities—of the memory of fear, of pride, of anger, of boredom which men take away from battle.

"The Man in the White Hat," Crane's final section of "With Greek and Turk," is an account of battle memories and understandings as they approach but fail to be translated into meaningful action. Here is a rather impressionistic story of a café revolution, of a crowd incited by a newspaperman who then marches on the king's palace only to be turned away by a guard.[16] Through Crane's irony one can sense the frustration of action, the unfortunate failure—both private and public—in translating apprehension into understanding and understanding into meaningful action. Here is the failure of the Greek cause which he was then reporting, but here also is the tragedy of Balkan history in Crane's time, and,

* It is interesting, and perhaps rather ominous in light of Crane's visions of communal misapprehensions which were soon to be recorded in the Whilomville stories, to note here again his representing a return to a communal apprehension which is associated with sleep. The same was true in both *The Red Badge* and "The Open Boat."

indeed, perhaps also a human inadequacy which for Crane had broader or even personal implications.[17]

Even from this brief glimpse at Stephen Crane's journalistic writing about Greece, it is apparent that his first look at war and at "how the men felt in those scraps" produced in him an awareness of the facts of war and of battle which was at once broader and more somber than had been manifest in *The Red Badge of Courage*. At the same time, perhaps, he could be sure that he had been right in his earlier war novel, at least about the apprehension of the individual soldier. But Crane's first experience in battle produced for him an understanding of the sensitive individual in battle which took him well beyond that manifest in *The Red Badge of Courage* or in his journalistic writing about the Greek War. That understanding is most clearly embodied in the fiction which was the product of his sojourn in Greece.

Only two works of fiction came out of Crane's Greek experience, a less than adequate novel and one short story, which critics have found to be seriously flawed. That story, "Death and the Child," is for this reason not often closely examined, yet it remains one of Crane's most challenging and provocative works. Written late in 1897, well after he had left Greece and had taken up residence in England, the story also represents a further distillation of his war experience.[18] It can, in fact, be read as a fictionalized autobiographical account of Crane's own day of battle—an account to which is appended a most curious ending. And perhaps the story represents even more, for in "Death and the Child" Crane imaginatively came to terms with the understanding which, as I have said, must precede that of "the mental attitude of the men." He came to terms with the meaning of war for himself, and with the implications of the search for that meaning.

At first reading, "Death and the Child" seems to be only a restatement of the themes of *The Red Badge of Courage*, a story of initiation to war, although this time an initiation of an Italian war correspondent of Greek family and sympathies, a man of sensibility, education, and maturity considerably beyond those of the young American farmboy-turned-soldier, Henry Fleming. Like Crane's American soldier, Peza, the Italian correspondent, has his romantic visions of war exploded by war's realities. And also like Henry Fleming, Peza flees from the field of battle. But at this point similarities end.[19] For if in *The Red Badge of Courage* Henry's initiation to war's actuality achieves for him a place in a community, Peza's initiation in "Death and the Child" deepens his isolation from his fellowman.

At the beginning of the story Peza is presented as an acutely sensitive and highly educated young man, come to the battlefield to apprehend for himself the reality of war. The isolation implicit to such a man at such a task is established at the outset, when Peza is set in opposition to the natural flow of humanity, which is in flight from war. "The peasants who were streaming down the mountain trail had, in their sharp terror, evidently lost their ability to count. The cattle and the huge round bundles seemed to suffice to the minds of the crowd if there were now two in each case where there had been three. This brown stream poured on with a constant wastage of goods and beasts. . . . It was as if fear was a river. . . . It was a freshet that might sear the face of the tall quiet mountain" (*Virginia*, V, 121). In contrast to the apprehension of these peasants, inexact and fearful as it is, there is another way of seeing, an apprehensional state in which the senses are acute and objective and the emotions are disengaged. And the narrating voice of the story ironically and suddenly imposes this alternative by, as it were, turning around and, presumably with its back to these fleeing peasants, describing in quite a different style what these peasants do not see. Now the reader is presented, not with a "stream" but with another body of water.

> The blue bay, with its pointed ships, and the white town lay below them, distant, flat, serene. There was upon this vista a peace that a bird knows when, high in the air, it surveys the world, a great, calm thing rolling noiselessly toward the end of the mystery. Here on the height one felt the existence of the universe scornfully defining the pain in ten thousand minds. The sky was an arch of stolid sapphire. Even to the mountains raising their mighty shapes from the valley, this headlong rush of fugitives was too minute. The sea, the sky, and the hills combined in their grandeur to term this misery inconsequent. Then, too, it sometimes happened that a face seen as it passed on the flood reflected curiously the spirit of them all, and still more. One saw then a woman of the opinion of the vaults above the clouds. When a child cried it cried always because of some adjacent misfortune, some discomfort of a pack-saddle or rudeness of an encircling arm.

There is here a radical—an absurd—dichotomy between the human creature and the natural universe, a dichotomy which, if it is to be bridged, must be bridged by means of an individual human understanding. Peza, who like Crane has formulated the purpose of apprehending and perhaps even interpreting, stands somewhere between these two possibilities, in the position in which that individual human understanding is possible. Peza is an intellectual, and the objectivity of his apprehension separates him from the fleeing peasants just as distance separates him from the warring soldiers.[20] His purpose is to diminish that distance without losing the objectivity of his apprehension. Crane's purpose is to test whether such an undertaking is possible.

Peza's movement toward confrontation involves the shortening of emotional as well as physical distance. Yet, as he

moves to the top of the first hill in the first stage of his progress to the crest of the mountain and to his confrontation
with the actuality of war itself; he has as his Virgil in this
Dantesque journey an officer whose experience, restraint, and
limits of vision contrast sharply with Peza's innocence, enthusiasm, and ambition for full understanding.[21] The officer
is "quiet and confident, respecting fate, fearing only opinion,"
while Peza's observation soon turns to sympathy, and his
desire to apprehend soon becomes a search for actual participation. The officer, whose dust-covered uniform contrasts
with Peza's freshly new clothing, attempts to restrain the
correspondent, even to warn at one point that "there is no
time for this" as Peza's sympathy overflows. Soon, however,
Peza has left his companion behind and gone on from the
artillery positions on the plain to a mountain howitzer position and finally to the infantry and their line of battle atop
the mountain.

Peza has, of course, set out to see war, and throughout
his progress up the mountain everything is presented in the
language of seeing. The reader's attention is constantly called
to characters' eyes—to the "flash of eyes" of the lieutenant,
to the fact that Peza's "eyes glistened." Battle wounds are
seen in ironic contrast to the illustrated instructions printed
on the cloth provided to bind them. Shifts in perspective
are meticulously recorded, as Peza occasionally pauses in his
ascent to observe the panorama of battle.

As Peza moves up the mountain, however, "the full lens
of his mind" is exposed to a number of obstacles to vision.
One, of course, is the simple satiation of sight. He recognizes
that the experience of seeing the battle is similar to that of
the visual satiation one sometimes encounters after too long
in a picture gallery, and, as he lights a passing soldier's cigarette, he recognizes in the soldier's eyes the same satiation.

And the experience of battle brings with it another limitation, a limitation not unlike that of the lieutenant—or of the peasants fleeing down the mountain. For Peza also soon becomes aware that "his whole vision was focussed upon his own chance." Another obstacle is, of course, the artificial order which participants always impose upon the natural chaos of battle; this is perhaps best symbolized by the rituals of military conduct, which are often described in Crane's story. When the lieutenant, Peza's guide, leaves the correspondent, "they bowed punctiliously, staring at each other with civil eyes," and, when Peza then climbs farther up the mountain, he comes upon an artillery unit whose conduct is extremely formalized and mannerly. Come to "look this phenomenon [war] in the face," Peza continually finds his apprehension blocked by the formal manners of professional soldiers.

The obscuring rituals are lessened as Peza climbs to the even higher infantry position. But now these obstacles are replaced by another, by something within Peza himself—his own animal fear. At the top of the mountain he finally has his opportunity to confront and to apprehend the actual hand-to-hand fighting. As he approaches, he first behaves in a courageous, even reckless manner. He sees an attack forming and runs along the crest of the mountain to meet it ("it was incredible recklessness thus to call to himself the stare of thousands of hateful eyes"). When he finally arrives at the Greek infantry position, he is given an opportunity to join in the fight. But before he begins to participate, he must confront directly that necessary ingredient—indeed that essence —of war which Crane himself had confronted in the body of the Greek soldier. Peza is told to equip himself by removing the bandoleer from a corpse, but when he turns to this ultimate confrontation, this touching of death itself, he falters. He is frozen with fear, is unable even to remove the blanket which covers the corpse. A soldier must retrieve the needed equipment for him.*

Peza masters his fear for a moment and dons the bandoleer, but then an experience—more intense even than sight—seizes Peza's imagination, and, in one of Crane's most grotesquely rendered passages, the reader sees Peza completely immobilized by an audio-tactile fantasy.

> Peza, having crossed the long cartridge-belt on his breast, felt that the dead man had flung his two arms around him.
>
> A soldier with a polite nod and smile gave Peza a rifle, a relic of another dead man. Thus, he felt, besides the clutch of a corpse about his neck, that the rifle was as inhumanly horrible as a snake that lives in a tomb. He heard at his ear something that was in effect like the voices of those two dead men, their low voices speaking to him of bloody death, mutilation. The bandoleer gripped him tighter; he wished to raise his hands to his throat, like a man who is choking. The rifle was clammy; upon his palms he felt the movement of the sluggish currents of a serpent's life; it was crawling and frightful.
>
> *Virginia*, V, 138-39

Again the quality of Peza's apprehension is established by contrast with that of his companions, whose experience at that moment, far from being fantastic, is very real, very comradely, and even very gustatory.

> All about him were these peasants, with their interested countenances, gibbering of the fight. From time to time a soldier cried out in semi-humorous lamentations descriptive of his thirst. One bearded man sat munching a great bit of hard bread. Fat, greasy, squat, he sat like an idol made of tallow. Peza felt dimly that

* This ultimate confrontation would be later developed in Crane's final war story, "The Upturned Face."

there was a distinction between this man and a young student who could write sonnets and play the piano quite well. The old blockhead was coolly gnawing at the bread, while he, Peza, was being throttled by a dead man's arms.

He looked behind him, and saw that a head by some chance had been uncovered from the blanket. Two liquid-like eyes were staring into his face. The head was turned a little sideways as if to get a better opportunity for scrutiny. Peza could feel himself blanch; he was being drawn and drawn by these dead men slowly, firmly down as to some mystic chamber under the earth where they could walk, dreadful figures, swollen and blood-marked. He was bidden; they had commanded him; he was going, going, going.

Here the corner of Peza's war experience is turned. Now, failing in the attempt to participate and to objectify, he withdraws from participation and apprehension, away from present actuality and into the isolation of his terrifying private fantasy. As that fantasy—in all its synaesthetic horror—overpowers Peza and obliterates his sense of reality, and as point of view is simultaneously shifted, the narrative voice reports that the correspondent bolts and runs. The final image of the section establishes another isolating fact, another difference between Peza's way of seeing and that of the other men. "The soldier with the bread placed it carefully on the paper beside him as he turned to kneel in the trench."

Crane's conclusion to "Death and the Child," although somewhat clumsily handled, is to my mind not "sentimental," as Stallman and other critics have suggested.[22] Rather, by virtue of its ending, "Death and the Child" becomes profoundly tragic. In the final section, Crane employed a rather innocent and unconditioned point of view, a point of view rather gratuitously and intrusively established earlier in the story, to set the terms of Peza's tragedy. Earlier, Crane had

described a child, left behind by its refugee parents and playing on the top of the mountain and within hearing distance
of the battle. Now the child is used as a point of view to
describe what happened to Peza and to voice a compellingly
and dramatically ironic question.

> The child heard a rattle of loose stones on the hill-
> side, and facing the sound, saw a moment later a man
> drag himself up to the crest of the hill and fall panting.
> Forgetting his mother and his hunger, filled with calm
> interest, the child walked forward, and stood over the
> heaving form. His eyes, too, were now large and in-
> scrutably wise and sad. . . .
> After a silence, he spoke inquiringly. "Are you a
> man?"
> Peza rolled over quickly and gazed up into the fear-
> less and cherubic countenance. He did not attempt to
> reply. He breathed as if life was about to leave his body.
> He was covered with dust; his face had been cut in some
> way, and his cheek was ribboned with blood. All the
> spick of his former appearance had vanished in a gen-
> eral dishevelment, in which he resembled a creature
> that had been flung to and fro, up and down, by cliffs
> and prairies during an earthquake. He rolled his eyes
> glassily at the child.
> They remained thus until the child repeated the
> words "Are you a man?"
> Peza gasped in the manner of a fish.

Like Harry of Ernest Hemingway's "The Snows of Kilimanjaro," Peza has come to the top of the mountain.* Here
he has confronted, in a child's innocent question, the fact of
his own dehumanization, the result of the experience he him-

---

* Peza's mountain, however, is either entirely imagined or is relocated by
Crane. The village of Velestinon lies on an inland plain and has only a few
low, unpopulated hills in its immediate vicinity. The opening scene of
Crane's story is rather clearly a representation of peasants fleeing from the
villages on the slopes of Mt. Pelion, on the outskirts of Volos and thus
some eighteen kilometers from Velestinon. Pelion, however, is the mountain
nearest to Velestinon.

self had sought. For Peza's sensibility, so acute at the beginning of the story, has been violated precisely because of its responsiveness. Now Peza, fish-like, is hardly more aware than were the animal-like peasants of the story's opening paragraph.

One of Crane's more perceptive recent critics, Eric Solomon, sees "Death and the Child" as a mockery of the intellectual, but to me Crane's awareness here is profoundly more negative than that. For it is Peza's very capacity to apprehend which has defeated and dehumanized him. And, although Crane was to see many more battles and to write of them in his few remaining years, he would describe no more keen sensibilities on his battlefields. For, with the muddled exception of his Greek war novel, *Active Service*, Crane's heroes in his remaining war stories would henceforth be seasoned and stoical veterans.[23]

I shall consider *Active Service* only briefly, and the book deserves little more than that. It was ill-conceived from the very beginning, and difficult for Crane to write (he began it in late 1897 and did not finish it until May of 1899). When he had finally completed it, he was dissatisfied with the result ("I wish it were a better novel," he wrote).[24]

Unfortunately, the author's judgment of *Active Service* was correct. Crane had never learned to construct a novel dealing with more than one developing character, nor had he learned to sustain the development of the complexities of an individual character over extended space. Thus, though *Active Servce* is less fragmentary than *The Third Violet*, its characters remain only types—the rigid professor, his vindictive wife, his innocent daughter, the rich student, the rascally servant. Even Rufus Coleman, the correspondent-hero, is a bit too mechanical and rather unbelievably devoid of feeling, and only his relationship with Nora Black, the most interesting character in the book, strikes any fire.[25]

Certainly another important problem in the novel lies in its inconsistency of tone. Or perhaps the problem lies in the fact that, after "Death and the Child," any novel in which Crane undertook to deal with the awful reality of his experience in the Greek war must almost inevitably be conducted from the distance of parody. Eric Solomon has capably demonstrated how *Active Service* begins as a skillful parody of the love and adventure story. The absurd plot, the marvelously sardonic, almost Nathaniel Westian, account of the journalists and the baby without arms, the caricature of Hearst, Rufus Coleman's awareness of his role—all are elements in this parody.[26] But after this parody is established, after the absurdity of the plot is revealed and the seriousness of the characters is deflated, Crane confronted the problem critical to the successful execution of the parodic novel: What does one do after the parody is established at the expense of believability? It is a problem Crane never successfully solved; his other parodic novel, *The O'Ruddy*, was unfinished at his death. In *Active Service* the problem forced Crane to alter his posture in relation to the novel. In the end, *Active Service* becomes the very thing its first chapters have ridiculed.

Perhaps the real problem lies in the novel's subject. The *Times Literary Supplement* has said that *Active Service* "fails because it tries to go beyond war."[27] Certainly this is unfair to Crane, but if one recognizes the remarkable autobiographical elements in the novel which Stallman has identified,[28] it is apparent that *Active Service* isn't about a confrontation with war at all, but about two love relationships. In fact, at its center, the novel seems to dramatize some unresolved conflicts in Crane's own relationships—with Cora, for example. In the novel, Nora Black's advances are successfully resisted by the correspondent, who prefers an innocent college girl. Indeed, *Active Service* seems to lead Crane, who could never successfully write a love story anyway, into areas of private conflict from which almost any writer would willingly retreat.

Yet there is one moment in the novel in which Crane—perhaps returning one last time to that corpse on the battlefield at Velestinon—does clearly expose his own response. It comes when the novel's newspaperman-protagonist himself confronts the actuality of battlefield death.

> They [the newspaperman Coleman, his dragoman, and his carriers] finally came up with one of these black bodies of men and found it to be composed of a considerable number of soldiers who were idly watching some hospital people bury a dead Turk. The dragoman at once dashed forward to peer through the throng and see the face of the corpse. Then he came and supplicated Coleman as if he were hawking him to look at a relic and Coleman, moved by a strong, mysterious impulse, went forward to look at the poor little clay-covered body. At that moment a snake ran out from a tuft of grass at his feet and wriggled wildly over the sod. The dragoman shrieked, of course, but one of the soldiers put his heel upon the head of the reptile and it flung itself into the agonizing knot of death. Then the whole crowd pow-wowed, turning from the dead man to the dead snake. Coleman signalled his contingent and proceeded along the road.
>
> *Novels,* 472

A passage like this certainly does not belong in a parodic or a satiric novel. But it does reveal, in its muted grotesquerie, just how far Crane's attitude toward war had come by 1899. If one remembers "The Snake," Crane's little description of an instinctive killing written several years earlier, one can guess at Crane's purpose here. For here snake and Turk (and even Greek) are interchangeable; war is only an instinctive killing, conducted and then marveled at by a gawking crowd. For the sensitive man, for a man very much like Crane himself, there is only one possible response. From this intolerable reality he can only turn away.*

Crane had gone to Greece to find out whether *The Red Badge of Courage* was "all right" and had found it to be so. But there he had also found out something of the monstrous actuality of war, and he had also begun to find out something of the inability of sensitive men to tolerate even the apprehension of that actuality. And, perhaps most important, Crane found out what happened when they really tried.

---

* In "The Upturned Face," Crane's great final war story, the only thing to do with a battle corpse is—with appropriate ritual—to cover it with dirt.

X
Past and Present: Whilomville and London

I have tried to observe closely, and to set down what I have seen in the simplest and most concise way.

Stephen Crane in a letter to
DeMorest's Family Magazine, 1896

In the final three years of his career Stephen Crane produced material diverse in subject, in genre, and in quality. There was one period of intense creativity—between his returning to England from Greece to settle in Limpsfield in June of 1897, and his setting out for Cuba in April of the following year. Perhaps for Crane it was a final period of unqualified commitment to his art. The period may have begun with the recognitions after his dark night at sea and after his day on the battlefield in Greece; it would have ended with the violations to the eye, sensibility, and body which were to be his lot in America's "splendid little war" in Cuba. In any event, in the months between Greece and Cuba Crane wrote "The Blue Hotel," "The Bride Comes to Yellow Sky," "Death and the Child," "The Monster"—in fact, most of the short stories for which he is today remembered. After Cuba, and his curious withdrawal to Havana which followed his final war experience, Crane returned to England and took up residence at Brede Place. Now again there was much writing, but too much of it was hurried and of little literary significance. Appropriately, one of the finest of these later stories was "The Upturned Face."

Throughout the final years, however, and from 1897 until the end, Crane's imagination remained committed to the three subjects which he had previously explored. In writing out of the early memories of his own communal experiences, he considered man's apprehension of his fellows and how man's associations altered that apprehension. In his memories of the American West and of his own experiences there, Crane found contrasts in the way of seeing things which were the results of oppositions of cultures, and he also discovered stories which embodied man's fundamental problems in apprehending his world. When he came again to experience and to write of man at war, Crane explored the individual's confrontation with the absolutes of life and death. Because of the diverse nature of his writings in these final years, I shall consider his work in a sequence determined by his choice of subject. Here I shall consider how Stephen Crane —after his experience in Greece—first returned in his fiction to the locus of his childhood to find the material to embody in fiction his reinforced sense of the inadequacies of man's vision and the distortions imposed on that vision by the pressures of man's own fragile communities.

After he moved to England, Crane reported his own apprehensions of his new environment in a number of newspaper and magazine sketches before he settled down again to writing fiction. Many of these pieces were reminiscent of the early New York sketches of 1893 and 1894, and yet there was a difference. The author of *The Red Badge of Courage* was by now quite well known on both sides of the Atlantic, so he was able to write very much the kind of journalism he wished to write, to address himself to those subjects which interested him, and to be free of the pressures and competitions which he had experienced in Greece. The journalistic pieces which he produced in the early months of his stay in England gave good evidence of his movement away from the conventions of journalism to a more radical impressionism in which his new concerns were apparent. For now it was not with the innocent eyes of a Bowery girl that he confronted reality, but with his own. Now Crane's concern with the event of apprehension became even more intense, and he approached it with less distance and with a considerably diminished and altered irony.

The first of Crane's English sketches was familiarly ironic. It was written just after his first visit to England and on his way to Greece, and it concerns that aspect of the English which perhaps most startles the American on his first visit— the English use of the English language. The English slang word *bounder* and its curious ambiguity of meaning are the subjects of Crane's ironically hyperbolic piece. Perhaps it is not so much a word as a subtlety of apprehension on the part of its users—an apprehension which is unavailable to the uninitiated and is thus unavailable to Crane himself—which is the subject in "New Invasions of Britain." "Good slang is subtle and elusive. If there is a quick equivalent for a phrase, it is not good slang, because good slang comes to fill a vacancy. It comes to cover some hole in the language. Hence it is not easy to find out about bounders"[1] (*Writings*, 247).

Later in the summer of 1897, after his return from the Greek war, Crane really began to describe his own confrontations in England. One sketch—perhaps partly Cora's—was "Fresh Bits of Gossip on European Affairs," in which, after his own tourist's praise of the beauties of Buckingham Palace gardens, Crane allows the point of view of two Scotswomen and their discussion of Queen Victoria's jubilee to deflate his own romanticism.[2] But more significant is "London Impressions," a set of sketches which appeared serially in three issues of Frank Harris' *Saturday Review* in July and August.[3]

"London Impressions" comprises eight reflections upon Crane's experience when he first arrived in the English city. In it he describes himself catching a cab at a railroad station, the cab ride to his hotel, the fall of the harnessed cab horse, its righting, his arrival at the hotel, his ascent in the elevator. And along the way Crane reflects on the top hat of the horse's rescuer, London street noise, and London billboards. But in the midst of this variety of impressions, a common theme is apparent. Throughout, Crane is concerned with the differences between expectations and apprehensions of reality.

In "London Impressions" again Crane is his own protagonist, an innocent abroad whose range of apprehension is sharply limited at first and gradually expands to a full and freshened vision. Again Crane was concerned with learning to be an apprehender if not an interpreter, but this time it is not the color of the sky which is unavailable at first; it is the reality of the city itself. "I was born in London at a railroad station, and my new vision encompassed a porter and a cabman. They deeply absorbed me in new phenomena, and I did not then care to see the Thames Embankment nor the Houses of Parliament. I considered the porter and the cabman to be more important" [4] (*Work*, XI, 131).

Throughout "London Impressions," and as his apprehension expands, Crane tests the reality before him against his previous experiences and expectations: the symbolic significance of a top hat in London as opposed to its significance in the American West, the unexpected slowness of the hotel elevator, the sounds of London, for which no illustrator had prepared him. And throughout, Crane reflects upon the capacities and conditions of his apprehension. It almost seems that at one moment in the piece—when Crane is describing himself in his cab in the London fog—he is at the same time representing his view of the human condition of apprehension, a view which has informed not only *The Red Badge of Courage* and "The Open Boat" but much of what he had written earlier and of what was to come.

> The cab finally rolled out of the gas-lit vault into a vast expanse of gloom. This changed to shadowy lines of a street that was like a passage in a monstrous cave. The lamps winking here and there resembled the little gleams at the caps of the miners. They were not very competent illuminations at best, merely being little pale flares of gas that at their most heroic periods could only display one fact concerning this tunnel—the fact of general direction. But at any rate I should have liked to observe the dejection of a searchlight if it had been called upon to attempt to bore through this atmosphere. In it each man sat in his own little cylinder of vision, so to speak. It was not so small as a sentry-box nor so large as a circus tent, but the walls were opaque, and what was passing beyond the dimensions of his cylinder no man knew.[5]

This unusual grotesque passage has a considerable impact, for Crane's reader has been constantly made aware of how often man finds himself within similar cylinders of vision, in situations in which one's way of seeing is determined and limited by one's position in time and space. In Crane's stories these situations, as Crane's syntactical echo of the dying Mercutio's speech in *Romeo and Juliet* would suggest here, are tragic, or, at least, can sometimes be mortally dangerous. Crane's prose writing presents the imperfection of innocence which must somehow be contested in an effort at seeing. "London Impressions" is inspired journalism and in many ways is more strikingly imagined than all but the finest of Crane's fiction.*

In August and September of 1897 Crane and Cora vacationed in Ireland with Harold Frederic and his wife.[6] The experiences of the trip were set down in several sketches. In the first, a *tour de force* of impressionism, Crane describes the passage of a locomotive from the Euston Station in London to Glasgow. "The Scotch Express" contains some remarkably vivid passages, and at least one—about the city of Glasgow—grotesquely suggests a social reality not unlike that of *Maggie* or of some of the New York sketches. "The flames of pauseless industries are here and there marked on the distance. Vast factories stand close to the track, and reaching chimneys emit roseate flames. At last one may see upon a wall the strong reflection from furnaces, and against it the impish and inky figures of workingmen. A long, prison-like row of tenements, not at all resembling London, but in one way resembling New York, appeared to the left, and then sank out of sight like a phantom"[7] (*Work*, XI, 164). But the social reality is not Crane's central subject in "The Scotch Express." Rather, he was concerned with apprehension, with seeing at a speed of sixty-five miles an hour (which is brilliantly dramatized throughout), with apprehension superimposing memory. "The Scotch Express" closes in the Glasgow station. "The porters and the people crowded forward. In their minds there may have floated dim images of the traditional music-halls, the bobbies, the 'buses, the 'Arrys and 'Arriets, the swells of London" (*Work*, XI, 165).

---

* Crane tried to revitalize the inspiration early the next year in a sketch of a theatre queue being entertained by itinerant performers. The moment described in "At the Pit Door," just before entrance, is reminiscent of "The Men in the Storm," and the sketch does seem to represent Crane's only attempt to infuse a London sketch with social meaning. But the result is only flatly descriptive and strikes little fire. See *Writings*, 444–47.

Out of his experiences in Ireland came a sequence of five sketches published in the *Westminster Gazette* in October.[3] These "Irish Notes" are essentially travel writing. The first, "Queenstown," which records Crane's arrival in the wet and foggy port city (now known as Cork) is in its opening again rather reminiscent of one of Whistler's impressionistic portscapes, and the remaining four ("Ballydehob," "The Royal Irish Constabulary," "An Old Man Goes Wooing," and "A Fishing Village") employ strikingly impressionistic renderings in describing life and work in the Irish villages near where the Cranes and the Frederics spent their holiday.

> The melancholy fisherman made his way through a street that was mainly as dark as a tunnel. Sometimes an open door threw a rectangle of light upon the pavement, and within the cottages were scenes of working women and men, who comfortably smoked and talked. From them came the sounds of laughter and the babble of children. Each time the old man passed through one of the radiant zones the light etched his face in profile with touches flaming and sombre, until there was a resemblance to a stern and mournful Dante portrait.*
>
> *Work*, XI, 176 (from "An Old Man Goes Wooing")

But again Crane's interest was not purely descriptive; everywhere in "Irish Notes" the interest is engaged in the way the Irish see. In "Queenstown" Crane was concerned— as he was in "The Blue Hotel"—with how the social isolation of a constable affects his apprehension. "A separated people will beget an egotism that is almost titanic. A world floating distinctly in space will call itself the only world. The progression is perfect" (*Work*, XI, 174). And in "A Fishing Vil-

---

* Again, what at first seems to be pure impressionism has upon closer reading a grotesque and symbolic quality. For as the sketch develops, one surmises that the "tunnel" of the fisherman suggests something of the limitations of his apprehensional world, and "Dante" suggests something of its hellish quality.

lage" Crane dramatized those events which occur both outside and inside the mind of a young fisherman to bring him
to the decision to emigrate. It is always what and how an
Irishman sees which fascinated Crane, and thus in "Ballydehob" he praised the Irish apprehension. "For amid his
wrongs and his rights and his failures—his colossal failures—
the Irishman retains this deliberate blade for his enemies,
for his friends, for himself, the ancestral dagger of fast sharp
speaking from fast sharp seeing—an inheritance which could
move the world" (*Work*, XI, 170–71). It is just these qualities
with which Crane was to characterize his rollicking Irish hero
in *The O'Ruddy*, the satiric romance which Crane left unfinished and which Robert Barr completed after Crane's
death.[9]

There were two other English stories, both written at Brede
Place in Crane's final year. One of them—"Manacled"—is a
nightmarish account of an actor who is left chained on stage
in a theatre fire. The story is probably—as Stallman asserts—a
record of a nightmare of unusual emotional impact.* In
"Manacled" Crane employed much of the same kind of
grotesque fire imagery which he had used earlier (and
which I shall soon consider) in "The Monster." Language
like "he heard the hum of flames" and "beautiful flames
flashed above him; some were crimson, some were orange, and
here and there were tongues of purple, blue, green," and the
reported fact that just before unconsciousness the chained
actor "felt very cool, delightfully cool" show Crane going to
extreme lengths in grotesque rendering to achieve dramatically impressionistic effects.[10] Or perhaps Crane's impressionism is really not that at all but something quite beyond it.
For Crane's dream, and the impact it had upon him, and

* Stallman reports that the story was written after a small domestic
fire, and that before writing "Manacled" Crane had himself chained to see
how it felt. See Stallman, 470.

the story in which the dream is rendered may all be accounted for by his own ambiguous attitudes toward Brede
Place and his extravagant life there. "Manacled" can thus
be read as an expressionistic fantasy which is indeed a far
cry from the social realism of 1894.

"The Squire's Madness," Crane's other Brede Place story,
is also founded in fantasy,[11] but this time not so vividly
rendered. The protagonist is a wealthy poet, the heir of
"Oldrestham Hall," who has returned after ten years "of
incomprehensible wandering" with his wife (again the story
is founded in parody—this time of gothic romance). He
is first seen in his study and at work on a rather Keatsian
ballad.

> The garlands of her hair are snakes;
> Black and bitter are her hating eyes.
> A cry the windy death-hall makes—
> O, love, deliver us.
> The flung cup rolls to her sandal's tip;
> His arm—
>
> *Stories and Sketches*, 774–75

But Linton, Crane's protagonist, is interrupted—at the moment when his imagination has also run dry—by his wife,
who vigorously insists upon the fact that her husband is ill.

In view of Crane's own situation and the progress of his
own illness* at the time of writing it, "The Squire's Madness" is rather ominous indeed. Again it seems that Crane's
intentions might well have been expressionistic, that the story
was to be a rendering and embodiment of his own anxieties.
Unfortunately, however, these intentions must remain un-
clarified, since he never finished the story. Cora finished it;
she later explained that she had " 'conceived' the finish." [12]
And her completion—in which an eminent London brain

* "The Squire's Madness"—Crane's part of it—was written early in
1900, after Crane's first hemorrhage. See Stallman, 446.

specialist reports to Linton that " '*It is your Wife who is Mad! Mad as a Hatter!*' " (*Stories and Sketches*, 779) — reduces the story from the complex ironies of Crane's parodic expressionism to flat if rather Thurberesque farce.

The locus of the Irish sketches is an Irish town as undistinguished as Maggie's tenement. But while Crane was in Ireland in September of 1897, he was completing a novelette set in a location partly imagined and partly wished for—the place where Crane was "from," the locus of his memory.[18] Whilomville, the name Crane assigned his Port Jervis, is the setting for "The Monster" and would remain a fertile ground for a number of curiously realistic stories which Crane would continue to produce until only a few months before his death.

All three of Crane's major biographers—Thomas Beer, John Berryman, and R. W. Stallman—have set forth historical sources for the events and characters in "The Monster" and in the other stories of Whilomville. Yet many of these assertions remain unsupported and conjectural. What is perhaps more important is the degree to which these stories are imagined rather than remembered. Whilomville is not a setting for a local colorist but an idealized setting in which characters are as free as possible to determine their own way of seeing—free, at least, of the economic, and natural, and psychic determinants which shape the apprehensions of Maggie, and the correspondent, and Peza.

Yet in spite of this freedom, "The Monster" embodies for Crane a considerably darkened and inward-turned vision. For "The Monster," the story of ostracism in the American small town of Crane's memory, is, in part, a reenactment of the real expatriation to which Crane had himself been driven after the Dora Clark affair and the imagined ostracism which he and Cora would necessarily expect from a Port

Jervis or a Hartwood.[14] But "The Monster" is also the story of a compelled confrontation, and unlike *The Red Badge of Courage* or "The Open Boat," this confrontation, and the knowledge to be gained from it, leads not to community but away from it. Here confrontation leads to madness, and knowledge leads to isolation.

Crane's intentions in "The Monster" are in part disclosed by its remarkable similarity to Henrik Ibsen's *An Enemy of the People.* William Dean Howells, Crane's former mentor, had called the American public's attention to Ibsen in 1891, and Beerbohm Tree had presented *An Enemy of the People* in London in 1893 and in the United States in the spring of 1895. The reaction (both in the theatre and in the press) had been sharp, so Crane probably knew the play. Crane's story, like Ibsen's drama, is about a doctor who is ostracized by his community for a socially responsible act. In both works the doctors' families and practices suffer. In both there appear poignant scenes showing the absence of expected guests, and distinguished citizens excuse their conduct by invoking the pressures of public opinion. Crane's Judge Denning Hagenthorpe, the bachelor leader of Whilomville, is an echo of Ibsen's bachelor, Peter Stockmann.[15]

Crane's style in "The Monster" seems affected by his awareness of Isben's dramatic writing. The prose is more "normal," less colorful, and less color-charged than in the earlier work.[16] Unlike the earlier stories, narrative viewpoint is not so important. "The Monster" is developed dramatically, with plot and action realized in carefully arranged scenes.[17] Yet there is at least one scene which is as far from Ibsenian realism as it is possible to be. That is Crane's remarkably grotesque representation of that moment in which Henry Johnson, the Negro hostler, who has entered the burning house to save Dr. Trescott's son, Jimmie, falls and receives the chemical burn which destroys his face.

Johnson halted for a moment on the threshold. He cried out again in the negro wail that had in it the sadness of the swamps. Then he rushed across the room. An orange-colored flame leaped like a panther at the lavender trousers. This animal bit deeply into Johnson. There was an explosion at one side, and suddenly before him there reared a delicate, trembling sapphire shape like a fairy lady. With a quiet smile she blocked his path and doomed him and Jimmie. Johnson shrieked, and then ducked in the manner of his race in fights. He aimed to pass under the left guard of the sapphire lady. But she was swifter than eagles, and her talons caught in him as he plunged past her. Bowing his head as if his neck had been struck, Johnson lurched forward, twisting this way and that way. He fell on his back. The still form in the blanket flung from his arms, rolled to the edge of the floor and beneath the window.

Johnson had fallen with his head at the base of an old-fashioned desk. There was a row of jars upon the top of this desk. For the most part, they were silent amid this rioting, but there was one which seemed to hold a scintillant and writhing serpent.

Suddenly the glass splintered, and a ruby-red snakelike thing poured its thick length out upon the top of the old desk. It coiled and hesitated, and then began to swim a languorous way down the mahogany slant. At the angle it waved its sizzling molten head to and fro over the closed eyes of the man beneath it. Then, in a moment, with mystic impulse, it moved again, and the red snake flowed directly down into Johnson's upturned face.

Afterward the trail of this creature seemed to reek, and amid flames and low explosions drops like red-hot jewels pattered softly down it at leisurely intervals.

Virginia, VII, 24

Here is, indeed, "realism with a difference." [18]

Fire had been a subject for Crane as early as 1894, when he composed—purely from his own imagination—a "report" of a tenement house fire.[19] In 1896 in "The Veteran"

Henry Fleming perishes in an attempt to save some colts in a barn fire, and two years after "The Monster," "Manacled," which we have already seen, was to be a record of a nightmarish fire. Apparently the event of fire was associated in Crane's mind with some threatening and chaotic principle of the universe. In any event, fire was in Crane's work one of those recurring symbols—like war and its deaths, like the sea and its indifference. Fire is threatening to man, yet it is a destructive principle which man must confront. Like Henry Fleming, whose final (and perhaps, apotheosizing) confrontation is fiery, his namesake's, Henry Johnson's, confrontation with fire disfigures and maddens him.* Jimmie, who also is face to face with the fire, escapes unscathed and remains innocent.

For it is neither Jimmie nor Henry who must take responsibility for acknowledging the fire's existence and for coming to terms with its effects. Jimmie is "only a child," though his innocent imagination is destructive from the very first. In the opening scene the boy, playing railroad, destroys a peony. After the fire, his innocence becomes cruelty, as is apparent when Jimmie, at the head of a mob of boys, teases the disfigured Henry. Yet Crane was aware that in the American town childish innocence—no matter how destructive or cruel—is always permitted.

Henry Johnson is no child, rather an adult Negro. As Crane (and Ralph Ellison) was fully aware, he is an "invisible man," denied a real identity by the people of Whilomville.[20] Crane's representation of Henry's minstrel-

---

* It is interesting to note that the name Henry Johnson is composed, perhaps, from Henry Fleming's and Maggie Johnson's names. Or, perhaps, from Johnson Smith, an alteration or misspelling of Johnston Smith, Crane's pseudonym in the 1893 *Maggie*. See Stallman, 69; Katz, *Maggie*, xv–xvi; Levenson, *Virginia*, VII, p. xxii; Berryman, 194. Or perhaps, as Berryman and Levenson also suggest in their discussions, if "Jimmie Johnson" is really the name imagined by Crane as that of his alter ego, his identity is divided between the unmarked Jimmie and the disfigured Johnson.

esque walk about the town in his lavender trousers and straw hat with bright silk band and his being mistaken for a Pullman porter would suggest something of the way a Negro is denied identity by his fellow townspeople and even collaborates in that denial. But when the fire—the disordering and disclosing principle—burns away that Negro's face, the embodiment of the identity which Henry is already denied, the townspeople refuse to look. For that facelessness is at once the symbol of their denial and a tribute to the disorder which they have refused to acknowledge in their universe. The center of the horror is what it would disclose to the observer about himself.

It is Judge Hagenthorpe who is the first to refuse to see the monstrous Henry. And what he avoids is the horror of being stared at by Henry's unblinking eye. "On the second floor he entered a room where Doctor Trescott was working about the bedside of Henry Johnson. The bandages on the negro's head allowed only one thing to appear, an eye, which unwinkingly stared at the judge. The latter spoke to Trescott on the condition of the patient. Afterward he evidently had something further to say, but he seemed to be kept from it by the scrutiny of the unwinking eye, at which he furtively glanced from time to time" * (*Virginia*, VII, 31). And other of Whilomville's townspeople are terrified and offended by the very appearance of the monster. Usually they are able to avoid him, but occasionally he appears, and his appearance wreaks havoc in the community. Dr. Trescott is held responsible, and loses a patient when Henry frightens a little girl at a birthday party. "Hearing a noise behind her at the window, one little girl turned to face it. Instantly she screamed and sprang away, covering her face with her hands"

* Here Crane restates and dramatizes the horror implicit in the child's chant which has just preceded it. "Nigger, nigger, never die, / Black face and shiny eye" (*Virginia*, VII, 30).

(*Virginia*, VII, 45). Another glimpse of Henry brings disorder, ironically enough even to Watermelon Alley: "She
shielded her eyes with her arms and tried to crawl past it,
but the genial monster blocked the way" (*Virginia*, VII, 47).

Now a monster, Henry embodies the social reality to
which the fire is the equivalent natural fact. And the community of Whilomville cannot allow this manifest and
monstrous facelessness to exist.* First Henry's death is announced in the newspapers. Then the community's leaders
demand that he be sent "somewhere off up in the valley."
Henry himself, his brain damaged by his wound, cooperates
in ignoring the fact of his facelessness and going "courting"
and grotesquely and unconsciously thereby parodying the
hypocritical social relationships dramatized in his earlier
evening walk. Given this situation, Henry's humanity, his
sexual identity, must at all costs be denied ("Was it a man?
She didn't know. It was simply a thing, a dreadful thing."),
and in this Crane ironically cooperates by calling the monster
"it." Given these denials, of course, Henry ceases even to be a
character, and ceases thereby to bear any responsibility for
acknowledgment of the reality he has confronted.

There is, however, one character who by circumstance is
compelled to acknowledge the humanity of this Negro, his
facelessness, and the social and natural facts which it con-
firms. And this is Dr. Trescott, who is "free, white, and
twenty-one" and in every sense fully responsible. He is thus,
by a kind of default, Crane's protagonist in "The Monster."
It is he who acknowledges his debt to Henry, the saver of his
son and a servant-member of his household; he uses his
medical skills to save Henry's life, finds Henry a home, and,
when all else fails, receives the crazed and disfigured Negro

---

* It is interesting to compare Crane's only description of the monstrousness
of Henry—"He now had no face"—to Melville's description of his white
whale—"I say again he has no face."

again into his household. Dr. Trescott, in short, acknowledges both Henry's humanity and the irrational horror of which Henry's disfigurement is the result. And, like Ibsen's Dr. Stockmann, social ostracism and isolation are the rewards for his unblinking apprehension. When the doctor resists community pressure to remove from its presence this "out of the ordinary" "thing," his practice declines and his wife is subjected to rebuff. After several representations of these facts, Crane concludes the story with an impressionist's irony in a scene which dramatizes in a single image the empty loneliness of the Trescotts' life in Whilomville.

> "Why—didn't Anna Hagenthorpe come over?"
> The mumble from his shoulder continued, "She wasn't well enough."
> Glancing down at the cups, Trescott mechanically counted them. There were fifteen of them. "There, there," he said. "Don't cry, Grace. Don't cry."
> The wind was whining around the house and the snow beat aslant upon the windows. Sometimes the coal in the stove settled with a crumbling sound, and the four panes of mica flushed a sudden new crimson. As he sat holding her head on his shoulder, Trescott found himself occasionally trying to count the cups. There were fifteen of them.
>
> *Virginia*, VII, 64–65

It is not, however, only Jimmie's and Henry's confrontations and Dr. Trescott's tenacious apprehension which are important. For throughout "The Monster" Crane was concerned with the varying refusals and inabilities of vision and understanding in Whilomville's townspeople. In "The Monster" Crane calls our attention repeatedly and ironically to the technology of seeing—to "the shimmering blue of the electric arc-lamps" on the main street, for instance. There is the spectacle of the fire at Dr. Trescott's and the excitement of the crowd, whose vision is always less than accurate, whose delusions are always ironically apparent. "But a great rumor went among the crowds. It was told with hushed voices. Afterward a reverent silence fell even upon the boys. Jimmie Trescott and Henry Johnson had been burned to death, and Doctor Trescott himself had been most savagely hurt. The crowd did not even feel the police pushing at them. They raised their eyes, shining now with awe, toward the high flames" (*Virginia*, VII, 28). Then immediately the reader learns of the crowd's exchanges of rumors and discovers how the observers have misapprehended what they have seen.

After the accident which renders Henry monstrous, the town is less willing to look. The heroic Negro, mindless as well as faceless, soon ceases to be a character and comes to be only a visual affront to the community. After the fire, Henry is presented only when he is being observed by one of the townspeople. After Dr. Trescott, Judge Hagenthorpe is the first to see the monstrous Henry, but his lawyer's mind, which refuses the absurd reality which the fire embodies, must refuse this evidence of its destructive existence as well; the judge questions the propriety of the doctor's saving Henry and is soon in the vanguard of those who would have Henry sent away.

Some of the citizens of Whilomville make tentative efforts to come to terms with the human suffering before them. Reifsnyder, the barber, and one of his patrons consider the doctor's problem and Henry's agony.

> "Supposing you were in his place," said one, "and Johnson had saved your kid. What would you do?"
> "Certainly!"
> "Of course! You would do anything on earth for him. You'd take all the trouble in the world for him. And spend your last dollar on him. Well, then?"

"I wonder how it feels to be without any face?" said Reifsnyder, musingly.

Virginia, VII, 41

As a number of critics have pointed out, Martha Goodwin, the town gossip, is modeled upon a Port Jervis lady for whom Crane had apparently conceived a passionate and permanent dislike. Martha, "the mausoleum of a dead passion," is certainly despised by Crane, as is "the grave of a stale lust" about whom he had written in a letter from Port Jervis.[21] And yet, ironically, it is Martha Goodwin, who, in her perverse effort to belittle her companions, on one occasion defends Dr. Trescott.[22]

The children of Whilomville, their imaginations less insulated, make tentative attempts at approaching the disfigured Henry, but again their confrontation is for wrong reasons. It is on a dare that Jimmie Trescott, who leads the group, who "bravely" approaches the now veiled monster, and Willie Dalzel, trapped in the dare himself, follows suit. Neither boy, concerned as each is for his reputation for courage, can really consider the thing which he has confronted. At the end there is only Dr. Trescott, who has seen the monster for what he is. And it is ironic to note—in the face of the acceptance which his still innocent boy has received for his boldness in the community of Whilomville children—how the doctor's much more courageous confrontation is rewarded.

In "The Monster" Crane has experimented with new implications to his concern and his pattern of action. In *The Red Badge*, "The Open Boat," and elsewhere a return to community follows the moment of confrontation. But for Dr. Trescott there is no return to community—only the emptiness of his teacups.[23] Now the pattern of action is truncated; the movement to isolation is one way only. And the community is more a source of delusion than a refuge.

Isolation, long an identifying condition for the protagonist of American fiction, is here a consequence of apprehension. In one sense Crane has taken his reader beyond Natty Bumpo or Hawthorne's Robin, even perhaps beyond Ethan Brand and Ahab, and to an American protagonist whose identifying condition is social and whose movement is toward, rather than away from, isolation. For in Crane's Dr. Trescott we approach Fitzgerald's Dick Diver, Ellison's Invisible Man, even Salinger's Seymour Glass.[24]

"The Monster" was to appear in a volume with "The Blue Hotel," and in the spring of the following year—on board the press boat en route to Cuba, and later in Havana —Crane wrote another Whilomville sketch, "His New Mittens," which would later be used to fill out the Harper's volume.[25] In "His New Mittens" Crane returned to his point of departure in "The Monster" and to a subject recreated from his own Port Jervis experiences—to Whilomville as experienced by a child. And his concern with this subject was an old one—"How environment shapes lives regardless," how the Whilomville of the child shapes the apprehension of the man.

"His New Mittens" turns upon the pattern of action discovered in *The Red Badge*. The story's child protagonist, who "runs away from home," makes an abortive escape from his family only to be returned at the end. But in the story Crane's newly darkened imagination provided his protagonist, Horace Glenn, with no moment of confrontation, no apprehension, no insight. For, as is evident from the very first, Horace's flight is an escape from the conflict between opposed authorities. On the one hand is a hierarchial community of children, which demands participation in fantasy games and enforces these demands with ridicule and a threat of ostracism. On the other are the equally strong assertions of Horace's mother, whose demands have moral authority, and who uses love and its deprivation (in the form of food) to achieve her results.

Thus, in his angry response to his mother's punishment for dirtying his mittens in a game required of him by his peers, Horace "runs away," but only into a storm, a storm of "blue snow" (like that in which the deluded Swede will find himself in "The Blue Hotel")—a storm in which anger and fear and an accustomed isolation keep his eyes turned toward the house he has left behind and make any kind of new apprehensional event impossible. "Evidently the storm had increased, for when he went out it swung him violently with its rough and merciless strength. Panting, stung, half-blinded with the driving flakes, he was now a waif, exiled, friendless, and poor. With a bursting heart, he thought of his home and his mother. To his forlorn vision they were as far away as Heaven" (*Virginia*, VII, 91).

So Horace returns home—by way of a butcher shop where Stickney, the family butcher, "was whistling cheerily and assorting his knives." He returns to the household of women and makes his surrender, he is received, and all is forgiven. As Horace is enfolded in his doting mother's arms, and as his aunt—rather ominously in light of the way nourishment has been used before[26]—offers root beer to the boy's rescuer, what Aunt Martha says of the root beer might well apply to the boy's capacity for apprehending his world—" 'We make it ourselves.' " For in Crane's ironically "happy" ending all is right again—except for Horace's capacity for autonomous apprehension of reality.

"His New Mittens" is not Crane's first study in the causes of the failures of the eye. But it opened for him a new approach to his subject. For after "The Monster" and "His New Mittens" Crane was constrained to examine in depth the shaping of the imagination by early environment. In subsequent stories he chose the available setting, Whilomville, and for his protagonist the child whose capacity for apprehension in "The Monster" was already severely blunted. Jimmie Trescott appears in all but one of the thirteen Whilomville stories which *Harper's* published in consecutive issues beginning in August of 1899.* And, although Jimmie is not always at the center of the action, the reader is always aware of his presence. For in Jimmie Trescott he is observing the growth, nurture, and shaping of an American delusion.

If Jimmie is important to the Whilomville stories, what is also important—and in all but two is the motive force for their central actions—is communal opinion. There are three communities in Whilomville, a white adult community, a community of children, and—only briefly seen—a community of Negroes. And in all three everything seems to turn upon individual acceptability to the group and individual status within it. In Whilomville parents adhere rigidly to the formal demands of their rituals; children fight or submit themselves to indignities in order to obtain acceptance by their peers. And in "The Knife," the one published story in the series in which Crane showed Negroes interacting with one another, living up to one's status and loyalty to race entirely determine conduct in crisis.[27] Such conduct is hardly to be regarded as fatuous, for in Whilomville acceptability is of real importance. As elsewhere in Crane's works, isolation—whatever else it may bring—is always dangerous. Whilomville's communities—whether child or adult—are savage to outsiders.

What is more important, however, is how these communities of Whilomville so rigidly enforce, not only patterns of behavior, but patterns of imagination upon their members. Throughout the Whilomville stories is recurring evidence of the banality and derivative nature of the imaginations of the town's child and adult citizenry. No one in Whilomville as-

* Crane wrote them between January and early November of 1899.

serts original fantasies or experiments with direct confrontations with reality or with new ways of seeing. Among Whilomville's children there are many Tom Sawyers, but there is
no Huck Finn.

In Crane's town even apprehensional experience in nature
is blunted by communal pressure. In "Lynx-Hunting" (the
first of the stories Crane wrote)[28] two youthful hunters are
so conditioned by their literary experiences that they set out
improbably after a lynx in the New York countryside. And
when they shoot Henry Fleming's cow by mistake, and lie
elaborately to protect themselves from the farmer's wrath,
a final admisssion that they had mistaken a cow for a lynx
brings only incredulous laughter—from, of all people, Henry
Fleming and a Swede. Jimmie Trescott and his friend live
in such an atmosphere of lies and derived fantasy that the
truth is strange and difficult to arrive at, and, once it is confronted, it is recognized neither by the boys who are too
afraid to see, nor by the adults, who no longer care.*

The Whilomville stories, however, are centrally concerned
with how distortions of apprehension are engendered and
enforced by a child's relationships with his peers and with
his parents. In "The Carriage-Lamps," after breaking car-
riage lamps and stoning Peter Washington, the Negro hostler who tells on him, Jimmie is confined to his room to await
his punishment. But he is fatuously forgiven by his father
when—in a travesty of what Crane considered the travestied
ending of *Huckleberry Finn*[29]—Dr. Trescott observes an
elaborately literary escape plot conceived by Jimmie's comrades in their effort to free their friend. If the story is somewhat overplotted and perhaps a bit too clever, Crane's point
is clear.

* As Levenson suggests, "Lynx-Hunting" is really a kind of Sullivan
County sketch, a last representation of man's confrontation with Nature,
which, like the others, is resolved in comic anticlimax.

In a remarkably imaginative departure from the resources of his own experience, Crane caused a little girl named Cora, the spoiled and willful daughter of a New York artist, to appear in two of the stories. The name should be more significant than it has been to Crane's biographers, for in both "The Angel-Child" and "The Stove" it is the little girl's willfulness which upsets the rather rigid and unreasonable pretensions and rituals of the adults.[30] "The Angel-Child," the first of the *Harper's* series, describes in mock-heroic language the rape of a number of locks when little Cora (the spoiled city cousin of Jimmie Trescott) obtains too much birthday money from her indulgent father and, after an ice cream feast, takes the children of the town on a visit to the barber. The almost mindless barber ("upon his face a grin of almost inhuman idiocy"), who is perhaps something of an absurd reality himself, gives haircuts which shear away the fashionable curls from the children's heads and shock and anger the parents. In Cora's other story, "The Stove," she and Jimmie Trescott, playing at a child's fantasy, roast turnips in a cellar and reduce a pretentious adult tea party to chaos. As Eric Solomon points out, "The Stove" suggests parallels between the children's games and those of their parents, for in both, form exceeds content. And, when the fantasy of one violates the ritual of the other, all are left in a cellar and in a kind of confused despair from which not even the noble Dr. Trescott can clearly save them. For such a comic story, "The Stove" concludes with a distinctly hollow ring. "Trescott arose and extended his hands in a quiet but magnificent gesture of despair and weariness. He seemed about to say something classic and, quite instinctively, they waited. The stillness was deep and the wait was longer than a moment. 'Well,' he said, 'we can't live in the cellar. Let's go up stairs' " (*Virginia*, VII, 206).

There are other remarkable similarities between the worlds

of children and of parents. For in Whilomville the community of children imposes rigid demands upon the behavior and imaginations of its members. Most of the children's rituals are derived rather than conceived, and more effort is expended in ordering status and conforming to preconceived patterns—in learning "how" to do it—than in conception—or in apprehension. A number of the Whilomville stories represent the nature of these childish rituals and the rigidity with which their demands are enforced. And when one considers their full implication, the child's world of Whilomville is an ominous one indeed.

In one of the darker of these stories Cora is again involved, although she is not present. "The Lover and the Tell-Tale" describes how ridicule is used to inhibit the expression of feelings and to enforce conformity to the repressive standards of the community of children. In it, Jimmie is caught writing a love letter to his beloved Cora and is ridiculed by the other children. Goaded into a rage, he attacks them in a scene of animalistic violence which, as Eric Solomon suggests, prefigures William Golding's *Lord of the Flies*.[31] And, as in Golding's novel, the violence is interrupted only by the intervention of adult authority, the teacher who punishes Jimmie. But the real villainess of the piece is not the teacher, but the tell-tale, Rose Goldege, a miniature of the female gossip upon whom Crane had lavished special hate in *The Third Violet* and "The Monster." [32] Again, it is the origins of her behavior—the way in which Rose is conditioned to engage the world in which she lives—in which Crane is interested.

> But this small Rose Goldege happened to be of a family which numbered few males. It was in fact one of those curious middle-class families that hold much of their ground, retain most of their position, after all their visible means of support have been dropped in the grave. It contained now only a collection of women who

existed submissively, defiantly, securely, mysteriously, in a pretentious and often exasperating virtue. It was often too triumphantly clear that they were free of all bad habits. However, bad habits is a term here used in a commoner meaning because it is certainly true that the principal and indeed solitary joy which entered their lonely lives was the joy of talking wickedly and busily about their neighbors. It was all done without dream of its being of the vulgarity of the alleys. Indeed it was simply a constitutional but not incredible chastity and honesty expressing itself in its ordinary superior way of the whirling circles of life and the vehemence of the criticism was not lessened by a further infusion of an acid of worldly defeat, worldly suffering and worldly hopelessness.

Virginia, VII, 145

It is no surprise then, as Crane's final image in the story represents, that after Jimmie's struggle is all over, "he saw gloating upon him the satanic black eyes of the little Goldege girl."

Other of the stories record similar enforcements. Crane had long been interested in the psychology of the dare. He marveled at the risk which an individual would take in an attempt to make good a challenged boast, to support an endangered pretension. "A Mystery of Heroism," "The Five White Mice," and "The Monster" all consider the taking of a risk on dares. In one of the Whilomville stories, " 'Showin' Off,' " Crane considered how the dare is used to provoke foolhardy conduct. Here Horace Glenn is trapped by his own bravado and hyperbole into a dangerous velocipede ride which wrecks his vehicle. Horace—like his predecessors in Crane's fiction—has risked physical injury to keep his pretensions intact and to remain acceptable to his peers.

In "Shame," one of the more complex and profound of the stories, Jimmie Trescott finds himself caught between two sets of expectations and, after considerable maneuvering, escapes for a time into a rather irrational fantasy. In this story, Jimmie, in order to join the other children at a picnic, must somehow obtain a packed lunch. He approaches the family cook and, after considerable discussion, persuades her to provide him with a sandwich in a lunch pail. But at the picnic Jimmie discovers that his lunch pail has made him the object of ridicule.*

" 'Oh, mamma! Oh, mamma! Jimmie Trescott's got his picnic in a pail!' Now there was nothing in the nature of this fact to particularly move the others—notably the boys, who were not competent to care if he had brought his luncheon in a coal-bin; but such is the instinct of childish society that they all immediately moved away from him. In a moment he had been made a social leper" (*Virginia*, VII, 167). Now Jimmie is caught—between the two worlds. "He did not know what to do. He knew that the grown folk expected him at the spread, but if he approached he would be greeted by a shameful chorus from the children—more especially from some of those damnable little girls."

Suddenly Jimmie's isolation and dilemma is relieved—or apparently so—by a beautiful lady who comes to sit beside him, to feed him, to save him from embarrassment. Of course, one might conjecture on the frequency of female characters as significant forces—for the good or for the bad—in the disturbance of emotional or communal order in Whilomville.† Suffice it to say that Jimmie falls in love with this

---

* Levenson suggests that to the middle-class children the lunch pail is the badge of the working class. *Virginia*, VII, p. lvi.

† Perhaps a subsequent biographer may someday elucidate the paradoxically sexual sense of sin and protection which Crane seemed to derive from sometimes rather shadowy (in both senses) women who were somewhat older than himself. Perhaps inadvertently, Crane was alluding to its origins here. In this connection, one cannot but think of the "fairy lady" of the fire which blocked Jimmie's and Henry's path in "The Monster" (after Jimmie's cry for " 'Mam-ma.' "). Crane's own emotional life was heavily engaged with such women. There were Helen Trent, Lily Brandon Munroe,

beautiful lady," but even this fantasy is of no protection, and the illusion is only temporary. For when the picnic ends, Crane leaves Jimmie still caught between two expectations, fearfully awaiting his father's return after the discovery of the hidden and uneaten sandwich which the cook had so grudgingly prepared for the boy.

Probably the most ominous of the Whilomville stories—especially in light of the fact that within six weeks following its composition Crane would write "The Upturned Face" and there represent the real event which the Whilomville children here imitate in their play[33]—is "The Trial, Execution, and Burial of Homer Phelps." The story tells of a child's game which demands a scapegoat and of how that scapegoat is obtained. Willie Dalzel's gang (Jimmie Trescott is a senior member) is playing at war, and when Homer Phelps asks to join, the price of admission is that he play defendant in a court-martial. When he botches the job of prisoner at the "execution," he is again excluded, and in order to gain reacceptance, Homer agrees to submit himself to "burial." The cruel ritual is chilling in its implications, for the burial suggests just how high the price of acceptance in Whilomville can sometimes be.

And the price is high because the protection offered is great. Just how great, how threatening and vulnerable is the outsider, and how complex the ritual of initiation is shown in two stories which dramatize the disorder and violence which are the results of the arrival of a new boy in town. In "The Fight" the new boy is required to fight with Jimmie Trescott

---

perhaps Amy Leslie, and certainly Cora herself. See Berryman, 28, 45, 146–49; Beer, 59–77; Stallman, *passim*. Donald B. Gibson (*The Fiction of Stephen Crane*, 140–42) discusses the "dark ladies" of Crane's fiction and their place beside their sisters in the works of other nineteenth-century American writers as the embodiment of forces threatening consciousness. Perhaps, along with little Cora of "The Angel-Child," this "beautiful lady" is another—though hardly a significant—example.

in order that his place in the elaborate hierarchy of children be established. And when he not only defeats Jimmie but Willie Dalzel, the current chief of the tribe of children, the new boy becomes a threat to the very order of the children's universe. For the sensibility of the child's community is primitive, and the outsider is threatening to it precisely because of the fact that his potential is unknown. His potential must therefore be either eliminated or rendered knowable. And throughout the story, Crane's metaphors acknowledge the primitive quality of the children's response. Here is an example: "He approached slowly the group of older inhabitants and they had grown profoundly silent. They looked him over; he looked them over. They might have been savages observing the first white man or white men observing the first savage. The silence held steady" (*Virginia*, VII, 217).

Order is reasserted in "The City Urchin and the Chaste Villagers" when Johnnie Hedge (one must always observe Crane's names) and Willie Dalzel fight twice again. For finally Willie emerges triumphant as Jimmie Trescott adjusts nimbly to the shifting hierarchies. But Crane never lets us forget the almost gratuitous cruelty of the children to any outsider. In this story, when the Negro hostler Peter Washington tries to separate the combatants, he is assaulted with the cry of " 'Nig-ger-r-r! Nig-ger-r-r!' " from Johnnie's younger brother. There are few heroes in Whilomville, and, lest the reader become too admiring of the victorious Willie, Crane closes the story as he is subjected to the humiliation of having his ears publicly boxed by his mother.

Thus the reader has seen Jimmie's education. He has observed the boy as his encounters with Nature are prejudiced and distorted, as his emotional life is disturbed, as he escapes briefly from the cruel demands of his communities into isolation, as he learns the price the isolate must pay. The reader has also been made to recognize (in a perfectly straightforward story like "Making an Orator") that the pain of his experience in Whilomville is remembered pain, that the lessons which are intended are never the lessons learned. Jimmie has, however, become nimble and adroit in his relationships. If the boy has learned nothing else, he has learned how to lie —how to misrepresent his intentions—to others and even to himself. However, these questionable capabilities bring Jimmie no closer to reality—or to the "Christmas" of "A Little Pilgrim"—than before. For in spite of the boy's adroit maneuvering for membership in the Sunday school which he expects to celebrate Christmas properly, in Whilomville in this final story all Christmas parties are canceled.*

As Crane's biographers have made clear, all of the Whilomville stories have their origins in Crane's memory of the events of his own childhood.[34] And there can be no doubt that he conceived of the Whilomville stories as parts of a single, organized whole. The stories were presented serially in a chronological sequence and covered a period of around two and one-half years; the same sequence was maintained in Harper's book publication.[35] But it is also clear that the stories have a thematic organization as well. Solomon speaks of "a clear pattern of developing seriousness." I would also suggest that in the course of the stories, as Jimmie becomes older, he becomes increasingly less autonomous, more duplicitous. In the early stories Jimmie opposes the communities of Whilomville; in the later stories he joins them and adopts their techniques. Like Henry Fleming, Jimmie became more of a member than an individual.

* "A Little Pilgrim" (or "A Little Pilgrimage," a name by which it is also known, see *Virginia*, VII, 255; and *Stories and Sketches*, 765) is, as George Monteiro has pointed out, a skillfuly wrought jeremiad against the hypocrisies of the church in Whilomville. And to achieve this satire Crane employed a subtle, almost Joycean use of imagery. See "Whilomville as Judah: Crane's 'A Little Pilgrimage.'" *Renascence*, XIX (Summer, 1967), 184–89.

Thus the Whilomville stories seem to betray in Crane an intention which was not unlike that of James Joyce in *Dubliners* a few years later. For the Whilomville stories seem designed to show something of the causes of the apprehensional paralysis in the life of an American small town. Unfortunately, Crane's stories never rose to Joyce's achievement. They were, in the first place, too hastily written. Their inner relationships were not carefully worked out, they were irregular in quality, and none of them show the care in execution—the skill in impressionistic rendering—to which the reader has become accustomed in Crane's better work. But the Whilomville stories, as explanation though not as justification of the apprehensional climate of "The Monster," open the possibility of a subject which, though Crane would have no more time to explore it, could have been incredibly rich. Indeed one might reasonably surmise that the imaginative possibility Crane embodied in Whilomville is richer by far than that of *The Red Badge,* and the subject of war to which he committed so much effort in his final years.

XI

Showdowns:
Crane's West Remembered

*Brevity is an element that enters importantly
into all pleasures, of life.*
                    Stephen Crane to Cora Stewart,
                    November, 1896

In June of 1897 Stephen Crane was a long way from San
Antonio. Much had occurred between the time when the
rather disoriented young journalist had departed from that
city on his way to Mexico more than two years before. Yet
now Crane, newly arrived in England with his own "bride,"
remembered that trip and wrote his brother Edmund to retrieve two western stories he had left behind him in Hartwood, New York.[1] In September he began writing about the
West again; he immediately produced "The Bride Comes to
Yellow Sky," and three months later, after writing "Death
and the Child," he returned to his memories of the West
and, this time recalling a Nebraska snowstorm, he began
"The Blue Hotel." [2] That imaginative return west bore Crane
real fruit; these, the products of his final ordering of that
experience, were two of his least realistic and most accomplished stories, stories in which he was able to exploit the
possibilities of his earlier apprehensions of reality to an extraordinary extent.

225

Crane began "The Bride Comes to Yellow Sky" shortly after he settled in with Cora at Ravensbrook and probably shortly before his first meeting with Joseph Conrad.[3] The story seems to have gone well from the very beginning; it was not long before Crane was calling it a "daisy," his favorite word of approval. And it was also well received in his new circle of friends. As he reported to his brother, "All my friends come here say it is my very best thing. I am so delighted when I am told by competent people that I have made an advance." [4]

Like "The Blue Hotel," "The Bride" finds its origins in parody. For Crane's story turns upon a comic representation of that event which is climactic and essential to the western romance, the showdown. Unlike most showdowns, however, Crane's is conducted between a drunken old cowboy and a recently married marshal; it is concluded with words and without guns; and in it the winner is motivated, not by his honor, but by visions of the comforts of a Pullman car. And though Crane's parody in "The Bride" is decidedly more comic than that of "The Blue Hotel," this showdown makes his reader wistfully aware that, historically if not conventionally, Crane's comic version is more accurate; the vision of the Pullman was to replace the heroic imagination, and the city's institutions did replace the Old West's traditions and rituals.

Yet beyond its parodic inception, "The Bride Comes to Yellow Sky" is a story owing much to Crane's recently discovered pattern of action. For "The Bride" is the story of the return to his community of Marshal Jack Potter, who earlier had departed somewhat furtively from it, had seen San Antonio, and had gotten married. These facts alone are sufficient reason to expect that Potter will confront orders of reality which he had not previously imagined. Yet the marshal is not the story's only initiate. As the story opens, Potter's bride is enjoying her first train ride; in the second section an Easterner is about to see western violence for the first time; and at the end of the story Scratchy Wilson experiences an initiation of his own.

"The Bride Comes to Yellow Sky" is a story of two kinds of orders—of two American civilizations—one of the East and the city, whose collective imagination is dedicated to machines, manufactured objects, and institutions; the other the West of the frontier town, its communal imagination dominated by Nature, animals, and individual violence.[5] And in the opening paragraph, in shifting visual perspective, is set forth the central opposition of the story. "The great Pullman was whirling onward with such dignity of motion that a glance from the window seemed simply to prove that the plains of Texas were pouring eastward. Vast flats of green grass, dull-hued spaces of mesquite and cactus, little groups of frame houses, woods of light and tender trees, all were sweeping into the east, sweeping over the horizon, a precipice" (*Virginia*, V, 109). "The Bride Comes to Yellow Sky" is indeed based upon the historical fact of the "pouring eastward" of the western plains. Crane in his journey west had observed that with the coming of the railroad, the nomadic, independent, heroic conditions of existence of the region were fast disappearing. With the railroad came a mercantile, impersonal, interdependent civilization (and indeed, as Crane apocalyptically suggested, that horizon may well be "a precipice").

In "The Bride" Crane was concerned with the confrontation, or the "showdown" of these two opposed orders. Yellow Sky is, in fact, at the nexus, the point of tangency of the river and the railroad, the two symbols around which his story is ordered. "To the left, miles down a long purple slope, was a little ribbon of mist where moved the keening Rio Grande. The train was approaching it at an angle, and the apex was Yellow Sky." The reader sees Jack Potter in the first scene with an imagination newly in thrall to the bedazzlements of the Pullman, but he will learn later that Scratchy Wilson, Potter's antagonist, is "about the last of the old gang that used to hang out along the river here." When Potter and Scratchy meet, the reader will be concerned with considerably more than just a parody of a cowboy "showdown." [6]

The first two sections of the story represent the naive apprehensions of these two orders. And of these the first is the more remarkable. The story, opening as it does with a scene in which Marshal Jack Potter, lawman of Yellow Sky, is returning with his new bride to his community, shows him examining with astonished eyes the trappings of his new environment. Crane's imagery is vivid and fresh in describing that vision. "He pointed out to her the dazzling fittings of the coach; and in truth her eyes opened wider as she contemplated the sea-green figured velvet, the shining brass, silver, and glass, the wood that gleamed as darkly brilliant as the surface of a pool of oil."

But what is more important is the curiously reflexive quality of Potter's apprehension. As the "dazzling fittings," the "darkly brilliant" wood, the steel buttons of his bride's dress, as well as the "numerous mirrors," the sardonically observant fellow passenger, the porters, and the two rows of waiters all suggest, this is one of Crane's nearer approaches to pure expressionism. For here is a grotesque rendering of the peculiarly reflexive quality of the modern condition. Jack Potter is seeing, but at the same time is intensely aware that he is being seen; he is intensely concerned with his "image."

> He, the town marshal of Yellow Sky, a man known, liked, and feared in his corner, a prominent person, had gone to San Antonio to meet a girl he believed he loved, and there, after the usual prayers, had actually induced her to marry him, without consulting Yellow Sky for

any part of the transaction. He was now bringing his bride before an innocent and unsuspecting community.

Of course people in Yellow Sky married as it pleased them, in accordance with a general custom; but such was Potter's thought of his duty to his friends, or of their idea of his duty, or of an unspoken form which does not control men in these matters, that he felt he was heinous. He had committed an extraordinary crime. Face to face with this girl in San Antonio, and spurred by his sharp impulse, he had gone headlong over all the social hedges. At San Antonio he was like a man hidden in the dark. A knife to sever any friendly duty, any form, was easy to his hand in that remote city. But the hour of Yellow Sky—the hour of daylight— was approaching.[7]

Virginia, V, 111

Potter and his modern apprehension seem curiously unsuited to the role which he must reclaim for himself, the role of lawman in Yellow Sky.

The importance of Potter's reasserting authority, however, becomes clear when in the second section the reader anticipates—and this time point of view is established in the eyes of a naive traveling salesman from the East—the impending disorder which Potter's absence makes possible. For if Potter is an absent lawman, Scratchy Wilson is the lord of Yellow Sky's misrule. Scratchy's imagination is of the river as surely as Potter's is of the Pullman; as Potter is thoughtful so Scratchy is drunk; as Potter's eyes render him passive ("like a man waiting in a barber's shop"), so the delusions of Scratchy (he of "the creeping movement of the midnight cat") infect him with the potential for violent action. And that potential, and the dangerous disorder it wreaks, is made startlingly apparent in the third section, as point of view again shifts so that it is balanced between a faintly ironic narrator and Scratchy Wilson himself. When Scratchy enters the story, the reader sees an innocent on the edge of initiation. "A simple child of the earlier plains," Scratchy has reinforced with alcohol his anachronistic understanding of the reality of his West. He is isolated—the town has emptied in anticipation of his arrival—and is living in a fantasy world which he can control (the town "was a toy for him"). But Scratchy is unaware of the falseness of his delusions, unaware that his maroon shirt was "made principally by some Jewish women on the East Side of New York," and that his boots are "of the kind beloved in winter by little sledding boys on the hillsides of New England." And even as Scratchy reveals his terror, first to animal and then to man, the reader recognizes that Scratchy's natural violence cannot hold sway for long. Clearly a showdown is close at hand.[8]

The "hideous rite" of that showdown is the climax of Crane's story. Now Jack Potter, who with his bride and his new self-consciousness seemed so terribly inadequate to his task in the first section, must confront this disordering principle in his community and, by overcoming this disorder, reassert his own place as marshal and peace officer in that community. Yet now Potter seems curiously more armed than the reader at first believed. For he has at his side that curiously faceless and mechanical bride, the embodiment of the new estate to which he has committed himself,[9] and he has before his inner eye an image embodying a new order to which he has now committed his imagination.

> Potter looked at his enemy. "I ain't got a gun on me, Scratchy," he said. "Honest, I ain't." He was stiffening and steadying, but yet somewhere at the back of his mind a vision of the Pullman floated: the sea-green figured velvet, the shining brass, silver, and glass, the wood that gleamed as darkly brilliant as the surface of a pool of oil—all the glory of the marriage, the environment of the new estate. "You know I fight when it comes to

fighting, Scratchy Wilson, but I ain't got a gun on me. You'll have to do all the shootin' yourself."

Virginia, V, 119

Jack Potter has learned a new way of seeing. He has a new commitment for his eye. And if Scratchy Wilson can terrorize Yellow Sky, he cannot eradicate Potter's new vision nor violate his new belief. It is with Potter's steadfastness that Wilson's own fantasy is destroyed. Now and finally, Scratchy must accept his insignificance and the ritualized artificiality of his vision.

> "Married!" said Scratchy, not at all comprehending.
> "Yes, married. I'm married," said Potter distinctly.
> "Married?" said Scratchy. Seemingly for the first time, he saw the drooping drowning woman at the other man's side. "No!" he said. He was like a creature allowed a glimpse of another world. He moved a pace backward, and his arm with the revolver dropped to his side. "Is this—is this the lady?" he asked.
> "Yes, this is the lady," answered Potter.
> There was another period of silence.
> "Well," said Wilson at last, slowly, "I s'pose it's all off now."

Jack Potter's showdown with Scratchy Wilson, however, involves more than simply the assertion of a new way of seeing in Yellow Sky. For Potter at least, the confrontation involves an apprehension of self as well. George Monteiro has pointed out that there is evidence in "The Bride Comes to Yellow Sky" to suggest that the violent nature in Scratchy Wilson which Jack Potter has faced down perhaps also is really himself in disguise.[10] Part of the evidence is to be found in the recurrent colors of black and red in the images of the "red tops" of Wilson's boots, his "maroon-colored flannel shirt," his "blue-black revolver" and of Potter's "new black clothes," "reddened" face and "brick-colored hands." The new order, the new vision, and the "new estate" all require a new kind of master, and in facing down Scratchy Wilson, what Potter may really be achieving is a new image of self to serve that new order.*

The idea that "The Bride Comes to Yellow Sky" is, at least in part, a monodrama may seem somewhat less surprising if one considers that at least two of Crane's close associates in England, Joseph Conrad ("The Secret Sharer") and Henry James ("The Jolly Corner") were later to write similar stories, and that Crane himself had been reading Poe ("The Man of the Crowd"?) on his western trip.[11] Shortly before writing "The Bride," Crane had himself arrived somewhat guiltily in England with his own "bride," thus returning to his own "community," the English-speaking world. Somewhat later, it is also interesting to note, Crane was reported as entertaining his guests by imitating—and no doubt caricaturing—Scratchy Wilson.[12]

But what is also revealing—as was the case with Henry Fleming—is subsequent history. For neither Scratchy Wilson nor Jack Potter were to die, but both reappeared in a story to be discussed later—"Moonlight on the Snow," which Crane wrote at Brede Place in 1899. The story has interesting thematic parallels to "The Bride," and this time Potter's new condition is officially recognized. "The foremost was Jack Potter, a famous town marshal of Yellow Sky, but now the sheriff of the county." And his deputy? "The other was Scratchy Wilson, once a no less famous desperado" (*Virginia*, V, 188).

The success of "The Bride Comes to Yellow Sky" is only

---

* It is interesting to note that James Agee, in his sensitive rendering of "The Bride" as a film script, was fully aware of the potential of the story as monodrama. To this end he opened his film version with a scene in which Jack Potter, en route to San Antonio, arranges an "honor system" for a prisoner. Also, Agee makes Scratchy Wilson, the scapegoat-king, a cleaner of cesspools ("That's a job ye do yourself—and nobody ought to have to do it for him," says one character). See *Agee on Film: Five Film Scripts* (Boston, 1964), 355–90.

partly due to the profundity of its theme. Also important is the economical clarity of Crane's organization and execution. For Crane's arrangement of the three scenes of contrasting location (the Pullman car, the saloon, the street) and his setting of eastern characters against western, indoor scenes against outdoor, sharpen the effect of that contrast and opposition which is central to "The Bride's" theme.[13] And the division of the story into four parts—each of the first three being centered upon one innocent, the final part presenting the final double confrontation—clearly objectifies Crane's statement. "The Bride Comes to Yellow Sky" is perhaps Crane's most formally correct, perhaps even his finest story.

"The Blue Hotel," a "daisy" of a darker hue, was conceived in an English snowstorm in late November, when Crane, depressed and nearing on to the end of "Death and the Child," made his way home from the Conrads'.[14] Perhaps Crane remembered the limits to man's vision set by the natural violence of a Nebraska blizzard, and perhaps he recalled his own earlier feelings about these limits.[15] Perhaps there were more specific memories—of his attempt to intervene in a barroom fight in Nebraska, or even of a blue hotel, which asserted itself against its background, but which could not be seen a hundred yards away in a blizzard.[16] In any event, Crane built a story out of these memories, laboriously polished it, and finally sent it to his agent in early February of 1898.[17] Many years late, H. L. Mencken said that that story was "better, perhaps, than any other of his stories." [18]

Whether or not it is Crane's best story, "The Blue Hotel" is certainly one of his most grotesque. Shifting from one scene to another sharply in contrast, full of distorting emotions, contrived lighting effects, and blurring snow, replete with moments of sudden distorting movement and flashings of emotion and incongruous imagery, "The Blue Hotel" has a dreamlike, almost purely expressionistic quality—a climactic demonstration of Crane's development beyond realism.[19] But in spite of its peculiar richness in grotesque, "The Blue Hotel"—in theme at least—can be meaningfully regarded as a counterpart to the more restrainedly realistic "The Open Boat." For, as Joseph N. Satterwhite has pointed out, if the theme of "The Open Boat" is the coming to understand one's stake in the human condition, "The Blue Hotel" is about the failure of an initiation into an awareness of one's humanity and the consequences of that failure.[20] The protagonist of this story fails to apprehend the reality in which he finds himself. He is isolated, and, when he attempts to demand a place for himself in a community, he finds only rejection and death. Here the irony with which Crane reports this story of illusion, the distance between what is and what is seen, is so great that Crane's very representation is radically distorted.

The protagonist of Crane's story is a Swede, a foreigner, who is filled with illusions of the West and now has come to confront the reality itself. Unfortunately, the Swede's first experience in the West takes place in a "blue hotel." Like most hotels, this one (the "Palace" of Fort Romper) is unlike the world outside. Crane describes it as having been painted blue in an attempt "to declare its position against any background" (*Virginia*, V, 142), to make it different from the world of Nature. And as long as one stays inside the hotel, reality can be made to conform to illusion. Yet even illusions —the illusions of the innocent and those of the initiate— can conflict. Inside the blue hotel, the Swede is at first terrified by his own illusion of a "wild" West, which he believes he sees confirmed in the blue hotel. But Scully, the proprietor of this inn of fantasy, asserts another ordered vision—that of the civilized community. And in his attempt to alleviate the Swede's fears he offers his guest a drink which is meant to initiate the guest into the company of the hotel's occupants. But the Swede's response is hardly a friendly one. "The Swede laughed wildly. He grabbed the bottle, put it to his mouth, and as his lips curled absurdly around the opening and his throat worked, he kept his glance burning with hatred upon the old man's face" (*Virginia*, V, 151).

From the ritualistic quality of this drink it would at first seem that the Scully's "initiation" of the Swede in the blue hotel constitutes an admission to the community of the West. But in Crane true initiation rarely brings one into a community and always involves more than just ritual. Adequate apprehension and clear understanding are critical, and the Swede achieves neither. So the Swede's initiation—as Crane's ironic treatment of his grotesque behavior indicates —is only a hollow formality.

It is doubly hollow because the Swede does not accept Scully's ordered vision, nor is Scully able to impose it for long. For the Swede, almost immediately, begins to see himself in the role of hero in a western romance—that genre which Crane is carefully parodying.[21] Brash and arrogant when he rejoins the others after his ritual drink, the Swede assumes "the air of an owner." At dinner he "fizzed like a fire wheel." Acting his part well enough to convince himself in the compliant world of the hotel, the Swede asserts apparent control over his environment. He arranges a card game, pounds upon the table, accuses one of the players— Scully's son—of cheating, defeats him in a fight in the snow, and departs indignantly. In Scully's blue hotel the Swede has acted out his self-assigned role, and even outside, in the snowstorm, he succeeds for a time in imposing his vision. He has accused Johnnie of cheating, and he makes the accusation stick by defeating the boy in a fight. But, as we are yet to see, the Swede's apprehension of reality is imperfect. And before long he has lost the protections of the blue hotel and finds himself totally alone in a blinding snowstorm.[22]

Thus Crane has been true to his pattern of action; the Swede has moved out of the illusions of the community and into a condition of isolation. It seems for a moment that, like Henry Fleming and the men in the open boat, the Swede, after experiencing for a time the illusions of arrogance, may achieve his own apprehension of reality.[23] * But the Swede's exceeds the pomposity of either Henry or the men in the boat. The Swede's arrogance seems really to be a sort of insolence toward Scully, toward his companions, toward the storm, and even toward fate itself. Indeed, as Winifred Lynskey has suggested, the Swede's defiant insolence amounts to a kind of *hybris*, and "The Blue Hotel" seems to emanate, thematically, a tragic quality.[24]

This *hybris*, this refusal to see his place in his universe (as one of the "lice which were caused to cling to a whirling, fire-smote, ice-locked, disease-stricken, space-lost bulb") isolates the Swede, and makes his return to the community impossible. Yet somehow this same arrogance gives him the conceit necessary for survival in a blinding blizzard.

> He might have been in a deserted village. We picture the world as thick with conquering and elate humanity, but here, with the bugles of the tempest pealing, it was hard to imagine a peopled earth. One viewed the existence of man then as a marvel, and conceded a glamour of wonder to these lice which were caused to cling to a whirling, fire-smote, ice-locked, disease-stricken, space-lost bulb. The conceit of man was explained by this storm to be the very engine of life. One was a coxcomb not to die in it.[25]
>
> *Virginia*, V, 165

* We have seen the same pattern in *The Red Badge* and in "The Open Boat." John Berryman, in one of the most striking statements in his challenging book on Crane, suggests that Crane often combined in one character both the *Alazon*, the man who pretends to be more than he is, and the *Eiron*, the man who pretends to be a fool. I submit that both qualities—

"However," says Crane in the next sentence, "the Swede found a saloon." Here is shelter from the storm, in which conceit is necessary for survival. But here is no blue hotel, in which reality is willed. Indeed, "in front of it [the saloon] an indomitable red light was burning," and here reality no longer conforms to the requirements of the Swede's illusion.[26] The Swede now tries to play out his role in his own fantasy (and in the western Crane is parodying). But when the Swede attempts to assert his will to gain a new acceptance in the community of the saloon, and to force the inhabitants to drink with him (Crane knew the clichés well), the results are quite different. Now at the hands of an utterly unvillainous and almost faceless gambler, the Swede is killed. And it is with an irony of rhetoric—a rhetoric deliberately overblown and then deflated by a diminishing simile—an irony which is at this point characteristic of the story—that Crane reports the Swede's death: "This citadel of virtue, wisdom, power, was pierced as easily as if it had been a melon. The Swede fell with a cry of supreme astonishment" (*Virginia*, V, 169). This ultimate isolation and blindness are in part the result of the Swede's failure to see things as they are, and Crane ends the eighth section of the story with "The corpse of the Swede, alone in the saloon, had its eyes fixed upon a dreadful legend that dwelt a-top of the cash-machine: 'This registers the amount of your purchase.' "

"The Blue Hotel," however, is not simply the account of one man's presumptuous vision and its consequences. For it is not only the Swede whose perception fails him. Indeed,

of arrogance and of fear—contribute to the delusion of Crane's innocents. See Berryman, 278–80.

In quite a different context, and in radically different terms, Daniel Weiss speaks of "the Swede's emotional swing from apprehensive depression to manic elation" which "reflects, internalized, the same battle-field as that on which Henry Fleming fought his fears." " 'The Blue Hotel': A Psychoanalytic Study," in Maurice Bassan (ed.), *Stephen Crane*, 162, also 154–64.

motifs of delusion and isolation and conceit are apparent everywhere in the story. In fact, as "The Blue Hotel" develops, one soon gets the feeling of an inadequacy of community—of the representation of a group of people who are only living together, at once in a state prior to community, and—if we remember Scully's representations to the Swede about the "ilictric streetcars"—in a state too modern for any real cohesiveness or sense of brotherhood.* Crane is here anticipating not only his own Whilomville stories but one of the major assertions of twentieth-century drama and fiction. But in "The Blue Hotel" the inadequacy of community is founded upon failures of a shared apprehension and a common understanding.

"The Blue Hotel" opens with a declaration of separateness—with the image of the hotel asserting itself against its background. This hotel is soon populated by strangers—by an Easterner (Mr. Blanc),[27] a cowboy, an innkeeper, and a Swede—and none of these strangers seem to understand one another very well. Throughout the story the reader is reminded of their failures of communication.

> "I don't know nothin' about you," answered Johnnie, "and I don't give a damn where you've been."
>
> "I don't understand you," he [the Easterner] said, impassively.
>
> "Now," said Scully, severely, "what does this mane?"
>
> "He ain't no Swede," said the cowboy, scornfully.
>
> "Well, what is he then?" cried Johnnie. "What is he then?"
>
> "It's my opinion," replied the cowboy deliberately, "he's some kind of a Dutchman." [28]

These failures bring about a disruption of order. A fight begins during a card game, and soon everything is blindness

---

* R. W. Stallman points out that in "The Blue Hotel" quarrels and fights, which are ubiquitous, in fact pattern the story. See Stallman, 488.

and confusion. The spilled cards "gazed with their silly eyes at the war that was waging above them"; the fight between Johnnie and the Swede is conducted in a blinding storm in which no one can see or hear clearly. Thus it comes as no surprise to the reader when, after the Swede has rejected this apparent community which seemed to him to have conspired to deny him safety or identity, after he has wandered out into the "deserted village" of a snowstorm and there found even less protection, and after he has taken refuge in a saloon, a gambler (a citizen whose place in his community is superfluous at best) refuses the Swede's offer of a drink with, "My friend, I don't know you." So the Swede's death, which follows, is not only the result of his deluded understanding, it is also the result of the failure of the others to accept him or even to form a viable community to receive and protect him.

It is this failure of community which Crane ironically considers in the final section of the story, in which the cowboy and the Easterner discuss the problem of the "responsibility" for the Swede's death. Here the reader learns that, even in the relative simplicity of the blue hotel, where members of an apparent community seem able to act willfully to achieve results, causation is so complex as to be ultimately indecipherable, random, and absurd (" 'Yes, a thousand things might have happened,' said the Easterner, tartly"). Yet the reader also discovers that any one of the hotel's occupants—Scully, the Easterner, the cowboy—could have acted to prevent the Swede's death. Now Crane has gone beyond simple determinism to a more sophisticated and paradoxical understanding of causation.*

---

* Stallman says that the "ironic" and the deterministic endings stand at odds with one another, that thus "The Blue Hotel" is flawed. See Stallman, 488–89. It seems rather that the opposition is deliberate and that in this tension Crane approaches an even more profoundly ironic paradox. Levenson, however, has this to say of the last sentence:

Thus we arrive at the final irony of Crane's story, and perhaps the most terrible of all. For the reader of the final pages of "The Blue Hotel" must sense, along with the multiplicity of causation which Mr. Blanc proposes, the utter randomness, the utter absence of cause, which—in spite of all this self-serving prattle about causation—pervades the story. Crane had been interested in the absurd and random nature of reality in other stories, especially, perhaps, in "The Five White Mice" and in several of the earlier western stories. And now, in "The Blue Hotel," the very notion of causation seems man's ultimate conceit. It is fully, if ironically, in keeping with this story of causation and chance, of individual and communal blindness and fear and conceit, that, after Mr. Blanc's assertions about sins being the results of collaborations, the cowboy should misunderstand, withdraw again into his delusion, and say, "Well, I didn't do anythin', did I?" [29] *

"The Blue Hotel" has been variously interpreted (one critic has even read it as a satire),[30] and in part this disagreement is the result of the story's radically grotesque quality. But in spite of Crane's ironic representation—both in rhetoric and in imagery—of distortions of pride and per-

---

The one bond which unites men is their dark complicity, and even so they remain apart. Thus each of the three lines of thought in the story leads to equivocal argument. From one point of view, events are fortuitous except for an occasional feat—like painting the hotel an arresting blue—whereby the assertion of identity seems to bring identity into being. From another point of view, man makes his own destiny, if it is a proof of human agency that Wild West illusions about Nebraska make the Wild West fantasy come true. And, finally, all men share responsibility even doing nothing—or at least they do so if they think they do. Given the facts as presented, the story constructs a universe which defies every quest for certain meaning.

Virginia, V, pp. xcvii–xcviii
Perhaps that defiance is Crane's final ironic negation.

* This is, of course, an ironic repetition of Johnnie's earlier "Well, what have I done?" (*Virginia*, V, 149).

ception—this remarkably nightmarish story demonstrates for Crane a movement away from an earlier and more simplistic view of causation. More important, however, is the evidence which "The Blue Hotel" offers of Crane's darkening imagination. For this story, written just after "Death and the Child," offers a vision of man in a universe apprehensionally unavailable to him, a universe in which communities offer little or no comfort, a universe in which the very possibility of the coherence of assumed causation is now seriously in doubt.

"Moonlight on the Snow," which Crane wrote late in 1899, is another manifestation of the darkening of Crane's imagination. As a sequel to "The Bride Comes to Yellow Sky," it deals in the less comic aspects of the "civilizing" of the West. "Moonlight on the Snow" is the story of Tom Larpent, a western gunman who, after killing a man in a saloon,[31] is about to be lynched by the citizens of a town named Warpost: This town (a rival of Yellow Sky) is also becoming "civilized," and its citizens wish to hang Larpent in order to preserve its "reputation"—or, as Larpent has it, to protect "a real-estate boom." But during this "outing of real-estate speculators" a stagecoach full of Easterners arrives, and the occupants are horrified by the preparations for the lynching. Now "the rough West stood in naked immorality before the eyes of the gentle East." The citizens of Warpost waver, and the hanging of the sardonic Larpent is delayed. Then Jack Potter and Scratchy Wilson appear and save the day by charging Larpent with grand larceny and taking him off to Yellow Sky. The citizens of Warpost are left in the ironic position of springing to Larpent's defense in an effort to claim their victim. Again—and this time with the aid of Scratchy Wilson—the western way of seeing things gives way to the opposed eastern order of apprehension and evaluation.

In "Moonlight on the Snow" the names of places and characters remind one of Henry James. "Larpent" sounds a good bit like "serpent," "Pigram's store" in the western town becoming eastern could suggest "Pilgrim's store," and "Ike Boston" drives the coachload of Easterners.[32] The fact that the lynching is to occur, not from a tree, but from a fixed wooden crane in front of the store, that the gallows is no longer natural but is now a "commercial" gallows, is a nice touch. But for all Crane's cleverness, "Moonlight on the Snow" is a bit artificial; the irony is too heavy, too much at the expense of characterization.* What is perhaps most significant about it is the cynicism with which Crane regards the commercializing "Easternization" of Warpost.

Crane's other 1899 western story was published only a few months before his final illness.[33] † "Twelve O'Clock" is a grotesque and bloody tale of a slaughter which is the absurd result of a group of naive cowboys coming to a hotel to see a cuckoo clock. Again Crane is concerned with a confrontation of a civilized, "Easternized" western townspeople and the children of the earlier plains, the cowboys. The disaster which is the result of the arrogance of a drunken cowboy and the fear and commercial avarice of the townspeople is concluded only in a horrible slaughter. Central to the story is a clock (watches, clocks, and time are important in many

---

* It is a bit unbelievable, for instance, that even the hardened Tom Larpent could remain ironically detached at his own lynching. But perhaps the model is really Col. Sherburne of Mark Twain's *Huckleberry Finn.* See Levenson, *Virginia,* V, p. cxxiv.

† There is one other story, a tall tale about the workings of chance entitled "A Poker Game," which, although it was not set in the West, is identified as a western story by Levenson. It appeared posthumously, in *Last Words* (1902). See *Virginia,* V, pp. cxxxi–cxxxii, 192–94.

of Crane's western stories),* and time—running out as it is for the West—is central to Crane's theme. Here the cowboys' misunderstanding about a clock brings disastrous results, and the absurd cuckoo signaling in the final sentence with its twelve calls marks the end of an order.

Somehow "Twelve O'Clock" is told without the distancing irony that we have come to expect from Crane. It is a much too desperate story. As John Berryman has suggested, it is a nightmarish caricature of Crane's own earlier work,[34] perhaps of the more tragic "The Blue Hotel." The bloody ending of "Twelve O'Clock" is almost devoid of meaning.[35] The story is an almost complete surrender to a vision of the absurd which, in the final year, was becoming increasingly significant in Crane's imagination.

* "The Bride Comes to Yellow Sky," "The Five White Mice," and "The Wise Men" are three examples.

XII

"The Glazed Vacancy": Crane's Last Wars

"But to get the real thing!" cried Vernall, the war-correspondent. "It seems impossible!"

War is death, and a plague of the lack of small things, and toil.
                                        Stephen Crane, War Memories, 1899

In a sense, Stephen Crane's great subject was war. Throughout his career, it was the apprehension of man on the battlefield which was Crane's most consistently fertile subject. In Greece, Crane apprehended the reality of battle for himself, or, at least, he recognized the limits of his—or any man's—capacity to tolerate that apprehension. Yet in that day on the battlefield Crane had glimpses of that reality—of its fortuitousness, its absurdity, its incomprehensibility. In his other writing during his English years he explored the causes of man's failures of apprehension of reality, and he also considered the absurd and incomprehensible nature of the universe itself. And when, after describing the death of Peza in "Death and the Child," he again returned to the subject of man in battle, it was with an altered awareness and concern. Now he turned increasingly away from man's apprehension of the thing itself to represent the essential absurdity of that reality and to commit himself and his own apprehension to an articulation of that essential absurdity by acknowledging man's inability to fully comprehend it.[1]

244

Crane's final experience with war was considerably fuller than his Greek experience had been. He had set out for New York from Queenstown, Ireland, on April 14, 1898, and—having signed up with Pulitzer's *World* as a correspondent—was in Key West on the 26th, one day after the United States declared war on Spain.[2] He was to be a first-hand observer of all of the land action, and he would also be on hand for the arrival of the Americans in Havana. Indeed, he was not to return to his English home and to Cora until mid-January of 1899, after almost nine months away.[3] Out of these experiences came a large number of journalistic accounts, a semi-fictional summary, and a book of stories and sketches. But after that book, *Wounds in the Rain*, there would still be more war stories which would draw from Crane's experience in the Spanish-American War. In almost all of this writing there is apparent a shift in emphasis. Now it is the ordinary soldier, fighting steadily and without fanfare, doing his job, who is at the center of Crane's attention. Now the stoic virtues, not the keen awarenesses, are praised. And now the style is barer, the irony drier, the tone more resigned.

The first pieces Crane wrote after leaving England were the product of his experiences at sea. En route to New York, Crane described the British shipbuilding industry on the Isle of Dogs. After he had made his way to Key West there were descriptions of a captured Spanish ship's captain and of the coastline of Cuba as seen from Admiral Sampson's flagship, the *New York*.[4] In these Crane is still the impressionist, and often he is still centrally concerned with the experience of acute apprehension; in his short profile of the American spy C. H. Thrall, "The striking thing about him now is his eyes . . . peculiarly wide open as if strained with watching. . . . They stare at you and do not seem to think, ..."[5] But more and more Crane's interest can be seen to shift to the ordinary sailors, to the effects upon them of the lack of action, to their language, to their point of view.[6] And also, Crane was now increasingly turning to events of gratuitous, meaningless danger—to the near-ramming of the *World*'s dispatch boat, the *Three Friends*, by an American gunboat which had borrowed food from her a short time earlier, or—after the fashion of the Sullivan County sketches—to the dissipation of fear when a pursuing ship proves to be American instead of Spanish.[7]

When Crane first landed on Cuban soil—along with the Marines on June 7, his change in attitude and in interest became more apparent.[8] And several of the pieces for the *World* reflect these changes. Now Crane reported false rumors, gallant blunders, useless deaths, and mistakes in armament policy, all of which suggest the absurd and gratuitous nature of the events of the war.[9] There are, of course, still other pieces which are more objectively impressionistic; Crane's descriptions of military actions are always full of vivid detail, of "every man in sight . . . eating pieces of white cocoanut" or of an overturned bathtub in a village yard.[10] But everywhere, even in these sketches, Crane turned again to the ordinary soldier—to his feelings and apprehensions and to the simple fact of his unyielding courage.

One can see the logic behind Crane's new attitude in a piece which describes Captain Elliott's expedition to capture a well at Cuzco ("really the tightest, best fight of the war," Crane calls it).[11] In his report (*"The Red Badge of Courage Was His Wig-Wag Flag"*) Crane begins with the preparations for and the progress into battle and takes special notice of the attitude of the men. "One could note the prevalence of a curious expression—something dreamy, the symbol of minds striving to tear aside the screen of the future and perhaps expose the ambush of death. It was not fear in the least. It was simply a moment in the lives of men who have staked themselves and have come to wonder which wins—red or black?" (*War Dispatches*, 142).

But as the moment of battle approaches, such attitudes become irrelevant, irrelevant to the giant absurdities of war, irrelevant because they disclose nothing and because they change nothing. "The sky was speckless, the sun blazed out of it as if it would melt the earth. Far away on one side were the white waters of Guantanamo Bay; on the other a vast expanse of blue sea was rippling in millions of wee waves. The surrounding country was nothing but miles upon miles of gaunt, brown ridges. It would have been a fine view if one had had time" (*War Dispatches*, 144). When the shooting begins, the soldiers become workmanlike and are in fact analogized to workmen. The analogy produces some remarkable grotesques. "He made no outcry; he simply toppled over, while a comrade made a semi-futile grab at him. Instantly one Cuban loaded the body upon the back of another and then took up the dying man's feet. The procession that moved off resembled a grotesque wheelbarrow" (*War Dispatches*, 145). War is only an event—an event which men work and die to create—which always comes to an end, and which occasionally generates distinctive images, images of bravery. "And—mark you—a spruce young sergeant of marines, erect, his back to the showering bullets, solemnly and intently wig-wagging to the distant Dolphin." This Marine sergeant signaling under fire was for Crane the most striking event of the Cuzco action—so much so, that one of Crane's memorable war sketches, "Marines Signalling Under Fire at Guantanamo," is entirely devoted to him. It is his courage and not his apprehension which is important, a courage which is the one unyielding fact in an event which is too absurd even to yield to apprehension. This courage, the stoic virtue, is all that is left for Crane to celebrate.

"Regulars Get No Glory" is another case in point. This

piece (the last written for the *World* before Crane's illness forced him to retire from the island) is an account of an ordinary soldier and of how he dies.[12] "He goes into battle as if he had been fighting every day for three hundred years. If there is heavy firing ahead he does not even ask a question about it. He doesn't even ask whether the Americans are winning or losing. He agitates himself over no extraneous points. He attends exclusively to himself" (*War Dispatches*, 189). As the piece develops, the reader soon discovers that Crane is not the least ironic in his attitude toward the qualified perception of this ordinary soldier (this "Private Nolan"). Rather there is an almost Kiplingesque and sentimental acceptance and praise for him.[13] ". . . Nolan, no longer sweating, swearing, overloaded, hungry, thirsty, sleepless, but merely a corpse, attired in about 40 cents' worth of clothes. Here's three volleys and taps to one Nolan, of this regiment or that regiment, and maybe some day, in a fairer squarer land, he'll get his picture in the paper, too"* (*War Dispatches*, 190).

When, after his convalescence at Old Point Comfort, Crane returned to Puerto Rico and the tail-end of the war, it was for a different paper, Hearst's *Journal*.[14] For the *Journal* there were to be only three pieces, but all three are distinctively Crane's. The first, "The Wonders of Ponce," evinces Crane's confrontation with the fact of his own mortality.[15] In another ("A Soldier's Burial That Made a Native Holiday") he tells of the utter meaninglessness of an American military funeral to the Puerto Rican citizenry. He reports the citizens' laughter as the funeral volleys are fired, and their

* It is perfectly true, as Stallman points out, that Crane's sketch is partly in reaction to the press's constant romanticizing of the society soldier in the war. But Nolan, who would reappear in "The Private's Story" and "Memoirs of a Private" (two proto-fictions from Crane's war experiences) as well as in "The Price of the Harness," is too important to Crane's imagination to be put off that easily. See Stallman, 385, 404; and *War Dispatches*, 188n.

unconcern for the final bugle call. In the other, "The Porto Rican "Straddle,' " he describes how surly Puerto Ricans became friendly after the occupation of their town by American soldiers. Now it is not apprehension which is important, rather the simple fact of power.[16]

Most of Crane's reporting for the *Journal* was done after the armistice and from his curious retreat in Havana, and a good number of the pieces are concerned with representing and anticipating Cuban attitudes toward the Americans there.[17] He also observed the citizens of the Cuban city and their peculiar responses to reality.[18] He contrasted the Cuban way of apprehending things with the American,[19] and in one remarkable sketch ("How They Leave Cuba") he utilized ironically contrasting points of view to describe the leave-taking of a homeward-bound Spaniard and his Cuban woman and their child (all of which is observed by a curious boatman).[20]

Many of the sketches are merely vignettes, Havana scenes and accounts of trivial events in the city.[21] But as time passed, Crane soon turned to political events, to the activities of the armistice commission. He was constantly annoyed by Spanish duplicity and by the officious bumbling of the Americans, and there are several critical, even vituperative pieces criticizing the Spaniards and the slowness of the negotiations.[22] But there is again the good word for "the wheel horse," now the ordinary career diplomat, always uncelebrated, who nevertheless "stands . . . ready to pull the next high-stepper out of a mudhole." [23]

As he had done after the Greek war for the *Westminster Gazette* in "With Greek and Turk," Crane brought his materials of the Spanish-American War together to shape a unified presentation of his experience. The result, "War Memories," first appeared in Lady Randolph Churchill's *Anglo-Saxon Review* of December, 1899.[24] It is not divided into distinct parts, as is "With Greek and Turk," and it is, at first reading, more discursive, less thematically structured. What is more important is Crane's method of organization. "With Greek and Turk" is organized around a single compressed unit of time, a single battle day, but "War Memories" is organized around a series of single images, all of which are thematically related.

The images as well are here used by Crane in a new way. In "War Memories" it is interesting to observe that the purely descriptive image—the image as element in purely impressionistic rendering—is less frequently present and less significant. Occasionally—as in earlier work—images are metaphorically employed to support Crane's highly imaginative assertions of similarities. One notable example is in *"The Red Badge of Courage* Was His Wig-Wag Flag," where there appears the image of a corpse—curiously compared to a wheelbarrow—which is carried from the field by Cuban soldiers—whom Crane compared to workmen; these images and associations are retained in "War Memories." [25] But more frequently now, Crane rendered things in isolation. Images in "War Memories" often gratuitously occur, set apart from their background and represented almost as if they are the real concretization of recollection.

Indeed, these images dramatize the process of memory, the memory of Vernall, the war correspondent who is only slightly characterized and is, of course, only the thinnest of disguises for Crane himself. But more significantly, these images, although they are less startling and more frequent, bear meaning in much the same way as Crane's earlier grotesque images. Now, however, as the ironic distance between narrator and perceiver shortens, and Crane's dramatic impressionism converges upon expressionism, these images become parts of a system which bear crucial thematic import.

"War Memories" opens with one of these images. For

after Crane-Vernall introduces himself with a denial of the possibility of apprehending the thing itself (" 'But to get the real thing! . . . It seems impossible' "), Vernall says,

> When I climbed aboard the dispatch-boat at Key West, the mate told me irritably that, as soon as we crossed the bar, we would find ourselves monkey-climbing over heavy seas. It wasn't my fault, but he seemed to insinuate that it was all a result of my incapacity. There were four correspondents in the party. The leader of us came aboard with a huge bunch of bananas, which he hung like a chandelier in the centre of the tiny cabin. We made acquaintance over, around, and under this bunch of bananas, which really occupied the cabin as a soldier occupies a sentry box. But the bunch did not become really aggressive until we were well at sea. Then it began to spar. With the first roll of the ship, it launched its honest pounds at McCurdy and knocked him wildly through the door to the deck-rail, where he hung cursing hysterically. Without a moment's pause, it made for me.
>
> *Virginia*, VI, 223

As the ravages of the swinging bananas are recounted, the reader begins to recognize that this incident is more than pure farce. For this gratuitous but dangerous bunch of bananas, brought on board by the leader of the correspondents, rather closely resembles Hearst's little war. And in the final sentence of the paragraph the reader's suspicion is reinforced. "You see? War! A bunch of bananas rampant because the ship rolled." [26]

Vernall returns to this image again as "War Memories" proceeds, and with other similar images he attempts to "get" the "real thing" of the war to which its men must, willy-nilly, relate. Part of the massive blindness of the force of war is suggested by the *Machias* (the American warship which almost rams the *Three Friends*). "Down upon our quarter swung a monstrous thing larger than any ship in the world—the U.S.S. *Machias*. She had a freeboard of about three hundred feet, and the top of her funnel was out of sight in the clouds like an Alp" (*Virginia*, VI, 224–25). The fact that the full impact of war's horrors must remain only incompletely known by any individual participant is likewise suggested by a description—Crane's ironic account of polite naval officers aboard the *New York* observing a bombardment. "The shell went carousing off to the Cuban shore, and from the vegetation there spirited a cloud of dust. Some of the officers on the quarter-deck laughed. Through their glasses they had seen a Spanish column of cavalry much agitated by the appearance of this shell among them" (*Virginia*, V, 226).

In "War Memories," as in much of his war writing, Crane's procedure is that of the closing vision. First the correspondent is off the coast, then he participates in a landing and experiences briefly—although he cannot observe it because of "impenetrable darkness"—the death of Dr. Gibbs, Vernall's friend. Finally the reality of that death is disclosed.

> At length, the land brightened in a violent atmosphere, the perfect dawning of a tropic day, and in this light I saw a clump of men near me. At first I thought they were all dead. Then I thought they were all asleep. The truth was that a group of wan-faced exhausted men had gone to sleep about Gibbs' body so closely and in such abandoned attitudes that one's eye could not pick the living from the dead until one saw that a certain head had beneath it a great dark pool.
>
> *Virginia*, VI, 227

Here is Vernall's first look at death, the center of war's reality—death hidden among the unseeing, sleeping soldiers.*

* It is not unlike an image in "War's Horrors and Turkey's Bold Plan," one of Crane's Greek war reports. See *War Dispatches*, 40; and Chap. 9, *supra*.

There are, of course, other images which suggest other aspects of the war's essence. A notable pair are those of the man in the Panama hat with his walking stick—Crane associates him with Mars, the war-god—and "the balloon of our signal corps," the impersonal American machine of war. "The balloon of our signal corps had swung over the tops of the jungle's trees toward the Spanish trenches. Whereat the balloon and the man in the Panama hat and with a walking-stick—whereat these two waged tremendous battle" (*Virginia*, V, 245). But finally, at the end of the final description of battle, there occurs an image which embodies war's ultimate reality.

> Lying near one of the enemy's trenches was a red-headed Spanish corpse. I wonder how many hundreds were cognizant of this red-headed Spanish corpse? It arose to the dignity of a landmark. There were many corpses, but only one with a red head. This red-head. He was always there. Each time I approached that part of the field I prayed that I might find that he had been buried. But he was always there—red headed. His strong simple countenance was a malignant sneer at the system which was for ever killing the credulous peasants in a sort of black night of politics, where the peasants merely followed whatever somebody had told them was lofty and good. But, nevertheless, the red-headed Spaniard was dead. He was irrevocably dead. And to what purpose? . . . Well, there you are, buried in your trench on San Juan Hill. That is the end of it. Your life has been taken—that is a flat, frank fact. And foreigners buried you expeditiously while speaking a strange tongue. Sleep well, red-headed mystery.
>
> *Virginia*, VI, 249–50

Of course, the image immediately calls to mind the corpse which Henry Fleming confronts in the forest chapel, or, perhaps, that of the dead young Greek volunteer in "With Greek and Turk." But Crane's treatment of this image manifests a slightly altered concern. Now it is not the grotesque terror of the event of apprehension that Crane wishes to communicate, nor even the delusion which leads the soldier to his death. Rather, Crane is here concerned with the gratuitous, the absurd meaninglessness of the fact of death. The event is without significant cause or effect, is expeditiously hidden; the fact remains undescribed and is finally a "mystery."

And the human response to it? One response, ineffectual though it may be, is to attempt to cure. So—almost as if it were written to oppose the image of the redheaded corpse—Crane set down a few pages later another vivid scene, this one in a church at El Caney which has been converted into a hospital for the Spanish wounded.

> The interior of the church was too cavelike in its gloom for the eyes of the operating surgeons, so they had had the altar-table carried to the doorway, where there was a bright light. Framed then in the black archway was the altar-table with the figure of a man upon it. He was naked save for a breech-clout, and so close, so clear was the ecclesiastic suggestion, that one's mind leaped to a fantasy that this thin pale figure had just been torn down from a cross. The flash of the impression was like light, and for this instant it illumined all the dark recesses of one's remotest idea of sacrilege, ghastly and wanton. I bring this to you merely as an effect—an effect of mental light and shade, if you like; something done in thought similar to that which the French Impressionists do in color; something meaningless and at the same time overwhelming, crushing, monstrous. "Poor devil; I wonder if he'll pull through?" said Leighton. An American surgeon and his assistants were intent over the prone figure. They wore white aprons. Something small and silvery flashed in the surgeon's hand. An assistant held the merciful sponge close to the man's nostrils, but he was writhing and moaning in some horrible dream of this artificial sleep.
>
> *Virginia*, VI, 254

Here again Crane's soldier is asleep, but his image is nevertheless vividly—even grotesquely—presented. It would almost seem that Crane is undertaking, by the vitalization—now of the reader's apprehension—to realize an event which may in some small way counter the absurdity of war's death.*

After this image most of the rest of "War Memories" is anticlimax. There is a rather comic account of "Bo's'n," Vernall's thieving servant, of a prisoner exchange, finally of Vernall's yellow fever and his return to the States after rather brutish treatment by a ship's officer. One has a sense, as Crane moves his reader gradually away from the war zone, that the absurd reality of war is even less understandable as one increases his temporal and spatial distance from it. Crane's final image is from a veranda in Old Point Comfort, as a column of the wounded pass before it on their way to the hospital. "Did they smirk and look as if they were bursting with the desire to tell everything which had happened? No, they hung their heads like so many jail-birds. Most of them seemed to be suffering from something which was like stage-fright during the ordeal of this chance but supremely eloquent reception" (*Virginia*, VI, 263). No interpreters here. And as for Vernall, the correspondent, he also seems to know that he cannot "get" the real thing. His ending is flat and negative. "The episode was closed. And you can depend upon it that I have told you nothing at all, nothing at all, nothing at all."

In October of 1900, after Crane's death in Germany, "War Memories" appeared again in the company of ten other sketches, all under the striking title of *Wounds in the Rain*.[27] The sketches (most of which were written after Crane's return to England in January of 1899)[28] are of varying quality

---

* Colvert, *Virginia*, VI, pp. xxxii–xxxiii, sees this description as elaborating a pattern of imagery ultimately originating in "Four Men in a Cave."

and reproduce Crane's war experience in various degrees of fictional disguise. *Wounds in the Rain* bears a curious and paradoxical relationship to Crane's other late series, the Whilomville stories. For if the Whilomville stories represents Crane's coming to terms with the communally shaped delusions of his past, *Wounds in the Rain* is the result of a summary attempt to order the experiences and significances of his confrontation with an absurd reality. In *Wounds in the Rain* Crane made a halting beginning toward the transformation of his disillusionments and his admirations in the Spanish American War into a formulated ethic for man in an absurd universe.

Some of the *Wounds in the Rain* sketches are simple reworkings of Crane's war pieces with little or no fictional veneer. "Marines Signalling under Fire at Guantanamo," for example, is an expansion of a single image from *"The Red Badge of Courage* Was His Wig-Wag Flag," a war dispatch I have already discussed. The sketch tells of the bravery of Sergeant Quick and Private Clancy in their flag signaling at Cuzco.[29] " 'God Rest Ye, Merry Gentlemen' "[30] is an only slightly fictionalized summary of the last phase of Crane's experiences in the Cuban campaign. The sketch turns on the innocence of "Little Nell,"* the war correspondent (a self-parody) and the blind misunderstanding by his New York editor of his actions in covering the war.[31] "This Majestic Lie" is a fictional rendering of the career of C. H. Thrall, the American businessman-spy whom Crane had portrayed earlier in a piece for the *World*, and whose career is imagined out of Crane's own postwar experiences in Cuba.[32] The story is trivial enough—of an American spy who is blackmailed by a Havana restaurant and who wreaks a postwar revenge.

---

* Crane's war stories are still usually initiations; somebody must experience battle for the first time, even if the initiation must be fictionalized. Crane had seen battle before Las Guasimas; Crane's Little Nell had not.

Other sketches of the *Wounds in the Rain* collection are simply "low-pressure writing," inferior work written in a time of illness and need, hardly pulled "together into [the] sharp design" which is so characteristic of Crane's best work.[33] "The Revenge of the *Adolphus*" is such a piece—framed out of Crane's nautical reportage by means of a weak plot, with hardly discernible form or theme and with only occasional sparks of good writing.[34] "The Lone Charge of William B. Perkins" has somewhat more shape and at least a shadowy theme. In this account of a war correspondent in his first combat, Crane described a skirmish absurdly set off by the explosion of a jammed cartridge. Perkins, the correspondent, is saved by the unexplained presence on the battlefield of a rusting boiler in which he hides. He endangers himself because of a dare of the sort that figures in "A Mystery of Heroism" and in " 'Showin' Off.' "[35] Here is another rendering of the gratuitousness of the events of war, a gratuitousness before which Crane's sensitive innocent is so confused that he cannot "distinguish between a 5-inch quick-firing gun and a nickel-plated ice-pick," and finds himself in the middle of a battlefield because he thinks that a dried palm branch is a Spanish guerrilla.[36] Of course, in this uncomprehended reality Perkins is alone ("Save for sharp inquiring glances, no one acknowledged his existence"). But Crane fails to focus his story sharply enough to give its occurrence a significance. Perkins survives, but the reader never knows how his experience has affected him. It is unclear whether anything has really or meaningfully happened. "The Serjeant's Private Mad-house" also presents a world controlled by gratuitousness. It turns on the delusion of a fear-crazed soldier whose fantasy of Spanish soldiers massed for attack threatens to provoke disaster. When the Spanish do attack, however, the mad soldier's singing frightens them away. Here again

Crane represented fantasy-perceptions of the imaginative man in battle, their inaccuracies and their dangers. They perhaps indicate just how far the ideal embodied by Lieutenant Peza —the ideal of the apprehending hero—has slipped since "Death and the Child." [37] Unfortunately, neither Cuban story has sufficient thematic focus to radiate much heat.

If some of the *Wounds in the Rain* stories are "low-pressure writing," others are more fully achieved—stories in which Crane began to grope for new possibilities of meaning and of value. And this groping can occur in what are very unpretentious stories indeed. "The Second Generation" is perhaps Crane's most sardonic war story. And the object of his scorn is the gentleman-soldier, the "hero" of so much newspaper writing during the Spanish-American War, whom Crane felt had unjustly stolen the "glory" from the regular soldier.[38] "The Second Generation" is the story of the son of a United States Senator who fails to "do his duty" after his father has obtained a commission for him. But young Caspar Cadogan's real failure—exemplified by his refusal to give his canteen to a feverish soldier—is a failure of selfishness, a failure of love. For this failure, the punishment is exclusion from the military brotherhood (" '—the other men, you know. I couldn't get along with them, you know. They're peculiar, somehow; odd; I didn't understand them, and they didn't understand me.' " *Virginia*, VI, 284). It is the disclosure of that denial which provokes the father's final scornful judgment. The father and his coming-to-awareness of the impropriety of his seeking special treatment for his worthless son is pathetic; the son—perhaps the ultimately degraded apprehending hero[39]—is only contemptible.

Willa Cather wrote, " 'The Price of the Harness' just misses being a fine story." Certainly it is one of Crane's better performances in the collection. And in it there is clearer evidence of Crane's search. For Private Nolan (who had appeared earlier as the typical army "regular")* and his companions provide for Crane a hero quite different from Henry Fleming or Lieutenant Peza.[40] Nolan is the common soldier, the ordinary fighting man of no unusual perception, whose apprehension is incomplete or inaccurate, and for whom war is a reality by which is tested, not his apprehension, but his capacity to perform his duty selflessly. Indeed, Nolan is, like Henry at the end of *The Red Badge*, not a man but a member, one of four companions in the story who share the experience of war and the point of view of the story. These four companions provide a point of view broader than that by which the war was described in *The Red Badge of Courage*. And central to Crane's story is the comradeship of the four men. It is this community itself, and its violation by the event of death, with which Crane was concerned.

The experience of war is a painful one for all four of Crane's soldiers. Companions as the story opens, they are soon separated by their injuries. Martin is hit in the arm, joins the column of wounded (endless and ubiquitous in Crane's war stories), contracts yellow fever, and meets his friend Grierson in the yellow-fever tent. Grierson tells of Watkins' probably mortal lung wound. And, in a chillingly brilliant scene in which Crane's unusual sympathy for the failures of perception just saves him from the bad taste of an insensitive irony, Nolan dies of a battle wound, and the companionship is violated—yet violated only by death. Here Crane has subdued his irony, and he simultaneously has established the superior importance of human love to circumstantial fact, by a remarkable and sudden shift in narrative distance—a shift

* Nolan appears as the antithesis to the socialite-soldier in "Regulars Get No Glory" (see *supra*, 249, 248). Possibly also it is Nolan who is the narrator of "Memoirs of a Private," and who is Crane's *persona* in "The Private's Story" (see *supra*, 248 *n*.)

which as it vitalizes the event, disorients the reader and blunts his critical objectivity.

"Well, it is damp," said Nolan, with sudden irritability. "I can feel it. I'm wet. I tell you—wet through—just from lyin' here."

They answered hastily. "Yes, that's so, Jimmie. It *is* damp. That's so."

"Just put your hand under my back and see how wet the ground is," he said.

"No," they answered. "That's all right, Jimmie. We know it's wet."

"Well, put your hand under and see," he cried, stubbornly.

"Oh, never mind, Jimmie."

"No," he said in a temper. "See for yourself." Grierson seemed to be afraid of Nolan's agitation, and so he slipped a hand under the prostrate man, and presently withdrew it covered with blood. "Yes," he said, hiding his hand carefully from Nolan's eyes, "you were right, Jimmie."

"Of course I was," said Nolan, contentedly closing his eyes. "This hillside holds water like a swamp." After a moment he said, "Guess I ought to know. I'm flat here on it, and you fellers are standing up."

He did not know he was dying. He thought he was holding an argument on the condition of the turf.

Virginia, VI, 111–12

The objective fact, the real "condition of the turf" (or the color of the sky, for that matter), is not important here. Nolan could probably not tolerate the knowledge of the nature of that wetness were it available to him, and to know would not change things anyhow. What is important is the generosity of Nolan's friends, their easing of the inevitable event, Nolan's death.

Crane's is a mature style in this story. Willa Cather calls it postimpressionist, and its advance over the purer early impressionism is clearly apparent. Now selected images are in focus and are intrinsically meaning bearing and yet are at once more suggestive and less specific than the earlier grotesques or even more recent symbolic images.

> There was something distinctive in the way they carried their rifles. There was the grace of an old hunter somewhere in it, the grace of a man whose rifle has become absolutely a part of himself. Furthermore, almost every blue shirt-sleeve was rolled to the elbow, disclosing forearms of almost incredible brawn. The rifles seemed light, almost fragile, in the hands that were at the end of these arms, never fat but always with rolling muscles and veins that seemed on the point of bursting.[41]
>
> *Virginia,* VI, 100

Still, in spite of such new sophistications, there is everywhere apparent Crane's continuing concern for the absurd disparity between reality and man's apprehension of it. Repeatedly in the story Crane contrasted actual war to the official one—the real to the apparent ("Officially, the battalion had not yet fired a shot"); there is the house on the battlefield which, like the lifesaving station in "The Open Boat," may or may not be occupied.* [42]

The story was written late in 1898 and was simultaneously published in the December issues of *Blackwood's Edinburgh Magazine,* and *Cosmopolitan.* In the American monthly, it appeared under the title of "The Woof of Thin Red Threads." This title was a phrase taken from the story itself. "To the prut of the magazine rifles was added the under-chorus of the clicking mechanism, steady and swift as if the hand of one operator was controlling it all. It reminds one always of a loom, a great grand steel loom, clinking, clanking,

---

* These buildings appear frequently in Crane's battle landscapes. One finds them, for example, in "War Memories," in the skirmishes of "The Kicking Twelfth" which I shall consider later), and there is, of course, the abandoned house which had been the home of the child in "Death and the Child."

plunking, plinking, to weave a woof of thin red threads, the cloth of death" (*Virginia*, VI, 109). But Crane objected to it; he was apparently dissatisfied with the emphasis it placed upon the story's determinism. As he wrote his agent, Paul Revere Reynolds, "The name of the story is 'The Price of the Harness' because it *is* the price of the harness, the price the men paid for wearing the military harness, Uncle Sam's military harness; and they paid blood, hunger and fever." [43] It is the men and their relationships, and not the absurd reality they occupy, which is important here.[44]

Where "The Price of the Harness" is clear, "Virtue in War" is ambivalent. On its face, the story has as its hero the "highly educated and strictly military Gates," a West Pointer retired from the army who returns to service, finds his way circuitously to a position of command over a battalion (Crane directed much of his irony here at the ritual irrationalties of military life), prepares a regiment for combat, and dies stoically in battle. And, of course, the true report of Gates's death is lost in the correspondents' discussion of mint juleps.[45] But, if Major Gates is one protagonist, the story certainly has another in Private Lige Wigram, whose friendliness transcends rank (as his unannounced and informal visit to the Major, which outrages the officer, suggests), whose sense of battlefield comradeship ignores the imperative of command, who tries to save the wounded Gates, and who at the end is engaged in the effort of properly identifying the Major's corpse.[46] Perhaps, as again Crane's alternate title would suggest,* exactly what is virtue in war is the question which Crane poses to his reader.

"The Clan of No-Name" is certainly Crane's most ambitious undertaking in the *Wounds in the Rain* collection.

---

* When it appeared in *Frank Leslie's Popular Monthly* in November of 1899, the story was entitled "West Pointer and Volunteer." See *Virginia*, VI, pp. cxlvi–cxlix.

The story is conducted in what is perhaps the book's most elaborate plot arrangment—an envelope structure with two separate plots, one contained within the other.[47] The story opens and closes with an account of Margharita, who receives and decides to accept the proposal of marriage of a Mr. Smith of Tampa. Upon deciding, she destroys the photograph of Manolo Prat, a soldier to whom she had previously pledged her love. The intervening sections tell Manolo's story, a story of his first battle, his bravery, and his death in a militarily insignificant skirmish. But this romance of love and death, which Eric Solomon calls "a bad pastiche of Kipling," [48] may also represent Crane's most serious attempt in *Wounds in the Rain* to articulate an ethic appropriate for the individual confronting such an absurd reality as war.

The central action of the story is Manolo Prat's. And this first lieutenant's initiation to battle and his death take place on a typically Cranean field of war in a struggle which, as Berryman says, is "atrocious." The battle here is between insurgent Cubans and guerrillas, a civil war in which no quarter is given. The action, like so many of Crane's battles, is not of central military importance. There is the discrepancy between the real and the reported ("The importance lay not so much in the truthful account of the action as it did in the heroic prose of the official report"). Yet Crane's impressionism in "The Clan" is perhaps somewhat altered; here the auditory image seems more important than the visual, and there is little of the heavy irony. And again there is evidence of Crane's shifting concern. In "The Clan of No-Name," Crane almost assumed the absurdity, the "atrocity" of the universe; the real subject is Manolo's conduct, not his vision.

Throughout the story there is reference to custom. In the frame we discover that it is the custom of polite people to permit no lapse in conversation and that the form of Smith's proposal is important to him. But in the main body of the story Manolo is also seriously and critically concerned with good form. "There was a standard, and he must follow it, obey it, because it was a monarch, the Prince of Conduct" (*Virginia*, VI, 127). Like Margharita's Mr. Smith, Manolo Prat conforms strenuously to a rigid pattern of behavior. But unlike Mr. Smith, Prat's conformity is meaningful. In what is to be a characteristic refrain—to be repeated later in the story for ironic purposes—Manolo's attitude is described thus:

> He was of a kind—that seemed to be it—and the men of his kind, on peak or plain, from the dark northern ice-fields to the hot wet jungles, through all wine and want, through all lies and unfamiliar truth, dark or light, the men of his kind were governed by their gods, and each man knew the law and yet could not give tongue to it; but it was the law, and if the spirits of the men of his kind were all sitting in critical judgment upon him even then in the sky, he could not have bettered his conduct; he needs must obey the law, and always with the law there is only one way. But from peak and plain, from dark northern ice-fields and hot wet jungles, through wine and want, through all lies and unfamiliar truth, dark or light, he heard breathed to him the approval and the benediction of his brethren.
>
> *Virginia*, VI, 131

This law leads the new lieutenant to bravery and to brotherhood with the brave. Manolo's courage is acknowledged by a recognized hero, Bas, and "the new officer [Prat] had early achieved a part of his ambition—to be called a brave man by established brave men" (*Virginia*, VI, 127). But the same law—which demands the subjugation of self-concern to duty —also leads Manolo Prat a step beyond. It leads him to recognize what Neal Osborn calls the "mystic tie uniting all men." [49] More specifically, it leads him to a saucerlike hollow in the battlefield and a position beside a wounded soldier, a peasant who is "not of his kind." Prat knows that both are doomed, but when he takes his place to die beside that peasant, he has achieved a capacity for love which neither Margharita's self-serving infidelity, nor Mr. Smith's selfish desire, nor the general's ambition allow them. And by achieving this capacity, Manolo Prat has earned something which no other Crane hero has yet achieved. He has earned the right not to see. It is without apparent irony that Crane describes Lieutenant Prat's death. "There was a stir in the grass at the edge of the saucer, and a man appeared there looking where lay the four insurgents. His negro face was not an eminently ferocious one in its lines, but now it was lit with an illimitable blood-greed. He and the young lieutenant exchanged a singular glance; then he came stepping eagerly down. The young lieutenant closed his eyes, for he did not want to see the flash of the machete" (*Virginia*, VI, 132). It would thus seem that "The Clan of No-Name" is a pure celebration of Manolo Prat's achievement. But Crane could not resist the slight shift of attitude and a resulting final irony. For, with its envelope structure, the story does not end with Manolo Prat's death, but with Mr. Smith's proposal. Here are the other "laws"—now less heroic than the laws of courage. Here is a law of conversation and a proper way for polite men to propose marriage. And when the refrain is repeated in a final paragraph, the reader is struck by the possibility of ironic meaning, and is left with an uneasy doubt as to whether Manolo Prat was an absurd saint or simply a fool of his own illusions. "For the word is clear only to the kind who on peak or plain, from dark northern ice fields to the hot wet jungles, through all wine and want, through lies and unfamiliar truth, dark or light, are governed by the unknown gods; and, though each man knows the law no man may give tongue to it" (*Virginia*, VI, 136).

If Crane was asserting an ethic here, it is a tentative one at best. Here is another of those final ambiguities which grace the endings of Crane's finest stories. One thinks back to "The Bride" for a moment and wonders, who, after all, was caught in delusion, Scratchy Wilson or Potter? And one thinks of "The Open Boat" ("They felt that they could then be interpreters." Could they?). Yet, ambiguous though he may be, Crane here was at least groping toward an ethic of the absurd which goes well beyond that which other writers were to formulate several decades later. And what is perhaps even more significant for Crane, "The Clan of No-Name" may well be the articulation of what he had failed to achieve in the final chapter of *The Red Badge of Courage*.

In the final desperate months Crane continued to write of wars, but too much of the result was hack work. There were the Wyoming Valley tales—rapid revision of an earlier manuscript and from a book by Crane's own grandfather, the Reverend Dr. George Peck[50]—and there were also nine accounts of the *Great Battles of the World*, to be collected for Lippincott—"such sure quick money," Crane called them in a letter to Pinker. These were done with Kate Frederic's assistance—or one should say, *by* Kate Frederic, with Crane writing only a few transitional passages. But the project dragged on and became a burden.[51] The last serious war writing—drawn from Crane's Cuban experiences—describes an imaginary conflict between "Spitzbergen" and "Rostina." [52] And in these stories, as in "An Episode of War," Crane again returned to his concern with the paradox of apprehension and love.

The "Spitzbergen Tales," as they were called in *Last Words*,* are executed in a purified style. The flash of

* *Last Words* is the first publication in which the four tales were printed together, and they did not appear there in proper sequence. In fact, it was not until Wilson Follett's Knopf edition that the four were placed in correct order, and there they were rather eccentrically titled. See Williams and Starrett, *Stephen Crane: A Bibliography*, 56–64; and *Work*, IX, 137–71.

impressionistic image has been darkened; the language is bare and functional, never decorative.[53] And Crane's focus is a relentlessly closing one. Beginning in "The Kicking Twelfth" and "The Shrapnel of Their Friends" with a whole regiment as protagonist, Crane reduced his subject to sixteen men in the third sketch and in "The Upturned Face" concluded with the burial of a single soldier.* Moreover, in this very economical set of stories, Crane was also economical of character. There is only one character in the set who appears in more than one story and is considered in any depth—whose apprehension is of significance to Crane's theme. This is Lieutenant Lean, an officer who, although he appears in the first two stories of the set, stands quietly in the background and is moved to the center of the action only in the final crucial moments.

The first two of the stories are concerned with the initiation of a regiment to combat. In the first, "The Kicking Twelfth,"—the Twelfth Regiment of the Line of the Spitzbergen infantry—recruits for war, goes into battle, and gains glory in its first engagement. The reader is introduced to Lieutenant Lean, watches the "Kicking Twelfth" as it bravely captures a hill ("They did not seem to think of being killed; they seemed absorbed in a desire to know what would happen and how it would look when it was happening." *Virginia*, VI, 290). Then the regiment advances to capture another enemy position. Lieutenant Lean leads the charge, and after this first fight is over, even as the general commends the colonels, the colonel commends his lieutenant. All is well in the "Kicking Twelfth"; like Henry Fleming's regiment, it has successfully endured its baptism of fire. But as was

* There is extant the manuscript of a fifth Spitzbergen tale, "The Fire Tribe and the White-Face," which remained unfinished at Crane's death and has never seen print. Stallman asserts that it "concludes the action of the sequence" but is "a fictional fizzle" which Crane recast as drama. See Stallman, 531, 605, 623.

also the case with Henry, the realities of war are later to be quite different and considerably darker.

The next sketch is a step closer to the awful reality. As "The Shrapnel of Their Friends" opens, one sees the regiment proud of itself for its earlier bravery ("Corps prides met each other face to face at every step." *Virginia*, VI, 301). But the soldiers are also anxious, and they watch their general to determine their fate (vision remains always significant). When the regiment is called to attack a second time, war—the reality which the men are now confronting—is less orderly, less safe, less reasonable. Now the regiment occupies a position which comes under the fire of its own artillery. Enraged and terrified by this danger and its absurdity, the "Kicking Twelfth" almost breaks and flees; now the regiment is cursed by its general. But again all comes right in the end; the men do not flee, the colonel of the Twelfth is apologetically decorated, and the soldiers even find an opportunity afterwards to curse the errant artillery battery.

In the third sketch, " 'And If He Wills, We Must Die,' " as the men of the "Kicking Twelfth" move yet another step closer to the horror at the center of the experience of war, Crane's focus narrows. He was concerned here, not with the whole regiment, but with one squad, which attempts to hold one house. Now the soldiers cannot see their enemy,[54] and in this story the very purpose of the military action is called in question ("Another private explained to a comrade: 'This is all nonsense anyhow. No sense in occupying this post. They . . .' "). Indeed, there is everywhere a growing sense of behavioral and environmental disorder. Soldiers are caught stealing and are not punished; the sergeant is disdainful of the deserted house which he occupies (" 'These people must have lived like cattle' "). Throughout, snatches of confused conversation are recorded. And this time the squad fails, its sergeant is killed, the position is lost.

The final and climactic sketch of "The Kicking Twelfth" is "The Upturned Face." It is a work justly famous but too often read without its companions, for although the sketch has a Goyaesque quality which, as John Berryman has said, makes it "unlike . . . all Crane's other stories," [55] "The Upturned Face" is nevertheless the logical outcome, not only of its three companion sketches, but of much of what Crane had experienced, thought, and written before it. In this final Spitzbergen tale Crane, again closing focus, turned his attention to the young officer whom we have met earlier, Lieutenant Lean. As "The Upturned Face" begins, Lean is in the company of an adjutant and some privates, and all are confronting the corpse of a dead companion. The story opens with the adjutant's asking a question—the question logically to follow after the increasing chaos, absurdity, and destruction described in the first three parts of "The Kicking Twelfth." " 'What will we do now?' said the adjutant, troubled and excited. 'Bury him,' said Timothy Lean" (*Virginia*, VI, 297).

It is the question to follow apprehension, the question which Crane himself had finally come to ask.[56] And it is Timothy Lean who answers it by an imperative for the performing of a ritual. Lieutenant Lean asserts the law and insists upon the order of the burying of the dead. On its face, the ritual is a rather futile one. It is directed at the ordering of the experience of one who is no longer alive to apprehend. But it is also a ritual of recognition—of the mutability which one shares with the dead. Moreover, here this ritual requires even more horrible apprehension. The body must be touched; the dead face must be looked into. And this work must be performed under the rattle of gunfire. Ritual is a means of dealing with chaos, a means of asserting order, but ritual requires confrontation even as it makes such confrontation bearable.

First there must be touch. The body is searched, the corpse is placed in the grave. The adjutant attempts, by joking, to insulate himself from the confrontation, but Lean, whose role here is almost that of a priest, will not permit such turning away. " 'Well,' he said humorously to Lean, 'I suppose we had best tumble him in.' 'Yes,' said Lean. The two privates stood waiting, bent over their implements. 'I suppose,' said Lean, 'it would be better if we laid him in ourselves.' " When the body is placed in the grave, even Timothy Lean falters ("Both were particular that their fingers should not feel the corpse"), and when Lean and the adjutant attempt to recite the service for the burial of the dead, they both fail. Neither can remember all the words of the service, and there is no book. So there are only a few remembered lines—a request for mercy from a god of "superb heights."

When it is time for the grave to be filled—when the apprehension of death is to be concluded—the experience of confrontation paradoxically becomes more intense. Now, as Lean looks down into the upturned face, the apprehension is consummate. For now what Lean sees in the grave he identifies with himself. The recognition of the finitude he shares with the corpse is so intense, that, when the first shovelful of dirt strikes the feet rather than the face, "Timothy Lean felt as if tons had been swiftly lifted from off his forehead." This final process of ritual is to be experienced individually and without assistance. When one of the privates is wounded, Lean takes the shovel himself. Again the adjutant attempts to turn away—to insulate himself with words, and again Lean will not permit it. This time Lieutenant Lean breaks rules—he violates both courtesy and military protocol—to silence the adjutant.[57] " 'Damn you,' said Lean, 'shut your mouth.' He was not the senior officer."

But there is yet a final moment of confrontation—with the "chalk-blue" face of the corpse,* the last of the body remaining uncovered. And at the final moment, Lean—who is finally more a man than a priest—stutters and flinches. And at that moment his companion, the adjutant, who understands the lieutenant's reluctance, encourages Lean so that he can complete the covering of the corpse. There is a terrible relief in the final sentence. "Lean swung back the shovel; it went forward in a pendulum curve. When the earth landed it made a sound—plop." [58] Like another lieutenant in "The Clan of No-Name" Timothy Lean has earned the right, finally, to cover over the reality of death and to turn away.

In "The Kicking Twelfth" Crane has taken a regiment and one of its lieutenants, Timothy Lean, through an initiation into the absurdity of war perhaps not unlike that which he himself had experienced.[59] Lean and Crane have then moved to a consideration of the next question—of "What will we do now?" Timothy Lean attempts to assert order in his chaotic universe and to do service to a dead companion. In that assertion—now by ritual and not by "interpretation" (as in the final sentence of "The Open Boat"), Lean has

---

* One has seen enough of Crane's use of blue to recognize its central significance to the writer's imagination. It was Blue Billie who threatened George near the end of *George's Mother*, and in *The Red Badge*, Henry Fleming repeatedly noticed the blue battle line of the Union forces and felt his own insignificance. Crane wrote a poem about "Blue Battalions," and the same color isolated the blue hotel from its background. Snow—in "The Blue Hotel" and elsewhere—is often presented as having a bluish tinge. In the Greek war writing and in the Cuban pieces appear blue shirtsleeves, blue moonlight, and brilliant blue seas. But most noticeable of all is the blue "color of the sky" finally apprehended by the men in "The Open Boat." It is the color which constantly reminds Crane's characters of their own insignificance in a universe from which they are essentially alienated. One also wonders whether Crane's blue—like Melville's white—might not mask some terrible and supreme reality, a reality necessarily incomprehensible to man, a reality for which man can feel only awe. In another frame of reference, however, blue can be said to be the color of the absurd.

come, privately, to confrontation with the final reality, death itself. With the assistance of another man he has, however, completed his task and thus earned the right to avert his eyes. Crane has here achieved a statement as succinct and perhaps as profound as any other in his work. "The Up-turned Face" should have been Crane's final story.[60]

XIII
Conclusions

A *man said to the universe:*
"Sir, I exist!"
"However," replied the universe,
"The fact has not created in me
A *sense of obligation."*
Stephen Crane, War is Kind, 1899

L'absurde naît de cette confrontation entre l'appel humain et le silence déraissonable du monde.
Albert Camus, Le mythe de Sisyphe, 1942

"The Upturned Face" was, for Stephen Crane, the end of a complex and compressed development. When he began as a writer, Crane was aware of a dichotomy—a difference between human apprehension of reality and reality itself. It was an awareness which arose out of the intellectual environment of his own time. His imagination was shaped in the waning years of the nineteenth century, a time when a number of writers were becoming increasingly uncomfortable with their awareness of the rapidly widening dichotomy between subject and object which had been generated out of the secularization and diffusion of the romantic vision.* One consequence of this awareness and dissatisfaction, as Professor Miller has pointed out, is nihilism. Man and his subjective awareness are separated from objective reality; man grants existence to that which he apprehends; thus he threatens to "drink up the sea." Soon he will wander in the nothingness of his own ego or—as the vision is set forth in

---

* The idea and the terminology are obviously J. Hillis Miller's. See *Poets of Reality*, 1–4.

one of Crane's most nihilistic images—alone in a blinding snowstorm on a Nebraska plain.

Crane countered that vision in his awareness of man's impulse to "walk barefoot into reality," * or to reengage reality by apprehending its objective nature objectively— beyond the distortions of the will. Yet, he was simultaneously and ironically aware of man's many delusions, his protective and often self-serving denials of that impulse. As his experience widened, Crane also came to know of the limits of man's very capacity for apprehension beyond the will's delusions. It was his awareness of and service to that impulse which gave life to Crane's personal vision.

Stephen Crane's earliest journalistic writing and his first experiments in fiction took ironic note of the dichotomy between reality and the ordinary man's usual apprehension of it. The Asbury Park sketches are populated by such figures as James A. Bradley looking out over his ocean and the resorters gazing uncomprehendingly at the union marchers. In the Sullivan County sketches Crane set his "little man" in a natural environment and considered how that man saw and failed to see that environment, how fear and pride diminished his capacity to see and tell of it. At the end of several of these sketches Crane also showed his early awareness of the unstable nature of man's apprehension; often he recorded shifts of attitude in altered awarenesses of the environment.

Crane's first novel, *Maggie*, is also centered around the experience of apprehension. And here the protagonist's vision is also distorted—but this time not so much by fear of what she is seeing as by fear of what she has seen. Maggie's fear and distorted apprehension of reality lead her to isolation and death, and her story is told in an impressionistic

* The phrase is Wallace Stevens' but it is to be found in Professor Miller's *Poets of Reality*, 7.

language which records the alteration of reality by the eye in renderings which are often sharply grotesque. If Crane's was a style influenced by Hamlin Garland's "veritism" or even by Crane's associations with painters in New York and by his observation of the techniques they employed in their work, it was also a literary method fit to dramatize his own and his characters' awarenesses.

Stephen Crane continued in the development of that method in his realistic writing on social themes in his years in New York. But even as he was developing his capabilities as a writer, he was broadening the dimensions of his awareness and concern. His characters in these socially engaged sketches and stories are constantly moving to events of apprehension, are constantly pressing beneath the surfaces of appearance to confront the thing itself. And they are constantly threatened as well by new dangers to the clarity of their vision, and now not only by fear but by the solipsism attendant upon isolation, by the barriers of social class, by the early conditioning of psychological orientation, by the bedazzlements of naiveté.

Yet, although Crane's development was considerable in these sketches, it was in *The Red Badge of Courage* that he first discovered a pattern of action whereby he could dramatize his awareness. *The Red Badge* is a story of a young soldier's learning to see a complex reality—the reality of war—in the most difficult of conditions. Here Henry's apprehension is threatened by fear, by confusion, by rumor, by constantly shifting perspectives, and by his own prejudices and presumptions. Yet after he flees from the communal and limited awareness of his regiment, he comes to confront alone and in Nature the fact of war—paradoxically the very reality from which he had fled. And after this flight from his regiment, and his consequent isolation and confrontation, he returns—to his companions and to his share of their delu-

sions. Henry's return to community is complex in its implications, for if his becoming "not a man but a member"
saves him from the solipsism of isolated vision, it also subjects him again to communal delusions. Crane in the final
chapter failed to come to terms with the paradox inherent in
this contradiction. Yet, although *The Red Badge* may not be
wholly successful as a work of art, it does establish for its
author a pattern of action which would serve him throughout his career.

This discovered action was important to Crane in his work
of 1895 and 1896. In his first writings about the West,
Crane's awareness of the essential disorientation of man in
the universe, of the complex implications of his communal
experience, and of the impact of that experience upon the
individual in the formation and shaping of apprehensional
capability produced work which concerned the contrasting
ways of seeing in East and West. *The Third Violet*, Crane's
next novel, failed, perhaps because its author's now intensified commitment to the event of apprehension made the
conduct of his novel within the conventions of American
realism impossible. And the socially engaged city sketches of
1896 also show a tension between Crane the realist and the
Crane committed imaginatively to the event of apprehension
and to the tensions between the private and the communal
imagination which are dramatized in that event. Crane also
wrote a number of war stories in these years, and here again
he dramatized the oppositions between group expectation
and communal response.

Some of the unresolved tensions inherent in Crane's early
work were to some extent resolved in his writing of "The
Open Boat." In this story, as he approached the full
maturity of his style, he moved also toward a recognition of
new implications for his pattern of action. Again Crane's
apprehending characters must be isolated before they can

see the thing itself, yet at the end of the story these characters effect their return to their community, to life on the shore. In "The Open Boat" Crane's imagination engaged the communal implications for individual apprehension; here his attention was not only upon how one comes to know the color of the sky, but also upon how one can come to "interpret" it, for one's self and for others.

There was another experience which was critical in the formation of Stephen Crane's imagination; that was his first experience in battle in the Greek war. In his Greek war journalism Crane began to manifest a recognition of the ultimate impossibility of "interpretation," or even of apprehension, of a reality as complex as that of battle. And the one short story to come out of the war, "Death and the Child," represents again—and for the last time in a war story—the movement into isolation of a sensitive protagonist who is seeking to confront unblinkingly the thing itself. Yet this movement is rewarded with no tolerable knowledge. Rather, the reality—which Peza finally cannot bear to confront—is ineffable, alien, and absurd; the effort to apprehend it brings only dehumanization. In the later inadequate novel of the Greek war, *Active Service*, there is at odd moments evidence of Crane's dark awareness of the dangers of apprehension.

Thus, after "The Open Boat" and "Death and the Child," Crane's was a paradoxical awareness. He recognized the necessary impulse of man to reestablish his place in the universe by apprehending objective reality and his recurring effort to do so, first by laying aside the protections and illusions provided by his communities and setting out alone to seek confrontation and apprehensional engagement, then by returning to his community to be an "interpreter." He was also aware, however, of man's essential incapacity to tolerate such an apprehensional engagement, he was aware of man's inability to sustain a real confrontation with an essential reality, and he was aware of the dangers inherent in such an undertaking.

This paradoxical awareness generated the work of Crane's final years. In these years his writing took several directions, but his awareness was embodied in stories about three subjects. Working at times in extremely difficult conditions Crane wrote of life in modern cities and towns (the American towns of his childhood and the London of his present life), of the American West, and of war.

When Crane wrote of man in city and in town, his darkened imagination again manifested itself, but his old concerns remained apparent. In the city sketches of London Crane's interest in the event of apprehension—in the capabilities and the limitations of the eye—was so intense that it superseded his commitment to represent the reality he observed. But when he turned to the small town of his own memory, which he called Whilomville, and pursued there in "The Monster" and in the Whilomville stories the origins of limitation upon the eye and the understanding, Crane's darkened awareness caused a truncation of his pattern of action, and the writer demonstrated a newly intensified sense of the limitations upon apprehension imposed by the community. Now sensitive characters are simply driven from their place in their community into isolation; yet it is only when such a character has thus escaped the blindnesses and bedazzlements of family or social group that he can even hope to see clearly. Dr. Trescott is the only exception here, and of the others, no one really escapes. It was in these Whilomville stories that Crane explored the nature and impact of communal delusion as it enforced itself upon Whilomville's citizens, and first upon its children.

The years after the Greek war were also the years of Crane's great western stories, stories which showed complex developments and doublings of his pattern of isolation, confrontation, and return. In "The Bride Comes to Yellow Sky" Crane dramatized the replacement of one order of communal apprehension with another; in other stories he considered the consequences of that replacement. In "The Blue Hotel" the failures of the communal and private understandings and apprehensions bring death to the Swede; "Moonlight on the Snow" is about the commercialization of the imagination in a western town; in "Twelve O'Clock," the last of the western stories, Crane represented a kind of absurd apocalyptic vision of apprehensional failure.

But it was in his final war, and in the writing that was to come out of it, that Crane began to approach the formulation of an answer to his terrible enigma. In Cuba the reality of war seemed simply not available. The reality itself was fragmented and absurd, and to confront it led only to isolation and madness. Having recognized this impossibility, Crane again turned to the third step in his pattern of action to find new possibilities—possibilities which for him had been inherent in that return as early as *The Red Badge*. To return to one's community was to recommit one's self, not only to the dangers of delusion but also to the possibilities of relationship with one's fellows, to a kind of salvation through the surrender of self.* In these possibilities— inherent in the ethic of service and in the rituals of obliga-

* J. Hillis Miller speaks of the walk barefoot into reality as "abandoning the independence of the ego. Instead of making everything the object for the self, the mind must efface itself before reality, or plunge into the density of an exterior world, dispersing itself in a milieu which exceeds it and which it has not made. The effacement of the ego before reality means abandoning the will to power over things. This is the most difficult of acts for a modern man to perform. It goes counter to all the penchants of our culture. To abandon its project of dominion the will must will not to will" (*Poets of Reality*, 8). Crane in "The Upturned Face" did not remotely approach this, "the new realm of the twentieth century poem." Perhaps, however, Crane's tentative exploration there of the possibilities of self-surrender might be taken as a gesture in that direction. If so, Stephen Crane is more "modern" than anyone has ever imagined.

tion—Crane seemed to be on the verge of finding something which might serve as an alternative to the effort of confrontation which—in the face of an absurd reality—now seemed so futile. If, as in "The Upturned Face," man submitted himself to these new values, he might, still paradoxically alone, come both to a tolerable glimpse of reality and achieve the right, finally, to turn away. However, before Crane could explore and seek answers to the contradictions inherent in this possibility, death intervened.

The event of apprehension—although it may be most significant in American literature—is the property of no one writer, of no time, of no place, of no language. If one considers only American writers, one would easily recall the importance of Walt Whitman's contemplation of a blade of grass, or of Huck Finn's several and grotesque apprehensions of his father, or of the always recurring and often formally dramatized scenes of confrontation in Henry James's work—in *The Portrait of a Lady* (which Crane admired) or perhaps even more significantly in *The Ambassadors*. And later there would be Sister Carrie looking at the lights of the lake front, and Cowperwood in *The Financier* and his two apprehensions, the first of a lobster destroying a squid, the second of the stars above his prison yard. Later Gatsby would see the green light on Daisy's dock, and—one could go on and on with such a catalogue.

But what is significantly unusual about the scenes of confrontation in Crane's fiction, what makes them of such defining importance in his own time, is not only their pervasiveness but their quality of uncertainty. For in Crane's stories and novels one can never be entirely sure just what it is that has been seen or whether anything has really been seen and understood at all. Crane is at the critical moment always a bit too ironic, or the possibilities which he presents are a bit too multiple, for the reader ever to be sure.

Of course, what one is finally unsure of is the nature of the reality which Crane's characters confront. Ultimately—an awareness which Crane seemed to experience more intensely in his later works—the reality which these characters confront is unknowable because it is too alien to be known. For what is also notable in Crane's work is the degree and frequency with which his characters are dislocated in their isolation. There are first of all the men who continually find themselves in unaccustomed environments in the woods and caves and swamps of Sullivan County; then there is the dependent Maggie Johnson, first in the unaccustomed brilliance of restaurant and music hall, then forced to fend for herself on the streets. There are also George and his mother, both country people in the city, and, elsewhere, a young, middle-class man making his experiments in misery and in luxury.

Later there are four men in an open boat, and Scratchy Wilson, wearing his manufactured shirt in the wrong time, and Potter in the Pullman, and a Swede in a blue hotel in Nebraska. And there is a Greek youth in his high, straight collar, dead on a battlefield, and there is Crane himself in London, and a college professor in the middle of a war, and a Spanish peasant dead in Cuba, and a lieutenant wielding a shovel on burial detail. No one belongs where he is; everything is incongruous and alien. "The whole affair is absurd." * [1]

* *Virginia*, V, 77. This is hardly an isolated appearance of the word or of its conception in Crane's work; rather, both word and idea appeared frequently. He used *absurd* in adverbial form, again in "The Open Boat" (*Virginia*, V, 88), and—for another example—in "The Five White Mice." Here, Crane's protagonist sees the unsuspected concluding turn of events as "an absurd imposition" (*Virginia*, V, 51). Moreover, Crane used many other words to express the same notion—*preposterous* in "The Open Boat" (*Virginia*, V, 77), *meaningless* (in describing the church hospital in "War Memories" as "something meaningless and at the same time overwhelming," *Virginia*, VI, 254), and, in the same work, *curious* (*Virginia*, VI, 246), ironically to describe a battle wound.

It would thus seem that simply to label Crane a naturalist, or even to proceed to a reading of Crane's fiction after a consideration of some formulaic definition of literary naturalism, is a bit misleading. In the first place, naturalism can mean different things to different readers. To some, naturalism is simply "pessimistic determinism"; to others, the naturalist is essentially a social reformer.[2] Still others follow a middle course; C. C. Walcutt, as I have said, observed a "divided stream" in American literary naturalism, one optimist, one pessimist, both of which proceed out of the assumptions of philosophical monism.[3] Yet whether literary naturalism is in effect an awareness of the chains of determinism, an inquiry into social causation, or the product of a philosophy of unity, all would agree that literary naturalism assumed a relational union—causal or physical—of man and his environment. It is precisely that relationship of which Crane was unsure.

For if Crane's characters are always alien to their environment, always dislocated, never physically connected to the reality which they confront—never, in Camus' phrase, "a tree among trees," they are also rarely causally enmeshed in that reality.[4] Instead, they live in a world of gratuitous event, a world in which chance or accident is constantly violative of causation. Although Jim Conklin and Billie Higgins die, Henry Fleming and the correspondent live, and there is no explanation. "The whole affair is absurd," thinks the correspondent in "The Open Boat," and it is this absurdity—and not the causal process of damage occurring to a ship, its foundering, and the lowering away of boats (which Crane so carefully explained in his newspaper account of the sinking of the *Commodore* and so completely excluded from "The Open Boat")—which is Crane's fictional theme.[5] The events of "The Five White Mice" are governed by a throw of the dice. Where causation is described, it is presented as too complex to be unraveled. Since everyone in the blue hotel that day is responsible for the Swede's death, no one of them is responsible. And though there must certainly be a cause for the fire in Dr. Trescott's house, Crane never bothers to explain it, and the reader simply is made to assume that it would be inappropriate and irrelevant to conjecture upon it.

It would, of course, be inappropriate for me here to pause to trace a history of the concept of the absurd, even from Kierkegaard to the present. I can only assert that in what is often taken to be the classic modern definition of the term, Albert Camus' *Le mythe de Sisyphe*, the word *absurde* appears in connection with several descriptions and partial definitions, but no precise single meaning is achieved for it. However, if Camus did not formally define the notion, he did describe it at considerable length.

> Ce divorce entre l'homme et sa vie, l'acteur et son décor, c'est proprement le sentiment de l'absurdite.
>
> Mais ce qui est absurde, c'est la confrontation de cet irrationel et de ce désir éperdu de clarté dont l'appel résonne au plus profond de l'homme. L'absurd dépend autant de l'homme que du monde.
>
> L'absurde est essentiellment un divorce. Il n'est ni dans un ni dans l'autre des elements compares. Il naît dans leur confrontation.
>
> . . . je puis donc dire que l'Absurde n'est pas dans l'homme (se une parielle metaphore pouvait avoir un sens) ni dans le monde, mais dans leur presence commune.[6]

Such circling of definition led John Cruickshank to conclude, "By the absurd Camus generally means the absence of correspondence or congruity between the mind's need for coherence and the incoherence of the world which the mind experiences."[7]

There is, as Cruickshank admitted, considerable difference of opinion concerning Camus' intentions in using the term.[8] But Cruickshank's definition—if it does not represent Camus' meaning—certainly represents a condition with which Stephen Crane would have had a familiar sympathy. For throughout Crane's career—and increasingly after "The Open Boat"—he asserted in his writing an awareness of the risible yet maddening incoherence of the universe and man's need to apprehend and to understand it, of man's loss of role and his search for place and reason. It is this awareness, and not Crane's "naturalism," which best characterizes his vision.

For everywhere opposing this absurdity is a pressure for order, a pressure for apprehension and for understanding. The pressure is apparent from the very beginning in Crane's style, in his early painterly renderings, later in his dramatization of characters' emotions through the use of impressionistic techniques, at the end in his increased use of vividly and intensely rendered expressionistic images. It is apparent also in Crane's early experiment in the formalization of emotional response to color and in his later efforts at the composition of colors in nature. And it is apparent in his efforts at syntactic patterning, in his rhythmic arrangements, and in his verbal repetitions and refrains.

The pressure is also apparent in Crane's complex ironic relationships to his subjects. His irony was intense—so intense that it generates tonal discordances which damage, sometimes irreparably, certain of his works—and it was only in the final years that he gained a consistent control over that irony. But its object was always clear; Crane directed his irony at self-delusion, at the too-easy acceptance of facile or self-serving explanations of reality—in short, at refusals to see.

And the pressure is also apparent in the recurrent actions in Crane's fiction and in the patterns by which those actions are governed. Repeatedly in Crane's work an effort at seeing takes the protagonist out of his community and into a condition of isolation. And after meaningful confrontation occurs, there is often a return to the community from which that protagonist has come, a return in which the confrontation experienced takes on social significance. As Crane continued to write, the protagonist's capability—and the confronted reality's availability—for meaning came to be increasingly less sure. For over the course of his short career Crane came to be aware of too many dangers to clear seeing, and in time he even became more aware of the essential dichotomy between man and the universe, a dichotomy which made any comprehension impossible. At the end Crane's protagonists were left with rituals, with formal efforts at confrontation and at the submission of self which, when performed for one another, could reward the individual with the consolations of love, with a tolerable glimpse at the universe, and, finally, with a right to turn away.

It is this pressure to see which remains the characteristic phenomenon of Stephen Crane's prose writing. And the identification of the nature and the consequences of that pressure thus becomes one key, one means of access, to the central vision of this most available and at the same time this most obscure of the writers of his time. It is not only Crane's awareness of man's impulse to "walk barefoot into reality," but it is also his central vision of that reality, and the intensity of the pressure that opposed it, which makes Stephen Crane one of the most intensely modern of the American writers of his century.

Notes

CHAPTER I

1. Hamlin Garland's obituary opinion in *The Saturday Evening Post*, CLXXIII (July 28, 1900), 16–17, is fairly representative. Garland saw Crane as an undisciplined genius, an uncontrolled and minor talent who died young: "Crane's mind was more largely subconscious in its workings than that of most men. He did not understand his own mental processes or resources. When he put pen to paper he found marvelous words, images, sentences, pictures already [sic] to be drawn off and fixed upon paper. . . . Such a man cannot afford to enter the white-hot public thoroughfare, for his genius is of the lonely and the solitary shadow-land."

2. Vincent Starrett called Crane an "imagist" in *Buried Caesars* (Chicago, 1923), 73–86. See also H. E. Dounce, "Stephen Crane as a Craftsman," New York *Evening Sun*, January 8, 1917, p. 8.

3. Alexander Woollcott, "Woollcott Presents," *Saturday Review of Literature*, XVI (October 23, 1937), 14.

4. Thomas Beer, *Stephen Crane: A Study in American Letters* (New York, 1923). Beer's biography, hereinafter cited as Beer, though maddeningly undocumented, is intensely provocative as a "primary" source for Crane scholars. The other was Thomas L. Raymond's *Stephen Crane* (Newark, 1923). It received no wide acceptance.

5. Granville Hicks, for example, said in 1935, "Crane's virtues as a writer come from the honesty and the clarity with which he recorded what he saw; his weaknesses are the result of his failure to discover why he saw as he did." See Hicks, *The Great Tradition: An Interpretation of American Literature since the Civil War* (Rev. ed.; New York, 1967), 160. Jean Cazemajou has pointed out that some critics of the 1930s saw Crane as a "champion of the cause of the common man," although Professor Cazemajou provides us with no examples. See Cazemajou, *Stephen Crane* (Minneapolis, 1969), 6.

6. Alfred Kazin (Rev. ed.; Garden City, 1956), 48–52.

7. Their memory was no doubt jogged at that time by the enthusiastic support of a writer of the heroic stature of Ernest Hemingway. See Hemingway (ed.), *Men at War* (New York, 1942).

8. See Jean Cazemajou, "Stephen Crane: Deux decennies de redecouverte (1948–1968)," *Les Langues Modernes*, LXIII (1969), 54–60.

9. John Berryman, *Stephen Crane* (New York, 1950), hereinafter cited as Berryman. "Introduction," *Stephen Crane: An Omnibus*, ed. R. W. Stallman (New York, 1952), xix–xlv, hereinafter cited as *Omnibus*. Recently Daniel Weiss has returned to a highly sophisticated psychoanalytical criticism of Crane in "*The Red Badge of Courage*," *Psycho-*

analytical Review, LII (Summer, 1965) 32–52, LII (Fall, 1965), 130–54; and with Kermit Vanderbilt in "From Rifleman to Flagbearer: Henry Fleming's Separate Peace in *The Red Badge of Courage*," *Modern Fiction Studies*, XI (Winter, 1965–66), 371–80.

10. See James T. Cox, "Stephen Crane as Symbolic Naturalist: An Analysis of 'The Blue Hotel,'" *Modern Fiction Studies*, III (Summer, 1957), 147–58 and Joseph X. Brennan, "The Imagery and Art of *George's Mother*," *CLA Journal*, IV (December, 1960), 106–15. But see Philip Rahv, "Fiction and the Criticism of Fiction," *Kenyon Review*, XVIII (Spring, 1956), 276–87.

11. See James B. Colvert, "Structure and Theme in Stephen Crane's Fiction," *Modern Fiction Studies*, V (Autumn, 1959), 199–208.

12. See Robert F. Gleckner, "Stephen Crane and the Wonder of Man's Conceit," *Modern Fiction Studies*, V (Autumn, 1959), 271–81.

13. Only one example of the many source studies of *The Red Badge of Courage* is Thomas A. Gullason's "New Sources for Stephen Crane's War Motif," *Modern Language Notes*, LXXII (December, 1957), 572–75.

14. See John E. Hart, "*The Red Badge of Courage* as Myth and Symbol," *University of Kansas City Review*, XIX (Summer, 1953), 249–56.

15. This very fruitful approach to Crane has many proponents. One distinguished example is Peter Buitenhuis' "The Essentials of Life: 'The Open Boat' as Existentialist Fiction," *Modern Fiction Studies*, V (Autumn, 1959), 243–50.

16. Eric Solomon, *Stephen Crane: From Parody to Realism* (Cambridge, Mass., 1966), hereinafter cited as *Stephen Crane*, and Donald B. Gibson, *The Fiction of Stephen Crane* (Carbondale and Edwardsville, Ill., 1968).

17. Lillian Gilkes, *Cora Crane* (Bloomington, Ind., 1960).

18. For a brief discussion of texts, see my Preface, *supra*. Joseph Katz, *The Poems of Stephen Crane* (New York, 1966), hereinafter cited as *Poems*.

19. See T. A. Gullason, "The New Criticism and Older Ones: Another Ride in 'The Open Boat,'" *CEA Critic*, XXXI (June, 1969), 8; Matthew J. Bruccoli, "*Stephen Crane: A Biography*," *Stephen Crane Newsletter*, III (Winter, 1968), 9–10; Lillian Gilkes. "Corrections of R. W. Stallman's *Stephen Crane: A Biography*," *Stephen Crane Newsletter*, III (Spring, 1969), 6–7; and Lillian Gilkes, "Stephen and Cora Crane: Some Corrections, and a 'Millionaire' Named Sharefe," *American Literature*, XLI (May, 1969), 270–77.

20. V. L. Parrington, "The Beginnings of Critical Realism in America," *Main Currents in American Thought* (New York, 1930), III, 323–29.

21. C. C. Walcutt, *American Literary Naturalism: A Divided Stream* (Minneapolis, 1956), 66–86.

22. Donald Pizer, "Stephen Crane's *Maggie* and American Naturalism," *Criticism*, VII (Spring, 1965), 175, also 168–75.

23. Parrington, *Main Currents in American Thought*, III, 323–27; Harry Hartwick, *The Foreground of American Fiction* (New York, 1934), 21–44; Oscar Cargill, *Intellectual America* (New York, 1941), 48–175.

24. George W. Meyer, "The Original Social Purpose of the Naturalistic Novel," *Sewanee Review,* L (October–December, 1942), 563–70.
25. Walcutt, *American Literary Naturalism,* 3–29.
26. Thus Lars Ahnebrink in "Toward Naturalism in American Fiction," *Moderna Sprak, LIII* (1959), 365–72, has emphasized the scientific method to which naturalism was committed.
27. "Stephen Crane and His Work," *Friday Nights* (New York, 1922), 209. Garnett's judgment was originally uttered, however, before the London Academy on December 17, 1898.
28. R. W. Stallman and Lillian Gilkes (eds.), *Stephen Crane: Letters* (London, 1960), No. 213, p. 155, hereinafter cited as *Letters.*
29. Beer, 23.
30. Berryman, 263–93; *Omnibus,* xliii–xlv.
31. Orm Øverland, "The Impressionism of Stephen Crane: A Study in Style and Technique," in Sigmund Skard and Henry H. Wasser (eds.), *Americana Norvegica* (Philadelphia, 1966), I, 239–85.
32. Sergio Perosa, "Naturalism and Impressionism in Stephen Crane's Fiction," in Maurice Bassan (ed.), *Stephen Crane* (Englewood Cliffs, N.J., 1967), 85. Perosa calls this notion one of "the basic canons of impressionistic writing." I am indebted to his remarkably comprehensive article for much of my understanding of the sources of Stephen Crane's impressionism.
33. Joseph J. Kwiat has discussed this environment and this orientation at length in "The Newspaper Experience: Crane, Norris, and Dreiser," *Nineteenth-Century Fiction,* VIII (September, 1953), 99–117.
34. Joseph Conrad, "Preface," *The Nigger of the 'Narcissus,'* Uniform edition (London, 1929), VII, pp. ix, x. See Conrad's account of his meeting in his introduction to Beer. For the dating of Conrad's preface see Edward Garnett (ed.), *Letters from Joseph Conrad, 1895–1924* (Indianapolis, 1928), 101.
35. J. Hillis Miller, *Poets of Reality* (Cambridge, Mass., 1965), 3–4.
36. *Ibid.,* 13–67, 18–19.
37. *Ibid.,* 61, 63.
38. See Conrad's introduction to Beer, and Joseph Conrad, *Notes on Life and Letters* (New York, 1921), 49–52. As Stallman points out, however, Conrad's memory of dates seems inaccurate. See R. W. Stallman, *Stephen Crane: A Biography* (New York, 1968), 320, hereinafter cited as Stallman.
39. Eric Solomon, *Stephen Crane in England* (Columbus, Ohio, 1964), 91–118.
40. Austin M. Fox, in "Stephen Crane and Joseph Conrad," *Serif,* VI (December, 1969), 16–20, has undertaken a preliminary study, has set forth the chronology, and has suggested a few of the more obvious parallels to be drawn.

CHAPTER II

1. Stallman, 10–20. Berryman, 12–32.
2. Berryman makes much of "The King's Favor," which he sees as evidence

of Crane's special psychic orientation. See Berryman, 312, 322. See also Stallman, 23–31. Thomas A. Gullason, *The Collected Stories and Sketches of Stephen Crane* (New York, 1963), 49–52, hereinafter cited as *Stories and Sketches.* Olov Fryckstedt (ed.), *Stephen Crane: Uncollected Writings* (Uppsala, Sweden, 1963), 3–6, hereinafter cited as *Writings.*

3. D. G. Hoffman, "Stephen Crane's First Story," *Bulletin of the New York Public Library,* LXIV (May, 1960), 273–78. *Stories and Sketches,* 56–60.

4. *Stories and Sketches,* 60–61. Although Gullason includes "Dan Emmonds" as a work possibly of 1891 (*Stories and Sketches,* 61–65), Lillian Gilkes has made a rather convincing case for "Dan Emmonds" as a work of 1897 in spite of Stallman's objection (see *supra* Chap. 1, n. 19 for reference). In the biography (15, 537–39, 565), Stallman's position is that if there were an earlier sketch called "Dan Emmonds," the published version, at least, is the result of a radical 1897 revision. Solomon, *Stephen Crane,* 149, wisely described it as having its "date unknown." In the most recent discussion of the "Dan Emmonds" mystery George Monteiro suggests convincingly that the sketch is a later foreshortening of a proposed novel of the same name, announced and subsequently abandoned in 1896. See George Monteiro, "Stephen Crane's Dan Emmonds: A Case Reargued," *Serif,* VI (March, 1969), 32–36. I therefore exclude both the sketch and the lost novel from consideration here.

5. Stallman, 31–32; *Writings,* 7–8.

6. *Stephen Crane,* 7. Solomon was first, but more recently there have been articles like Neville Denny, "Imagination and Experience in Stephen Crane," *English Studies in Africa,* IX (March, 1966), 28–42, which have followed a similar path.

7. Stephen Crane covered Hamlin Garland's lecture on William Dean Howells, "Howells Discussed at Avon-by-the-Sea," for the August 18, 1891 edition. This was the occasion for his first meeting with Garland. See R. W. Stallman and E. R. Hagemann (eds.), *New York City Sketches of Stephen Crane* (New York, 1966), 267–68, hereinafter cited as *New York City Sketches;* and Stallman, 34.

8. James B. Colvert has examined them briefly in "The Literary Development of Stephen Crane" (Ph.D. dissertation, Louisiana State University, 1953), 9–19. In addition to the sketches discussed in my text, there appeared pieces by Crane on July 2 ("Meetings Begun at Ocean Grove"), July 3 ("Crowding Into Asbury Park"), July 24 ("On the New Jersey Coast: Summer Dwellers at Asbury Park and Their Doings"), August 5 ("Along the Shark River"), August 29 ("The Seaside Assembly's Work at Ocean Grove"), and September 11 ("The Seaside Hotel Hop"). See Stallman, 47, 49, 51, 52, and 570; *Writings,* 3–31; and *New York City Sketches,* 265–86. See also Marston LaFrance, "The Ironic Parallel in Stephen Crane's 1892 Newspaper Correspondence," *Studies in Short Fiction,* VI (Fall, 1968), 101–103, who points out that in the series of summer sketches Crane is concerned with drawing an ironic parallel between the worshippers at Ocean Grove and the vacationers at Asbury Park, who are both ignoring reality and are bedazzled by jimcracks and personalities.

9. The "Joys of Seaside Life" appeared unsigned in the *Tribune* on July 17, 1892.
10. New York *Tribune*, August 14, 1892, p. 17.
11. See Stallman, 53–57. For a time there was a delightful theory abroad about the election of 1892, with Whitlaw Reid, the *Tribune's* owner, as the Republican vice-presidential candidate on Benjamin Harrison's ticket. According to this theory, Crane's story threw New York, the key state in the election, into the Democratic column and thus elected Grover Cleveland to the presidency. Though Beer (88–90) did not follow it, the theory was first explicitly refuted by Willis Johnson in "The Launching of Stephen Crane," *The Literary Digest International Book Review*, IV (April, 1926), 288–90, and later by Melvin Schoberlin in his introduction to *The Sullivan County Sketches of Stephen Crane* (Syracuse, 1949), 6–11, hereinafter cited as *Sullivan County Sketches*. See also Beer, 89–90; Berryman, 44; and Stallman, 53–57.
12. See Stallman, 60–64.
13. *Ibid.*, 60.
14. Stallman also identifies "The Reluctant Voyagers" (a comic tale about two resorters who are carried out to sea on a derelict raft with which they are playing, and finally end up in a New York City taxicab in their bathing suits) as a result of the 1892 summer, although, as Stallman, Linson, and Gullason agree, it was actually set down in the spring of 1893. See *Stories and Sketches*, 121–36; Stallman, 63, 571; and Linson, *My Stephen Crane* (Syracuse, 1958), 18–20; Maxwell Geismar, *Rebels and Ancestors: The American Novel, 1890–1915* (Boston, 1953), 131.
15. Stallman says that Linson's memory of Crane's composition of "The Pace of Youth" was "two years later." However, Linson clearly identifies the writing as taking place in the spring of 1893 in *My Stephen Crane*, 26n., 27, 28. See also J. C. Levenson, "Introduction," in Fredson Bowers (ed.), *The University of Virginia Edition of the Works of Stephen Crane* (Charlottesville, 1969), V, pp. xxiii–xxiv, hereinafter cited as *Virginia*.
16. *Writings*, 90–94.
17. Willis F. Johnson, "The Launching of Stephen Crane." Probably, as Donald Pizer points out, Johnson's memory is not entirely accurate, but the date Johnson assigns to Crane's showing him the Sullivan County sketches may well be correct. For, although there may be some dispute as to just which of the Sullivan County pieces are to be classified as the sketches, there can be no doubt that Crane's publication of Sullivan County reports began in the *Tribune* in February of 1892. See *Maggie: A Girl of the Streets*, ed. Donald Pizer (San Francisco, 1968), "Introduction," xivn.
18. In R. W. Stallman (ed.), *Sullivan County Tales and Sketches* (Ames, Iowa, 1968), hereinafter cited as *Sullivan County Tales*, there are assembled some nineteen sketches, and the editor mentions in "Acknowledgements," viii, another ("Jack," a dog sketch) which he has not included. In Thomas A. Gullason, "A Stephen Crane Find: Nine News-

paper Sketches," *Southern Humanities Review*, II (Winter, 1968), 1–37, there is one addition to their number, "Two Men and A Bear."

Gullason includes in his gathering two newly discovered pieces, "Not Much of A Hero" (*Tribune*, May 1, 1892) and "A Reminiscence of Indian War" (*Tribune*, June 26, 1892). "Not Much of A Hero" is an ironic juxtaposition of fancy and reality again; this time the heroic legendary identity of an Indian fighter of Pike County is set against his historical identity as a sadistic murderer. "A Reminiscence of Indian War" is an account of an historical incident of the Revolutionary War in Pike County, based upon a history by Crane's grandfather and not unlike Crane's "Wyoming Valley Tales," which were published in Crane's *Last Words* (London, 1902). This latter discovery may lend support to Hans Arnold's contention that the "Wyoming Valley Tales" are early work. See *infra*, Chap. 12, n. 50.

19. Stallman, 37.
20. *Sullivan County Tales*, 55.
21. See Gullason, "A Stephen Crane Find."
22. Of the three, only one, "The Mesmeric Mountain," appeared in Crane's time, and that posthumously in *Last Words*. The other two did not see print until Melvin Schoberlin published them from manuscript in 1949 in *Sullivan County Sketches*.
23. Schoberlin has identified the four characters as Crane and three companions who together had tramped the woods. See "Introduction," *Sullivan County Sketches*, 18; and Stallman, 43–44. Curiously, the "little man," whom Schoberlin identifies as Louis E. Carr, Jr., is referred to as "Billie" in at least three of the stories in *Sullivan County Tales*, 113, 119, 120, 127.
24. Colvert, *Virginia*, VI, pp. xvi–xxiii, sees the sketches as fundamentally about the distortions imposed upon a sombre and remote natural reality by the deluded human imagination, about man's hysterical fear of a threatening nature and his impulse to seek its secret meaning. He sees *The Red Badge of Courage* as an expansion of the myth of man's inability to apprehend the mysterious world which is first established in the Sullivan County sketches.
25. See Donald B. Gibson, *The Fiction of Stephen Crane*, 5, also 3–24. Gibson, in an original reading of the Sullivan County sketches, sees "Four Men in a Cave" as being "on one level, a story about birth," about "the ability to face the object of fear [which] manifests the strengthening consciousness." Gibson sees the entire set of stories as dramas of the development of the consciousness in the escaping from protection and in the facing down of fear.
26. See *ibid.*, 15–16. Gibson sees the campfire here as "the light of consciousness." But see also xvii.
27. Solomon apparently sees it as a parody of Poe. But Bierce's *Tales of Soldiers and Civilians* was more current, published in 1891, and Crane's early admiration of Bierce is fairly clear. See "Introduction," *Sullivan County Sketches*, 16; *Letters*, No. 32A, pp. 50–51; and Berryman, 41.

28. Take, for instance,

    > Once I saw mountains angry,
    > And ranged in battle-front.
    > Against them stood a little man. . . .

    or

    > There was set before me a mighty hill,
    > And long days I climbed
    > Through regions of snow.
    > When I had before me the summit-view,
    > It seemed that my labor
    > Had been to see gardens
    > Lying at impossible distances.

    Poems, 24, 28

    See also Colvert, *Virginia,* VI, pp. xix—xxiii.

29. See Gibson's remarkable reading of "The Holler Tree" in *The Fiction of Stephen Crane,* 17–19.

30. In "The Launching of Stephen Crane," 289, Johnson called it "one of the best pieces of writing that Stephen ever did."

31. Berryman, 284.

32. Eric Solomon characterizes the passage thus in *Stephen Crane,* 3. Gibson sees a similar disparity of diction in *Maggie.* See his *The Fiction of Stephen Crane,* 31.

33. Stallman, *Sullivan County Tales,* 73, 89, 110.

34. *Ibid.,* 88, 89, 102.

35. Thus I exclude from consideration here "How the Donkey Lifted the Hills," which Stallman includes in his collection. This piece, along with "The Victory of the Moon," and "The Voice of the Mountain," is rather clearly identified with Crane's Mexican trip, Stallman's arguments to the contrary notwithstanding. See "Appendix," *Letters,* No. 17, p. 323; Joseph Katz's review, "Stephen Crane: Sullivan County Tales and Sketches," in *Stephen Crane Newsletter,* III (Fall, 1968), 10–11; and Bernice Slote, "Stephen Crane in the Nebraska *State Journal,* 1894–1896," *Stephen Crane Newsletter,* III (Summer, 1969), 4–5.

36. See Stallman, *Sullivan County Tales,* viii, 79n.; and R. W. Stallman (ed.), "Stephen Crane: Some New Stories," *Bulletin of the New York Public Library,* LXI (January, 1957), 36–46; and *Stories and Sketches,* 107–109.

37. Stallman, 116–17.

38. In a letter to Copeland and Day, written probably in June of 1895, Crane offered the Sullivan County sketches as "eight little grotesque tales of the woods which I wrote when I was clever," *Letters,* No. 74, p. 59. See Colvert, *Virginia,* VI, pp. xi–xvi.

39. *Letters,* No. 34, p. 32. James B. Colvert in "The Origins of Stephen Crane's Literary Creed," *Studies in English* (University of Texas), XXXIV (1955), 179–88, has argued rather convincingly that Kipling—and, more particularly, his *The Light That Failed*—had significant influence on Crane's early work.

Chapter III

1. *Letters*, No. 34, pp. 31–32. The first *sic* is Stallman's, the second my own. Crane asserted that this renunciation took place "when I left you"; presumably he referred to a parting which occurred at the end of the summer of 1892 (see Stallman, 61; and *Letters*, Nos. 28, 29, 29A, pp. 18–23). At the end of this time most of the Sullivan County writing was complete, and Crane had turned to the revision of *Maggie*. See *infra*, n. 3.

2. "On the New Jersey Coast" appeared on August 21, and the letter of complaint appeared three days later. Probably Crane and Lily had not yet parted.

3. Here we confront the increasingly complex issue of the time of composition of *Maggie*. Earlier Crane scholars date the composition variously, but it is now apparent that the *Maggie* published in 1893 was written somewhat later than was previously believed.

    Frank Noxon reported the earliest composition—of a story about a prostitute, which was written at the Delta Upsilon fraternity house at Syracuse in the spring semester of 1891, when Crane was in residence. See Stallman, 32; "Appendix," *Letters*, No. 24, p. 335, also pp. 334–39; and Frank Noxon, "The Real Stephen Crane," *Step Ladder*, XIV (January, 1928), 4–9. Willis Johnson remembered seeing a manuscript of *Maggie* later that year (see Johnson, "The Launching of Stephen Crane," 289). But Colvert is probably correct in distrusting these recollections and doubting that any completed draft of any novel closely resembling the 1893 *Maggie* was written in 1891. Were there such a draft, Crane almost certainly would have shown it to Hamlin Garland— a well-known writer whom Crane admired and who was an advocate of realism—when they met in August of 1891. See Colvert, "Introduction," *Virginia* I.

    Maggie, then, was almost certainly not completed in draft before August of 1891. Colvert suggests that Crane began to visit the Bowery in preparation for the writing of the novel in the fall of 1891; then he roamed the streets, the saloons, the flophouses, and the tenements of that quarter (like a good realist) and reported his adventures to Helen Trent. If Wallis McHarg's memory of Crane's assertion that he "wrote it in two days before Christmas" is correctly applied to Christmas of 1891 (see Beer, 81; Stallman, 66), then there must have been a draft of the novel by January, 1892. And, if Stallman is correct, another draft was written at Edmund's house during that spring and summer. But all this seems problematical. Crane was busy with the Sullivan County sketches in early 1892, and there is no clear recollection on the part of Hamlin Garland of ever seeing the novel in manuscript. Yet Crane and Garland almost certainly saw one another several times in August of 1892. See Donald Pizer, "The Garland-Crane Relationship," *Huntington Library Quarterly*, XXIV (November, 1960), 75–82.

    However, Richard Watson Gilder remembered that in March of 1892 Crane offered him a manuscript of *Maggie* (Beer, 83), and if Beer's rather vivid account of that incident is correct, then there was certainly a complete draft by that date. Colvert supports this claim, and its validity would certainly support the fact of subsequent private publication, for Gilder rejected the novel long before its 1893 publication. But it is also possible, as Donald Pizer has suggested, in his introduction to his facsimile *Maggie,* that Beer (or Gilder) misremembered the year, and that the draft which Gilder saw was executed in the fall and winter of 1892–93. There was certainly a full rewriting of the novel that winter. Frederick Lawrence's letter of 1923 gives support to this assertion, for Lawrence says that Crane wrote *Maggie* in the Pendennis Club, where he and Crane were living at the time. See "Appendix," *Letters,* No. 21, p. 331. If Pizer is right then, the curious March 23 recommendation of Crane by Garland to Gilder (*Letters,* No. 22, p. 16) does not apply to *Maggie* at all (see Pizer's introduction, xiii and note), or perhaps it refers to a draft shown to Garland in 1892 and subsequently replaced by the final draft completed at the Pendennis Club (hence Crane's curious notation. See Stanley Wertheim, "The Saga of March 23rd: Garland, Gilder, and Crane," *Stephen Crane Newsletter,* III [Winter, 1968], 1–3). It is clear, however, that the novel did not receive its title until after it was copyrighted on January 19, 1893. See *Letters,* No. 16, pp. 13–14. *Maggie,* in its famous mustard yellow cover, appeared sometime in late February or early March of 1893. See Stallman, 69; T. A. Gullason, "The First Known Review of Stephen Crane's 1893 *Maggie,*" *English Language Notes,* V (June, 1968), 300–302.

So, regardless of which theory is correct, it is clear that the 1893 *Maggie* as we know it was undertaken *after* Crane's first meeting with Garland, and that it was fully rewritten after Crane's "renunciation" of 1892. Crane himself regarded *Maggie* as a work of late 1892 and/or early 1893. "The three months which have passed have been months of very hard work to S. Crane . . . . I wrote a book," he wrote Lily Brandon Munroe in March or April of 1893. *Letters,* No. 28, p. 20; Berryman dates the letter in March (Berryman, 52), Stallman in April. "At 20 I began *Maggie* and finished it when I was somewhat beyond 21." *Letters,* No. 146, p. 117. Crane's twenty-first birthday was November 1, 1892.

R. W. Stallman's argument in "Crane's *Maggie:* A Reassessment," *Modern Fiction Studies,* V (Autumn, 1959), 251–59, and in Stallman, 32, 77–79, that *Maggie* is inspired by Crane's reading of *Madame Bovary* at Syracuse does not directly conflict with my claim that the "certain re-adjustment of his point of view victoriously concluded some time in 1892" (*Letters,* No. 80, p. 62) is clearly manifest in *Maggie.* In fact, whether or not there were drafts of *Maggie* (or even of *George's Mother*) before the summer of 1892, it is clear that Crane considered neither of these novels to be of his "clever period."

4. *New York City Sketches,* 267–68; Stallman, 34. See also Donald Pizer, *Realism and Naturalism in Nineteenth Century American Literature* (Carbondale, 1966), 114–20; and his "Crane Reports Garland on Howells," *Modern Language Notes,* LXX (January, 1955), 37–39. As Pizer points out, Garland in this period was describing himself as "an

impressionist, perhaps, rather than a realist." Perhaps, then, Garland's influence on Crane was a double one.

5. See *New York City Sketches*, 271. Stallman, 32; Beer, 157; Berryman, 20, 24 *et passim*. Of Zola, see *infra*, n. 10.

6. Edwin H. Cady, *Stephen Crane* (New York, 1962), 104.

7. Solomon, *Stephen Crane*, 7–8.

8. Parrington, *Main Currents in American Thought*, III, 328–29.

9. Walcutt, *American Literary Naturalism*, 67–72. Cady, *Stephen Crane*, 102–11, describes Walcutt's approach as one which surrounds more than it defines naturalism.

10. Ahnebrink's demonstration has been frequently disputed. No one seems to be able to establish definitely whether or when Crane read Zola, and it is just as possible, as one critic has suggested, that Crane's "naturalism" is the result of his association with the hard-bitten journalists of such periodicals as B. O. Flower's *Arena*, who were inclined to take an ironic view of a universe which they saw as monistic, amoral, a product of forces without personality. See Lars Ahnebrink, *The Beginnings of Naturalism in American Fiction* (Cambridge, Mass., 1950), and Colvert, "The Literary Development of Stephen Crane," 77–83. Edward Stone cites internal evidence in an attempt to show that Crane had read John Stirling's translation of *L'Assommoir*. See Stallman, 178.

11. David Fitelson, "Stephen Crane's *Maggie* and Darwinism," *American Quarterly*, XVI (Summer, 1964), 182–94; William T. Lenehan, "The Failure of Naturalistic Techniques in Stephen Crane's *Maggie*" in Maurice Bassan (ed.), *Stephen Crane's "Maggie": Text and Context* (Belmont, Calif., 1966), 166–73.

12. Maxwell Geismar, "Naturalism Yesterday and Today," *College English*, XV (January, 1954), 196; Robert M. Figg III, "Naturalism as a Literary Form" Pt. 2 of Louis D. Rubin, Jr. (ed.), "Three Modes of American Fiction: A Symposium," *Georgia Review*, XVIII (Fall, 1964), 314, also 308–16.

13. *Letters*, No. 17, p. 14, also No. 18, p. 14, and No. 58, p. 49.

14. Pizer, "Stephen Crane's *Maggie* and American Naturalism," 169, also 168–75.

15. R. W. Stallman, "Crane's *Maggie*: A Reassessment," *The Houses That James Built and Other Literary Studies* (East Lansing, Mich., 1961). This essay, in earlier states, also appeared as "Stephen Crane's Primrose Path," *New Republic*, CXXXIII (September 19, 1955), 17–18, and revised as "Crane's *Maggie*: A Reassessment" in *Modern Fiction Studies* as previously cited. See Stallman, 66–79.

16. Colvert, "Structure and Theme in Stephen Crane's Fiction," 203, also 199–208.

17. Cady, *Stephen Crane*. Crane's irony in *Maggie* has received recent critical emphasis. See, for example, Maurice Kramer, "Crane's *Maggie*: A Girl of the Streets*," *Explicator*, XXII (February, 1964), Item 49; or H. Wayne Morgan, "Stephen Crane: The Ironic Hero," *Writers in Transition* (New York, 1963), 1–22. However, it was Thomas Beer

who called *Maggie* "the first ironic novel ever written by an American."
Beer, 85.

More recently, Solomon in *Stephen Crane*, 23–44, and others have
emphasized the parodic elements in *Maggie*. E. H. Cady, revising somewhat his earlier opinion, has called attention to the pictorial quality of
the novel's exposition. See his "Stephen Crane: *Maggie, A Girl of the
Streets*," in Hennig Cohen (ed.), *Landmarks of American Writing*
(New York, 1969), 172–81. See also Malcolm Bradbury, "Romance and
Reality in *Maggie*," *Journal of American Studies*, III (July, 1969), 111–
21, an interesting examination of *Maggie* as an artifact in American
cultural history, in which Professor Bradbury states that as a student of
American studies he is concerned with "the understanding of reality
people can have."

18. Joseph X. Brennan, "Ironic and Symbolic Structure in Crane's *Maggie*,"
Nineteenth-Century Fiction, XVI (March, 1962), 303–15; and "Stephen
Crane and the Limits of Irony," *Criticism*, XI (Spring, 1969), 183–
200; Janet Overmyer, "The Structure of Crane's *Maggie*," *University of
Kansas City Review*, XXIX (October, 1962), 71–72; Pizer in *Realism
and Naturalism in Nineteenth Century American Literature*, 114–20.

19. Pizer, "Stephen Crane's *Maggie* and American Naturalism," 175.

20. *Letters*, No. 137, p. 110, also pp. 108–10.

21. Sergio Perosa, "Naturalism and Impressionism in Stephen Crane's Fiction," Bassan (ed.), *Stephen Crane*, 85, also 80–94.

22. For *Maggie*, Professor Bowers had wisely used the 1893 *Maggie* as his
copy-text, and has ignored William M. Gibson's argument that Crane's
revision for Appleton was connected with Crane's renunciation of "the
clever school." As we have seen, the renunciation certainly occurred
before Crane's final revision of the 1893 *Maggie*. See "Textual and
Bibliographical Note," in William M. Gibson (ed.), *"The Red Badge of
Courage" and Selected Prose and Poetry* (New York, 1956), xvi–xviii.
On the other hand, he has recognized that some of Crane's changes
for the 1896 edition were intentional and has thus kept balance in the
face of Joseph Katz's compelling argument that the revision for the 1896
edition is essentially a bowdlerization in "The *Maggie* Nobody Knows,"
Modern Fiction Studies, XII (Summer, 1966), 200–12. See also Bassan
(ed.), *Stephen Crane's "Maggie*," "Textual Note," xiii–xvi. Bassan's
excellent casebook is also based on the 1893 edition. There are two
facsimiles of the 1893 edition: *Maggie: A Girl of the Streets: A Story
of New York*, ed. Joseph Katz (Gainesville, Fla., 1966); and *Maggie:
A Girl of the Streets: A Story of New York*, Donald Pizer (ed.).

23. It was Walcutt, *American Literary Naturalism*, 72, who first noted
Crane's "spirited and intentional distortion of the grotesque world that
he has exactly seen."

24. David Weimer, who comments perceptively on this passage in his *The
City As Metaphor* (New York, 1966), 52–64, speaks of "Crane's expressionism" on p. 64. He is not precisely accurate.

25. Willaim Dean Howells, *Criticism and Fiction*, ed. Clara M. Kirk and
Rudolf Kirk (New York, 1959), 68; Stallman, 78. Janet Overmyer,
however, argues a structural organization for *Maggie* in "The Structure

of Crane's *Maggie*"; and C. B. Ives, in "Symmetrical Design in Four of Stephen Crane's Stories," *Ball State University Forum*, X (Winter, 1969), 17–26, traces a pattern of action which leads him to assert that the novel is neat and symmetrical.

26. Stallman, 76.

27. Gordon O. Taylor, *The Passages of Thought: Psychological Representation in the American Novel, 1870–1900* (*New York*, 1969) 110–35, has seen in Maggie a heroine psychologically determined by her environment and in Henry Fleming a hero psychologically disengaged from his environment.

28. He may have had a model for it in books by Charles Loring Brace or Thomas de Witt Talmage. See Stallman, 73.

29. Joseph X. Brennan examines this passage with care and intelligence in his "Ironic and Symbolic Structure in Crane's *Maggie*," 308–309. In "Maggie's Last Night," *Stephen Crane Newsletter*, II (Fall, 1967), 10, Matthew Bruccoli speaks of the "two time-schemes," literal and symbolic, in this passage.

30. Perhaps Crane believed the "huge fat man" to be a bit overdrawn, or perhaps the author feared offending his reader's sense of propriety. Or perhaps the Appleton editor objected. At any event the fat man does not appear in the 1896 version. For a discussion and evaluation of Crane's choice, see R. W. Stallman, "Stephen Crane's Revision of *Maggie: A Girl of the Streets*," *American Literature*, XXVI (January,) 1955), 528–36; William M. Gibson (ed.), *The Red Badge of Courage and Selected Prose and Poetry*, xvi–xviii; and "Introduction," *Maggie*, ed. Joseph Katz, v–xxiii.

31. *Letters*, No. 178, p. 133.

CHAPTER IV

1. Maurice Bassan, "An Early Draft of *George's Mother*," *American Literature*, XXXVI (January, 1965), 518, also 518–22.

2. *Ibid.*, but see Stallman, 210, 585. The fact that "The Reluctant Voyagers" (which Corwin Linson describes as being written in the late winter of 1893 in *My Stephen Crane*, 18–20) also appeared on *verso* of "The Holler Tree" manuscript seems hardly to preclude the possibility of Bassan's 1891–92 dating, though it would seem to me that *George's Mother* would hardly have been written before Crane's mother's death on December 7, 1891. See also C. K. Linson, "Stephen Crane," *Saturday Evening Post*, CLXXVI (April 11, 1903), 19–20.

3. Crane wrote Hamlin Garland on November 15, "I have just completed a New York book that leaves *Maggie* at the post. It is my best thing." *Letters*, No. 46, p. 41; and Stallman, 210.

4. Bassan, "An Early Draft of *George's Mother*," 219; and Stallman, 585.

5. Stallman, 44, 76, 212.

6. Richard Chase, "Introduction," *"The Red Badge of Courage" and Other Writings* (Boston, 1960), xv, quoted in Bassan's "An Early Draft of *George's Mother*, 520.

7. Beer, 225, quoted in Bassan, "An Early Draft of *George's Mother*," 219–20; Berryman, 304, 308, 318–20.
8. Stallman, 212.
9. Solomon's phrase. See his *Stephen Crane*, 60–61, also 45–67.
10. See Brennan, "Stephen Crane and the Limits of Irony."
11. Donald B. Gibson says, "*George's Mother* is a story about the conflict that occurs when a certain young man reaches that stage in his life when he feels that he must free himself from parental authority." See *The Fiction of Stephen Crane*, 40.
12. Crane's publications in that year were still "clever" and still committed to parody. Along with "Why Did the Young Clerk Swear?" there were two parodies done in dramatic form, "At Clancy's Wake" and "Some Hints for Playmakers." See *New York City Sketches*, 22–30.
13. There had already appeared in the *Herald* of January 4, 1892, a short sketch about three juvenile malefactors in police court, which is closely related to the opening scene of *Maggie*. See Stallman, 68; and "Youse Want 'Petey' Youse Do." *New York City Sketches*, 62–63.

    In light of C. K. Linson's unimpeached testimony in *My Stephen Crane*, 39, and Crane's own letter, *Letters*, No. 29A, p. 23, I would agree with Berryman, 67, and disagree with Solomon, *Stephen Crane*, 47, and Gullason, *Stories and Sketches*, 154–63. It seems that preponderant evidence suggests that at least two of the "baby sketches," "An Ominous Baby" and "A Dark Brown Dog," were completed before June of 1893, although Stallman's inconsistent suggestion that "A Dark Brown Dog" in which Crane took a rather different and sentimental attitude toward his subject (perhaps he was pandering to a popular expectation), may be somewhat later. It was apparently offered for publication by Cora, when the Cranes were in a rather tight fix financially, in 1900; *Letters*, No. 326, p. 259. But just how old was the manuscript which Cora offered to Pinker must remain a matter of conjecture. See Stallman, 100–102, 480, 496–97.
14. *New York City Sketches*, 130–31.
15. Like much of the early work, "A Desertion" remained unpublished until after Crane's death—in *Last Words* of 1902. For an early manuscript version, see Donald J. and Ellen B. Greiner (eds.), *The Notebook of Stephen Crane* (Charlottesville, Va., 1969), x, 52–55, hereinafter cited as *Notebook*.
16. Stallman has corrected his erroneous *Omnibus* dating in his biography. See *Omnibus*, 11; and Stallman, 94–95. Berryman, 81, sets it in March. Much of the confusion about dates which arises in this period may perhaps be blamed on Hamlin Garland's own confusion in his *Roadside Meetings* (New York, 1930), 189–206. Garland, for instance, remembered that *The Red Badge* manuscript was redeemed from pawn in 1893. It is clear from *Letters*, No. 32, p. 30, that this redemption took place in 1894. See also *Letters*, No. 37, p. 36.
17. Maurice Bassan, "Misery and Society: Some New Perspectives on Stephen Crane's Fiction," *Studia Neophilologica*, XXXV (1963), 104–20.

    Thomas Beer, 98, reports that Crane "could stand through nights in a blizzard of late March to write 'Men in the Storm' or sleep in a Bowery shelter to get at the truth of 'An Experiment in Misery.' " Linson, *My Stephen Crane*, 58–63, tells the same story in more detail, and it seems clear that "An Experiment in Misery" was generated by Crane's own experience.

Bassan has also provided a close and valuable reading of the too rarely examined "An Experiment in Misery." See Maurice Bassan, "The Design of Stephen Crane's Bowery 'Experiment,' " *Studies in Short Fiction*, I (Winter, 1964), 129–32, revised for Bassan (ed.), *Stephen Crane*, 118–22.

18. *Ibid.*, 119.
19. See Stallman, 99–100. Maurice Bassan in his studies of the "Experiments" seems to assume that the two protagonists are intended to be distinct characters. But Crane's mention of "another social study" in the frame of the second sketch (*New York City Sketches*, 47), the many comparisons drawn by the young man between the condition of the rich which he now observes and that of the poor, and even at the end, the memory of "a wail of despair of rage [that] had come from the night of the slums" lead me to disagree.
20. *New York City Sketches*, 76–83, 86–87. There was also an affectionate description of the building itself—in two versions, neither of which were published during Crane's life. The original manuscript version of this description is reproduced in *Notebook*, vi–vii, 6–16; Stallman and Hagemann's flawed text in *New York City Sketches*, 14–16; and a shortened variant as "A Mournful Old Building," *New York City Sketches*, 16–17. See Stallman, 80–82.
21. "Howells Fears Realists Must Wait" appeared in the New York *Times* of October 28, 1894. There was also a rather straightforward biographical account of a singer, "Miss Louise Gerard—Soprano," which appeared in *The Musical News* of December, 1894. See *New York City Sketches*, 88–91, 117–19.
22. "The Gratitude of a Nation," an unpublished Decoration Day tribute which Crane offered in lieu of an eyewitness report of a parade, was refused by the *Press*. See Stallman, 108.
23. "Coney Island's Failing Days" and "In a Park Row Restaurant," *New York City Sketches*, 70–75, 83–86; *Notebook*, ix, 36–45.
24. *New York City Sketches*, 97–102, 107–11; and *Notebook*, 56–75, where "When a Man Falls" appears in the shortened form in which it was published as "A Street Scene" in *Last Words*. "Matinee Girls," which appears in Crane's notebook (see *Notebook*, v–vi, 34–35), was not published during his lifetime. In fact, it did not appear until R. W. Stallman published it, first in the *Bulletin of the New York Public Library*, LX (September, 1956), 455–62, and later in *New York City Sketches*, both times inaccurately.
25. *New York City Sketches*, 103–107, 185–89. See *Notebook*, xiii, 46–51.
26. One sketch, "Sixth Avenue," was apparently too hot for the *Press* to handle. See *New York City Sketches*, 117; and Stallman, 102–103.

27. *New York City Sketches,* 111–17. Gibson, *The Fiction of Stephen Crane,* 57–59, 117, compares the story, which he says "questions the desirability of valor uninformed by discretion," to "The Blue Hotel." See also *Notebook,* x, **26–33.**
28. *New York City Sketches,* 125–28.
29. *Ibid.,* 51–57. "A Christmas Dinner" was published, improbably enough, in *The Plumbers' Trade Journal, Gas, Steam, and Hot Water Fitters' Review* of January 1, 1895. See *New York City Sketches,* 119–25.
30. *New York City Sketches,* 66, also 63–70.
31. Robert W. Schneider, although he is not the first to note Crane's social awareness, comments lucidly upon it and summarizes other understandings of it in his *Five Novelists of the Progressive Era* (New York, 1965), 60–111.

CHAPTER V

1. John Berryman goes to some length to label it "great." See Berryman, 282–93.
2. See W. Gordon Milne, "Stephen Crane: Pioneer in Technique," *Die Neueren Sprachen,* VII (July, 1959), 297–303.
3. "Introduction," *Omnibus,* xix–xlv.
4. James B. Colvert, "Style and Meaning in Stephen Crane's 'The Open Boat,'" *Texas Studies in English,* XXXVII (1958), 40, also 34–45.
5. As early as 1895 the reviewers of *The Red Badge of Courage* were describing Crane as an impressionist. See especially Anonymous, "*The Red Badge of Courage,*" *Critic,* n.s. XXIV (November 30, 1895), 363. Besides Conrad, many of the early critics considered Crane's impressionism, including Edward Garnett, "Mr. Stephen Crane: An Appreciation," *Academy,* LV (December 17, 1898), 483–84; and H. G. Wells, "Stephen Crane from an English Standpoint," *North American Review,* CLXXI (August, 1900), 233–42.
6. See Charles R. Metzger, "Realistic Devices in Stephen Crane's 'The Open Boat,'" *Midwest Quarterly,* IV (Autumn, 1962), 47–54.
7. Robert L. Hough's n. 2 in "Crane and Goethe: A Forgotten Relationship," *Nineteenth-Century Fiction,* XVII (September, 1962), 135–36, presents a succinct history of this argument. In sum, the influence of painting was assumed until 1949, when Melvin Schoberlin denied it. Berryman and C. K. Linson (who was one of Crane's "Indians") agreed, but Joseph Kwiat has insisted on the influence in "Stephen Crane and Painting," *American Quarterly,* IV (Winter, 1952), 331–38. More recently, Stanley Wertheim has argued that Crane's impressionism has nothing to do with French painting but is rather an example of Garland's "veritism" put into practice. See Wertheim's "Crane and Garland: The Education of an Impressionist," *North Dakota Quarterly,* XXXV (Winter, 1967), 23–28. For a provocative reminiscence of Crane's days with his painters, see Henry McBride, "Stephen Crane's Artist Friends," *Art News,* XLIX (October, 1950), 46.
8. See Hough, "Crane and Goethe," 138–39.

9. H. G. Wells also saw Whistler's influence in Crane's descriptions: "There is Whistler even more than there is Tolstoy in *The Red Badge of Courage*," in "Stephen Crane from an English Standpoint," 233–42, 234. It is also interesting to note that (*contra* Wertheim) at least one of Crane's artist associates, Gustave Verbeck, was at the time a professing and practicing impressionist. See McBride, "Stephen Crane's Artist Friends," 46.

10. Ford Madox Ford, "Techniques," *Southern Review*, I (July, 1935), 31, also 20–35.

11. A number of critics—notably Philip Young, *Ernest Hemingway: A Reconsideration* (University Park, Pa., 1966); Carlos Baker, *Hemingway* (Princeton, 1956); and Charles P. Weeks, "The Power of the Tacit in Crane and Hemingway," *Modern Fiction Studies*, VIII (Winter, 1962–63), 415–18—have discussed the parallels between the two, as men and as writers.

12. Gorham Munson, "Prose for Fiction: Stephen Crane," *Style and Form in American Prose* (Garden City, 1929), 163. See also Gullason, "A Stephen Crane Find." 1–37, especially 6–7.

13. Milne, in "Stephen Crane: Pioneer in Technique," discusses these stylistic relationships.

14. Russell Roth in "A Tree in Winter: The Short Fiction of Stephen Crane," *New Mexico Quarterly*, XXIII (Summer, 1953), 192, also 188–96, speaks of Crane as "the *essential* Puritan."

15. "Dan Emmonds," *Stories and Sketches*, 63; "Killing His Bear," *Sullivan County Tales*, 67; "The Men in the Storm," *New York City Sketches*, 95.

16. Brennan, "The Imagery and Art of *George's Mother*," 107. See also his "Stephen Crane and the Limits of Irony."

17. Solomon, *Stephen Crane*, 55–60.

18. Maurice Bassan has shown a similar technique in "An Experiment in Misery." See his "The Design of Stephen Crane's Bowery 'Experiment.'"

19. See Edward Garnett, *Friday Nights*, 201–17. The fullest single consideration of Crane's irony, perhaps, is Eric Solomon's. In his *Stephen Crane* his concern is really with a special definition of Crane's irony.

20. Berryman, 279. Colvert puts it this way ("The Literary Development of Stephen Crane," 200): "The narrative design of Crane's best fiction is defined by the tension between two ironically divergent points of view: the narrowing and deluding point of view of the actors and the enlarging and ruthlessly revealing point of view of the observer-narrator." But, as we shall see, it is not clear to me that Crane was really sure that his own vision was "ruthlessly revealing."

21. Munson, "Prose for Fiction," 159.

22. Colvert, "Style and Meaning in Stephen Crane," 41.

CHAPTER VI

1. For a concise and well-documented account of the inception of *The Red Badge of Courage*, see Joseph Katz's introduction to his 1895 facsimile edition. Stephen Crane, *The Red Badge of Courage* (Columbus,

Ohio, 1969), v-xiii. For a fuller account, see William L. Howarth, "*The Red Badge of Courage* Manuscript: New Evidence for a Critical Edition." *Studies in Bibliography*, XVIII (1965), 229-47.
2. Louis C. Senger reported Crane as saying of *The Red Badge*, "I deliberately started in to do a pot-boiler, something that would take the boarding-school element—you know the kind. Well, I got interested in the thing in spite of myself, and I couldn't, I couldn't. I *had* to do it my own way." "Appendix," *Letters*, No. 12, pp. 318–19. See Stallman, 168.
3. *Letters*, No. 17, p. 14.
4. Linson, *My Stephen Crane*, 37.
5. Gibson, *The Fiction of Stephen Crane*, 61, also 60–89.
6. Solomon, *Stephen Crane*, 68–98.
7. Øverland, "The Impressionism of Stephen Crane," 262. See also Brennan, "Stephen Crane and the Limits of Irony," in which this technique is criticized.
8. Solomon, *Stephen Crane*, 73–74.
9. Øverland, "The Impressionism of Stephen Crane," 261–62.
10. W. Gordon Milne calls attention to the "clinking, clanking, plunking, plinking" of the "great grand steel loom" of rifle fire, as it weaves its "cloth of death," in "Stephen Crane: Pioneer in Technique," 297–303, 301.
11. Howarth, in "*The Red Badge of Courage* Manuscript: New Evidence for a Critical Edition," offers convincing evidence for the insufficiency of a text based solely on the Appleton 1895 edition of *The Red Badge of Courage*. There have been facsimile editions of the syndicated newspaper version of 1894, such as Stephen Crane, *The Red Badge of Courage*, ed. Joseph Katz (Gainesville, Fla., 1967); and of the Appleton edition of 1895, such as Stephen Crane, *The Red Badge of Courage*, ed. Joseph Katz (Columbus, Ohio, 1969). And there have been several texts which have been based upon examination of the extant manuscript as well as the Appleton text. John T. Winterich's edition of *The Red Badge of Courage* (London, 1951), and R. W. Stallman's text in *Omnibus* (1952) are early examples. But both of these editions appeared before the recovery of the eight most recent of the fifteen holograph pages missing from the *Red Badge* manuscript delivered to Willis Brooks Hawkins by Crane in 1896. See *Letters*, No. 134, p. 107. R. W. Stallman edited *The Red Badge of Courage* (New York, 1960) from the manuscript and the 1895 edition, but several errors in this edition have been subsequently located. Frederick C. Crews edited *The Red Badge* (Indianapolis, 1964), and the edition edited by Thomas A. Gullason in *The Complete Novels of Stephen Crane* (Garden City, N.Y., 1967), hereinafter cited as *Novels*, was also based on manuscript examination. But Crews's edition, which appeared before Howarth's article, gave authority to the Appleton edition. Thus, while I await Professor Fredson Bowers' definitive University of Virginia edition of the novel, I have chosen Gullason's as my text.
12. See, for the classic example, Stallman, *Omnibus*, 199, and his *Stephen Crane*, 168–88. See also his "Stephen Crane" in John W. Aldridge

(ed.), *Critiques and Essays on Modern Fiction, 1920–1951* (New York, 1952), 268–69, and Rahv, "Fiction and the Criticism of Fiction," 276–99. Or see Stanley B. Greenfield, "The Unmistakable Stephen Crane," *PMLA*, LXXIII (December, 1958), 562–72; and Scott C. Osborn, "Stephen Crane's Imagery: 'Pasted Like a Wafer,'" *American Literature*, XXIII (November, 1951), 362.

13. Marston LaFrance, in a study of *The Red Badge* which parallels my own at several points, makes a similar assertion about Crane's symbolism. See "Stephen Crane's Private Fleming: His Various Battles," in Marston LaFrance (ed.), *Patterns of Commitment in American Literature* (Toronto, 1967), 116, 124, also 113–33.

14. *Novels*, 218, 251. James Trammell Cox, "The Imagery of *The Red Badge of Courage*," *Modern Fiction Studies*, V (Autumn, 1959), 215, also 209–19, considers these figures. See also Mordecai and Erin Marcus, "Animal Imagery in *The Red Badge of Courage*," *Modern Language Notes*, LXXIV (February, 1959), 108–11; and Norman Lavers, "Order in *The Red Badge of Courage*," *University Review*, XXXII (Summer, 1966), 287–95.

15. But see John W. Rathbun, "Structure and Meaning in *The Red Badge of Courage*," *Ball State University Forum*, X (Winter, 1969), 8–16, who argues that, while Henry sees war as a "red god," Crane, recognizing war to be a part of nature, uses animal imagery to describe it.

16. Edward Stone, "The Many Suns of *The Red Badge of Courage*," *American Literature*, XXIX (November, 1957), 322–26. See also Cox, "The Imagery of *The Red Badge*," 212. See also O. W. Fryckstedt, "Henry Fleming's Tupenny Fury: Cosmic Pessimism in Stephen Crane's *The Red Badge of Courage*," *Studia Neophilologica*, XXXIII, No. 2 (1961), 265–81, who asserts Henry's relation to the sun to be the central and emblematic relationship of the novel. See Howarth, "*The Red Badge of Courage* Manuscript."

17. Hart, "*The Red Badge of Courage* as Myth and Symbol," 254, for instance, has also suggested that the motif of eating, apparent in this image, is often repeated and is of symbolic significance.

18. "Appendix," *Letters*, No. 24, p. 336. Berryman, 24, suggests, "Conceivably he came on this passage in his psychology course [at Syracuse]."

19. Hough, "Crane and Goethe: A Forgotten Relationship," 135–48.

20. *Goethe's Theory of Colours*, trans. C. L. Eastlake (London, 1840), 304.

21. See Berryman. See also Stephen Crane, "The Art Students League Building," *New York City Sketches*, 16, also 14–16; *Notebook*, 6–16; and *Letters*, No. 216, pp. 158–59. I have come across no clear evidence that before 1893 Crane had any direct experience with Emerson's writings.

22. Ralph Waldo Emerson, *Nature*, Scholars' Facsimiles and Reprints, ed. Kenneth Walter Cameron (New York, 1940), 14.

23. Øverland, "The Impressionism of Stephen Crane," 248.

24. *Omnibus*, 185.

25. Hough, "Crane and Goethe," 144.

26. *Goethe's Theory of Colours*, 306.
27. I cannot agree with Cox, "Imagery of *The Red Badge*," 213, that "yellow is consistently associated with death." Henry is not reflecting upon death in the tent. See John J. McDermott, "Symbolism and Psychological Realism in *The Red Badge of Courage*," *Nineteenth-Century Fiction*, XXIII (December, 1968), 324–31, who also discusses the symbolic values of red and white in the novel, and assigns values more nearly in agreement with my assertions.
28. Emerson, *Nature*, IV, 34.
29. Crane uses the metaphor frequently—*Novels*, 209, 215, and elsewhere.
30. In the fifties and early sixties many critics, especially those following Berryman, saw Crane as a symbolic colorist. See, for example, Stone, "The Many Suns of *The Red Badge*"; or Cox, "The Imagery of *The Red Badge of Courage*"; Claudia C. Wogan, "Crane's Use of Color in *The Red Badge of Courage*," *Modern Fiction Studies*, VI (Summer, 1960), 168–72; or Hart, "*The Red Badge of Courage* as Myth and Symbol." These writers differ in specifics. See also Isaac Rosenfeld, "Stephen Crane as Symbolist," *Kenyon Review*, XV (Spring, 1953), 310–14.
31. Stanley Wertheim, "Stephen Crane and the Wrath of Jehova," *Literary Review*, VII (Summer, 1964), 505, calls *The Red Badge of Courage* "an aborted initiation myth." He argues that Henry never fully matures nor achieves full integration into his community.
32. Seymour Gross calls the church which Robin visits "the church of the city of night" in "Hawthorne's 'My Kinsman, Major Molyneux': History as Moral Adventure," *Nineteenth-Century Fiction*, XII (September, 1957), 103, also 97–109.

    Neither Professor Gross nor I am offering Hawthorne as a source for Crane's war novel, however, although to resist such an offering is exceedingly difficult, for the list of suggested sources and analogues is a long one. Crane, even in his own time, was annoyed by source hunters (see *Letters*, No. 217, pp. 159–60), but despite his denials (see *Letters*, 173), critics and scholars have persisted. Several, such as Cargill, in *Intellectual America*, 86; and Robert E. Spiller, *Literary History of the United States*, ed. Spiller, Thorp, and others, II (3rd ed., rev.; New York, 1963), 1022, still claim Zola's *La Débâcle* as a source, although Stallman denies that Crane even finished reading it; see *Letters*, n. 140, p. 158. James B. Colvert has suggested that Crane's source might have been a review of Zola's book in "*The Red Badge of Courage* and a Review of Zola's *La Débâcle*," *Modern Language Notes*, LXXI (February, 1956), 98–100. V. S. Pritchett has seen Tolstoy, whom Crane much admired, as a source; and Lars Ahnebrink has seen Tolstoy's novels, *War and Peace* and *Sebastopol* as sources. See V. S. Pritchett, *The Living Novel and Later Appreciations* (New York, 1964), 232; *Letters*, No. 111, p. 78; and Ahnebrink, *The Beginnings of Naturalism*, 343–60.

    Some American sources and analogues have been suggested. H. T. Webster has proposed Wilbur Hinman's *Corporal Si Klegg* in "Wilbur

F. Hinman's *Corporal Si Klegg* and Stephen Crane's *The Red Badge of Courage,*" *American Literature,* XI (November, 1939), 285–93. Oscar Cargill, *Intellectual America;* and Percy Boynton, *Literature and American Life* (Boston, 1936), 677–78, have suggested Bierce. Van Wyck Brooks, *The Confident Years: 1885-1915* (New York, 1952), 137–38, has mentioned Whitman's *Specimen Days.* And as an analogue, Eric Solomon has discussed Joseph Kirkland's *The Captain of Company K* in "Another Analogue for *The Red Badge of Courage,*" *Nineteenth-Century Fiction,* XIII (June, 1958), 63–67. A painter, Winslow Homer; a photographer, Brady; Crane's teacher, General John B. Van Petten of Claverack Academy; and even Crane's father have been mentioned. See Lyndon Upson Pratt, "A Possible Source of *The Red Badge of Courage,*" *American Literature,* XI (March, 1939), 1–10; Thomas F. O'Donnell, "John B. Van Petten: Stephen Crane's History Teacher," *American Literature,* XXVII (May, 1955), 196–202; and Gullason, "New Sources for Stephen Crane's War Motif."

Two scholars have even tried to locate a source for the novel's title. See Abraham Feldman, "Crane's Title from Shakespeare," *American Notes and Queries,* VIII (March, 1950), 185–86; and Cecil D. Eby, Jr., "The Source of Crane's Metaphor, *Red Badge of Courage,*" *American Literature,* XXXII (May, 1960), 204–207. And some critics, not satisfied with only one source discovery, have suggested a second. See Eric Solomon, "Yet Another Source for *The Red Badge of Courage,*" *English Language Notes,* II (March, 1965), 215–17.

But even though the list of proposed sources and analogues continues to grow, H. G. Wells has anticipated all of them. Of the possibility of Tolstoy's influence, Wells protested, "There still remained something entirely original and novel," in "Stephen Crane from an English Standpoint," 234. See also R. W. Stallman, "The Scholar's Net: Literary Sources," *College English,* XVII (October, 1955), 20–27.

33. See Daniel G. Hoffman, *Form and Fable in American Fiction* (New York, 1961), 113–25.

34. Eric Solomon sees Henry's ironic initiation as a parody of the conventions of the war novel in *Stephen Crane,* 68–98. To me Crane's irony is more profound.

35. Orm Øverland, "The Impressionism of Stephen Crane," 251, emphasizes the impressionistic character of Crane's presentation of Henry's confusion.

36. Gordon O. Taylor, in an extremely acute essay on *The Red Badge,* in which the central importance of the perceptual process is recognized, discusses the apprehensional importance of fear in Crane's novel. *Psychological Representation in the American Novel, 1870–1900* (New York, 1969), 110–35. See also Colvert, *Virginia,* VI, pp. xxi–xxiii, who sees *The Red Badge of Courage* as an expansion of the myth of the "little man" of the Sullivan County sketches, who masks with bravado an almost hysterical fear of a threatening nature, but who is driven to the impossible task of apprehending that nature in its ineffableness.

37. See Donald B. Gibson, *The Fiction of Stephen Crane,* 19–20, 74.

38. I have already mentioned the symbolic significance of this incident. See 90–91, and n. 15 *supra*.
39. It is interesting to note that Crane's most emphatically ironic figures are frequently liturgical. In "War Memories," a long, journalistic piece which Crane wrote about his Spanish-American War experiences, we find, at a climactic moment, the image of a wounded Spanish soldier treated as a *pietá*. See Chap. 12.
40. Crane fortunately revised his *Red Badge* manuscript to exclude a too-specific explanation of the meaning of Henry's confrontation. In the manuscript the following paragraph concludes the seventh chapter and thus explains Crane's three ironic symbols. See *The Red Badge of Courage*, ed. Stallman, 54, 210. "Again the youth was in despair. Nature no longer condoled with him. There was nothing, then, after all, in that demonstration she gave—the frightened squirrel fleeing aloft from the missile. He thought as he remembered the small animal capturing the fish and the greedy ants feeding upon the flesh of the dead soldier, that there was given another law which far-over-topped it—all life existing upon death, eating ravenously, stuffing itself with the hopes of the dead. And nature's processes were obliged to hurry . . . [incomplete]." In the Appleton edition, Crane chose instead to depend upon the irony of juxtaposition to convey meaning, and after ending the chapter with "A sad silence was upon the little guarding edifice," he opens the next with "The trees began softly to sing a hymn of twilight. The sun sank until slanted bronze rays struck the forest. There was a lull in the noises of insects as if they had bowed their beaks and were making a devotional pause. There was silence save for the chanted chorus of the trees" *Novels*, 236. See Gibson, *The Fiction of Stephen Crane*, xvi, 64, 74–75.
41. *Omnibus*, 199.
42. Neal J. Osborn, "William Ellery Channing and *The Red Badge of Courage*," *Bulletin of the New York Public Library*, LXIX (March, 1965), 182–96. See also McDermott, "Symbolism and Psychological Realism in *The Red Badge of Courage*."
43. Rosenfeld, "Stephen Crane as Symbolist," 313.
44. See Donald B. Gibson, *The Fiction of Stephen Crane*, 78.
45. Nor, indeed an "ascension" for himself. As James Trammell Cox and Bernard Weisberger have reminded us, Conklin's body only "seemed to bounce a little way from the earth." See Cox, "The Imagery of *The Red Badge*," 209; and Bernard Weisberger, "*The Red Badge of Courage*," in Charles Shapiro (ed.), *Twelve Original Essays on Great American Novels* (Detroit, 1958), 104; and *Novels*, 243.
46. The scene anticipates a similar ironic awareness of the ultimate inadequacy of human assistance or protection in "The Open Boat," when the correspondent, safe in the shallow water at last, and with a bit of salt water in his eye perhaps, sees, belatedly, a man running toward him: "He was naked—naked as a tree in winter; but a halo was about his head" (*Stories and Sketches*, 358). See my discussion of "The Open Boat" in Chap. 8.

47. I shall confine further comment on the now stale wafer of Crane's final sentence in Chap. 9 to this footnote. First, I would suggest again that the significance lies, not in the objective meaning of the symbol, but in its significance as the object of the boy's anger. The field is indeed an embattled one, occupied by such figures as Joseph Hergesheimer, *Work*, I, p. x; Stallman, *Omnibus*, 199–200; and his "The Scholar's Net"; his "Fiction and Its Critics," in his *The Houses that James Built*, 247–48; Rahv, "Fiction and the Criticism of Fiction," 276–99; Osborn, "Stephen Crane's Imagery: 'Pasted Like a Wafer,' " 362; Colvert, "The Origins of Stephen Crane's Literary Creed," 183; Carlson, "Crane's *The Red Badge of Courage*, IX," *Explicator*, XVI (March, 1958), Item 34; and Cecil D. Eby, Jr., who denies any symbolic intent whatsoever, in "Stephen Crane's 'Fierce Red Wafer,' " *English Language Notes*, I (December, 1963), 128–30. But in Stallman's biography, 171–76, Stallman's position is again asserted and developed further.

   A still, small voice in *College English*, who suggests that the wafer which Crane had in mind was that red seal affixed to a document and implying finality, seems—in spite of Professor Stallman's somewhat illogical objection—to be closest the truth. See Rudolph Von Abele in "Symbolism and the Student," *College English*, XVI (April, 1955), 427.

   Crane's wafer simile, by the way, in its fresh and diminishing effect, is in no way atypical of Crane's style (the boat as bathtub in "The Open Boat" will be another example). But regardless of the simile, the sun—occurring as it does here and elsewhere in the novel—is again symbolically significant.

48. Eric Solomon, "The Structure of *The Red Badge of Courage*," *Modern Fiction Studies*, V (Autumn, 1959), 231. Joseph Conrad had suggested the same thing earlier. See Conrad, "His War Book," *Last Essays* (Garden City, 1926), 121. Hart, "*The Red Badge of Courage* as Myth and Symbol," 249, speaks of "The progressive movement of the hero, as in all myth . . . that of separation, initiation, and return." See Ives, "Symmetrical Design in Four of Stephen Crane's Stories."

   It is interesting in this regard to note that Donald B. Gibson, *The Fiction of Stephen Crane*, 80–81, sees "the man of the cheery voice" as a wizard who can miraculously lead the youth through the confusion of war, a Virgil to Henry's Dante. But see G. L. Williams, "Henry Fleming and the 'Cheery Voiced Stranger,' " *Stephen Crane Newsletter*, IV (Winter, 1969), 4–7.

49. See William P. Safranek, "Crane's *The Red Badge of Courage*," *Explicator*, XXVI (November, 1967), Item 21. Here the parallel between Fleming and Wilson is discussed.

50. See Vanderbilt and Weiss, "From Rifleman to Flagbearer."

51. See William Joseph Free, "Smoke Imagery in *The Red Badge of Courage*," *CLA Journal*, VII (December, 1963), 148–52.

52. Donald B. Gibson, *The Fiction of Stephen Crane*, 85–86, points out that the animal images in the description of the first battle after Henry's

return suggest that "still the youth is acting instinctively, not exhibiting true courage."
53. Crane was unsure of his ending. See *supra,* 115n.
54. Walcutt, *American Literary Naturalism,* 66–86, 222–23; Winifred Lynskey (ed.), *Reading Modern Fiction* (4th ed.; New York, 1968), 173–77; Vanderbilt and Weiss, "From Rifleman to Flagbearer"; Clark Griffith, "Stephen Crane and the Ironic Last Word," *Philological Quarterly,* XLVII (January, 1968), 83–91; Donald Gibson, *The Fiction of Stephen Crane,* 60–68.
55. R. B. Sewall, *"The Red Badge of Courage," Explicator,* III (May, 1945), Item 55. See also McDermott, "Symbolism and Psychological Realism in *The Red Badge of Courage.*"
56. In the biography, Stallman has amplified his position. See Stallman, 170–71.
57. Cox, "The Imagery of *The Red Badge*"; and Weisberger, *"The Red Badge of Courage,"* 105–106.
58. Solomon, *Stephen Crane,* 96–98.
59. See Greenfield, "The Unmistakable Stephen Crane," n. 16, p. 568; and R. W. Stallman's rebuttal in "Notes Toward an Analysis of *The Red Badge of Courage,*" in Sculley Bradley, R. C Beatty, and E. H. Long (eds.), *The Red Badge of Courage,* Norton Critical Edition (New York, 1962), 254n. Greenfield rejects C. C. Walcutt's reading of an ironic conclusion to the novel (see *supra,* n. 54) yet sees in the conclusion "an irony which neatly balances two major views of human life. . . ." Greenfield, adroitly comparing this conclusion to that of Chaucer's *Troilus and Criseyde,* claims for Crane a simultaneous acceptance of a deterministic universe and an individual responsibility for one's own honesty. But see Mordecai Marcus, "The Unity of *The Red Badge of Courage,*" in Richard Lettis, Robert F. McDonnell, and William E. Morris (eds.), *The Red Badge of Courage: Text and Criticism* (New York, 1960), 189–95. It hardly seems that the twenty-fourth chapter of *The Red Badge,* taken as it stands, can support Greenfield's cleverly constructed reading.

In Thomas M. Lorch's study, "The Cyclical Structure of *The Red Badge of Courage,*" *CLA Journal,* X (March, 1967), 229–38, several patterns demonstrate cyclical movement in the novel. He believes that Crane in the final chapter describes a change in Henry Fleming but leaves the question of whether this change is permanent in doubt.

In a provocative and original critical conjecture, Malcolm Bradbury and Arnold Goldman, "Stephen Crane: Classic at the Crossroads," *Bulletin of the British Association for American Studies,* No. 6 (June, 1965), 42–49, argue that Crane's failure, here as elsewhere, is the failure of his hero and of his age, the failure of the intellectually uncommitted who avoid choice by losing themselves in action. A similar (but not identical) position is taken by John W. Rathbun in his "Structure and Meaning in *The Red Badge of Courage.*"
60. Norman Friedman, in "Criticism and the Novel," *Antioch Review,* XVIII (Fall, 1958), 358, 360–61, has expressed the "irony" of the statement thus:

To be sure, on the next day he fights heroically, but the point
to be made here is that not only has he not returned to his
regiment by deliberate moral choice, but has also persisted in the
convenient deception that he was wounded by the enemy in action.
Nor does he ever (except in the movie version) reveal that he had
run away from battle and that his wound is spurious. To say that
Conklin's death has sown the seed in him of heroic resolve, or has
initiated him into manhood, is to exceed the evidence.

And later,

It is true that he [Henry] is now a "man," but only in the sense
that he has seen the war and learned what he can do rather than
in the sense that he has formed more noble resolves and strengthened
his will in reaching for them. The essential change around which
this plot turns, then, is from ignorance to knowledge rather than
from cowardice to heroism. It is acting both as coward and hero
that enables Fleming to know himself, and not achieving self-
knowledge which allows him to become courageous.

61. Donald B. Gibson, *The Fiction of Stephen Crane*, 61, 90, argues that
neither "The Veteran" nor the passages which Crane expunged from the
final version of the novel can be regarded as anything other than "external
evidence." I would agree, but I cannot thereby ignore external evidence.
The fact that an author excises certain language from a manuscript does
not necessarily establish that the *content* of that language is contrary to
his purpose. He may—and in perhaps more cases is—rejecting the language on *stylistic* grounds, excluding it because he is dissatisfied with its
overexplicitness, prolixity, or simply its form. And if an author reintroduces
a character into a later work, we can, I believe, reasonably assume that—
there being no evidence to the contrary—the author remains true to his
original conception of that character.

62. See *Novels*, 288; and *Stories and Sketches*, 291.

63. Harold R. Hungerford, " 'That Was at Chancellorsville': The Factual
Framework of *The Red Badge of Courage*," *American Literature*, XXXIV
(January, 1963), 520–31, has demonstrated conclusively that Crane in
The Red Badge is reproducing the action at Chancellorsville in the spring
of 1863. See *Stories and Sketches*, 292. As Hungerford points out
(530): "No one called the battle Chancellorsville in the book because
no one would have known it was Chancellorsville. No impression is
more powerful to the reader of Civil War reports and memoirs than
that officers and men seldom knew where they were. They did not
know the names of hills, of streams, or even of villages."

64. But see Warren D. Anderson, "Homer and Stephen Crane," *Nineteenth-
Century Fiction*, XIX (June, 1964), 84–85, also 77–86, who uses "The
Veteran" to demonstrate that Crane is concerned with Henry's courage
in *The Red Badge* and that the novel is, therefore, not mere determinism.
Jean Cazemajou, *Stephen Crane*, 20, says that in "The Veteran"
Henry purges himself of the sins of lying and cowardice by confession
and a selfless act of heroism.

CHAPTER VII

1. *New York City Sketches*, 51–57, 119–25.
2. And possibly Kansas City as well, although "Art in Kansas City," which has been recently rediscovered, and which was almost certainly written on the way west, is really only a playful fantasy. See Joseph Katz " 'Art in Kansas City' A New 'Uncle Clarence' Story," *Stephen Crane Newsletter*, II (Fall, 1967), 3–4.
3. Willa Cather's account of her meeting with Crane is highly fictionalized. See "When I Knew Stephen Crane," *The Library* (June 23, 1900), 17–18, reprinted in *Prairie Schooner*, XXIII (Fall, 1949), 231–36. For a historically accurate account see Bernice Slote, "Stephen Crane and Willa Cather," *Serif*, VI (December, 1969), 3–15; "Stephen Crane: A Portfolio," *Prairie Schooner*, XLIII (Summer, 1969), 175–204; and Bernice Slote, "Stephen Crane in the Nebraska *State Journal*, 1894–96," 4–5.
4. Joseph Katz, *Stephen Crane in the West and Mexico* (Kent, Ohio, 1970), 3–14; see also his "Introduction," xiii–xiv; and Stallman, 132.
5. See Katz, *Stephen Crane in the West and Mexico*, xv–xvi; Levenson, *Virginia*, V, pp. xxiii–xxiv.
6. "Seen at Hot Springs," *Stephen Crane in the West and Mexico*, 14–20.
7. "Grand Opera in New Orleans" and "The Fête of Mardi Gras," *Stephen Crane in the West and Mexico*, 20–23, 24–30; and Katz's introduction, xviii; and George Monteiro, " 'Grand Opera for the People': An Unrecorded Stephen Crane Printing," *Papers of the Bibliographical Society of America*, LXIII (First Quarter, 1969), 29–30.
8. "Galveston, Texas, in 1895," *Stephen Crane in the West and Mexico*, 30–35; also see xviii–xix.
9. "Patriot Shrine of Texas," *ibid.*, 35–41.
10. "Stephen Crane in Mexico: I," *ibid.*, 41–51.
11. "Stephen Crane in Mexico: II," "In Free Silver Mexico," "A Jag of Pulque is Heavy," "The Dress of Old Mexico," and "The Main Streets of this City," *ibid.*, 52–69. See Stallman, 140–44.
12. Katz, *Stephen Crane in the West and Mexico*, 70–73; see also xx–xxii.
13. *Ibid.*, 74–77; also xxii–xxiii.
14. "The Voice of the Mountain," "How the Donkey Lifted the Hills," and "The Victory of the Moon," *ibid.*, 81–91.
15. Stallman, 137; Beer, 116–17; Levenson, *Virginia*, V, xxxvii–xxxix, xli.
16. Levenson, *Virginia*, V, pp. xlix–lii; Stallman, 218–19; *Letters*, No. 171, p. 128, and No. 175, p. 130.
17. *Letters*, No. 210, p. 154. Solomon, *Stephen Crane in England*, 118, lists it among Crane's best stories. Stallman, however, dissents. See Stallman, 327–28. Donald B. Gibson, *The Fiction of Stephen Crane*, 118, also 118–20, to whose sensitive reading I owe much, admires it as a "typical" story which is "among Crane's best work."
18. *Stories and Sketches*, 272–76; Stallman, 580; and *Writings*, 170–74.
19. Stallman, 146–48; and Levenson, *Virginia*, V, pp. xlii–lvi, clix, clx, clxix.

20. Ford called it "Three White Mice," in "Techniques," *Southern Review*, I (July, 1935), 30–35.
21. See Levenson, *Virginia*, V, xxxix, who discusses this theme in relation to the title of "One Dash—Horses."
22. Donald B. Gibson *The Fiction of Stephen Crane*, 121–22, quarrels with the logic and points out that causal sequence is antithetical to the logic of chance. I would disagree. If the *original* event in the sequence—that of the dice roll—is without cause, the logic of chance is not violated.
23. Wells, "Stephen Crane from an English Standpoint," 239. Wells calls "The Wise Men" "a perfect thing." Also see Stallman, 147; and *Stories and Sketches*, v, 419–29; and Levenson, *Virginia*, V, pp. xlii–xliii.
24. There were a few experiments, and among them were a theatrical sketch called "A Prologue" (Crane unsuccessfully sought a position as a drama critic for the Philadelphia *Press* in September of 1895; see Stallman, 154, 163, 545–46; and Levenson, *Virginia*, V, xl–xli) and another allegorical fable, "The Judgment of the Sage," which appeared in *The Bookman* of January, 1896. See *Writings*, 177–78. "A Tale of Mere Chance," an imitation of Poe's "The Tell-Tale Heart," which appeared in the *English Illustrated Magazine* of March, 1896, was also probably written in 1895. It was probably Crane's only experiment in first-person narration. But unlike Poe's narrator, Crane's protagonist is haunted by a visual fantasy—of white tiles stained by his victim's blood. When she talked to Crane in Nebraska, Willa Cather remembered that he carried in his pocket a small volume of Poe. See Stallman, 131, 584; *Stories and Sketches*, 249–51; and Berryman, 111.
25. Stallman, 166.
26. In a note tipped into a copy of the novel, C. K. Linson claimed that "Crane jocularly informed me that I was 'Hawker' in the book." See Joseph Katz, "Corwin Knapp Linson on *The Third Violet*," *Stephen Crane Newsletter*, III (Fall, 1968), 5; see Berryman, 123.
27. In 1935 Ford said of it, "I have been preaching the claims of that book for years and have never, so far as I know, made a single convert," "Techniques," 26. But Henry James, if one accepts hearsay evidence, approved. See Thomas Beer, "The Princess Far Away," *Saturday Review of Literature*, I (April 25, 1925), 702.
28. See Øverland, "The Impressionism of Stephen Crane," 248, who observes the impressionism in some of the passages.
29. "Sailing Day Scenes," 140–43, "Opium's Varied Dreams," 143–48, "New York's Bicycle Speedway," 149–51, "Evening on the Roof," 153–56, all in *New York City Sketches*.
30. "Yellow Undersized Dog," 157–58, "Stephen Crane at Asbury Park," 283–86, "The Devil's Acre," 298–302, *New York City Sketches*. See also Chap. 2, *supra*.
31. There was also a "story-sketch"—a rather curiously informal piece of reportage—about the discovery of a lumber raft lost six years at sea. It was variously entitled, "Six Years Afloat" and "The Raft Story." Stallman sees it as a prophecy of "The Open Boat." See *Writings*, 186–89; and Stallman, 589. And there was a review—"Ouida's Masterpiece." See *Writings*, 223–34; and Stallman, 243–44.

32. See Solomon, *Stephen Crane*, 49–50.
33. "A Detail," *Stories and Sketches*, 311–12, was the only one of these stories to be published during the year—in *The Pocket Magazine* (October, 1896). B. J. R. Stolper, in *Stephen Crane* (Newark, 1930), 12, corrects Ames W. Williams and Vincent Starrett, *Stephen Crane: A Bibliography* (Glendale, Calif., 1948), 92, in this date.
34. For accounts of the Dora Clark affair see Olov W. Fryckstedt, "Stephen Crane in the Tenderloin," *Studia Neophilologica*, XXXIV (1962), 135–63; and Stallman, 218–36. See also *New York City Sketches*, 215–63.
35. It appeared in the New York *Journal* of October 25, 1896. See *New York City Sketches*, 162–66.
36. New York *Journal*, November 1, 1896, p. 25. See *Writings*, 215.
37. Solomon, *Stephen Crane*, 20, also 19–22.
38. "A Mystery of Heroism" and "A Gray Sleeve" were the first to appear. See Colvert, *Virginia*, VI, xxv and note; but see Stallman, 137. And see *Virginia*, VI, pp. xxxvii–lxxix.
39. Colvert, *Virginia*, VI, p. xxv.
40. See C. B. Ives, " 'The Little Regiment' of Stephen Crane at the Battle of Fredericksburg," *Midwest Quarterly*, VIII (Spring, 1967), 247–60.
41. See Colvert, *Virginia*, VI, p. xxvii.
42. *Letters*, No. 146, p. 117; see Stallman, 194.
43. *Virginia*, VI, pp. lxxx–lxxxvii. But see Stallman, 298.
44. Stallman says of "An Episode of War," "The wound is the symbol of his change of vision." And later, "*An Episode* thus bears comparison with *The Upturned Face* and, in its theme of a change of vision, it links with *A Mystery of Heroism* and *The Red Badge of Courage*," *Omnibus*, 377. Berryman, *Stephen Crane*, 256, would disagree. He sees "An Episode of War" as a story defining an ethic. Of the "Episode's" protagonist he says, "How to act, wounded, is his [Crane's] Lieutenant's problem."
45. Before leaving, Crane visited Cambridge, Mass., for a foray into sports reporting. See "Harvard University Against the Carlisle Indians" and "How Princeton Met Harvard at Cambridge and Won, 12 to 0," *Writings*, 211–15 and 219–22. There was also a tribute—and a sort of valedictory—to Hearst's *Journal* ("A Birthday Word from Novelist Stephen Crane," New York *Journal*, November 8, 1896). See Stallman, 237–38. See also Joseph Katz, "Stephen Crane, 'Samuel Carlton,' and a Recovered Letter," *Nineteenth-Century Fiction*, XXIII (September, 1968), 220–25.

CHAPTER VIII

1. Grant C. Knight, in *The Critical Period in American Literature* (Cos Cob, Conn., 1968 [1951]), 118, spoke of 1897 as the year in which Crane stood at a "crossroad in his literary progress."
2. Berryman, 121–49. See also Beer, 130–38; and *Letters*, No. 158, pp. 123–24, 133–39; see also Katz, "Stephen Crane, 'Samuel Carlton,' and a Recovered Letter."

3. Stallman, 301, 598, seems irrefutable in his assertion that regardless of alleged or actual ceremonies in Greece or in England, both knew that because of Cora's earlier marriage no wedding ceremony was of contractual validity.

4. See Conrad's introduction to Beer's *Stephen Crane* for an account of his first meeting with Crane and of their friendship. Crane's other English associations are discussed in Berryman, 185–214, and in Beer, 159–79, but for a more recent and more thorough examination of Crane's English relationships and influences, see Solomon's *Stephen Crane in England*; Stallman, 237–335; Lillian B. Gilkes, "Stephen Crane and the Harold Frederics," *Serif*, VI (December, 1969), 21–48; and Chap. 1, *supra*.

5. According to Berryman, Crane had read James's criticism as early as 1895. See Berryman, 103. At any rate, he was reading and praising *The Portrait of a Lady* in Athens in 1897 and later. See Beer, 157; and Stallman, 294–95, 299, *et passim*.

6. As Stallman points out (244 and 589), Crane had written no less than five times previously about shipwrecks—in "The Raft Story," "The Captain," "The Wreck of the New Era," "Ghostly Spirit of Metedeconk," and "The Reluctant Voyagers." Of them, the last—probably written in the spring of 1893—was a comic treatment of the subject of two men adrift on a raft. See Stallman, 63, 84, 210; and Linson, *My Stephen Crane*, 18–20.

7. See A. J. Liebling, "The Dollars Damned Him," *New Yorker*, XXXVII (August 5, 1961), 48–72. See Crane's letters also. But Solomon, in *Stephen Crane in England*, sees other more significant influences. For a revision of Liebling's view of Crane's circumstances, see Matthew J. Bruccoli and Joseph Katz, "Scholarship and Mere Artifacts: The British and Empire Publications of Stephen Crane," *Studies in Bibliography*, XXII (1969), 277–87.

8. In the face of many arguments to the contrary, Russell Roth, " 'A Tree in Winter,' " 190, also 188–96, asserts that Crane's achievements came in "The Open Boat," "The Bride Comes to Yellow Sky," and "The Blue Hotel." He further asserts that *The Red Badge* does not measure up to these. I would agree with Mr. Roth.

9. See Øverland's "The Impressionism of Stephen Crane," 265.

10. Richard P. Adams, "Naturalistic Fiction: 'The Open Boat,' " *Tulane Studies in English*, IV (1954), 142–43, also 137–46, has counted nearly a hundred color terms in the story.

11. For a discussion of Crane's color symbolism in "The Blue Hotel," see Cox, "Stephen Crane as Symbolic Naturalist."

12. *Stories and Sketches*, 535 and 539. In the second occurrence, "from the dark northern" appears "from dark northern."

13. Buitenhuis, "The Essentials of Life," makes this comparison.

14. See Øverland, "The Impressionism of Stephen Crane," 262 ff. As Øverland points out, substitutionary speech has often been taken to be a hallmark of impressionism.

15. One critic even asserts that the broken peony (Virginia, VII, 10) in "The Monster" is such an image. See Thomas A. Gullason, "The Symbolic Unity of 'The Monster,'" *Modern Language Notes*, LXXV (December, 1960), 663–68. Another less plausible reading occurs in James Hafley's "'The Monster' and the Art of Stephen Crane," *Accent*, XIX (Summer, 1959), 159–65.
16. See Brennan, "Ironic and Symbolic Structure in Crane's *Maggie*," 303–15.
17. In his discussion of "The Open Boat," in *The Fiction of Stephen Crane*, 130, also 127–35, Donald Gibson sees the function of these images quite differently. See Øverland, "The Impressionism of Stephen Crane," 273–77.
18. Cox, "Stephen Crane as Symbolic Naturalist," has suggested a much more complex patterning of similes.
19. But see Wertheim, "Crane and Garland: The Education of an Impressionist."
20. See Munson, "Prose for Fiction," 159. Donald B. Gibson, who throughout his study takes Crane seriously to task for failures of tone, also recognizes Crane's achievement of tonal control—at least "to some degree." Gibson sees this control to be achieved in *The Red Badge*. See *The Fiction of Stephen Crane*, 105.
21. With near-prescience, Crane discussed his will with his lawyer brother, William, and appointed his literary executors in November of 1896, just before his departure for Florida. See Levenson, *Virginia*, V, pp. liii–lvi. See also Berryman, 166. Berryman reports the false obituaries and remarks that the seventy or eighty hours in the boat probably did Crane's potential tuberculosis little good. See Stallman, 235–57.
22. Buitenhuis, "The Essentials of Life," 244.
23. For an enlightening discussion of "The Open Boat" as an example of Crane's style and presentation of his narrative of apprehension, see Colvert's "Style and Meaning in Stephen Crane." Colvert recognizes the central issue in Crane's fiction when he says (40): "This ironic contrast suggests a theme so central to Crane's consciousness that it can be taken as almost a definition of his world view, the vision of life governed by his profound sense of the consequences of our faulty perceptions of reality. The grand subject of his fiction is man's struggle to bring into some sort of meaningful order the confusions and contradictions of experience."

    Charles R. Metzger, in "Realistic Devices in Stephen Crane's 'The Open Boat,'" 54, says that "the facts presented, the perspectives employed, the contrasts stated are all joined in the work to describe not only some impressive facts of life, but also to demonstrate some defensible generalizations, not only about human experience, but also about how that experience is apprehended and how, when it is apprehended, we react to it."
24. Ralph Ross, John Berryman, and Allen Tate, *The Arts of Reading* (New York, 1960), 280–84, have a quite different but also extremely interesting interpretation.

25. Andrew Lytle, " 'The Open Boat': A Pagan Tale," *The Hero with the Private Parts* (Baton Rouge, 1963), 63, also sees the four occupants of the boat as representative. Lytle's interpretation, however, is quite different from my own.
26. Gordon and Tate's term. See Caroline Gordon and Allen Tate, *The House of Fiction* (2nd ed.; New York, 1960), 213, 442. Also Stallman, 258–59.
27. But see Lytle, " 'The Open Boat': A Pagan Tale," 65; and James J. Napier, "Land Imagery in 'The Open Boat,' " *CEA Critic*, XXIX (April, 1967), 15.
28. See John T. Frederick, "The Fifth Man in 'The Open Boat,' " *CEA Critic*, XXX (May, 1968), 12–24, who sees a shift of imagistic emphasis from visual to tactile at the beginning of the second section.
29. Ross, Berryman, and Tate, *The Arts of Reading*, 285, observe the "subtle brotherhood" but do not comment upon Crane's ironic treatment of it.
30. Buitenhuis, "The Essentials of Life," 248.
31. Lavers, "Order in *The Red Badge*," 294, sees him as a false salvation symbol.
32. Lytle, " 'The Open Boat': A Pagan Tale," 71, calls this night a "dark night of the soul."
33. Buitenhuis, "The Essentials of Life," 249, identified the poem which the correspondent remembers as a poem with which Crane was familiar in his youth. The poem, entitled "Bingen," is by a Victorian poetess, Caroline Norton, and was published in *The Undying One; Sorrows of Rosalie; and Other Poems* (New York, 1854), 226–29. The correspondent—or Crane—misremembered or, as Buitenhuis suggests, edited the poem. See Solomon, *Stephen Crane*, 169–70. See also Brennan's unsympathetic reading, "Stephen Crane and the Limits of Irony," and Levenson, *Virginia*, V, pp. lxii–lxix.
34. In a very curious reading, Landon C. Burns, Jr., "On 'The Open Boat,' " *Studies in Short Fiction*, III (Summer, 1966), 455–57, has seen the haloed citizen as a being similar to Michelangelo's God in *The Creation*. Donald B. Gibson, *The Fiction of Stephen Crane*, 128–32, speaks of three distinct meanings for "nature" in "The Open Boat." But I doubt that either Crane's theology or his metaphysic was that conscious or systematic.
    Lloyd N. Dendinger, noting that in both works experience leads to moral certainty, although ironically for Crane, sees certain images as inversions of Coleridge's in "The Rime of the Ancient Mariner." See "Stephen Crane's Inverted Use of Key Images of 'The Rime of the Ancient Mariner,' " *Studies in Short Fiction*, V (Winter, 1968), 192–94.
35. See Griffith, "Stephen Crane and the Ironic Last Word," 86–87.
36. From Emerson's "The Poet," and from Whitman's "Song of Myself," section 25.
37. Robert Meyers, "Crane's 'The Open Boat,' " *Explicator*, XXI (April, 1963), Item 60, believes that the survivors were finally to become priests

in a new religion whose development Crane traces in "The Open Boat." But Crane's concern seems to me to be more aesthetic than theological. See also Lytle, " 'The Open Boat': A Pagan Tale," 74–75.

CHAPTER IX

1. *Stephen Crane Newsletter,* I (Winter, 1966), 8.
2. Beer, 147; Stallman, 260; and *Letters,* 139*n.*
3. Stallman, 260–70; see also Levenson, *Virginia,* V, pp. lxix–lxxii. I am indebted to Professor Stallman for my reiteration of the events of the Greek war. For his full account, also see Stallman, 270–93.
4. Stallman, 271–72; but see Gilkes, "Corrections of R. W. Stallman's *Stephen Crane: A Biography,*" 6–7.
5. See Gilkes's essay in *American Literature,* "Stephen and Cora Crane: Some Corrections, and a 'Millionaire' Named Sharefe." This is the last word in a rather complex and conjectural exchange between Gilkes and Stallman over the question of Crane's itinerary in his journey from London to Athens. See Gilkes, *Cora Crane,* 78–92, and her "Stephen Crane's 'Dan Emmonds': A Pig in a Storm," *Studies in Short Fiction,* II (Fall, 1964), 66–71; R. W. Stallman, "Was Crane's Sketch of the Fleet off Crete a Journalistic Hoax?: A Reply to Miss Gilkes," *Studies in Short Fiction,* I (Fall, 1964), 72–76; Lillian Gilkes, "No Hoax: A Reply to Mr. Stallman," *Studies in Short Fiction,* I (Fall, 1964), 77–83; and Stallman, in the biography, 260–69, 538–39. Miss Gilkes's modification of her position in the *American Literature* essay is the most graceful, and probably the most convincing argument.

   What is more significant is Stallman's convincing demonstration that, although he had requested a meeting, Crane did not actually make the acquaintance of Joseph Conrad (on the occasion of the meeting which Conrad misremembers in his introduction to Beer) until after Crane's return to London from Greece. See Stallman, 267, 320–21.
6. John Bass, "How Novelist Crane Acts on the Battlefield," New York *Journal,* May 23, 1897. See Stallman, 281. As Levenson points out, one of Crane's functions in Greece was to be a celebrity for other writers to cover. See *Virginia,* V, p. lxxiv.
7. These sketches often illustrate Crane's subjective or apprehensional concerns. See, for example, "The Dogs of War," an autobiographical sketch in which Crane described "a correspondent's curiously irrational concern for a puppy, which he acquired, lost, and recovered in the Thessalian campaign, even in the midst of the fighting." See Stallman, 197. In "The Eastern Question" Crane took a sardonic look at the powers of Europe who, because of their failure to understand the diplomatic issues, were duped by the wily Turks. See *War Dispatches,* 44–47, 54–59. See also "The War Correspondents," in B[ernice] D. S[lote] (ed.), "Stephen Crane: Two Uncollected Articles."
8. D. G. Hoffman, *The Poetry of Stephen Crane* (New York, 1957), 162–63, 187–88.
9. See Joseph Katz, " 'The Blue Batallions' and the Uses of Experience," *Studia Neophilolgica,* XXXVIII (1966), 107–16.

10. For a fuller description of their publication see *War Dispatches*, 60.
11. Published elsewhere as "Half a Day in Suda Bay" and as "Stephen Crane's Pen Picture of the Powers' Fleet off Crete," it was Crane's first writing of the Greek war for Hearst. See *War Dispatches*, 11–19, 60; and *Writings*, 249–56.
12. Crane had already reported the battle for the *Journal* in a rather straightforward account. See "Crane at Velestino," *War Dispatches*, 28–33. But "A Fragment" embodies what Crane later remembered of the experience.
13. In *The Fiction of Stephen Crane*, 120, Donald B. Gibson says, "Crane's method of beginning his stories is nearly always the same. He begins with a general description of some kind, gradually narrowing his focus to concentrate on the area most interesting him."
14. Elsewhere published as "My Talk with 'Soldiers Six.' " See *War Dispatches*, 60; and *Writings*, 284–93.
15. Crane's Athenian youth's fears were not realized. George I remained on the Greek throne until 1913, when he was assassinated.
16. See Stallman, 276, 594.
17. There are two other extant journalistic pieces which Crane wrote during his sojourn in Greece, and neither is of much consequence. "The Blue Badge of Cowardice," which appeared in the *Journal* of May 12, describes the evacuation of the Greek seaside resort of Volos after the battle of Velestinon. "Yale Man Arrested" (May 14) reports in less than 150 words the arrest of an American war correspondent in Athens. See *War Dispatches*, 33–37; *Writings*, 261–65; and Stallman, 284–85.

    Berryman suggests that Crane may also have ghost-written parts of Cora's journalistic pieces, which she did under the pseudonym of "Imogene Carter." See Berryman, 181–82.
18. A recent discovery of a manuscript page of "Death and the Child" (see Joseph Katz, "An Early Draft of 'Death and the Child,' " *Stephen Crane Newsletter*, III [Spring, 1969], 1) demonstrates that Crane developed the plot first, then the final language. "Death and the Child" was written quite late in 1897; it was finished in December. See Levenson, *Virginia*, V, pp. lxxvii–xcix.
19. See Stallman, 289; Levenson, *Virginia*, V, p. lxxxii; Colvert, *Virginia*, VI, p. xvi; and Geismar, *Rebels and Ancestors*, 106.
20. Solomon says that in "Death and the Child" "Stephen Crane is mocking the intellectual, the youth whom the universities have not taught the fundamentals of active life." See Solomon, *Stephen Crane*, 109. But, as I shall later explain, I do not quite agree.
21. The association is Solomon's. See *ibid.*, 108.
22. See Stallman, 325.
23. See Solomon, *Stephen Crane*, 109–13; and Cazemajou, *Stephen Crane*, 23.
24. Stallman, 205, 268, 293, and 311. In March of 1899 Crane wrote his agent, Pinker, "I am confident that it will be the most successful book that I have ever published." See *Letters*, No. 284, p. 218. But Crane must have been talking about money. For in May, just after the novel's completion, he wrote Mrs. Moreton Frewen of the novel's birth "in all

its shame," and he said, "may heaven forgive it for being so bad." Joseph Katz, "SC to Mrs. Moreton Frewen: A New Letter," *Stephen Crane Newsletter,* I ([Summer,] 1967), 6. Later, he wrote in another letter, "I hope that the new book will be good enough to get me to Colorado. It will not be good for much more than that." See Stallman, 472.

25. See Donald B. Gibson, *The Fiction of Stephen Crane,* 140–42.
26. Solomon, *Stephen Crane,* 135–44.
27. November 25, 1960. See Stallman, 600.
28. Stallman has identified Rufus Coleman partly as Crane and partly as Crane's journalistic rival, Richard Harding Davis. Nora Black is certainly Cora, at least in part, and, if so, the presentation is more than "Crane's jest at Cora." Stallman, 25, 266, 270, 290–93, 594. Also see Berryman, 228–30, who sees Nora as a combination of Cora and Amy Leslie; Geismar, *Rebels and Ancestors,* 109–12; and *Letters,* 133–39.

CHAPTER X

1. See Stallman, 267.
2. *Ibid.,* 305–306, 595–96, 598.
3. July 31, August 7 and 14, 1897. See *Saturday Review,* LXXXIV, 105–106, 132–33, 158–59.
4. Unfortunately "London Impressions" has not been republished in any of the recent Crane collections, though it does appear in Vol. XI of the Knopf edition (*Work*). Citations in the text are to this edition.
5. That this passage in "London Impressions" contains particular significance for Crane is suggested, not only by the repetition of the "cylinder" figure at least three times (*Work,* XI, 132, 135, 140), but also by the fact that the imagery of the passage recalls that of "In the Depths of a Coal Mine," which Crane had done back in 1894 with his friend C. K. Linson as illustrator.
6. Within six months Frederic was dead and Crane had written an obituary piece on him, "Harold Frederic," for the Chicago *Chap-Book* of March 15, 1898. See Stallman, 302. See also Gilkes, "Stephen Crane and the Harold Frederics," 21–48.
7. "The Scotch Express" has also been republished only in the Knopf edition.
8. Stallman, 598. Four of these sketches reappear only in the Knopf edition, and "Queenstown" is collected for the first time in *Writings,* 296–99.
9. *The O'Ruddy* was for Crane frankly a potboiler. But, realizing it would not be completed before his death, he convinced Robert Barr, a writer and a close personal friend, to complete it. So Crane gave him the uncompleted manuscript—65,000 words, according to Cora. See Gilkes, *Cora Crane,* 254 ff. The completion and publication of *The O'Ruddy* was the subject of a complex of problems—for Cora and for the Crane scholar. Although, when it was finally published, Barr credited Crane with only one-fourth of the work, Crane's letters seem to suggest that at the time of his death Crane had already presented to his agent over 40,000 of the book's projected 80,000 words (in its published state

The O'Ruddy is closer to 65,000 words in length), and Crane was also to some degree responsible for the plan of the unwritten portion. One scholar has submitted *The O'Ruddy* to a computer-assisted stylistic analysis in order to determine Crane's part in its writing. See Bernard O'Donnell, "Stephen Crane's *The O'Ruddy*: A Problem in Author Discrimination," in Jacob Leed (ed.), *The Computer and Literary Style* (Kent, Ohio, 1966), 107–15. For an account of the curious history of *The O'Ruddy*, see, in addition to *Cora Crane*, Lillian Gilkes and Joan H. Baum, "Stephen Crane's Last Novel: *The O'Ruddy*," *Columbia Library Columns*, VI (February, 1957), 41–48. See *Letters*, *passim*; and Stallman, *passim*.

10. *Stories and Sketches*, 763, 764, also 762–64.
11. *The O'Ruddy*, of course, is also replete with descriptions which apply to Brede Place, though it is not specifically set there. See Stallman, 450–51.
12. *Ibid.*, 558. But Stallman also asserts that "Cora completed ["The Squire's Madness"] from Stephen's notes dictated in his dying days."
13. See Levenson, *Virginia*, VII, xi–xiv; and Joseph Katz, "SC to Edmund B. Crane: Two New Letters," *Stephen Crane Newsletter*, I (Spring, 1967), 7–8.
14. Levenson, *Virginia*, VII, xi–xix. Port Jervis and Hartwood were very much on Crane's mind around the time of the writing of "The Monster." In October, a month after its completion, Crane was writing his brother, "My idea is to come finally to live at Port Jervis or Hartwood." See *Letters*, No. 201, p. 147.
15. See Howells, *Criticism and Fiction*, 20, 140; Hesketh Pearson, *Beerbohm Tree* (London, 1956), 72–73; Mrs. George Cran, *Herbert Beerbohm Tree* (London, 1907), 38–39, 108. See also Ahnebrink, *The Beginnings of Naturalism*, 378–81.
16. See Berryman, *Stephen Crane*, 192, 323–24. Exception must be taken, of course, for the burning laboratory scene. See Geismar, *Rebels and Ancestors*, 116–20.
17. Ives, "Symmetrical Design in Four of Stephen Crane's Stories," even sees a symmetrical plan for "The Monster," according to which the first twelve chapters have to do with the making of the monster, the latter twelve with his effect on the town.
18. The phrase is Levenson's. See *Virginia*, VII, pp. xiii–xiv.
19. "When Every One is Panic Stricken," *New York City Sketches*, 97–102. See Stallman, 123–25.
20. See Stallman, 334.
21. In a letter written from Port Jervis in December of 1894 Crane described the woman who was later to serve him as the model for Martha Goodwin.

> There is a feminine mule up here who has roused all the blood thirst in me and I don't know where it will end. She has no more brain than a pig and all she does is to sit in her kitchen and grunt. But every when she grunts something dies howling. It may be a girl's reputation or a political party or the Baptist Church but it

stops in its tracks and dies. Sunday I took a 13 yr. old child out driving in a buggy. Monday this mule addresses me in front of the barber's and says, "You was drivin' Frances out yesterday" and grunted. At once all present knew that Frances and I should be hanged on twin gallows for red sins. No man is strong enough to attack this mummy because she is a nice woman. . . . She is just like those hunks of women who squat on porches of hotels in summer and wherever their eye lights there blood rises. Now, my friend, there is a big joke in all this. This lady in her righteousness is just the grave of a stale lust and every boy in town knows it. She accepted ruin at the hands of a farmer when we were all 10 or 11. (*Letters*, No. 49, pp. 42–43.)

Crane, himself very much the victim of gossip (the old lady in question had in fact accused him of corrupting a child), described the old lady in her seat on the porch of a summer hotel in 1896 in *The Third Violet* and again in "The Monster." See Wilson Follett's introduction to *Work*, III, p. xvi. Sy Kahn, "Stephen Crane and the Giant Voice in the Night: An Explication of 'The Monster,'" in Richard E. Langford (ed.), *Essays in Modern American Literature* (Deland, Fla., 1963), 41–42.

22. See Kahn, "Stephen Crane and the Giant Voice in the Night," 41–43.
23. See Levenson, *Virginia*, VII, xxxi–xxxii.
24. Interpretation of "The Monster" is various and sometimes highly imaginative. See, for example, Hafley, "'The Monster' and the Art of Stephen Crane," 159–65, who believes that Henry Johnson, after his accident, became a God-like figure, the ultimately good man, a reality (to paraphrase T. S. Eliot) too much for humankind to bear. He therefore must go masked, and he is last seen looking toward the sky and "waving his arms in time to a religious chant." Sy Kahn has compared the eye, which stares out of the bandages at Judge Hagenthorpe—reinforced imagistically by the song of the small boys ("'Nigger, nigger, never die/ Black face and shiny eye.'")—to the eyes of Dr. Eckleburg, staring across the moral wasteland of Scott Fitzgerald's *The Great Gatsby* ("Stephen Crane and the Giant Voice in the Night," 40). Stallman has seen Henry as hero, has seen his monstrousness as a final comment on heroism, and has seen it as "an appeal for brotherhood between white and black," 334. And Levenson, in one of the most sensitive readings, has developed Berryman's earlier suggestions that "The Monster" is essentially a psychic reenactment for Crane. Levenson, *Virginia*, VII, pp. xi–xxxii.
25. Levenson, *Virginia*, VII, pp. xxxii–xxxiii; Stallman, 350.
26. Levenson, *Virginia*, VII, p. xxxv.
27. Crane wrote—or collaborated with Cora on—two other stories of Negroes, but these are set in Cora's South rather than in Whilomville. They were entitled "Brer Washington's Consolation" and "The Ideal and the Real," although neither was published. See Stallman, 479–80.
28. It was not the first published, however. "The Angel-Child," which was Crane's second composition, appeared before "Lynx-Hunting" in *Harper's* and in the collections of 1900. See Levenson, *Virginia*, VII, pp. liii–lvii, and 103–106.

29. Beer, 113; Stallman, 479.
30. See *Virginia*, VII, xliv–xlv, where Levenson develops the biographical parallel between the two Coras. Neither Geismar, Stallman, nor Berryman makes anything of the parallel.
31. Solomon, *Stephen Crane*, 215.
32. *Ibid.* 214 n; Stallman, 114; *Letters*, No. 49, pp. 42-43.
33. "The Trial, Execution, and Burial of Homer Phelps" was one of the stories Crane submitted to Pinker on September 22, 1899. On November 4 Crane sent Pinker that "double extra special good thing," "The Upturned Face." Levenson, *Virginia*, VII, p. liv; and Stallman, 486.
34. Stallman is notable in this respect. See Stallman, *passim.*
35. The first story, "The Angel-Child," occurs at "the advent of the warm season"; " 'Showin' Off' " is in colder weather; and "Shame"—the picnic story—occurs the following summer. "The Stove" is set in the Christmas season, "The Trial, Execution, and Burial of Homer Phelps" occurs when the snow is melting, "The Fight" and its sequel occur "near the first of April," and "A Little Pilgrim" is set in November. See Solomon, *Stephen Crane*, 207. Although it is not usually regarded as a part of the Whilomville sequence, "His New Mittens" precedes the others; it is set in winter. Because in a sense all of the stories explain it —"The Monster" may be assumed to come later.

CHAPTER XI

1. Levenson, *Virginia*, V, pp. lxxiii–lxxvi; Katz, "SC to Edmund B. Crane: Two New Letters," 7–8.
2. Levenson, *Virginia*, V, pp. xciv–cii.
3. "The Bride Comes to Yellow Sky" was written immediately after "The Monster," which Crane finished around September 9, 1897. See Stallman, 311; *Letters*, No. 201, p. 146. He had finished "The Bride" and delivered it to *McClure's* by October 29. The meeting with Joseph Conrad occurred on October 15, 1897. See Garnett (ed.), *Letters from Joseph Conrad*, 114–15.
4. *Letters*, No. 200, p. 145; No. 201, p. 146.
5. Since Robert Barnes, "Stephen Crane's 'The Bride Comes to Yellow Sky,' " *Explicator*, XVI (April, 1958), Item 39, many critics have recognized the "East-West conflict" as central to the story. Also since Solomon's *Stephen Crane*, 252–56, many critics are alert to Crane's uses of parody. See Stallman, 136.
6. For my awareness of the symbolic opposition of railroad and river, as well as much else of significance in "The Bride Comes to Yellow Sky," I am indebted to George Monteiro's brilliant analysis, "Stephen Crane's 'The Bride Comes to Yellow Sky,' " in Neil D. Isaacs and Louis H. Leiter (eds.), *Approaches to the Short Story* (San Francisco, 1963), 221–38. See also Neil D. Isaacs, "Yojimbo Comes to Yellow Sky," *Kyushu American Literature*, No. 10 (December, 1967), 81–86.
7. Geismar, *Rebels and Ancestors*, 101–103, and Berryman, 196, see expression of Crane's psychological conflict in Potter's guilt. See also Levenson, *Virginia*, V, pp. lxxiii–lxxvi.

8. Monteiro, "Stephen Crane's 'The Bride Comes to Yellow Sky,' " 224, sees Scratchy Wilson as a Lord of Misrule, reigning "in an intercalary period 'between the old and the new.' " He also describes the conflict between Potter and Wilson as an Appollonian-Dionysian opposition.

9. Barnes, "Crane's 'The Bride Comes to Yellow Sky,' " calls the bride herself Potter's "weapon."

10. Monteiro, *Approaches to the Short Story*, 234.

11. Stallman, 131.

12. *Ibid.*, 327.

13. Mark Schorer, *The Story: A Critical Anthology* (New York, 1950), 20. In his notes he calls "The Bride" a "story of contrast."

14. *Letters*, No. 224, p. 171.

15. Levenson, *Virginia*, V, pp. xciv–xcviii.

16. Beer, 113–14; Slote, in "Stephen Crane: A Portfolio," 192–99, describes in detail Crane's Nebraska travels, and doubts the credibility of Beer's report.

17. Katz, "An Early Draft of 'The Blue Hotel,' " 1–3; Levenson, *Virginia*, V, pp. xcviii–cii. See also Joseph Katz, "Introduction," "The Blue Hotel," Merrill Literary Casebook Series (Columbus, Ohio, 1969), 1–4.

18. In his "Introduction" to *Work*, X, p. xii.

19. See Hugh N. Maclean, "The Two Worlds of 'The Blue Hotel,' " *Modern Fiction Studies*, V (Autumn, 1959), 260–70.

20. Joseph N. Satterwhite, "Stephen Crane's 'The Blue Hotel': The Failure of Understanding," *Modern Fiction Studies*, II (Winter, 1956–57), 238, also 238–41. But see Bruce L. Grenberg, "Metaphysics of Despair: Stephen Crane's 'The Blue Hotel,' " *Modern Fiction Studies*, XIV (Summer, 1968), 203–13, who argues that the Swede correctly perceives the nature of Fort Romper, and that this correct perception tragically leads to his death. But this hardly explains the Swede's final actions in the barroom.

21. Stallman, 136; Solomon, *Stephen Crane*, 257–70.

22. Donald B. Gibson, " 'The Blue Hotel' and the Ideal of Human Courage," *Texas Studies in Language and Literature*, VI (Autumn, 1964), 388–97, points out that the Swede is no representative of mankind—that, indeed, the Swede is not even intended as a sympathetic character. The article has reappeared as part of Chap. 6 of Gibson's *The Fiction of Stephen Crane*, 106–18.

23. Gleckner's "Stephen Crane and the Wonder of Man's Conceit," makes much the same argument.

24. Lynskey (ed.), *Reading Modern Fiction*, 173.

25. A number of recent critics have commented on the significance of this last sentence. To Brennan, in "Stephen Crane and the Limits of Irony," it simply shows that Crane hated man. Narveson (see "Stephen Crane: A Portfolio," 187–91) sees conceit as the principal theme of the story; see also Levenson, *Virginia*, V, pp. xcvi–xcviii. Clark Griffith, in "Stephen Crane and the Ironic Last Word," speaks of Crane's awareness of two types of illusions—one destructive, the other creative—in man.

26. See Stallman, 488 (he describes the red-lit saloon as "hell"). See also Richard VanDerBeets, "Character as Structure: Ironic Parallel and Transformation in 'The Blue Hotel,'" *Studies in Short Fiction*, V (Spring, 1968), 294–95, who points out the ironic parallel between the characters in the hotel and those in the saloon.

27. Neal J. Osborn, "Crane's 'The Monster' and 'The Blue Hotel,'" *Explicator*, XXIII (October, 1964), Item 10, comments upon this name, which to him suggests that the names *Fort Romper* and the *Pollywog Club* imply something about the area's social and civic maturity.

28. *Stories and Sketches*, 487, 489, 492.

29. But see William B. Dillingham, "'The Blue Hotel' and the Gentle Reader," *Studies in Short Fiction*, I (Spring, 1964), 224–26, who argues that Crane's final sentence is an attempt to engage the reader's apprehension of the Swede.

30. Marvin Klotz, "Stephen Crane: Tragedian or Comedian in 'The Blue Hotel,'" *University of Kansas City Review*, XXVII (March, 1961), 170–74.

31. Beer, 178, reports that Crane heard and modeled the story of "Moonlight on the Snow" upon the theatrical irony of a gambler Crane had observed in Florida. See *Letters*, No. 233, p. 180. Stallman (who regards "Moonlight in the Snow" as a companion piece to "The Blue Hotel") also reports this source. See Stallman, 604; and *Stories and Sketches*, 710–19. See also Joseph Katz, "An Early Draft of 'Moonlight on the Snow,'" *Stephen Crane Newsletter*, III (Summer, 1969), 1–2; and Levenson, *Virginia*, V, pp. cxxi–cxxvi.

32. Osborn, "Crane's 'The Monster' and 'The Blue Hotel,'" has commented upon name puns in Crane.

33. Crane's first mention of this story, "Twelve O'Clock," occurs in a letter to a publisher dated by Stallman and Gilkes, February 28, 1899. But this letter treats the story with some familiarity. See *Letters*, No. 278, p. 214. Presumably the story was complete in August of 1899—before "Moonlight on the Snow." See Levenson, *Virginia*, V, p. cxx. It was published in December of 1899, also before "Moonlight on the Snow." See *Virginia*, V, pp. clxxxvi–cxciii; Berryman, 248; and Stallman, 452, 493, 580.

    Another bit of western writing—an account of the violence engendered by the appearance of a top hat in Tin Can, Nevada—comically prefigures "Twelve O'Clock." It appeared as a part of Crane's "London Impressions" in *Saturday Review* of August 7, 1897, 132–33. See Stallman, 580.

34. Berryman, 248.

35. Stallman partly recognizes the absurdity inherent in the story when he says of it, "His Western tale might be read as a parody of the extravagant and idiotic life at Brede Manor, except that it needed no cuckoo clock to tell Crane how senseless it was, a comic opera that was destined to end quite otherwise." Stallman, 493. But see Levenson, *Virginia*, V, pp. cxx–cxxi.

CHAPTER XII

1. See Solomon, *Stephen Crane*, 116–17, where a similar argument is made.
2. In March, before leaving, Crane did two journalistic pieces, "Concerning the English 'Academy'" (a satire for *The Bookman*) and "Harold Frederic" (an appreciation for *Chap-Book*). See *Writings*, 303–309.
   For a succinct account of Crane's experiences in the Spanish-American War, see Levenson, *Virginia*, V, pp. cv–cxvi.
3. Stallman, 361, also 350–442. The reason for Crane's extended stay in Havana has never been adequately explained by detractors like Frederick Lewis Allen, in *Paul Revere Reynolds* (New York, 1944), 62, who suggests it as a period of dissipation, or by Berryman, in *Stephen Crane*, 228, who says that Crane "had gone underground," or by Levenson, *Virginia*, VII, pp. xxxii–xxxix, whose suggestion of a period for work is similar, or by Stallman, 422–42, who only records the contradictory evidence. A contemporary account which supports Levenson's suggestion is to be found in "Stephen Crane: A Portfolio," 200–204. And see Joseph Katz, "Cora Crane to John Hay: A New Letter on SC's Havana Disappearance," *Stephen Crane Newsletter*, I (Spring, 1967), 2–3.
4. "The Little Stilettos of the Modern Navy Which Stab in the Dark," *War Dispatches*, 112–16 (in Crane's *Last Words* it appeared under the title of "The Assassin in Modern Battles"); "The Terrible Captain of the Captured Panama," *Writings*, 315–16; "Sampson Inspects Harbor at Mariel," *War Dispatches*, 117–20.
5. "Stephen Crane's Pen Picture of C. H. Thrall," *War Dispatches*, 129–30. "With the Blockade on Cuban Coast," *ibid.*, 120–23, is also an impressionistically conceived sketch.
6. See "Inaction Deteriorates the Key West Fleet," *Writings*, 319–20; and "Sayings of the Turret Jacks in Our Blockading Fleets," *Writings*, 324–26. "Hayti and San Domingo Favor the United States," *War Dispatches*, 131–33, concerned public attitudes toward the war on the part of various West Indian onlookers.
7. "Narrow Escape of the Three Friends," *War Dispatches*, 134–36; and "Chased by a Big 'Spanish Man-o-War,'" *War Dispatches*, 168–71.
8. See Stallman, 361–62.
9. See, for example, "Roosevelt's Rough Riders' Loss Due to a Gallant Blunder," *War Dispatches*, 159–60; or "Denies Mutilation of Bodies," *Writings*, 334–35; or "Captured Mausers for Volunteers," *War Dispatches*, 186–87. There was also, of course, reportage of an almost purely factual nature. See "Night Attacks on the Marines and a Brave Rescue," *War Dispatches*, 171–72; "Artillery Duel Was Fiercely Fought on Both Sides," *War Dispatches*, 167–68; or "Pando Hurrying to Santiago; Cubans Say They Will Stop Him," *Writings*, 354–55.
10. "Crane Tells the Story of the Disembarkment," *War Dispatches*, 137–40. "In the First Land Fight 4 of Our Men Are Killed," New York *World*, June 13, 1898, which Stallman assigns to Crane (Stallman, 364, 606), is a similarly impressionistic sketch, as is "Stephen Crane's Vivid Story of the Battle of San Juan," *War Dispatches*, 172–83.
11. Stallman, 369.

12. *Ibid.*, 385, 404; and *War Dispatches*, 187–90.
13. Crane's concern with the workmanlike heroism of the individual soldier is also apparent in other reportage. See *ibid.*, "Stephen Crane at the Front for the *World*," 154–59, where Crane celebrated the courage of the Rough Riders, or "Spanish Deserters Among the Refugees at El Caney," 183–86, where Crane's sympathy was with the ordinary victims of the war, or "Hunger Has Made Cubans Fatalists," 161–67, where the Cuban soldiers' and the American regulars' attitudes and experiences are contrasted.
14. For the story of Crane's break with Pulitzer's *World*, see Stallman, 406–407.
15. See Matthew J. Bruccoli, " 'The Wonders of Ponce': Crane's First Puerto Rican Dispatch," *Stephen Crane Newsletter*, IV (Fall, 1969), 1–3.
16. See *War Dispatches*, 190–96.
17. *Ibid.*, "Havana's Hate Dying, Says Stephen Crane," 199–201, "Stephen Crane Sees Free Cuba," 201–202, "Stephen Crane Fears No Blanco," 202–206.
18. *Ibid.*, "Stephen Crane in Havana," 217–18, and "How They Court in Cuba," 220–22.
19. *Ibid.*, "The Grocer Blockade," 211–13.
20. *Ibid.*, 218–20.
21. *Ibid.*, "Stephen Crane's Views of Havana," 206–208, "Stephen Crane on Havana," 222–25, "In Havana as It Is Today," 237–41.
22. *Ibid.*, "Americans and Beggars in Cuba," 208–209, "Stephen Crane Makes Observations in Cuba's Capital," 209–10, " 'You Must!'—'We Can't!' " 225–28, "Spaniards Two," 231–33.

    In an interview which he granted an *Outlook* reporter shortly after his return to England (see "Mr. Stephen Crane on the New America," *Writings*, 421–24), Crane voiced again many of these frustrations.
23. "Our Sad Need of Diplomats," *War Dispatches*, 236, also 233–36.
24. Stallman, 605; *Virginia*, VI, pp. cliv–clxii.
25. *Virginia*, VI, 231
26. See also *ibid.*, 226.
27. American and English publication was almost simultaneous. Stokes was the American publisher, and Methuen was responsible for the London edition. See Williams and Starrett, *Stephen Crane: A Bibliography*, 50–52; Stallman, 514; and *Virginia*, VI, pp. lxxxvii–cvii.

    See Willa Cather's introduction to *Work*, IX. But Thomas A. Gullason, "The Significance of *Wounds in the Rain*," *Modern Fiction Studies*, V (Autumn, 1959), 235–42, sees *Wounds in the Rain* as a set of thematically patterned sketches unified around the words "wound" and "rain." Gullason's interpretation, if one considers that several of the stories are closely related to Crane's actual experiences, may seem a bit forced until one remembers "The Open Boat."
28. All of the stories and sketches appeared in newspapers or magazines prior to their publication in the collection. See *Virginia*, VI, pp. lxxxvii–xc, cvii–clxxi.

29. The piece first appeared in *McClure's Magazine* of February, 1899. See *War Dispatches*, 148–54. "Marines Signalling Under Fire" apparently had some unusual influence. Although Sergeant Quick was not mentioned in the *Annual Report of the Colonel Commandant of the United States Marine Corps to the Secretary of the Navy, 1898* (Washington, 1898), and although under the "murderous" Spanish fire no marines were killed or wounded (three suffered sunstroke), Sergeant Quick (and later a Private Fitzgerald, whom Crane had apparently memorialized as "Clancy") were recipients of the Congressional Medal of Honor. Jane Blakeney, *Heroes: U.S. Marine Corps, 1861–1955* (Washington, 1957), 7, 8.
30. Crane's punctuation. Ernest Hemingway's "Christmas" story about an attempted self-castration and an incompetent doctor had a similar title, differently mispunctuated: "God Rest You Merry Gentlemen" (New York, 1933), printed in a limited edition of 300 copies. See *Virginia*, VI, 137.
31. See Beer, 189–90; Berryman, 222–23; Stallman, 378–83.
32. "Stephen Crane's Pen Picture of C. H. Thrall," New York *World*, May 8, 1898. See *War Dispatches*, 129–30, and *supra*, 245. For the text, see *Virginia*, VI, 201–21.
33. See Willa Cather, *Work*, IX, p. ix.
34. Berryman, 220, calls it a "charming account of a tiny naval action . . . [in which Crane] animates the ships, which scarcely any writer has been able to do." I remain unconvinced, however. See *Virginia*, VI, 155–71.
35. Colvert, *Virginia*, VI, pp. xxxiv–xxxv, points out that "The Lone Charge" is based on an actual incident which happened to Ralph Paine, one of Crane's fellow correspondents.
36. *Virginia*, VI, 114–18.
37. Solomon, *Stephen Crane*, 117–18. *Virginia*, VI, 172–79.
38. Stallman, 395.
39. *Ibid.*, 441; Cather, *Work*, IX, p. ix.
40. In Daniel Weiss, " 'The Blue Hotel': A Psychoanalytic Study," 156, also 154–64, Private Nolan is said to be "at once the passive spectator and the good soldier."
41. Gullason, "The Significance of *Wounds in the Rain*," 236–37, contrasts this passage with a similar scene in *The Red Badge* to demonstrate his contention that Crane's later writing gained depth and maturity.
42. ". . . from the brow of one of the knolls where stood a pagoda-like house." *Virginia*, VI, 104.
43. *Letters*, No. 250, p. 193. See *Omnibus*, 684.
44. See Colvert, *Virginia*, V, p. xxxv.
45. Eric Solomon sees the story as a burlesque and sees Gates as its hero. See *Stephen Crane*, 101, 118.
46. Stallman, 385–86, thinks Lige is the story's hero and sees the martinet Major Gates as a parody of Colonel Roosevelt.
47. Berryman, 253–55; Hoffman, *The Poetry of Stephen Crane*, 152–55. Both fail to recognize Crane's half-ironic ending, but Hoffman points out Crane's innovation of the verse epigraph and explores its relevance to

the story. For a more complete, if somewhat specially pleaded, explication
of the story, see Neal J. Osborn, "The Riddle in 'The Clan': A Key
to Crane's Major Fiction?" *Bulletin of the New York Public Library*,
LXIX (April, 1965), 247–58.
48. *Stephen Crane*, 118–19.
49. "The Riddle in 'The Clan,' " 250. Osborn argues here that Crane's
ethic is Christian and is derived from that of W. E. Channing.
50. See Williams and Starrett, *Stephen Crane: A Bibliography*, 57. The
"Wyoming Valley Tales" (three stories—"The Battle of Forty Fort,"
"The Surrender of Forty Fort," and " 'Ol' Bennet' and the Indians")
deal with an historical event of war—the massacre in the Wyoming
Valley (in Pennsylvania) of July 3, 1778, and with the aftermath of this
event. The tales were first published posthumously, in *Last Words*,
in 1902. Hans Arnold, "Stephen Crane's 'Wyoming Valley Tales': Their
Source and Their Place in the Author's War Fiction," *Jahrbuch für
Amerikastudien*, IV (1959), 161–69, argues convincingly that the three
tales are based upon a history by Rev. Dr. George Peck, Stephen's
grandfather, *Wyoming: Its History, Stirring Incidents, and Romantic
Adventures* (New York, 1858). The historical "Ol' Bennet" turns out to
be Stephen's great-great-grandfather.

Arnold suggests that the three tales are the same as the "curt, compressed tales of the Wyoming Valley" which Beer reports that Crane
sent Wallis McHarg in 1892. Beer, 81–82. Arnold further argues that
"the holographs [of the "Wyoming Valley Tales"] clearly show a youthful hand" (165) and concludes that Cora's letter to an unidentified
publisher of August 28, 1900 (see E. H. Cady and L. G. Wells [eds.],
Stephen Crane's Love Letters to Nellie Crouse [Syracuse, 1954], Appendix, 82), concerns the three tales and is a duplicitous attempt to
pass the old tales off as recent work. And see n. 18. Chap. 2, *supra*.
But, as Stallman asserts, even though Peck's *Wyoming* did not appear
in Crane's list of books at Brede Place (see Stallman, 471, 554–55),
the book was available to him after July of 1899, when Wilbur Crane
visited him. Crane also had plans for a novel on the American Revolution
with Stokes (*Letters*, No. 310, p. 238). It is therefore likely that when
Crane wrote Pinker, his friend as well as agent, on September 30, 1899,
"Here is the first story of a series which will deal with the struggles
of the settlers in the Wyoming Valley (Pennsylvania) in 1776–79 against
the Tories and Indians. Perhaps you had better hold it until I finish two
or three more and then deal with some wealthy persons for the lot,
eh?" (this "first story" being " 'Ol Bennet' and the Indians"), Crane
was here presenting material which had been through recent revision.
Pinker had all three stories a month later (see *Letters*, No. 307, p. 235),
but he was unable to place them, although Cora was concerned about
them (*Letters*, No. 313, p. 241; No. 366, p. 285; No. 368, p. 286).
In the last of these letters to Pinker, Cora, annoyed, twits the London
agent with "I'm sure Mr. Reynolds could sell the Wyoming stories in
U.S. Do try him with them." See Stallman, 497, 514, 527, 555, 615,
619–20.

Thus Gullason (in the introduction to his *Stories and Sketches*, 34–35) recognizes that "In his last years in England he borrowed hastily from his grandfather's *Wyoming*." Gullason compares passages to show the great extent of Crane's "borrowing." But whether or not there was "borrowing" (of which Arnold leaves little doubt), Crane's haste with the Wyoming material is certainly clear. Two of the sketches— "The Battle of Forty Fort" and "The Surrender of Forty Fort"—were written (though not altogether by Crane) in less than twenty days. See *Letters*, No. 303, pp. 232–33; and No. 307, p. 235. See also Stallman, 619–20. Cora completed "The Surrender of Forty Fort." See Stallman, 621–22.

51. Nine accounts were published by Lippincott in 1901—"The Battle of Bunker Hill," "Vittoria," "The Siege of Plevna," "The Storming of Burkersdorf Heights," two accounts ("Leipzig" and "Lützen") under the title of "A Swede's Campaign in Germany," "The Storming of Badajos," "The Brief Campaign against New Orleans," and "The Battle of Sol- ferino" (all of which Kate Frederic wrote as well as researched). See Stallman, 340, 459, 502, 503, 619. See also Joseph Katz, "*Great Battles of the World:* Manuscripts and Method," *Stephen Crane Newsletter*, III (Winter, 1968), 5–7.

52. The four I consider here appeared together in 1902 in *Last Words*, although they first appeared separately in various periodicals. See *Virginia*, VI, pp. clxxii–cxci.

53. Colvert, *Virginia*, VI, p. xvi.

54. Virginia, VI, 310, and Colvert, xxxv.

55. *Stephen Crane*, 257. This quality has been variously interpreted by Crane's critics. William B. Dillingham, in "Crane's One-Act Farce: 'The Upturned Face,'" *Research Studies: Washington State University*, XXXV (December, 1967), 324–30, sees this quality as comedy. Colvert, *Virginia*, VI, p. xvi, speaks of the "ambiguous crossing of horror and humor" in the story.

56. Stallman says, "It is the question of how to come to terms with the real thing." *Omnibus*, 375.

57. Solomon, whose reading of the Spitzbergen tales resembles my own, points out this breach of decorum in *Stephen Crane*, 124–28.

58. *Ibid.*, 128. Solomon finds that "plop" a "permanent note of calm despair that is at once realism and parody, a summing-up and a criticism of war." It is interesting to note that the word is one of the repetitions characteristic of Crane's final style; "plop" appears three times on the story's final page.

59. This may be specifically as well as generally the case. Stallman asserts that "The Upturned Face" is written from Crane's experience at the burial of Surgeon Gibbs, and that Crane's Lieutenant Lean was a Lieutenant Herbert Draper. Stallman, 363–64. As Solomon points out, *Stephen Crane*, 126–27, "the reader is supposed to consider the [third] episode as part of the lieutenant's increasing store of knowledge."

60. And it very nearly was. Though "The Upturned Face" was conceived as early as January, 1899 (as "Dead Man"—see Stallman, 444), it was

not delivered to Pinker complete until November 4 (Stallman, 486 —it was then called "Burial"). See *Virginia*, VI, pp. clxxviii–clxxix. On December 29 Crane collapsed with a lung hemorrhage, and after that there was little serious writing. Crane did write "A Dark Brown Dog" in early January; he began "The Squire's Madness," and worked on *The O'Ruddy* and the *Great Battles of the World* series, and in the first three months of the new year (1900) did some minor reporting for the New York *Journal* on the Boer War, which he could not get to ("Some Curious Lessons from Transvaal," "Stephen Crane Says: Watson's Criticisms of England's War Are Not Unpatriotic," "Stephen Crane says: The British Soldiers Are Not Familiar with the 'Business End' of Modern Rifles"—Crane's sympathies were anti-imperialistic and were with the Boers, as is apparent in another historical piece for *Cosmopolitan*, "The Great Boer Trek"). There were also two other short pieces for the *Journal*, one a satire ("Stephen Crane Says: Edwin Markham Is His First Choice for the American Academy"), the other a diplomatic potpourri ("The Talk of London"). See *Writings*, 424–44; and *War Dispatches*, 299–312.

On April 1–2, 1900, Crane experienced another pulmonary hemorrhage, and his condition remained critical until his death in Germany on June 5. See Stallman, 493, 496–97, 501, 516, *et passim*.

CHAPTER XIII

1. A number of critics—notably Peter Buitenhuis ("The Essentials of Life") and William Bysshe Stein ("Stephen Crane's *Homo Absurdus*")— have discussed the existential elements in some of Crane's work.
2. See Chap. 1, *supra*.
3. Walcutt, *American Literary Naturalism*, 3–29, 305–306. See Chap. 1, *supra*.
4. Justin O'Brien's translation (Albert Camus, *The Myth of Sisyphus and Other Essays* [New York, 1955], 51). Camus says, "si j'etais arbre parmi les arbres, chat parmi les animaux, cette vie aurait un sens ou plutôt ce probleme n'en aurait point car je ferais partie de ce monde." *Le mythe de Sisyphe* (Paris, 1942), 74.
5. R. W. B. Lewis speaks of " 'The Open Boat,' with its double discovery, first, of the remote indifference of the universal power ('She was indifferent, flatly indifferent') and of the absurdity of life ('the whole affair was absurd'); second, of the one irreducible value remaining— 'the subtle brotherhood of men . . . established on the seas.' " *The Picaresque Saint* (Philadelphia, 1959), 92.
6. Camus, *Le mythe de Sisyphe*, 18, 37, and 48.
7. John Cruickshank, *Albert Camus and the Literature of Revolt* (New York, 1959), 41.
8. *Ibid.*, 49.

References Cited

I. WORKS BY STEPHEN CRANE AND
   EDITIONS OF CRANE'S WORKS AND LETTERS

Bassan, Maurice, ed. *Stephen Crane's "Maggie": Text and Context*. Belmont, Calif.: Wadsworth Publishing Co., 1966.

Bowers, Fredson, ed. *The University of Virginia Edition of the Works of Stephen Crane*. Charlottesville: University Press of Virginia, 1969–. I, *Bowery Tales*, intro. James B. Colvert, 1969. II, *Tales of Adventure*, intro. J. C. Levenson, 1970. VI, *Tales of War*, intro. James B. Colvert, 1970. VII, *Tales of Whilomville*, intro. J. C. Levenson, 1969.

Bradley, Sculley, R. C. Beatty, and E. H. Long, eds. *The Red Badge of Courage*. Norton Critical Edition. New York: W. W. Norton and Co., 1962.

Cady, E. H., and L. G. Wells, eds. *Stephen Crane's Love Letters to Nellie Crouse*. Syracuse: Syracuse University Press, 1954.

Chase, Richard, ed. *"The Red Badge of Courage" and Other Writings*. Boston: Houghton Mifflin, 1960.

Crane, Stephen. *Last Words*. London: Digby, Long, 1902.

———. "On the Boardwalk." New York *Tribune*, August 14, 1892, p. 17.

Crews, Frederick C., ed. *The Red Badge of Courage*. Indianapolis: Bobbs-Merrill, 1964.

Follett, Wilson, ed. *The Work of Stephen Crane*. 12 vols. New York: Knopf, 1925–27.

Fryckstedt, Olov, ed. *Stephen Crane: Uncollected Writings*. Uppsala: Acta Universitatis Upsaliensis, 1963.

Gibson, William M., ed. *"The Red Badge of Courage" and Selected Prose and Poetry*. New York: Rinehart, 1956.

Greiner, Donald J. and Ellen B., eds. *The Notebook of Stephen Crane*. Charlottesville: The Bibliographical Society of the University of Virginia, 1969.

Gullason, Thomas A. "A Stephen Crane Find: Nine Newspaper Sketches." *Southern Humanities Review*, II (Winter, 1968), 1–37.

———, ed. *The Complete Novels of Stephen Crane*. Garden City, N.Y.: Doubleday, 1967.

———, ed. *The Complete Short Stories and Sketches of Stephen Crane*. New York: Doubleday, 1963.

Katz, Joseph. "'Art in Kansas City.'" *Stephen Crane Newsletter*, II (Fall, 1967), 3–4.

———, ed. *"The Blue Hotel."* Merrill Literary Casebook Series. Columbus, Ohio: Charles E. Merrill, 1969.

331

——, ed. *Maggie: A Girl of the Streets . . . A Facsimile Reproduction of the 1893 Edition*. Gainesville: Scholars' Facsimiles and Reprints, 1966.
——, ed. *The Poems of Stephen Crane*. New York: Cooper Square, 1966.
——, ed. *The Red Badge of Courage*. Columbus, Ohio: Charles E. Merrill, 1969.
——, ed. "SC to Edmund B. Crane: Two New Letters." *Stephen Crane Newsletter*, I (Spring, 1967), 7–8.
——, ed. "SC to William Howe Crane: A Recovered Letter." *Stephen Crane Newsletter*, I (Winter, 1966), 8.
——, ed. *Stephen Crane in the West and Mexico*. Kent, Ohio: Kent State University Press, 1970.
——, ed. "Stephen Crane to Mrs. Moreton Frewen: A New Letter." *Stephen Crane Newsletter*, I ([Summer], 1967), 6.
——, ed. "Stephen Crane to William Howe Crane: A New Letter." *Stephen Crane Newsletter*, II (Fall, 1967) 9.
Lettis, Richard, Robert F. McDonnell, and William E. Morris, eds. *The Red Badge of Courage: Text and Criticism*. New York: Harcourt, Brace & World, 1960.
Monteiro, George. " 'Grand Opera for the People': An Unrecorded Stephen Crane Printing." *Papers of the Bibliographical Society of America*, LXIII (First Quarter, 1969), 29–30.
Pizer, Donald, ed. *Maggie: A Girl of the Streets (A Story of New York)*. Chandler Facsimile Editions in American Literature. San Francisco: Chandler, 1968.
Schoberlin, Melvin, ed. *The Sullivan County Sketches of Stephen Crane*. Syracuse: Syracuse University Press, 1949.
S[lote], B[ernice] D. ed. "Stephen Crane: Two Uncollected Articles." *Prairie Schooner*, XLIII (Fall, 1969), 287–96.
Stallman, R. W., ed. *Stephen Crane: An Omnibus*. New York: Knopf, 1952.
——, ed. "Stephen Crane: Some New Stories." *Bulletin of the New York Public Library*, LX (September, 1956), 455–62; (October, 1956), 477–86; LXI (January, 1957), 36–46.
——, ed. *Stephen Crane: Sullivan County Tales and Sketches*. Ames, Iowa: Iowa State University Press, 1968.
Stallman, R. W., and Lillian Gilkes, eds. *Stephen Crane: Letters*. London: Peter Owen, 1960.
Stallman, R. W., and E. R. Hagemann, eds. *The New York City Sketches of Stephen Crane*. New York: New York University Press, 1966.
——, eds. *The War Dispatches of Stephen Crane*. New York: New York University Press, 1964.
Winterich, John T., ed. *The Red Badge of Courage*. London: Folio Society, 1951.

II. BIOGRAPHIES, CRITIQUES, AND REMINISCENCES CONCERNING STEPHEN CRANE AND HIS WORK.

Ahnebrink, Lars. *The Beginnings of Naturalism in American Fiction*. Cambridge, Mass.: Harvard University Press, 1950.

———. "Toward Naturalism in American Fiction." *Moderna Sprak*, LIII (1959), 365–72.

Adams, Richard P. "Naturalistic Fiction: 'The Open Boat.' " *Tulane Studies in English*, IV (1954), 137–46.

Aldridge, John W., ed. *Critiques and Essays on Modern Fiction, 1920–1951*. New York: Ronald Press, 1952.

Allen, Frederick Lewis. *Paul Revere Reynolds*. New York: Privately printed, 1944.

Anderson, Warren D. "Homer and Stephen Crane." *Nineteenth-Century Fiction*, XIX (June, 1964), 77–86.

Anon. Review of *The Red Badge of Courage*. *Critic*, n.s., XXIV (November 30, 1895), 363.

Arnold, Hans. "Stephen Crane's 'Wyoming Valley Tales': Their Source and Their Place in the Author's War Fiction." *Jahrbuch für Amerikastudien*, IV (1959), 161–69.

Barnes, Robert. "Stephen Crane's 'The Bride Comes to Yellow Sky.' " *Explicator*, XVI (April, 1958), Item 39.

Bassan, Maurice. "An Early Draft of *George's Mother*." *American Literature*, XXXVI (January, 1965), 518–22.

———. "The Design of Stephen Crane's Bowery 'Experiment.' " *Studies in Short Fiction*, I (Winter, 1964), 129–32.

———. "Misery and Society: Some New Perspectives on Stephen Crane's Fiction." *Studia Neophilologica*, XXXV (1963), 104–20.

———. "Our Stephen Crane." *Mad River Review*, I (Spring–Summer, 1965), 85–90.

———, ed. *Stephen Crane: A Collection of Critical Essays*. Englewood Cliffs, N.J.: Prentice-Hall, 1967.

Beer, Thomas. "The Princess Far Away." *The Saturday Review of Literature*, I (April 25, 1925), 702.

———. *Stephen Crane: A Study in American Letters*. New York: Knopf, 1923.

Berryman, John. *Stephen Crane*. New York: Sloane, 1950.

Berthoff, Warner. *The Ferment of Realism*. New York: Free Press, 1965.

Boynton, Percy H. *Literature and American Life*. Boston: Ginn, 1936.

Bradbury, Malcolm. "Romance and Reality in *Maggie*." *Journal of American Studies*, III (July, 1969), 111–21.

Bradbury, Malcolm, and Arnold Goldman. "Stephen Crane: Classic at the Crossroads." *Bulletin of the British Association for American Studies*, No. 6 (June, 1965), 42–49.

Brennan, Joseph X. "The Imagery and Art of *George's Mother*." *CLA Journal*, IV (December, 1960), 106–15.

———. "Ironic and Symbolic Structure in Crane's *Maggie*." *Nineteenth-Century Fiction*, XVI (March, 1962), 303–15.

———. "Stephen Crane and the Limits of Irony." *Criticism*, XI (Spring, 1969), 183–200.

Brooks, Van Wyck. *The Confident Years: 1885–1915*. New York: Dutton, 1952.

Bruccoli, Matthew J. "Maggie's Last Night." *Stephen Crane Newsletter*, II (Fall, 1967), 10–11.

————. "*Stephen Crane: A Biography.*" *Stephen Crane Newsletter*, III (Winter, 1968), 9–10.

————. " 'The Wonders of Ponce': Crane's First Puerto Rican Dispatch." *Stephen Crane Newsletter*, IV (Fall, 1969), 1–3.

Bruccoli, Matthew J., and Joseph Katz. "Scholarship and Mere Artifacts: The British and Empire Publications of Stephen Crane." *Studies in Bibliography*, XXII (1969), 277–87.

Buitenhuis, Peter. "The Essentials of Life: 'The Open Boat' as Existentialist Fiction." *Modern Fiction Studies*, V (Autumn, 1959), 243–50.

Burns, Landon C., Jr. "On 'The Open Boat.'" *Studies in Short Fiction*, III (Summer, 1966), 455–57.

Cady, Edwin H. *Stephen Crane.* New York: Twayne, 1962.

Carlson, Eric W. "Crane's *The Red Badge of Courage*, IX." *Explicator*, XVI (March, 1958), Item 34.

Cather, Willa. "When I Knew Stephen Crane." *The Library*, I (June 23, 1900), 17–18. Reprinted in *Prairie Schooner*, XXIII (Fall, 1949), 231–36.

Cazemajou, Jean. *Stephen Crane.* Minneapolis: University of Minnesota Press, 1969.

————. "Stephen Crane: Deux decennies de redecouverte (1948–1968)." *Les Langues Modernes*, LXIII (1969), 54–60.

Colvert, James B. "The Literary Development of Stephen Crane." Unpublished Ph.D. dissertation. Louisiana State University, 1953.

————. "The Origins of Stephen Crane's Literary Creed." *University of Texas Studies in English*, XXXIV (1955), 179–88.

————. "*The Red Badge of Courage* and a Review of Zola's *La Débâcle.*" *Modern Language Notes*, LXXI (February, 1956), 98–100.

————. "Structure and Theme in Stephen Crane's Fiction." *Modern Fiction Studies*, V (Autumn, 1959), 199–208.

————. "Style and Meaning in Stephen Crane's 'The Open Boat.'" *University of Texas Studies in English*, XXXVII (1958), 34–45.

Conrad, Joseph. *Last Essays.* Garden City, N.Y.: Doubleday, Doran, 1926.

————. *Notes on Life and Letters.* New York: Doubleday, Doran, 1921.

————. *Works.* Uniform Edition. Vol. VII. London: J. M. Dent, 1929.

Cox, James Trammell. "The Imagery of *The Red Badge of Courage.*" *Modern Fiction Studies*, V (Autumn, 1959), 209–19.

————. "Stephen Crane as Symbolic Naturalist: An Analysis of 'The Blue Hotel.'" *Modern Fiction Studies*, III (Summer, 1957), 147–58.

Dendinger, Lloyd N. "Stephen Crane's Inverted Use of Key Images of 'The Rime of the Ancient Mariner.'" *Studies in Short Fiction*, V (Winter, 1968), 192–94.

Denny, Neville. "Imagination and Experience in Stephen Crane." *English Studies in Africa*, IX (March, 1966), 28–42.

Dillingham, William B. " 'The Blue Hotel' and the Gentle Reader." *Studies in Short Fiction*, I (Spring, 1964), 224–26.

————. "Crane's One-Act Farce: 'The Upturned Face.'" *Research Studies: Washington State University*, XXXV (December, 1967), 324–30.

Dounce, H. E. "Stephen Crane as a Craftsman." New York *Evening Sun,* January 8, 1917, p. 8.

Eby, Cecil D. "The Source of Crane's Metaphor, Red Badge of Courage." *American Literature,* XXXII (May, 1960), 204–207.

————. "Stephen Crane's 'Fierce Red Wafer.' " *English Language Notes,* I (December, 1963), 128–30.

Evans, David L. "Henry's Hell: The Night Journey in *The Red Badge of Courage.*" *Proceedings of the Utah Academy of Sciences, Arts, and Letters,* XLIV (1967), 159–66.

Feldman, Abraham. "Crane's Title from Shakespeare." *American Notes and Queries,* VIII (March, 1950), 185–86.

Figg, Robert M., III. "Naturalism as a Literary Form" (Part II of "Three Modes of American Fiction: A Symposium." Ed. by Louis D. Rubin, Jr.). *Georgia Review,* XVIII (Fall, 1964), 308–16.

Fitelson, David. "Stephen Crane's *Maggie* and Darwinism." *American Quarterly,* XVI (Summer, 1964), 182–84.

Ford, Ford Madox. "Techniques." *Southern Review,* I (July, 1935), 20–35.

Fox, Austin M. "Stephen Crane and Joseph Conrad." *Serif,* VI (December, 1969), 16–20.

Frederick, John T. "The Fifth Man in 'The Open Boat.' " *CEA Critic,* XXX (May, 1968), 12–14.

Free, William Joseph. "Smoke Imagery in *The Red Badge of Courage.*" *CLA Journal,* VII (December, 1963), 148–52.

Friedman, Norman. "Criticism and the Novel." *Antioch Review.* XVIII (Fall, 1958), 343–70.

Fryckstedt, O. W. "Henry Fleming's Tupenny Fury: Cosmic Pessimism in Stephen Crane's *The Red Badge of Courage.*" *Studia Neophilologica,* XXXIII, (1961), 265–81.

————. "Stephen Crane in the Tenderloin." *Studia Neophilologica,* XXXIV (1962), 135–63.

Garland, Hamlin. "Stephen Crane: A Soldier of Fortune." *Saturday Evening Post,* CLXXIII (July 28, 1900), 16–17.

Garnett, Edward. *Friday Nights: Literary Criticism and Appreciations.* New York: Knopf, 1922.

————, ed. *Letters from Joseph Conrad, 1895–1924.* Indianapolis: Bobbs-Merrill, 1928.

————. "Mr. Stephen Crane: An Appreciation." *Academy,* LV (December 17, 1898), 483–84.

Geismar, Maxwell. "Naturalism Yesterday and Today." *College English,* XV (January, 1954), 195–200.

————. *Rebels and Ancestors: The American Novel, 1890–1915.* Boston: Houghton Mifflin, 1953.

Gibson, Donald B. " 'The Blue Hotel' and The Ideal of Human Courage." *Texas Studies in Language and Literature,* VI (Autumn, 1964), 388–97.

————. *The Fiction of Stephen Crane.* Carbondale and Edwardsville, Ill.: Southern Illinois University Press, 1968.

Gilkes, Lillian. *Cora Crane.* Bloomington: Indiana University Press, 1960.

———. "Corrections of R. W. Stallman's *Stephen Crane: A Biography*." *Stephen Crane Newsletter*, III (Spring, 1969), 6–7.

———. "No Hoax: A Reply to Mr. Stallman." *Studies in Short Fiction*, II (Fall, 1964), 77–83.

———. "Stephen and Cora Crane: Some Corrections, and a 'Millionaire' Named Sharefe." *American Literature*, XLI (May, 1969), 270–77.

———. "Stephen Crane and the Harold Frederics." *Serif*, VI (December, 1969), 21–48.

———. "Stephen Crane's 'Dan Emmonds': A Pig in a Storm." *Studies in Short Fiction*, II (Fall, 1964), 66–71.

Gilkes, Lillian, and Joan H. Baum. "Stephen Crane's Last Novel: *The O'Ruddy*." *Columbia Library Columns*, VI (February, 1957), 41–48.

Gleckner, Robert F. "Stephen Crane and the Wonder of Man's Conceit." *Modern Fiction Studies*, V (Autumn, 1959), 271–81.

Going, W. T. "William Higgins and Crane's 'The Open Boat': A Note about Fact and Fiction." *Papers on English Language and Literature*, I (Winter, 1965), 79–82.

Gordon, Caroline, and Allen Tate, eds. *The House of Fiction*, 2nd ed. New York: Scribner's, 1960.

Greenfield, Stanley B. "The Unmistakable Stephen Crane." *PMLA*, LXXIII (December, 1958), 562–72.

Grenberg, Bruce L. "Metaphysics of Despair: Stephen Crane's 'The Blue Hotel.'" *Modern Fiction Studies*, XIV (Summer, 1968), 203–13.

Griffith, Clark. "Stephen Crane and the Ironic Last Word." *Philological Quarterly*, XLVII (January, 1968), 83–91.

Gullason, Thomas A. "The First Known Review of Stephen Crane's 1893 *Maggie*." *English Language Notes*, V (June, 1968), 300–302.

———. "The New Criticism and Older Ones: Another Ride in 'The Open Boat.'" *CEA Critic*, XXXI (June, 1969), 8.

———. "New Sources for Stephen Crane's War Motif." *Modern Language Notes*, LXXII (December, 1957), 572–75.

———. "The Significance of *Wounds in the Rain*." *Modern Fiction Studies*, V (Autumn, 1959), 235–42.

———. "The Symbolic Unity of 'The Monster.'" *Modern Language Notes*, LXXV (December, 1960), 663–68.

Hafley, James. "'The Monster' and the Art of Stephen Crane." *Accent*, XIX (Summer, 1959), 159–65.

Hart, John E. "*The Red Badge of Courage* as Myth and Symbol." *University of Kansas City Review*, XIX (Summer, 1953), 249–56.

Hartwick, Harry. *The Foreground of American Fiction*. New York: American Book Co., 1934.

Hemingway, Ernest, ed. *Men at War*. New York: Crown Publishers, 1942.

Hicks, Granville. *The Great Tradition*. Rev. ed. New York: Biblo and Tannen, 1967.

Hoffman, Daniel G. *Form and Fable in American Fiction*. New York: Oxford, 1961.

———. *The Poetry of Stephen Crane*. New York: Columbia University Press, 1957.

———. "Stephen Crane's First Story." *Bulletin of the New York Public Library*, LXIV (May, 1960), 273–78.

Hough, Robert L. "Crane and Goethe: A Forgotten Relationship." *Nineteenth-Century Fiction*, XVII (September, 1962), 135–48.

Howarth, William L. "*The Red Badge of Courage* Manuscript: New Evidence for a Critical Edition." *Studies in Bibliography*, XVIII (1965), 229–47.

Hungerford, Harold R. " 'That Was at Chancellorsville'; The Factual Framework of *The Red Badge of Courage*." *American Literature*, XXXIV (January, 1963), 520–31.

Isaacs, Neil D. "Yojimbo Comes to Yellow Sky." *Kyushu American Literature*, No. 10 (December, 1967), 81–86.

Ives, C. B. " 'The Little Regiment' of Stephen Crane at The Battle of Fredericksburg." *Midwest Quarterly*, VIII (Spring, 1967), 247–60.

———. "Symmetrical Design in Four of Stephen Crane's Stories." *Ball State University Forum*, X (Winter, 1969), 17–26.

Johnson, Willis. "The Launching of Stephen Crane." *Literary Digest International Book Review*, IV (April, 1926), 288–90.

Kahn, Sy. "Stephen Crane and the Giant Voice in the Night: An Explication of 'The Monster.' " *Essays in Modern American Literature*. Ed. Richard E. Langford, and others. Deland, Fla.: Stetson University Press, 1963, pp. 35–45.

Katz, Joseph. " 'The Blue Batallions' and the Uses of Experience." *Studia Neophilologica*, XXXVIII (1966), 107–16.

———. "Cora Crane to John Hay: A New Letter on SC's Havana Disappearance." *Stephen Crane Newsletter*, I (Spring, 1967), 2–3.

———. "Corwin Knapp Linson on *The Third Violet*." *Stephen Crane Newsletter*, III (Fall, 1968), 5.

———. "An Early Draft of 'The Blue Hotel.' " *Stephen Crane Newsletter*, III (Fall, 1968), 1–3.

———. "An Early Draft of 'Death and the Child.' " *Stephen Crane Newsletter*, III (Spring, 1969), 1.

———. "An Early Draft of 'Moonlight on the Snow.' " *Stephen Crane Newsletter*, III (Summer, 1969), 1–2.

———. "*Great Battles of the World*: Manuscripts and Method." *Stephen Crane Newsletter*, III (Winter, 1968), 5–7.

———. "The *Maggie* Nobody Knows." *Modern Fiction Studies*, XII (Summer, 1966), 200–12.

———. "Stephen Crane, 'Samuel Carlton,' and a Recovered Letter." *Nineteenth-Century Fiction*, XXIII (September, 1968), 220–25.

K[atz], J[oseph]. "Stephen Crane: *Sullivan County Tales and Sketches*." *Stephen Crane Newsletter*, III (Fall, 1968), 10–11.

Kazin, Alfred. *On Native Grounds*. Rev. ed. Garden City, N.Y.: Doubleday, 1956.

Klotz, Marvin. "Stephen Crane: Tragedian or Comedian in 'The Blue Hotel.' " *University of Kansas City Review*, XXVII (March, 1961), 170–74.

Knight, Grant C. *The Critical Period in American Literature*. Cos Cob, Conn.: J. E. Edwards, 1968 [1951].

Kramer, Maurice. "Crane's *Maggie: A Girl of the Streets*." *Explicator*, XXII (February, 1964), Item 49.

Kwiat, Joseph. "The Newspaper Experience: Crane, Norris, and Dreiser." *Nineteenth-Century Fiction*, VIII (September, 1953), 99–117.

————. "Stephen Crane and Painting." *American Quarterly*, IV (Winter, 1952), 331–38.

LaFrance, Marston. "The Ironic Parallel in Stephen Crane's 1892 Newspaper Correspondence." *Studies in Short Fiction*, VI (Fall, 1968), 101–103.

————, ed. *Patterns of Commitment in American Literature*. Toronto: University of Toronto Press, 1967.

Lavers, Norman. "Order in *The Red Badge of Courage*." *University Review*, XXXII (Summer, 1966), 287–95.

Lewis, R. W. B. *The Picaresque Saint*. Philadelphia: Lippincott, 1959.

Liebling, A. J. "The Dollars Damned Him." *The New Yorker*, XXXVII (August 5, 1961), 48–72.

Linson, Corwin Knapp. *My Stephen Crane*. Ed. Edwin H. Cady. Syracuse: Syracuse University Press, 1958.

————. "Stephen Crane." *Saturday Evening Post*, CLXXVI (April 11, 1903), 19–20.

Lorch, Thomas M. "The Cyclical Structure of *The Red Badge of Courage*." *CLA Journal*, X (March, 1967), 229–38.

Lynskey, Winifred C., ed. *Reading Modern Fiction*. 4th ed.; New York: Scribner's, 1968.

Lytle, Andrew. *The Hero With the Private Parts*. Baton Rouge: Louisiana State University Press, 1966.

McBride, Henry. "Stephen Crane's Artist Friends." *Art News*, XLIX (October, 1950), 46.

McDermott, John J. "Symbolism and Psychological Realism in *The Red Badge of Courage*." *Nineteenth-Century Fiction*, XXIII (December, 1968), 324–31.

Maclean, Hugh N. "The Two Worlds of 'The Blue Hotel.'" *Modern Fiction Studies*, V (Autumn, 1959), 260–70.

Marcus, Mordecai and Erin. "Animal Imagery in *The Red Badge of Courage*." *Modern Language Notes*, LXXIV (February, 1959), 108–11.

Metzger, Charles R. "Realistic Devices in Stephen Crane's 'The Open Boat.'" *Midwest Quarterly*, IV (Autumn, 1962), 47–54.

Meyer, George W. "The Original Social Purpose of the Naturalistic Novel." *Sewanee Review*, L (October-December, 1942), 563–70.

Meyers, Robert. "Crane's 'The Open Boat.'" *Explicator*, XXI (April, 1963), Item 60.

Milne, W. Gordon. "Stephen Crane: Pioneer in Technique." *Die Neueren Sprachen*, VII (juli, 1959), 297–303.

Monteiro, George. "Stephen Crane's 'The Bride Comes to Yellow Sky.'" *Approaches to the Short Story*. Ed. Neil D. Isaacs and Louis H. Leiter. San Francisco: Chandler Publishing Co., 1963, pp. 221–38.

————. "Stephen Crane's Dan Emmonds: A Case Reargued." *Serif*, VI (March, 1969), 32–36.

————. "Whilomville As Judah: Crane's 'A Little Pilgrimage.'" *Renascence*, XIX (Summer, 1967), 184–89.
Morgan, H. Wayne. *Writers in Transition*. New York: Hill and Wang, 1963, pp. 1–22.
Munson, Gorham. *Style and Form in American Prose*. Garden City, N.Y., Doubleday, 1929.
Napier, James J. "Land Imagery in 'The Open Boat.'" *CEA Critic*, XXIX (April, 1967), 15.
Noxon, Frank. "The Real Stephen Crane." *Step Ladder*, XIV (January, 1928), 4–9.
O'Donnell, Bernard. "Stephen Crane's *The O'Ruddy*: A Problem in Authorship Discrimination." *The Computer and Literary Style*. Ed. Jacob Leed. Kent, Ohio: Kent State University Press. 1966, p. 107–15.
O'Donnell, Thomas F. "John B. Van Petten: Stephen Crane's History Teacher." *American Literature*, XXVII (May, 1955), 196–202.
Osborn, Neal J. "Crane's *The Monster* and *The Blue Hotel*." *Explicator*, XXIII (October, 1964), Item 10.
————. "The Riddle in 'The Clan': A Key to Crane's Major Fiction?" *Bulletin of the New York Public Library*, LXIX (April, 1965), 247–58.
————. "William Ellery Channing and *The Red Badge of Courage*." *Bulletin of the New York Public Library*, LXIX (March, 1965), 182–96.
Osborn, Scott C. "Stephen Crane's Imagery: 'Pasted Like a Wafer.'" *American Literature*, XXIII (November, 1951), 362.
Øverland, Orm. "The Impressionism of Stephen Crane: A Study in Style and Technique." *Americana Norvegica* Ed. Sigmund Skard and Henry H. Wasser. Philadelphia: University of Pennsylvania Press, 1966. I, 239–85.
Overmyer, Janet. "The Structure of Crane's *Maggie*." *University of Kansas City Review*, XXIX (October, 1962), 71–72.
Parrington, V. L. *Main Currents in American Thought*. 3 vols. New York: Harcourt, Brace, 1927–30.
Pizer, Donald. "Crane Reports Garland on Howells." *Modern Language Notes*, LXX (January, 1955), 37–39.
————. "The Garland-Crane Relationship." *Huntington Library Quarterly*, XXIV (November, 1960), 75–82.
————. *Realism and Naturalism in Nineteenth-Century American Literature*. Carbondale: Southern Illinois University Press, 1966.
————. "Stephen Crane's *Maggie* and American Naturalism." *Criticism*, VII (Spring, 1965), 168–75.
Pratt, Lyndon Upson. "A Possible Source of *The Red Badge of Courage*." *American Literature*, XI (March, 1939), 1–10.
Pritchett, V. S. *The Living Novel and Later Appreciations*. New York: Random House, 1964.
Rahv, Philip. "Fiction and the Criticism of Fiction." *Kenyon Review*, XVIII (Spring, 1956), 276–99.
Randel, William. "The Cook in 'The Open Boat.'" *American Literature*, XXXIV (November, 1962), 405–11.
Rathbun, John W. "Structure and Meaning in *The Red Badge of Courage*." *Ball State University Forum*, X (Winter, 1969), 8–16.

Raymond, Thomas L. *Stephen Crane.* Newark: Carteret Book Club. 1923.

Rosenfeld, Isaac. "Stephen Crane as Symbolist." *Kenyon Review,* XV (Spring, 1953), 310–14.

Ross, Ralph, John Berryman, and Allen Tate. *The Arts of Reading.* New York: Crowell, 1960.

Roth, Russell. "A Tree in Winter: The Short Fiction of Stephen Crane." *New Mexico Quarterly,* XXIII (Summer, 1953), 188–96.

Safranek, William P. "Crane's *The Red Badge of Courage.*" *Explicator,* XXVI (November, 1967), Item 21.

Satterwhite, Joseph N. "Stephen Crane's 'The Blue Hotel': The Failure of Understanding." *Modern Fiction Studies,* II (Winter, 1956–57), 238–41.

Schneider, Robert W. *Five Novelists of the Progressive Era.* New York: Columbia University Press, 1965.

Schorer, Mark. *The Story: A Critical Anthology.* New York: Prentice-Hall. 1950.

Sewall, R. B. "Crane's *The Red Badge of Courage.*" *Explicator,* III (May, 1945), Item 55.

Slote, Bernice. "Stephen Crane and Willa Cather." *Serif,* VI (December, 1969), 3–15.

――――. "Stephen Crane in the Nebraska *State Journal,* 1894–1896." *Stephen Crane Newsletter,* III (Summer, 1969), 4–5.

Solomon, Eric. "Another Analogue for *The Red Badge of Courage.*" *Nineteenth-Century Fiction,* XIII (June, 1958), 63–67.

――――. *Stephen Crane: From Parody to Realism.* Cambridge, Mass.: Harvard University Press, 1966.

――――. *Stephen Crane in England: A Portrait of the Artist.* Columbus: Ohio State University Press, 1964.

――――. "The Structure of *The Red Badge of Courage.*" *Modern Fiction Studies,* V (Autumn, 1959), 220–34.

――――. "Yet Another Source for *The Red Badge of Courage.*" *English Language Notes,* II (March, 1965), 215–17.

Spiller, Robert E., and others, eds. *Literary History of the United States.* 3rd ed. rev. New York: Macmillan, 1963.

Stallman, R. W. "Crane's *Maggie:* A Reassessment." *Modern Fiction Studies,* V (Autumn, 1959), 251–59.

――――. *The Houses that James Built and Other Literary Studies.* East Lansing: Michigan State University Press, 1961.

――――. "The Scholar's Net: Literary Sources." *College English,* XVII (October, 1955), 20–27.

――――. *Stephen Crane: A Biography.* New York: George Braziller, 1968.

――――. "Stephen Crane's Primrose Path." *The New Republic,* CXXXIII (September 19, 1955), 17–18.

――――. "Stephen Crane's Revision of *Maggie: A Girl of the Streets.*" *American Literature,* XXVI (January, 1955), 528–36.

――――. "Was Crane's Sketch of the Fleet off Crete a Journalistic Hoax?: A Reply to Miss Gilkes." *Studies in Short Fiction,* II (Fall, 1964), 72–76.

Starrett, Vincent. *Buried Caesars.* Chicago: Covici-McGee, 1923.

Stein, William Bysshe. "Stephen Crane's *Homo Absurdus.*" *Bucknell Review,* VIII (May, 1959), 168–88.

"Stephen Crane: A Portfolio." *Prairie Schooner,* XLIII (Summer, 1969), 175–204.

Stone, Edward. "The Many Suns of *The Red Badge of Courage.*" *American Literature,* XXIX (November, 1957), 322–26.

Taylor, Gordon O. *The Passages of Thought; Psychological Representation in the American Novel,* 1870–1900. New York: Oxford University Press, 1969.

VanDerBeets, Richard. "Character as Structure: Ironic Parallel and Transformation in 'The Blue Hotel.'" *Studies in Short Fiction,* V (Spring, 1968), 294–95.

Vanderbilt, Kermit, and Daniel Weiss. "From Rifleman to Flagbearer: Henry Fleming's Separate Peace in *The Red Badge of Courage.*" *Modern Fiction Studies,* XI (Winter, 1965–66), 371–80.

Von Abele, Rudolph, and Walter Havighurst. "Symbolism and the Student." *College English,* XVI (April, 1955), 424–34, 461.

Walcutt, C. C. *American Literary Naturalism: A Divided Stream.* Minneapolis: University of Minnesota Press, 1956.

Webster, H. T. "Wilbur F. Hinman's *Corporal Si Klegg* and Stephen Crane's *The Red Badge of Courage.*" *American Literature,* XI (November, 1939), 285–93.

Weeks, Charles P. "The Power of the Tacit in Crane and Hemingway." *Modern Fiction Studies,* VIII (Winter, 1962–63), 415–18.

Weimer, David. *The City as Metaphor.* New York: Random House, 1966.

Weisberger, Bernard. "*The Red Badge of Courage.*" *Twelve Original Essays on Great American Novels.* Ed. Charles Shapiro. Detroit: Wayne State University Press, 1958, pp. 96–123.

Weiss, Daniel. "*The Red Badge of Courage.*" *Psychoanalytical Review,* LII (Summer, 1965), 32–52; LII (Fall, 1965), 130–54.

Wells, H. G. "Stephen Crane from an English Standpoint." *North American Review,* CLXXI (August, 1900), 233–42.

Wertheim, Stanley. "Crane and Garland: The Education of an Impressionist." *North Dakota Quarterly,* XXXV (Winter, 1967), 23–28.

———. "The Saga of March 23rd: Garland, Gilder, and Crane." *Stephen Crane Newsletter,* III (Winter, 1968), 1–3.

———. "Stephen Crane and the Wrath of Jehova." *Literary Review,* VII (Summer, 1964), 499–508.

Williams, G. L. "Henry Fleming and the 'Cheery Voiced Stranger.'" *Stephen Crane Newsletter,* IV (Winter, 1969), 4–7.

Wogan, Claudia C. "Crane's Use of Color in *The Red Badge of Courage.*" *Modern Fiction Studies,* VI (Summer, 1960), 168–72.

Woollcott, Alexander. "Woollcott Presents." *Saturday Review of Literature,* XVI (October 23, 1937), 14.

III. BIBLIOGRAPHIES

Katz, Joseph. *The Merrill Checklist of Stephen Crane.* Columbus, Ohio: Charles E. Merrill, 1969.

Stolper, B. J. R. *Stephen Crane: A List of His Writings and Articles About Him*. Newark: Public Library, 1930.

Williams, Ames W., and Vincent Starrett. *Stephen Crane: A Bibliography*. Glendale, Calif.: John Valentine, 1948.

IV. OTHER SOURCES

Agee, James. *Agee on Film: Five Film Scripts*. Boston: Beacon Press, 1964.

Annual Report of the Colonel Commandant of the United States Marine Corps to the Secretary of the Navy, 1898. Washington, D.C.: Government Printing Office, 1898.

Baker, Carlos. *Hemingway: The Writer as Artist*. Princeton: Princeton University Press, 1956.

Blakeney, Jane. *Heroes: U.S. Marine Corps, 1861–1955*. Washington, D.C.: Blakeney, 1957.

Camus, Albert. *Le mythe de Sisyphe*. Paris: Gallimard, 1942.

————. *The Myth of Sisyphus and Other Essays*. Trans. Justin O'Brien. New York: Knopf, 1955.

Cargill, Oscar. *Intellectual America: Ideas on the March*. New York: Macmillan, 1941.

Clemens, Samuel Langhorne. *The Writings of Mark Twain*. Vol. XIII. Autograph Edition. Hartford: American Publishing Co., 1899.

Cran, Mrs. George. *Herbert Beerbohm Tree*. London: John Lane, 1907.

Cruickshank, John. *Albert Camus and the Literature of Revolt*. New York: Oxford University Press, 1959.

Eastlake, C. L., trans. *Goethe's Theory of Colours*. London: J. Murray, 1840.

Emerson, Ralph Waldo. *Nature*. Ed. Kenneth Walter Cameron. New York: Scholars' Facsimiles and Reprints, 1940.

Gross, Seymour. "Hawthorne's 'My Kinsman, Major Molyneux': History as Moral Adventure." *Nineteenth-Century Fiction*, XII (September, 1957), 97–109.

Kirk, Clara M., and Rudolf, eds. *Criticism and Fiction and Other Essays*. New York: New York University Press, 1959.

Miller, J. Hillis. *Poets of Reality*. Cambridge, Mass.: Harvard University Press, 1965.

Norton, Hon. Mrs. Caroline (Sheridan). *The Undying One; Sorrows of Rosalie; and Other Poems*. New York: C. S. Francis, 1854.

Pearson, Hesketh. *Beerbohm Tree*. London: Methuen, 1956.

Peck, Rev. Dr. George. *Wyoming: Its History, Stirring Incidents, and Romantic Adventures*. New York: Harper, 1858.

Young, Philip. *Ernest Hemingway: A Reconsideration*. Rev. ed. University Park, Pa.: Pennsylvania State University Press, 1966.

Index of Crane's Writings

"Above All Things," 122, 126
"Across the Covered Pit," 33. *See also* Sullivan County sketches
Active Service, 191–92, 277
"Adventures of a Novelist," 137
"Along the Shark River," 290
"Americans and Beggars in Cuba," 326
"And if He Wills, We Must Die," 267, 268. *See also* Spitzbergen tales
"The Angel-Child," 217, 221n, 321, 322. *See also* Whilomville stories
"Apache Crossing," 122n
"Artillery Duel Was Fiercely Fought on Both Sides," 325
"Art in Kansas City," 311
"The Assassin in Modern Battles." *See* "The Little Stilettos of the Modern Navy Which Stab in the Dark," 325
"At Clancy's Wake," 299
"At the Pit Door," 200n
"The Auction," 136, 137

Baby sketches, 64, 150, 299
"Ballydehob," 201, 202. *See also* "Irish Notes"
"The Battle of Bunker Hill," 329. *See also* Great Battles of the World
"The Battle of Forty Fort," 328, 329. *See also* Wyoming Valley tales
"The Battle of Solferino," 329. *See also* Great Battles of the World
"Bear and Panther," 28
"Billy Atkins Went to Omaha," 72, 120
"The Black Dog," 30. *See also* Sullivan County sketches

"A Blackguard as a Police Officer," 137n
The Black Riders, 30, 86, 119
"The Blue Badge of Cowardice," 318
"Blue Battalions," 176, 271n
"The Blue Hotel," 13, 14, 24n, 51, 59, 76, 82, 94n, 116n, 121n, 128, 130, 131n, 136, 140, 149, 152, 154, 155, 156, 157, 195, 201, 213, 225, 226, 233–41, 243, 271n, 281, 283, 301, 314
"Brer Washington's Consolation," 321
"The Bride comes to "Yellow Sky," 13, 22, 67n, 76, 83, 122n, 128, 130n, 140, 149, 154, 155, 157 195, 225, 226–33, 241, 243n, 266, 279, 281, 314, 322, 323
"The Brief Campaign against New Orleans," 328. *See also Great Battles of the World*
"The Broken Down Van," 36n

"Caged With a Wild Man." *See* "A Texas Legend"
"The Camel," 18, 19
"The Captain," 22, 314
"Captured Mausers for Volunteers," 325
"The Carriage-Lamps," 216. *See also* Whilomville stories
"The Cat's March," 133n
"Chased by a Big 'Spanish Man-o-War,'" 325
"A Christmas Dinner Won in Battle," 72, 120, 301
"The City Urchin and the Chaste Villagers," 222. *See also* Whilomville stories
"The Clan of No-Name," 79, 83,

343

The Clan of No-Name,—*cont'd*
153, 153n, 262–66, 271. *See also*
Wounds in the Rain

"Concerning the English 'Academy,' " 325

"Coney Island's Failing Days," 300

"Crane at Velestinon," 318

"Crane Tells the Story of the Disembarkment," 325

"Crowding Into Asbury Park," 290

"The Cry of a Huckleberry Pudding," 29, 31, 76. *See also* Sullivan County sketches

"Dan Emmonds," 290, 302

"A Dark Brown Dog," 65n, 76, 299, 330. *See also* Baby sketches

"Dead Man," 329

"Death and the Child," 51, 128, 153n, 156, 157, 170, 183–92, 195 225, 233, 241, 244, 258, 261n, 277, 281, 318

"Denies Mutilation of Bodies," 325

"A Desertion," 65, 299. *See also* Baby sketches

"A Detail," 136, 137, 138, 313

"The Devil's Acre," 312

"Diamonds and Diamonds," 138

"The Dogs of War," 317

"The Duel That Was Not Fought," 72, 130n

"An Eloquence of Grief," 138

"An Episode of War," 83n, 144, 266, 312

"An Evening on the Roof," 135, 312

"An Experiment in Luxury," 69

"An Experiment in Misery," 54, 66, 67–69, 70, 77, 84, 300

"An Explosion of Seven Babies," 30. *See also* Sullivan County sketches

"The Fight," 221. *See also* Whilomville stories

"The Fire Tribe and the White-Face," 267n. *See also* Spitzbergen tales

"A Fishing Village," 201–202. *See also* "Irish Notes"

"The Five White Mice," 22n, 83n, 129, 131, 219, 240, 243n, 281, 282

"Flanagan and His Short Filibustering Adventure," 83n, 158–59n

"A Foreign Policy in Three Glimpses," 18

"Four Men in a Cave," 29, 31, 32, 33, 80, 255n, 292. *See also* Sullivan County sketches

"A Fragment of Velestinon," 177, 179–82, 318. *See also* "With Greek and Turk"

"A Freight Car Incident." *See* "A Texas Legend"

"Fresh Bits of Gossip on European Affairs," 197

"Gay Bathing Suit and Novel Both Must Go," 20n

George's Mother, 14, 15, 37, 55–63, 64, 66, 74, 81, 83, 85, 86, 87, 100n, 130, 135, 271n, 281, 294, 297, 298

"Ghostly Spirit of Metedeconk," 314

"Ghosts on the New Jersey Coast," 24, 85

"A Ghoul's Accountant," 30, 78. *See also* Sullivan County sketches

" 'God Rest Ye, Merry Gentlemen,' " 256. *See also Wounds in the Rain*

"The Gratitude of a Nation," 299

"A Gray Sleeve," 140, 142, 142n, 313. *See also The Little Regiment*

Great Battles of the World, 149, 266, 330

"The Great Boer Trek," 330

"Great Bugs at Onondaga," 19

"A Great Mistake," 64. *See also* Baby sketches

"Greeks Waiting at Thermopylae," 173n

"The Grocer Blockade," 326

"Half a Day in Suda Bay," 318

"Harold Frederic," 325

"Harvard University Against the Carlisle Indians," 313
"Havana's Hate Dying, Says Stephen Crane," 326
"Hayti and San Domingo Favor the United States," 325
"Heard on the Street Election Night," 72
"Henry M. Stanley," 18
"His New Mittens," 213–14, 322. *See also* Whilomville stories
"The Holler Tree," 30, 31, 140, 293. *See also* Sullivan County sketches
"Howells Fears Realists Must Wait," 300
"How Princeton Met Harvard at Cambridge and Won, 12 to 0," 313
"How the Donkey Lifted the Hills," 293, 311
"How They Court in Cuba," 326
"How They Leave Cuba," 249
"Hunger Has Made Cubans Fatalists," 326
"Hunting Wild Hogs," 26, *See also* Sullivan County sketches

"The Ideal and the Real," 321
"An Illusion in Red and White," 76
"An Impression of the Concert," 177–79. *See also* "With Greek and Turk"
"Inaction Deteriorates the Key West Fleet," 325
"In a Park Row Restaurant," 300
"An Indiana Campaign," 143. *See also The Little Regiment*
"In Havana as It Is Today," 326
"In the Broadway Cars," 72
"In the Depths of a Coal Mine," 70, 319
"In the First Land Fight 4 of Our Men are Killed," 325
"In the Tenderloin," 138
"In the Tenderloin: A Duel Between an Alarm Clock and a Suicidal Purpose," 139

"Irish Notes," 201, 204

"Jack," 291. *See also Sullivan County* sketches
"Joys of Seaside Life," 22, 291
"The Judgment of the Sage," 312

"The Kicking Twelfth," 261n, 267, 269–72. *See also* Spitzbergen tales
"Killing His Bear," 31, 302. *See also* Sullivan County sketches
"The King's Favor," 18, 289
"The Knife," 215. *See also* Whilomville stories

"The Landlady's Daughter," 37n
"The Last of the Mohicans," 26. *See also* Sullivan County sketches
"The Last Panther," 26. *See also* Sullivan County sketches
Last Words, 30, 132n, 266, 266n, 292, 299, 300, 325, 328, 329
"Leipzig." *See* "A Swede's Campaign in Germany"
"A Little Pilgrim," 223, 223n, 322. *See also* Whilomville stories
"A Little Pilgrimage." *See* "A Little Pilgrim"
"The Little Regiment," 15, 141
The Little Regiment, 139, 140, 143
"The Little Stilettos of the Modern Navy Which Stab in the Dark," 325
"London Impressions," ii, 21, 198–200, 319, 324
"The Lone Charge of Willam B. Perkins," 257, 327. *See also Wounds in the Rain*
"A Lovely Jag in a Crowded Car," 72
"The Lover and the Tell-Tale," 218. *See also* Whilomville stories
"Lützen." *See* "A Swede's Campaign in Germany"
"Lynx-Hunting," 216, 216n, 321. *See also* Whilomville stories

Maggie: A Girl of the Streets, 9, 14, 15, 17, 18, 25, 33, 35–54, 57, 59,

Maggie: A Girl of—cont'd
61, 63, 64, 65, 66, 74, 76, 80,
82, 83, 85, 86, 87, 100n, 123,
125, 130n, 135, 140, 145, 147,
148, 152, 153, 154, 156, 200,
207n, 274, 281, 294, 295, 296,
297, 298
"This Majestic Lie," 256. *See also*
Wounds in the Rain
"Making an Orator," 223
"Manacled," 202–203, 202n, 207
"A Man and Some Others," 126,
127
"A Man by the Name of Mud,"
132n
"The Man from Duluth," 136, 136n
"The Man in the White Hat," 177,
182. *See also* "With Greek and
Turk"
"Marines Signalling Under Fire at
Guantanamo," 247, 256, 327. *See
also Wounds in the Rain*
"Matinee Girls," 72, 300
"Meetings Begun at Ocean Grove,"
290
"Memoirs of a Private," 248n, 259n
"The Men in the Storm," 66–67,
200n, 300, 302
"The Mesmeric Mountain," 30, 292.
See also Sullivan County sketches
"Miss Louise Gerard—Soprano," 300
"Mr. Bink's Day Off," 73
"Mr. Stephen Crane on the New
America," 326
"The Monster," 14, 116n, 150, 155,
156, 195, 202, 204–13, 218, 219,
220n, 224, 278, 315, 320, 321,
322, 324. *See also* Whilomville
stories
"Moonlight on the Snow," 122n,
232, 241–42, 279, 324
"A Mournful Old Building," 300
"A Mystery of Heroism," 31, 122n,
140, 141, 219, 257, 313. *See also*
The Little Regiment

"Narrow Escape of the Three
Friends," 325

"Nebraska's Bitter Fight for Life,"
121
"New Invasions of Britain," 197
"New York's Bicycle Speedway," 312
"Night Attacks on the Marines and
a Brave Rescue," 325
"A Night at the Millionaire's Club,"
70
"Notes About Prostitutes," 137n
"Not Much of a Hero," 292. *See also*
Wyoming Valley tales

"The Octopush," 30, 82. *See also*
Sullivan County sketches
" 'Ol Bennet' and the Indians," 328.
See also Wyoming Valley tales
"An Old Man Goes Wooing," 201.
See also "Irish Notes"
"An Ominous Baby," 64, 76, 80,
299. *See also* Baby sketches
"One Dash—Horses," 125
"On the Boardwalk," 21
"On the New Jersey Coast," 21, 78,
148, 294
"On the New Jersey Coast: Summer
Dwellers at Asbury Park and Their
Doings," 290
"The Open Boat," 9, 14, 15, 31,
82, 83, 83n, 118, 141, 148, 149,
150–68, 169, 170, 182n, 199, 205,
212, 234, 236n, 261, 266, 271,
271n, 276, 277, 281, 282, 284,
307, 308, 312, 314, 315, 316,
317, 326, 330
The Open Boat and Other Stories,
138
"Opium's Varied Dreams," 312
The O'Ruddy, 192, 202, 319, 320,
330
"Ouida's Masterpiece," 312
"Our Sad Need of Diplomats," 326

"The Pace of Youth," 22, 24, 80,
132, 291
"Pando Hurrying to Santiago; Cubans Say They Will Stop Him,"
325
"A Poker Game," 137n, 242n

"The Porto Rican 'Straddle'," 249
"The Price of the Harness," 248n, 258, 262. *See also Wounds in the Rain*
"The Private's Story," 248n, 259
"A Prologue," 312

"Queenstown," 201, 319. *See also* "Irish Notes"

"The Raft Story," 312, 314
The Red Badge of Courage, 9, 13, 15, 24, 30, 33, 51, 57, 58, 73, 74, 75, 76, 78, 83, 83n, 86–118, 119, 120, 125, 132, 139, 140, 141, 144, 147, 148, 150, 151–52, 156, 159, 160, 165, 167, 168, 169, 170, 175, 176n, 179, 181, 182n, 183, 184, 194, 196, 199, 205, 212, 213, 223, 224, 232, 236n, 253, 259, 266, 267, 271n, 275, 276, 279, 282, 292, 301, 302, 303, 306, 307, 314, 327
"*The Red Badge of Courage* Was His Wig-Wag Flag," 246, 250, 256
"Regulars Get No Glory," 247, 259n
"The Reluctant Voyagers," 291, 314
"A Reminiscence of Indian War," 292. *See also* Wyoming Valley tales
"The Revenge of the *Adolphus*," 257. *See also Wounds in the Rain*
"Roosevelt's Rough Riders' Loss Due to a Gallant Blunder," 325
"The Royal Irish Constabulary," 201. *See also* "Irish Notes"

"Sailing Day Scenes," 312
"Sampson Inspects Harbor at Mariel," 325
"Sayings of the Turret Jacks in Our Blockading Fleets," 325
"The Scotch Express," 200, 319
"The Seaside Assembly's Work at Ocean Grove," 290
"The Seaside Hotel Hop," 290
"The Second Generation," 258. *See also Wounds in the Rain*

"A Self-Made Man," 136
"The Serjeant's Private Mad-house," 257. *See also Wounds in the Rain*
"Shame," 219–21, 322. *See also* Whilomville stories
" 'Showin' Off,' " 219, 257, 322. *See also* Whilomville stories
"The Shrapnel of Their Friends," 267, 268. *See also* Spitzbergen tales
"The Siege of Plevna," 329. *See also Great Battles of the World*
"The Silver Pageant," 70
"Sixth Avenue," 300
"Six Years Afloat," 312
"The Snake," 33, 34, 147, 193–94. *See also* Sullivan County sketches
"A Soldier's Burial That Made a Native Holiday," 248
"Some Curious Lessons from Transvaal," 330
"Some Hints for Playmakers," 299
"Some Interviews," 177. *See also* "With Greek and Turk"
"Spaniards Two," 326
"Spanish Deserters Among the Refugees at El Caney," 326
"The Spirit of the Greek People," 173n
Spitzbergen tales, 266–72, 329
"The Squire's Madness," 203–204, 203n, 320, 330
"Stephen Crane at Asbury Park," 25n, 312
"Stephen Crane at the Front for the *World*," 326
"Stephen Crane Fears No Blanco," 326
"Stephen Crane in Havana," 326
"Stephen Crane Makes Observations in Cuba's Capital," 326
"Stephen Crane on Havana," 326
"Stephen Crane Says: Edwin Markham Is His First Choice for the American Academy," 330
"Stephen Crane Says Greeks Cannot Be Curbed," 173n

"Stephen Crane says: The British Soldiers Are Not Familiar with the 'Business End' of Modern Rifles," 330

"Stephen Crane Says: Watson's Criticisms of England's War Are Not Unpatriotic," 330

"Stephen Crane Sees Free Cuba," 326

"Stephen Crane's Own Story," 167n

"Stephen Crane's Pen Picture of C. H. Thrall," 325, 327

"Stephen Crane's Pen Picture of the Powers' Fleet Off Crete," 173n, 318

"Stephen Crane's Views of Havana," 326

"Stephen Crane's Vivid Story of the Battle of San Juan," 325

"Stories Told by an Artist," 70

"The Storming of Badajos," 329. See also *Great Battles of the World*

"The Storming of Burkersdorf Heights," 329. See also *Great Battles of the World*

"The Stove," 217. See also Whilomville stories

"A Street Scene," 300

"Sullivan County Bears," 27. See also Sullivan County sketches

Sullivan County sketches, 9, 14, 24–34, 36, 76, 82, 143, 147, 148, 216n, 246, 274, 281, 291, 292, 294, 306

"The Surrender of Forty Fort," 329. See also Wyoming Valley tales

"A Swede's Campaign in Germany," 329. See also *Great Battles of the World*

"A Tale of Mere Chance," 312

"The Talk of London," 330

"The 'Tenderloin' As It Really Is," 138

"A Tent in Agony," 25, 29. See also Sullivan County sketches

"The Terrible Captain of the Captured Panama," 324

"A Texas Legend," 128

The Third Violet, 15, 70, 132, 133, 152, 191, 218, 276, 321

"This Majestic Lie," 256

"Three Miraculous Soldiers," 142. See also *The Little Regiment*

"The Trial, Execution, and Burial of Homer Phelps," 221, 322. See also Whilomville stories

"Twelve O'Clock," 154, 242–43, 279, 324

"Two Men and a Bear," 28. See also Sullivan County sketches

"Uncle Jake and the Bell Handle," 18

"The Upturned Face," 9, 14, 34, 51, 128, 149, 154, 157, 171, 188n, 194n, 196, 221, 267, 269–72, 273, 279n, 280, 313, 322, 329. See also Spitzbergen tales

"The Veteran," 116–17, 116n, 140, 141, 206, 310. See also *The Little Regiment*

"The Victory of the Moon," 293, 311

"The Viga Canal," 122, 124

"Virtue in War," 262. See also *Wounds in the Rain*

"Vittoria," 329. See also *Great Battles of the World*

"The Voice of the Mountain," 311

War Is Kind, 273

"War Memories," 83n, 86, 249–55, 261n, 281, 281n, 307. See also *Wounds in the Rain*

War Memories, 244

"War's Horrors and Turkey's Bold Plan," 175n, 252n

"The Way in Sullivan County," 27

"When a Man Falls a Crowd Gathers," 72, 300

"When Every One Is Panic Stricken," 72

"Why Did the Young Clerk Swear," 37, 299

Whilomville stories, 116n, 143, 150, 195–224, 238, 256, 278, 322
"The Wise Men," 131, 243, 312
"With Greek and Turk," 177-83, 249, 250, 253
"With the Blockade on Cuban Coast," 325
"The Wonders of Ponce," 248
Wounds in the Rain, 245, 255–66, 326

"The Wreck of the New Era," 314
Wyoming Valley tales, 266, 292, 328

"Yale Man Arrested," 318
"Yellow Undersized Dog," 312
"Yen Nock Bill and His Sweetheart," 139
" 'You Must'—'We Can't,' " 326
"Youse Want 'Petey' Youse Do," 299. *See also* Baby sketches

General Index

Agee, James, 232n
Alger, Horatio, 136
Anglo-Saxon Review, 249
Arena, 64, 296
Art Students' League, 70, 107, 132, 300

Bacheller syndicate, 73, 124
Barr, Robert, 202
Bass, John, 174
Bierce, Ambrose, 65, 306; "The Boarded Window," 30; Tales of Soldiers and Civilians, 292
Blackwood's Edinburgh Magazine, 261
The Bookman, 325
Brace, Charles Loring, 298
Brady, Matthew, 306

Camus, Albert, 101, 282; Le mythe de Sisyphe, ii, 273, 283
Cather, Willa, 258, 260, 312
Channing, W. E., 328
The Chap-Book, 319, 325
Chatterton, Thomas: Stephen Crane as, 3
Chaucer, Geoffrey: Troilus and Criseyde, 309
Churchill, Lady Randolph, 249
Clark, Dora, 137, 138, 204, 313
Claverack College: Vidette, 18
Clemens, Samuel Langhorne (Mark Twain): The Adventures of Tom Sawyer, 216; The Adventures of Huckleberry Finn, 107, 216, 242n, 280
Cleveland, Grover, 21, 291
Coleridge, Samuel Taylor: "The Rime of the Ancient Mariner," 316
Conrad, Joseph, 6, 11, 12, 13–16, 127, 132n, 149, 226, 233, 317,

Conrad, Joseph—cont'd
322; introduction to Beer's Stephen Crane, 314; "The Heart of Darkness," 13, 14; The Nigger of the "Narcissus," 10, 15, 289; The Secret Agent, 13, 14; "The Secret Sharer," 232
Cooper, James Fenimore, 26; Leatherstocking Tales, 9, 213
Cosmopolitan, 28, 261, 330
Crane, Cora (Stewart), 5, 149, 158, 158n, 171, 173, 174, 175, 192, 197, 200, 203, 204, 221n, 226, 245, 299, 314, 318, 319, 320, 321, 322, 328
Crane, Edmund B., 63n, 225, 294, 320
Crane, Mrs. J. T., 56, 298
Crane, Townley, 19, 20, 21, 56
Crane, Wilbur, 328
Crane, William, 170
Crouse, Nellie, 3

Dante Alighieri, 186, 308
Davis, Richard Harding, 170, 174, 319
DeMorest's Family Magazine, 147, 195
Descartes, René, 11
Dreiser, Theodore: Sister Carrie, 280; The Financier, 280

Eliot, T. S., 321; The Waste Land, 12
Ellison, Ralph, 207; Invisible Man, 213
Emerson, Ralph Waldo, 9, 92, 94, 162, 304; "The Poet," 316

Fitzgerald, F. Scott, 80, 87n; The Great Gatsby, 280, 321; Tender Is the Night, 213

350

Flaubert, Gustave, 36; *Madame Bovary*, 295
Flower, B. O., 296
Ford, Ford Madox (Hueffer), 78, 129, 133, 149, 312
Frank Leslie's Popular Monthly, 262
Frederic, Harold, 149, 200, 319
Frederic, Kate, 200, 201, 266, 329
Frewen, Mrs. Moreton, 318–19

Gardner, Charles, 129
Garland, Hamlin, 34, 35, 87, 149, 275, 287, 294, 295, 298; lecture on Howells, 36, 290; inscription in his *Maggie*, 38
Garnett, Edward, 6, 82, 149, 289, 301, 302
Gelber, Jack: *The Connection*, 52
George I (of Greece), 182, 187
Gilder, Richard Watson, 294, 295
Goethe, von, Johann Wolfgang: *Farbenlehre* (*Theory of Colours*), 92–94, 94n, 151
Golding, William: *Lord of the Flies*, 218

Harper's, 215, 217
Harris, Frank, 198
Harrison, Benjamin, 291
Hawkins, Willis Brooks, 303
Hawthorne, Nathaniel, 15, 305; "Ethan Brand," 213; "My Kinsman, Major Molyneux," 95, 213; "Young Goodman Brown," 67
Hearst, William Randolph, 137, 192, 248, 251, 313. *See also* New York *Journal*
Hemingway, Ernest, 80, 153, 153n, 287, 302; "A Clean, Well-lighted Place," 83; *For Whom the Bell Tolls*, 153; "The Gambler, the Nun, and the Radio," 153n, "God Rest You Merry Gentlemen," 327; *In Our Time*, 26; "The Snows of Kilimanjaro," 190
Herzberg, Max J., 92
Hilliard, John Northern, 39

Hinman, Wilbur: *Corporal Si Klegg*, 305
Homer, Winslow, 306
Howells, William Dean, 34, 35, 36, 37, 42, 70, 87n, 133, 149, 205, 290, 297, 300; *Criticism and Fiction*, 35, 37, 42, 297
Hueffer, Ford Madox. *See* Ford, Ford Madox
Huneker, James G., 133

Ibsen, Hendrik: *An Enemy of the People*, 205, 210

James, Henry, 133, 149, 168; *The Ambassadors*, 280; "The Jolly Corner," 232; *The Portrait of a Lady*, 280, 314
Johnson, Willis Fletcher, 20, 25, 31, 291, 293, 294
Jones, James: *From Here to Eternity*, 106
Joyce, James, 223; *Dubliners*, 224
Junior Order of United American Mechanics, 21, 22

Keats, John, 203
Kierkegaard, Søren, 283
Kipling, Rudyard, 34, 248, 263; *The Light That Failed*, 293; "The Man Who Was," 106
Kirkland, Joseph: *The Captain of Company K*, 306
Konstantinos, Crown Prince (of Greece), 174, 175, 182

Lanthorne Club, 132
Lawrence, Frederick, 295
Leslie, Amy, 221n, 319
Leslie's Weekly, 75
Linson, C. K., 70, 298, 299, 301, 319
Livingstone, David, 18

McClure's Magazine, 116, 322, 327
McHarg, Wallis, 294, 328
Melville, Herman, 15, 271; "The March into Virginia," 169; *Moby Dick*, 9, 209, 213

Mencken, H. L., 233
Michelangelo Bounarroti: *The Creation*, 316
Monet, Claude, 76
Monroe, Lily Brandon, 22, 35, 220n, 294, 295
Munch, Edvard, 44
Munson, Gorham, 79, 85
The Musical News, 300

New York *Herald*, 299
New York *Journal*, 24, 137, 170, 174, 175, 176, 248, 249, 313, 330
New York *Press*, 24, 67, 69, 70, 158n, 300
New York *Times*, 300
New York *Tribune*, 19–20, 21, 22, 25, 28, 29, 291
New York *World*, 245, 246, 248, 256, 326
Nicholas II, Czar, 176
Nietzsche, Friedrich Wilhelm: *The Joyful Wisdom*, 11–12
Norton, Hon. Mrs. Caroline (Sheridan): "Bingen," 164, 316; *The Undying One; The Sorrows of Rosalie; and Other Poems*, 316
Noxon, Frank, 92, 294

Outlook, 326

Paine, Ralph, 32
Peaslee, Clarence Loomis, 119
Peck, Rev. Dr. George, 266, 328; *Wyoming: Its History, Stirring Incidents, and Romantic Adventures*, 328, 329
Philistine affair, 132
Pinker, James B., 266, 299, 318, 322, 328
Pisarro, Camille, 76
Plato, 21
The Plumbers' Trade Journal, Gas, Steam, and Hot Water Fitters' Review, 301
The Pocket Magazine, 313

Poe, Edgar Allan, 292; "The Man of the Crowd," 233; "The Tell-Tale Heart," 312
Pulitzer, Joseph, 245, 326. *See also* New York *World*

Quick, Sergeant John H., 327

Ralph, Julian, 175n
Reid, Whitelaw, 19, 291
Renoir, Pierre Auguste, 76
Reynolds, Paul Revere, 262, 328
Riis, Jacob, 36, 67
Rockefeller, John D., 54
Rousseau, Henri, 44
Russell, Lillian, 54

Salinger, J. D.: *The Catcher in the Rye*, 213
Sampson, Admiral William T., 245
The Saturday Review, 198
Scribner's Magazine, 158n
Shakespeare, William: *Romeo and Juliet*, 199
Stange, Emile, 139n
Stevens, Wallace, 274n
Stewart, Cora, *See* Crane, Cora
Stirling, John, 296
Syracuse University Herald, 18, 25, 28

Talmage, Rev. Thomas deWitt, 298
Times Literary Supplement, 192
Thrall, C. H., 245, 256
Thurber, James, 204
Tolstoy, Count Lev Nikolayevich, 36, 302, 305; *Sebastopol*, 305; *War and Peace*, 305
Tree, Beerbohm, 205
Trent, Helen, 220n, 294
Truth, 70n
Twain, Mark. See Clemens, Samuel Langhorne

Van Petten, General John B., 306
Verbeck, Gustave, 302

Virgil (Publius Vergilius Maro), 186, 308

Wells, H. G., 85, 131, 133, 302, 306, 312
West, Nathaniel, 192
Westminster Gazette, 172, 177, 201, 249
Whistler, James McNeill, 77, 201, 302

Whitman, Walt, 168; "Song of My-self," 280, 316; *Specimen Days*, 306
Willard, Josiah Flynt, 67
Woollcott, Alexander, 3, 287

Zola, Emile, 36, 37, 38, 296; *L'Assomoir*, 36, 38, 296; *La Debâcle*, 36, 305; *Nana*, 36, 38